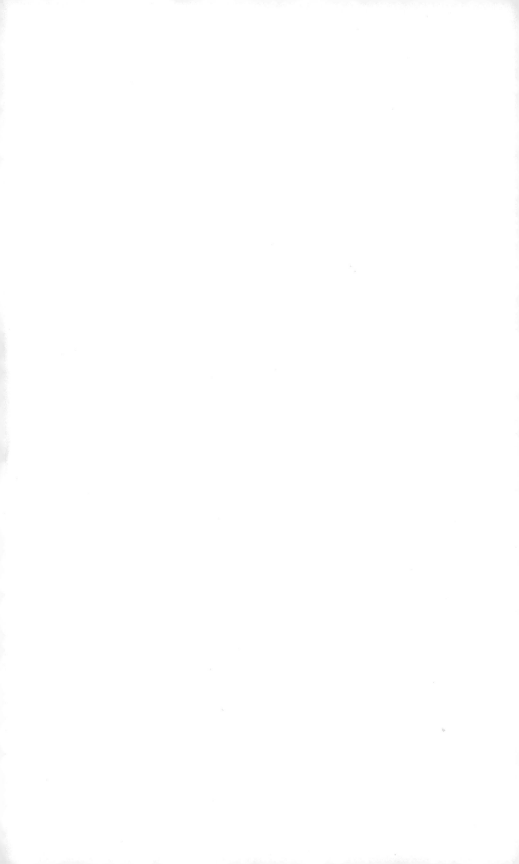

Here's the Deal

the Deal

A Memoir

Kellyanne Conway

THRESHOLD EDITIONS

New York   London   Toronto   Sydney   New Delhi

To the four chambers of my heart:
Georgie, Claudia, Charlotte, and Vanessa

Threshold Editions
An Imprint of Simon & Schuster, Inc.
1230 Avenue of the Americas
New York, NY 10020

First Threshold Editions hardcover edition May 2022

THRESHOLD EDITIONS and colophon are trademarks of Simon & Schuster, Inc.

For information about special discounts for bulk purchases, please contact Simon & Schuster Special Sales at 1-866-506-1949 or business@simonandschuster.com.

The Simon & Schuster Speakers Bureau can bring authors to your live event. For more information, or to book an event, contact the Simon & Schuster Speakers Bureau at 1-866-248-3049 or visit our website at www.simonspeakers.com.

Interior design by Jaime Putorti

Manufactured in the United States of America

10 9 8 7 6 5 4 3 2 1

Library of Congress Control Number: 2022935077

ISBN 978-1-9821-8734-7
ISBN 978-1-9821-8736-1 (ebook)

Contents

Introduction

Born to Run It

By every imaginable metric, I should have been a Democrat.

And a liberal. A feminist. Probably a man-hater, too.

I was raised in a house of all adult women. Four Italian Catholic women. In a small town in southern New Jersey between Philadelphia and Atlantic City. The only male in our all-female household was Pudgy the dog, and he stayed outside. (The inside dog, Beauty, was a girl.) This was the golden age of the women's liberation movement. *Roe v. Wade.* No-fault divorce. My father left us when I was three with no child support and no alimony. I was half Irish, half Italian. The men in my life—uncles, cousins, family friends—were union members.

All arrows pointed to me growing up at a time and in a way that should have had me, on January 20, 2017, my fiftieth birthday, ironing my pink pussy hat, printing my protest signs, and joining the "Women's March" in Washington, D.C. Instead, I wore a red hat and stood in front of the U.S. Capitol, steps away from President Donald Trump and Vice President Mike Pence as they were sworn into office, and then began my new job in the West Wing as counselor to the president. I should have been running Hillary Clinton's campaign or at least helping "the nation's first female president" find her way into the same White House Madonna said she "thought about blowing up" and where I now worked.

By then, I'd spent a quarter century as a fully recovered attorney, plying my trade as a pollster, a political strategist, and a TV talking head. I know all the reasons why some people become Republicans and other people become Democrats and a growing number join no party at all. I was a child of 1970s New Jersey, raised in a hardworking blue-collar area by a single mom whose friend sent her copies of *Ms.* magazine. Do I sound like a future Republican to *you*?

Yet there I'd been months earlier, on August 12, 2016, on the glittering twenty-sixth floor of Trump Tower in midtown Manhattan, staring across Donald Trump's battleship of a desk, on the verge of going to a place no woman had ever gone before. And I'd be going there with the highest-profile real estate developer, reality TV star, and business leader in America, whose immediate goal was stopping Hillary Clinton from becoming America's first female president while he became the nation's first president with no prior military or political experience. I had earned my way in, but it was the last place I imagined I could be.

I was already working on Trump's 2016 campaign as one of the five pollsters and a senior advisor to a thoroughly uninterested Paul Manafort. He literally fell asleep during my PowerPoint on how to close the gender gap with Hillary. (He must have still been on Ukraine time.) But the morning of the twelfth, I got a call from Manafort's deputy, Rick Gates, saying, "Mr. Trump is asking for you."

The candidate was recording videos for a few events he could not attend in person. The taping wasn't going so well. When I breezed in, there were a dozen anxious-looking people in the office and one hair-and-makeup artist who had just been told (by Trump) not to go near him. I could tell immediately he was in a fit of pique.

"Look at that," he said to me, motioning toward a video monitor. "Why am I pink? Who hired you people? Kellyanne, tell them I look like a pink, three-year-old baby."

Oh-kay, I thought to myself. *I've had babies. I've had three-year-olds. They were sorta pink. Let me see what we can do about this.* When the taping finally wrapped, Trump announced: "I want everybody out of here except Kellyanne."

"Are you coming on the plane to Pennsylvania?" he demanded as soon as the room cleared out.

"No, sir, I . . ."

"Why not? I thought you said you were."

"It's a smaller plane, I think. It's okay. I'll come next time."

"It's not okay," he corrected me. "Why do they keep putting the same people on the plane?"

"I don't know how that works," I answered. "I went on the road yesterday with Governor Pence. North Carolina looks like Trump country."

I took advantage of the extended pause. "But what's really going on?" I asked. Something had to be troubling him beyond the camera lighting and the airplane seating chart.

He leaned back in his huge leather chair and folded his arms. "Everybody tells me I'm a better candidate than she is."

I nodded and smiled. "That is empirically true."

"But she's got the better people."

"She's got many more people," I said. "She has a person whose only job is Lackawanna County."

One arched eyebrow.

"We have, like, one person in charge of Pennsylvania and three other states," I said. "So, yes, it is different."

That's when he got to what was really on his mind.

"Do you actually think we can do this?" he asked me, which I took to mean beat Hillary on November 8, less than three months away.

I didn't sugarcoat it.

"Yes, you can win, Mr. Trump—but right now we're losing. You've come this far. It's been remarkable. Look, she's too much Hillary and not enough Clinton. Bill was the charmer with the everyman appeal. People are skeptical of her. She rubs people the wrong way. She is seen as direct, but curt and not honest. Right now, sir, the entire conversation and election are about you."

"I know." He cracked a faint smile. "I get the best press coverage."

"You get the *most* press coverage," I retorted. "For you to win, the election needs to be about her, or at least more about her. The ballot won't say 'TRUMP' or 'NOT TRUMP.' People will have to actually suppress how they feel about her to vote for her."

"Go on."

"The polls are rough right now. And the window is closing. But, of course, you can win. I've been talking about the 'undercover, hidden Trump voter' for weeks now and met international ridicule. Those voters are real, and they will be there for you. The question is, are there enough of them? We also need to convince the fence-sitters, the crossover voters, and the conscientious objectors. They call themselves Independents not because they are not focused on politics but because they are. They don't like Washington, the career politicians, the system. They're on the outside, just like you."

I still had the floor.

I kept going, "I don't know a billion things about a billion things, sir, but I know consumers. I know voters. And I know polls." Then I dished up a quick version of the presentation Manafort had dozed through and others in campaigns past had ignored. "Look," I said, "women who are running for office usually have three distinct advantages, and Hillary can't claim any of them."

Trump always liked reviewing Hillary's deficits. He perked up at the prospect of hearing some new ones. "Women candidates are typically seen as fresh and new. There's a reason you've never heard of the 'Old Girls Network.' There isn't one. A couple of years ago, Joni Ernst cleared the primary threshold of fifty percent and then became U.S. senator. Iowa had literally never sent a woman to Washington before. The second advantage is that women are seen as less corruptible, more ethical, beyond reproach. Fairly or unfairly, often after a man is caught behaving badly in office, people immediately say, 'We need a woman. We need a woman.'"

Trump smiled at that, and I pressed on.

"Nobody sees Hillary as fresh and new," I said. "Nobody sees her as ethical and beyond reproach. In both cases, it's the opposite." And then there was the third advantage that Hillary lacked. "Women candidates are often viewed as peacemakers, earnest negotiators, consensus builders, as generally interested in how they can hammer out a deal with the other side. Who sees Hillary Clinton that way?"

"Nobody," Trump agreed.

As I laid all this out, I could tell I still had his attention, which was saying something. "Hillary's blue wall is real," I said finally. "But if we can break through it, you will win."

Then came the surprise question, the one I wasn't remotely expecting when I'd walked in the door. The world-famous dealmaker wanted to make one with me.

"You can do that?" he asked me.

"I can do that."

"Do you want to run this thing?"

"What do you mean, 'run this thing'?"

"The campaign."

"The campaign?"

He was serious. That made me nervous, so I just kept talking. "We need to focus on the states Obama-Biden carried twice with more than fifty percent and where Hillary is now polling below fifty and a Republican governor and/or senator was elected during the Obama years. We know people aren't allergic to Republican leaders in those states."

It wasn't the first time I had made that pitch, but it was the first time Trump had heard it, uninterrupted, and with less than one hundred days to go. He liked what he heard. Jared and Ivanka were on a cruise on the Danube. Don Jr. was hunting out west. This was a Friday, so Manafort's weekend in the Hamptons had begun a few days earlier.

Donald Trump waited for my response.

I wanted us both to succeed. So getting to yes required a few additional conditions that I wasn't even certain I could demand without sounding disrespectful or dissuaded. There was no use doing this if we couldn't do it right. "I'll need direct access to you at all times," I said. "Given the limited time before Election Day, we'll need one other new person in the C-suite. And I'll need the latitude to look at data more granularly, more situationally. Forget the national polls about the fiction of electability, which portends and pretends who can and can't win. The Electoral College is how you *do* or *don't* win."

Trump agreed to all of it. We had a deal.

"Who do I need to tell, sir? Who else needs to meet with me?"

Trump looked to either side and looked puzzled. "You talk to *me*. Just me."

If you're going to make history, who needs hierarchy?

The political warrior in me was elated. I'd just been handed the opportunity of a lifetime. I had earned it but never thought I'd achieve it. A man who'd been offered that job would have walked out of presidential nominee Donald Trump's office and immediately leaked the news to a favored reporter or commanded an impromptu press conference in the Trump Tower lobby. "I'm the new campaign manager," he'd have announced to the clicking cameras and klieg lights, exuding confidence through his jutted jaw and furrowed brow. "Everything's different now. We're going to win this thing." But I didn't do that. The political warrior was one thing, but I was also that girl from South Jersey, raised in a household of loving yet self-denying women, who had a hard time accepting yes for an answer. I had triumphed over some men but let other men trample all over me.

"You know what?" I said to Donald Trump. "We'll talk about it again tomorrow after you get back from Pennsylvania. See if you've changed your mind." I handed the legend Donald Trump, also my party's presidential nominee, a chance to rethink his offer and maybe even renege. What man would do that?

"Okay, honey," he said as I reached for the office door. "Leave it open, Kel," he added, a harbinger of things to come. "This is going to be great."

I was numb as I walked down the hallway toward the elevator, nodding goodbye to his trusted assistants Jessica and Rhona. Instead of hitting 14, where my office was, or lobby, where the press were, I reflexively hit 24 and changed elevators on the residence side. Would he tweet it? Had people overheard us? Would I blurt it out to the thirsty press corps corralled in the main lobby waiting for scoops and sound bites? Instead, I went down to the residence lobby and ran smack into Reince Priebus, chairman of the Republican National Committee. "Hey, Kellyanne, are you coming with us to Altoona?"

"No," I replied, avoiding eye contact and heading toward the side exit on 56th Street.

"So whadaya think? Can he really do this? It's too late—right?—the polls, the tweets."

"Yes, of course he can win this," I said. "I smell change in the air. Things are looking up. He's making some moves." I was as cryptic as Reince was frantic.

The only person I told that day about Trump's offer was my husband, George. "You're doing this," he said to me without a whiff of equivocation and with a tear in his eye. "This is your shot. I've listened to all these people deny you, dismiss you, and sell you short for all these years. They never took your advice, and maybe he will. You're going to do this."

I nodded, knowing George's support was genuine and unconditional.

"Kellyanne," George said, "Trump can actually win with you."

George was certainly right about the first part. I'd been cut down and cut off and cut out by some of the most famous and infamous men in business and politics. George had been around for plenty of it. He had little regard for the Republican consultancy that rewarded failure, operated like a walking RICO violation, and, lately, had never seen Trump and his appeal to a broad coalition of voters coming.

And so began the wildest adventure of my life, personally and professionally. I would certainly be changed by it, and so would America. I had talked my way into being Donald Trump's campaign manager. Now we'd see if I could talk him all the way into the White House. But first I had to talk myself into believing I was worthy of the historic moment.

I LIKE TO talk. Then again, that's not exactly breaking news.

I have spoken millions of words in public. On TV. In speeches. At rally podiums in front of roaring crowds. Before more modest but no less captive audiences in converted barns, in fancy living rooms, in hotel ballrooms, in wood-paneled boardrooms, on rooftops, and on hilltops. But I also like to listen. That's what good pollsters (and moms) do. We listen. Carefully.

Perhaps I've never had more to say than I do right now. When someone told me that a book like this one is usually around one hundred thousand words, my reaction was perfectly predictable: "Is that all? I've crammed that many into a single TV appearance."

Talking is what I love to do. It's also how I make things happen. It's a big part of who I am. I chat up strangers and find common bonds. I reconnect with old friends and reveal something new. The world is my focus group. I want to listen. And laugh. And learn.

Put it like this: I like to talk almost as much as my husband likes to tweet. On Twitter. About my boss, the president. George loved how I talked about Donald Trump, until he decided one day he couldn't stand it and chose to throw our lives into an uproar. Opposites may attract, but similars endure. I live my life mostly offline. George spends a major part of his day online. Then and now. That may be our greatest divide . . . and America's.

I've never had much of a filter between my brain and my lips. *No notes, no net:* That's been my MO all along. Announcing exactly how and where and among whom Donald Trump was going to win the presidency. Cheerfully appearing on five Sunday shows. Delivering unscripted speeches that make people ask, "Is she using a teleprompter? Is someone in her ear?" No, that is not the way I do it. But, yes, living on a limb like that also has its perils. When the whole world is listening and you're out there all alone—too little research, too little sleep—things don't always come out artfully or as intended. I made my bones in traditional media, live television, and ten-minute uninterrupted live radio, which is much more difficult than sitting around, writing, curating, editing, and tweaking the perfect tweet.

Alternative facts . . . remember those?

The jackals sitting on their asses lying in wait to pounce had for years played a one-way parlor game of parsing a phrase here or there from the millions of words I've spoken, hoping to denigrate and castigate me. No matter. They are the ones who often have thick skulls and thin skin (and marbles in their mouths when they speak). These elites were never my audience, anyway. The people are. I was speaking *to* them and sometimes *for* them. Rather than lash out and clap back at every mean post or miserable person, I decided to take the high road and the long view. That didn't happen quickly and that hasn't come easily, but it has kept me safe and sane, improved my outlook, and allowed me to retain joy on the journey of life.

I've been a little quiet lately, quieter than I usually am. I even took a long break from television. I jumped off while so many others were begging to get on. When I announced on Sunday night, August 23, 2020, that I was leaving the Trump administration as senior counselor to the president—one of Donald Trump's longest-serving senior aides— Election Day was still a few months away. I had decided to spend some much-needed time with my four growing children—ages ten, eleven, fifteen, and fifteen—and disconnect from Washington for a while. I'd given at the office. It was time to do more giving at home.

I went off the grid just as I'd promised to. George not so much, though he had vowed to give his poison Trump obsession a much-needed breather. I held my tongue, stayed out of the media, drove lots of carpools, and started nagging my children face-to-face again.

That time has been important, for all of us. But you knew I couldn't sit quietly forever. This book is called *Here's the Deal* for a reason. Rest assured, this is not one of those all-MAGA-all-the-time titles, packed with obsequious fawning, written by someone who lacked my daily proximity to or first-person perspective on President Donald Trump. This is also not another insufferable "tell-all" from an author spinning through a cycle of incredulity *who has decided to place profit over principle, fame over friendship, attitude over gratitude.*

Lots of people already know who I am. But not from where I've come, what makes me tick, how I found myself in the middle of incredible opportunities and wild dramas.

The Jersey girl, raised by independent women, who left home with hope and passion and strong beliefs. The young entrepreneur who made it to the highest levels of politics and media and did it on her own terms. The public servant who began at fifty and marveled at how decisions and actions could positively affect so many lives. The wife and mother who did her best under excruciating circumstances, as wives and mothers almost always do. The political professional who stared down entrenched careerists, petty jealousies, the old boys' network, the new boys' network, lies, personal attacks, and a man the president of the United States called the "husband from hell." Who else has had a life like mine? It's Quite The Story.

And it all began in a tiny town called Atco.

Part I

Jersey Girl

Chapter 1

Golden Time

I have an early memory of my father.

The two of us are eating pancakes together, sitting at the kitchen table like normal families do, acting as if the scene was certain to repeat itself a million times over. So here's what's strange about that father-daughter breakfast: I'm not sure if it really happened or if it's only wishful thinking on my part. But I cling to that early, early memory of us because it's the only one I have.

John Kainath Fitzpatrick was his name. I was three when he left for "the other woman" and "the other child." He and my two grandfathers had eight children with their wives and another eight children out of wedlock with their ... *nonwives*. The men in our family didn't just have side pieces. They didn't just have *comares*, as we say in Italian. They had side *families*. And it wasn't a secret to anyone. They all went off to be with those other families, leaving their original wives and children to face their own new normals and fend for themselves. Which is how I came to be raised by a houseful of strong, independent, wonderfully loving women who were pretty sure the whole world revolved around me.

I was born Kellyanne Fitzpatrick in Camden, New Jersey, on January 20, 1967. I favored my father's Irish side, with light skin and bright blue eyes, quickly becoming a stocky and curious little girl who was bursting with energy and thought almost everything was fun. My mother, Diane DiNatale Fitzpatrick, 100 percent Italian, the youngest of four sisters, had expected to devote her life to raising a big, happy family. Instead she was married at twenty-one, had me at barely twenty-three, and was divorced at twenty-six, never to seriously date again. When my father left, she got busy, not mad, ready to do whatever it took to provide for herself and especially for me—shielding me from adult problems and letting me be a kid.

Jobs at her father's Chrysler-Plymouth auto dealership, the local bank, and then a higher-paying position as a gaming supervisor at Atlantic City's Claridge Casino allowed her the dignity of work and an ability to spoil me by 1970s and 1980s New Jersey standards (read: inexpensively). We moved back in with her mother and two unmarried sisters at the old homestead, 375 Hendricks Avenue in tiny Atco, where the four women shared bedrooms so I could have my own.

My grandmother, Antoinette Lombardo DiNatale, was the unquestioned matriarch of our family. She, like my father's mother, Claire Muriel (Kainath) Fitzpatrick, had the selflessness, patience, and poise of a woman who had trudged through the Great Depression, foreign wars, and battles at home. Grandmom, as we called my mother's mother, suffered through a devastating car crash in her forties that took the life of her sister-in-law and left Grandmom bedridden for a year. She was told she would never walk again. She heard what the doctor said, then willed her way through it with prayers to St. Jude (the patron saint of lost causes), a fused hip, the hint of a limp, and zero self-pity.

My father's mother had crippling arthritis and buried two of her eight grandchildren, one from leukemia at age eight and another from an automobile accident at eighteen. Despite my father's long absence, I maintained loving relationships with his sisters, Aunt Gail and Aunt Ruth, and their children, Gaillynn, Tony, Sammy, Diana, A.J., and Jillese, and later my father's son Scott.

Grandmothers Antoinette and Claire did nothing for the glory, for the praise, for the honor, or for the money. Nothing. They were ladies with limited formal education and endless wisdom. They certainly had plenty to complain about. But to this day, I never remember either of my grandmothers complaining about anything. They smiled through their physical pain and emotional scars. They made our lives easier. And they would remain friends and travel buddies for decades past their children's divorce.

They were just spectacular.

That stone rancher at the corner of Route 30 (White Horse Pike) and Hendricks Avenue was bursting with love. Grandmom and my aunts Rita ("RoRo") and Marie ("MiMi") all took a daily hand in raising me, as did the aunts' married sister, GiGi (for Angela, whom we also called Angie), who stopped by nearly every afternoon with her two children, my first cousins and first friends, Renee and James ("Jay"). Together these vibrant women were South Jersey's version of TV's "Golden Girls," with housecoats, biting humor, late-night dessert benders, and life lessons. Grit was practically a genetic trait with them, but so was an ability to make everyone feel welcomed, special, and loved. Our wooden kitchen table was like the town square. Visitors filled their bellies and eased their burdens. Laughter was the theme song.

My mother's sisters were charitable with their time and modest treasure, frank in all their attitudes, and, as I can see looking back, way ahead of their time. Aunt Angie and her husband, Uncle Eddie, owned Mama D's Italian Specialties and the Country Farm Market, thirty yards in front of my house. Aunt Rita had been a technician in a doctor's office for decades and then owned a "custard" (soft-serve ice cream) shop and mini-golf course with Angie and Eddie next to the market. MiMi, who'd helped her father run his businesses, later returned to teaching eighth-grade math. She was known to her students as strict and mean because she didn't take excuses for late assignments and didn't try to be their friend. Then, years later, when they'd run across her around town, they'd often remark, "Thank you. You cared about us. You prepared me for high school. You taught me how to think."

These women didn't preach equality. They *lived it*. Why march in a parade or label yourself when your back door swings open for all comers, your heart and home open to all? My values and compassion for others were instilled by them, their careful nudging, our shared Catholic faith and their adherence to the Golden Rule. They knelt for the Lord and stood for the flag. Their love was unsparing and unconditional. What all that meant for me was an unshakably secure upbringing despite whatever circumstances might have pointed the other way. Whenever I felt awkward or unsure of myself, as all kids do, those women were right there for me, telling me how unique I was, that I could do and be anything, and that if I changed my mind (or couldn't cut it in "the real world"), I could always come home. Most parents and loved ones convey this to their kids. Mine absolutely meant it.

As millions of women know, you don't need to have a child of your own to love children. We all spoil someone else's son or daughter at some time. My aunts Rita and Marie forwent marriage and motherhood and instantly had the center of gravity in their home shift to the needs of a little one. GiGi found herself with a niece/third-child combo. Led by Mom and Grandmom, this circle of selfless women took all the love they had inside them and lavished it on me.

FROM THE DAY I started talking, I didn't stop. Probing. Pontificating. Polling people. Performing every chance I got. Constantly asking questions that started with "how come . . . ?" I'd line up my dolls and stuffed animals like I was in a courtroom and they were my jury. They all sat there in stunned silence as I played judge, prosecutor, defense counsel, and all the witnesses. I loved to mimic whatever I'd just seen on television, and we certainly watched a ridiculous amount of it. I had an aptitude for remembering names and numbers, dates and data. I had zero skills (still) for designing, decorating, or drawing anything. By the time I was four, everyone agreed I should grow up to be a lawyer.

My formal education got off to a bit of a rocky start when I dropped out of nursery school (pre-K). I went dutifully for a few weeks, then decided the whole thing was stupid and I'd rather hang out at home and get a real education from Grandmom. We folded clothes, cooked, and crocheted. I helped to roll the gnocchi and snap the string beans. We watched soap operas, more game shows, and, every night at six, the Channel 10 news with John Facenda or Channel 6 with Larry Kane and his successor Jim Gardner, the same Philadelphia newscasts Joe Biden was watching in Delaware. Grandmom would tell me stories about the old days and offer her perspective on handling different people and different situations. She'd sneak in a little crème de menthe or sloe gin. Her lessons seemed wise at the time, and they still do. Even as a little girl, I recognized that our family was different. Not different-bad, but different. When I entered kindergarten at St. Joseph's Catholic School in nearby

Hammonton, where I would stay for the next thirteen years, I was the only child of divorce in my class.

We didn't know what we didn't know, but our days and lives were constantly full. Five nights a week, we played poker, dominoes, pinochle, and Kings in the Corner at the kitchen table. Lifelong friends and new acquaintances from work or church slipped in the back door unannounced. It was 30th Street Station in there. God forbid that anyone thought of calling first. They knew a hot meal and warm conversation would always be waiting. Maybe they'd stay a night or three.

I realized later that the conversations were contemporary and the content somewhat controversial. Abortion, divorce, homosexuality/ AIDS, alcohol, drug and gambling addictions, adultery, arrest. The family friend who left his wife and five kids for another man. The nun who left the convent to get married. The local business owner who lost it all at the craps tables. Yet I cannot recall a single political conversation. Not one. I suppose the women of the house voted for Democrats, at least until Ronald Reagan came around, and certainly for that handsome young Catholic, John F. Kennedy. But the pictures that hung on our walls weren't of presidents or politicians. They were the pope and the Last Supper and my latest artwork from school, along with the crucifixes, scapulars, and saint statues that loomed in almost every room. I was taught to rely on God, my family, and myself—not some politician who would never know me . . . literally.

The one exception to the "politics-free" childhood occurred in August 1974. I was seven years old. The Watergate hearings were on TV. And I was prancing around the house with homemade "Impeach Nixon" buttons on my cotton dress. I'd cut them out of a piece of paper and used safety pins. I hardly knew who Nixon was. I certainly didn't grasp the concept of impeachment. I'd heard people saying Nixon should be impeached, and I guess I was following the crowd, annoyed that these tedious hearings had preempted our regularly scheduled game shows and soap operas.

My cousins Renee and Jay slept over almost every weekend. The three of us were less than three years apart, and I was the youngest. They were like siblings to me. The card players had us empty ashtrays and fetch mixed drinks. Saturday mornings meant Jay trying to pry me awake so that my nearby sleeping mother couldn't hear us, then us dumping an

entire box of sugary cereal and the entire sugar bowl into the biggest
Tupperware we could find, grabbing two ladles, and watching cartoons
for hours before Renee and I would leave for dance school. Renee guided
me through the female rites of passage and gave big-sister, tough-love
advice. We spent countless nights side by side in her canopy bed, dreaming and scheming, imagining our future husbands, children's names, and
destinies. Jay, ten months my senior, made me the brother he never had,
and I have all the scars on my knees and elbows to prove it. From sliding
into home plate on the concrete "field" to flying off his Huffy bike. From
Jay I also got an above-average knowledge of all things football and
became a field hockey fan who'd yell "Pandemonium!" from the sidelines.

Every winter, Grandmom and Aunt Rita headed to Florida for three
months. Mom and I would move in with Aunt Angie, Uncle Eddie, Jay
and Renee, so there would be someone to look after me while Mom was
at work. Uncle Eddie treated me like one of his own, including me on
hunting and fishing trips, even letting me call him "Uncle Daddy" when I
was terrified to participate in the Father's Day celebrations in elementary
school.

Once or twice, someone may have suggested show business as a possible career for me. I took dance and voice classes and did a stint at
modeling school. And my growing repertoire of imitations was vastly
expanded by the premiere of *Saturday Night Live*. I was allowed to stay
up late and watch because my aunts loved that show. By Sunday afternoon, I was slaying my small audiences with my killer reenactments of
Gilda Radner's Roseanne Roseannadanna and of Dan Aykroyd and Jane
Curtin's point-counterpoints on "Weekend Update."

"Dan, you pompous ass."

"Jane, you ignorant slut."

Shades of CNN and Fox segments to come, even if I wasn't entirely
sure yet what all those insults meant. But I had my doubts about showbiz
as a career for me, and a lot of it was how I looked. Until around fifth
grade, I was taller than the boys and chubbier than the girls. Thankfully,
nature and hormones did their thing. I slimmed out, the boys shot up,
and all was right with the world again.

The friends I made in those years would still be my friends decades
later, indeed some of my very closest friends in life. Christine Ordille and
I found each other in kindergarten. She was the youngest of seven. Her

father died when she was nine. She spent a lot of time with our family, and me with hers. We'd stay in my room for hours, experimenting with music and makeup and talking to boys on the phone. So many of us went through K–12 in the same school together: Linda, the Kathys, Sheri, Patty, Rohna, Francine, Antoinette, Steven, and Benjamin. My neighbors Jimmy Baker and Todd Ferster have been by my side for decades.

High school brought more friends and lots of Petrongolos, including Michaela, with whom I've shared life's biggest, best, saddest and funniest moments. She was the only person I'd ever met named Michaela, decades before every third girl seemed to have it, and her friendship came without jealousy or judgment. Since Michaela was one of ten children and I was one of one, we had very different backgrounds. There were Petrongolos in every grade. Her parents and siblings are in my life. Her sisters Marina and Angela are among my very close friends.

Given my father's disappearing act and the family tradition he was carrying on, I certainly could have developed an anti-male ethos. But my upbringing oriented me differently. Uncles, cousins, and male family friends provided strength, compassion, and life skills. And incredibly, the women never spoke ill of the men who had wounded them. The prevailing wisdom was that a family's dirty laundry should remain inside the house. What I saw as restraint, grace, resilience, and self-reliance, others might view as a failure to dump good-for-nothing jerks who'd refused to honor their wives as equals worthy of respect. What I got was an education—unspoken but potent—in women's empowerment. My mother, grandmother, and aunts made their own way on their own terms, independently and self-reliantly.

The fact is, I never heard a negative word about my father from any of them. That helped fortify me when, at age twelve, my father suddenly reappeared, watching from the back of St. Anthony of Padua Catholic Church as Jay and I and other parishioners received the Catholic sacrament of Confirmation. My mother had run into him somewhere and invited him.

Soon after that, my father asked if the three of us might meet for dinner. I agreed to go, more for my mom than for me. I was curious, but I could have gone either way. Then I had to decide whether to invite him into my life. Christine gave great advice. I said yes, got myself a father and a half brother, Scott, and learned the value of forgiveness, redemption, and second chances. He quickly became a cool dad, taking my friends and me to arcades, scary movies, and Phillies games, and would stay in my life and grow in my heart for the next forty years.

Though I wasn't even a teenager yet, I could see there was a certain unspoken tragedy to him, just leaving my mother the way he did. He missed out on a great wife. He stepped back into my life at an age when girls really need paternal attention and affection. When I finally had children of my own, I'd see no point in passing on any of that pain or regret to the next generation. We loved having PopPop John active in our lives.

OUR LITTLE ATCO wasn't even officially a town. It was just a speck on the map in Waterford Township, Camden County, a part of New Jersey that looks more toward Philadelphia than to New York. This was a part of New Jersey that deserved the slogan on the license plates: "Garden State." I always felt at home with the wide-open spaces, the solid traditions, and the genuine simplicity. Atco wasn't even named for a person or a geographical feature, the way most places are. It was named for a company. Local lore has it that, in 1904, when the Atlantic Transport Company of West Virginia placed an order for four large vessels with a shipbuilder in Camden, the surrounding township became known as Atco, a sign of appreciation for all the new jobs. To the extent that outsiders know the place at all anymore, it's often because of the high-octane Sunday afternoons at the Atco Dragway, New Jersey's first drag strip. My mother's father, a short, stocky man ironically nicknamed "Jimmy the Brute," had owned the Atco Speedway, another drag strip, which closed before I was born.

Though our house was only half a block off White Horse Pike, the old Route 30 between Philadelphia and Atlantic City, the scattered subdivisions hadn't yet crowded out all the fruit farms and other open spaces around us. I got my first summer job at twelve, packing blueberries at a farm just down the Pike in Hammonton, the self-proclaimed "Blueberry Capital of the World." The operation was owned by Billy DiMeo and his family. Billy and my mom were high school classmates and the adult leaders of our parish youth group. They may have regretted bringing impressionable tweens and teens to see movies like *Grease* and *Saturday*

Night Fever. In the early years, my friend Brenda would walk down the path from her grandmother's house to my grandmother's house by seven thirty every morning, and my mother or an aunt would drive us to the Indian Brand packing shed. For eight solid summers, I would do my best to uphold Hammonton's blueberry pride.

Blueberry packers took the pints filled by blueberry pickers and covered the containers one by one with cellophane, using a little square form to make sure the seal was even and tight, before wrapping everything with a rubber band and putting the pint into a crate. Each crate held a dozen pints. We were paid sixteen cents for each crate we filled, and I was so fast, people would come by to watch me. My mother stopped by sometimes to help, but we would usually end up firing her because she kept eating the blueberries instead of packaging them. They were delicious, plump, sweet, and warm from the sun.

The blueberry shed is where I learned the meaning of working hard. The DiMeos, Mike DeLuca, Gina, the Roseannes, Lynnie and Shelley, Renee, Jay, and Christine worked there, too. Whatever gifts God gives, I came to understand, depend on the rocket fuel of hard work. With that, almost anything is possible.

In our family, money was just a means to an end, not the end itself. My mother taught me this not only through her own prodigious work ethic but also by the way she always put her family first. No matter how much or little we had, I learned early on that what mattered was to give more than you take and to work harder than everyone else. If you outwork them, you'll probably outsmart them. There was so much to learn from my mother. When I got into my teens, sometimes I would wait up for her to drive home from her night shift, and we would talk while she ate a late dinner. Even though she was often working, she was always present and available to me. I called her at work regularly, almost as often as my kids FaceTime me now. Feeling neglected wasn't ever an issue as Diane's daughter.

Despite her warm and supportive nature, Mom was anything but a pushover. Her standards and sense of propriety were as plain as the gold crucifix around her neck. In the fall of 1981, my freshman year of high school, I was sitting on our powder blue velvet couch with Michaela, watching TV. Something came on—I can't remember what it was—that somehow offended fourteen-year-old me.

"*God damn it!*" I hissed from the living room couch.

My mother was stirring a pot in the kitchen. I could see her in the distance. The words had barely come out of my mouth when she came whipping around the corner and straight toward me. I swear that crucifix was bouncing off her chest.

"What did you say?" she demanded.

"I don't know," I answered. "What did I say?"

"I heard you. What did you say?" Her question was even sharper the second time, and now she was raising the wooden spoon she was gripping in her hand. Michaela looked terrified. I knew what she was thinking. She was thinking, *Your mother is going to hit you with that spoon!* My mother would never hit me, though she probably should have sometimes. I could see the sauce dripping from the spoon. She was steaming mad.

"Mom—"

"You took God's name in vain! Son of a bitch!"

"I just—"

"That's a commandment. Don't ever take God's name in vain again. I don't care if you say 'Motherfucker! To hell with this shit!' But don't you ever take God's name again."

It was a classic case: My mother, this loving woman who wore a gold crucifix and no other jewelry and had this humble, self-denying life, also had a drunken sailor's potty mouth. My father was the truck driver, but Mommy actually spoke like one.

Decades later, when the pre-K teacher would summon me the day after Easter to say that my sweet, well-mannered four-year-old son had acted out of the ordinary and said, "Son of *aaaa BITCH!*" complete with intonation and hand gestures, I would know exactly where that came from.

"Oh. He was mimicking his mommom. That's just what my mother said after Easter Mass yesterday when someone pulled in front of her in the church parking lot," I explained.

"At the church?" the teacher asked me, half amused, half in horror.

"Yes," I said. "I guess that's why we go."

Chapter 2

Beltway Bound

Y ou think I'm busy now? You should have seen me in high school.

I sang in the church choir and performed in the school plays. I took dance classes. I had field hockey practice from three to six every afternoon. I worked on the floats for our local parades. I was the homecoming princess for my grade and a staple of the first honor roll (all As). High school was a whirlwind. That doesn't mean I was particularly excellent at any of it except for my schoolwork, but I liked having a lot going on. The idea of skipping school or not having my work done never even occurred to me. When I turned sixteen, I got my farmer's driver's license, thanks to my still-roaring career in the blueberry packing shed at the DiMeos' farm. Finally, Brenda and I didn't need my mother to drive us on summer mornings anymore. We made the trip to Hammonton in my Subaru BRAT with the open-bed back and two backward-facing plastic seats, and, later on, in my far sportier Camaro Berlinetta with a T-top. My blueberry triumphs continued. I was crowned Blueberry Pageant Princess (no swimsuit portion, mercifully). I won first prize at the town's blueberry festival one year for packing thirty-nine crates and nine pints (477 individual pints) in thirty-five minutes, thanks in large part to the supervision and coaching of the DiMeos' niece and my lifelong friend, Donna Mortellite.

The summer of 1984, between my junior and senior years, I attended a program at Georgetown University, living on campus for three weeks and taking intermediate French and American government. The girls from Chicago, Miami, Los Angeles, and South America had style—panache—and designer goods I'd seen only in magazines. It wasn't my first time in Washington, but it was the first time I'd spent more than a couple of days there. *I like this place,* I thought to myself. Later that summer, our local paper, the *Hammonton News,* asked me to write a guest column about the Democratic and Republican national conventions. I was beyond excited that an Italian Catholic woman, Geraldine Ferraro, had been chosen to run for vice president on the Democratic ticket. I couldn't wait to sit in front of the TV and hear her rousing address to her party's convention in San Francisco. I planned to center most of my column around her speech. But then I watched President Ronald Reagan address the Republicans in Dallas. A man old enough to be my grandfather. More familiar with Hollywood than Hammonton. No common denominators whatsoever with my young life in South Jersey. And yet he had something I'd never heard from someone whom people described as a leader. He was aspirational and accessible. Patriotic. Resolute. It was like he was talking straight to me.

He became the lead in my column.

Then, on September 19, 1984, something amazing occurred. President Reagan came to Hammonton to campaign. This was a major deal for us. Our little corner of New Jersey didn't get a lot of presidents passing through on their way to the G7. Twenty-five thousand people packed downtown that Wednesday. The schools closed so the students could attend. In his speech, the visiting president even sang the praises of a local hero.

"America's future," Reagan said, "rests in the message of hope in songs of a man so many young Americans admire, New Jersey's Bruce Springsteen." The crowd roared! He definitely connected with his audience that long-ago September day. And for me, Reagan's speech wasn't even the best part. Since I was co-captain of the field hockey team and had been New Jersey Blueberry Princess, I was among the handful of young people who got a chance to meet him.

It wasn't any more than a polite hello and a handshake. But I was hooked.

A few months later, I came home from school one afternoon and announced to my family that Sister Alma Blume told me I would be the valedictorian of my 1985 St. Joseph's High School graduating class. I already had in my brain pieces of the speech I would deliver on June 6.

My mom, my grandmother, and aunts were all in their usual spots at the kitchen table, engrossed in another fierce game of cards. When I broke the news, and before I could preview my speech and postgraduate plans, Grandmom Antoinette looked up from her hand and smiled at me. "That's great, honey," she said. "We're so proud. There's a roast beef on the stove."

The other women smiled and nodded, too.

"It's your turn," one of them said, but not to me.

PARTLY, IT WAS the summer program at Georgetown. Partly, it was meeting President Reagan. Partly, it was because I could drive my car back and forth to New Jersey. At some point, the idea occurred to me: I should go to college in our nation's capital.

I got wait-listed at my first choice, Georgetown. The other "better schools" I was accepted by, including Boston College, the year after its star quarterback Doug Flutie won the Heisman Trophy and where applications were way up, weren't in Washington, and I hadn't applied to any other schools in D.C. Then my mother heard about Trinity College. Maybe that was the right fit for me. Founded by the Sisters of Notre Dame de Namur in 1897, it was the nation's first Catholic liberal arts college for women. The school had great professors, a proud academic tradition, and a roster of notable alumnae that included future Democratic Speaker of the House Nancy Pelosi (Class of 1962, when her last name was still D'Alesandro). By the time I arrived in the fall of 1985, enrollment had dipped a bit after some formerly all-male colleges went coed. But Trinity was less than three miles from the U.S. Capitol and an easy three-hour car ride from home.

In those days, the District of Columbia was infamously known as the "murder capital" of the United States. But to me, it looked like a magical city filled with fascinating people and endless opportunities. I could be independent but still close enough to Atco to take my laundry, angst, and newfound friends home on the weekends and then return with a trunk load of homemade goodies.

"I think that was a gunshot," Mom said anxiously as we settled into our room at the Holiday Inn the night she moved me down.

"I think it's just a, uh, an engine backfiring," I assured her. "It's fine."

The next morning, we had breakfast and I lazily watched a rerun of *The Bionic Woman* on TV as my mom ironed all my clothes (again) and stuffed twenty-dollar bills and love notes from different family members throughout my belongings. That day, my mother left her only child at college. And, God bless her, she did it alone. I'm sure she cried the whole way home. Thank you, Mommy.

I HAD LIFE-CHANGING experiences at Trinity, on and off the campus on Michigan Avenue NE. I gobbled up internships and lectures. I did research at the Library of Congress. I volunteered on Capitol Hill. I loved the halls of democracy and the people in them. I watched an oral argument in the United States Supreme Court. One of the best things about a small liberal arts college is that the education you receive really can be tailored to you. I know mine was. I was itching to explore the wider world around me.

I spent my entire sophomore year in England, studying in a program at Oxford University, where I met American graduate students named Peter Flocos and Frank Luntz, dear friends to this day. Frank was obviously bright, and he was a natural networker. He introduced me to one of his rumpled but brilliant and engaging British friends, Boris Johnson, who coedited the university's satirical magazine, *Tributary*, and would eventually become prime minister of England.

I visited a dozen countries that year abroad with fellow student and forever friend Mary-Ellen Pearce and returned to the States, eager to grab every opportunity I could. Semester-long internships. Non-blueberry summer jobs. Volunteer gigs to immerse myself in the Washington political scene. Spending time with new friends like Cathleen, E.J., Deborah, Maggie, Nicole, Dawn, Laura, Sylvia, Christine, and Tara. My friend Maureen Blum and I revived the College Republican Club on campus and urged our friend Tricia Callahan to revive the College Democrats. Friends who wished to remain politically neutral attended both clubs' activities. Our timing seemed promising, a year ahead of the next presidential election.

In the fall of 1987, I volunteered to work on Jack Kemp's Republican campaign for president. Kemp was a rising congressman from Buffalo, who'd come into politics after stints as a college and NFL quarterback. But when I showed up the Friday before Labor Day at the Kemp-for-president headquarters, I was dispatched instead to his congressional office, where I was brought in to meet the congressman's foreign policy legislative assistant, Raul Fernandez.

"Nice to meet you," Raul said, handing me a stack of passports with barely a glance.

Kemp was leading a large delegation of important people on a trip to Central America. This was months after the Iran-Contra scandal— President Reagan's secret attempt to broker freedom for American hostages in Lebanon by supplying arms to the Contras in the Nicaraguan civil war. Kemp's group was set to depart on Monday. My first task was to make sure that everyone had a valid passport, no one's was expired, and all of it was sorted out by takeoff time.

When I got to Raul's passport, I froze.

How was I going to tell him that his date of birth was wrong?

There was no possible way Raul Jose Fernandez Jr. had just turned twenty-one. No way this man who had an important job in Congress and was ordering other staffers to do important things was only seven months older than me.

No way.

Except that he was. And besides organizing international fact-finding missions, he was also using his Spanish-language and computer skills to help position Kemp as a conservative leader and heir apparent to the Reagan legacy. But if that meant that I was interning in an office where youth and energy were rewarded, how bad could that be? It gave me an incentive to work harder and smarter. Raul kept giving me more and more responsibility, and I enjoyed the challenge so much I never did go back to the campaign. When other volunteers groaned about having to run the copy machine, I jumped at the chance and read every document that passed through my hands. I stayed on as Raul's foreign policy intern for the entire semester. We became fast friends, and that friendship blossomed into romance. We would end up dating on and off for the better part of a decade, racking up memories and life-shaping experiences that are untouchable in the time capsule of those years of my life.

*   *   *

ATCO WOULD ALWAYS be my home, but Washington was becoming my city. And in those college years, there was nothing I enjoyed more than bringing my two worlds together the best way I knew how. At Thanksgiving. At Easter. On any random weekend. In Atco.

I loved introducing my hometown and my Golden Girls to my new college friends. Our house became the Ellis Island of Sundays and holidays. Grandmom fed the masses with four burners, two ovens, no pantry, no microwave, and no boxed or canned foods. She was organic before organic was cool.

Hopping into my Chevy for the three-hour drive north, my friends had heard I was an only child. Then they were greeted by dozens of people referred to as "aunt," "uncle," or "cuz," all huddled around makeshift tables and unmatching chairs, ready to feast. One Easter Sunday, the usual arguments about sports, movies, TV shows, and relationships were percolating and circulating around the table, competing with the noise of clanging platters and serving pieces, when my cousin Renee motioned to me to look at my visiting friend. The poor girl had nothing on her plate and a painful mix of terror and anguish on her face.

"What's wrong?" I asked her.

"Why is everyone mad at each other?" she wanted to know.

Now I had the contorted face. "MAD!? No one is mad. Pass the gravy! Mad at each other?"

"Then why is everyone yelling?"

"No one is yelling," I yelled. "We're *talking*." I wasn't even sure she could hear me over the decibels of explosive laughter and interruptions around the table.

"We're not mad, and we're not yelling," I repeated in a more reasonable tone. "We're just opinionated. We love to talk. We love to eat."

I started piling things onto her plate, explaining, "My cousin over there? He thinks the Dallas Cowboys are great. I love him, but he's wrong. The one across from us? He broke it off with the nicest girl we ever met. He's a *stunod* who likes the *puttanas*. You see the pretty brunette down the way with the hair? She has the nerve to say that the *Rocky* and *The Godfather* sequels are better than the originals. She's lucky we let her into the house." I started to attack the lasagna instead.

"*Capisce?*" I asked in Italian. "You understand? Does it make sense?"

It didn't, but she politely nodded, enjoyed her weekend, and returned to Washington with more leftovers than could possibly fit in her dorm fridge.

Another year at Thanksgiving, a different friend was eating everything put in front of him. An overflowing charcuterie board and hot hors d'oeuvres were the opening acts to a seated fish course, followed by homemade pepperoni bread (stromboli) and escarole (Italian wedding) soup, and then meat lasagna or manicotti. By the time the stuffed turkeys (plural) and seven sides arrived, my friend had the look of terror and anguish. He said, "I'm already so full I don't think I can have another bite." Everyone dropped their utensils to look at him with stunned disappointment, like he'd killed the family dog.

"What?" my aunt said. "It's Thanksgiving! You have to have turkey."

"I know," he fumbled. "I, I thought I smelled one cooking, but I mean, all this food, I figured you just ate other things."

"Don't insult my family," I implored. "Just keep eating. It's your fault for wearing a belt and pants with buttons."

No matter when I came home, who I brought with me, or what day of the week it was, full meals would appear as randomly as cousins of somebody's neighbor's cousin, and there were generally so many desserts it seemed that "one pie, one person" was enshrined in our house constitution.

Despite my repeated protests, MiMi insisted on giving up her room whenever I had guests. "Honey, I made up the beds for you," she would say, ignoring the reality that my friends and I always ended up sacking out like newborn puppies on the living room carpet. Stepping over us one morning after yet another needless night on the sofa, MiMi finally surrendered: "I'm getting too old for this shit," she announced. "No more making beds. I'll just vacuum better from now on."

How fortunate I was to be raised in this hive of activity where conversation was easy and friendships lasting! From early childhood through college and beyond, I was exposed to a wide variety of views and beliefs. Nuns and priests showed up for Sunday dinner after Mass, met at the table by "Uncle" Hyman Rosen or "Aunt" Esther Malinsky, who taught me cool words like *kibitz* and *mazel tov* and introduced me to knishes, lox, and bagels. Or a wild-child cousin who had hitchhiked to get there.

Or mechanics from Puerto Rico and Yugoslavia (and their families) who worked at Grandpop's Chrysler-Plymouth agency, or "Uncle Willie" and his family from the neighboring town. All those cousins from Philly and Trenton. The names and the memories still make me smile. These men, women, and children all laid the foundation for the vocation I would eventually choose. Listening to them talk prepared my ears for anyone and opened my mind to what I call our "unifying differences."

WHILE RAUL MENTORED and loved me, I also learned polling at the knees of a master while I was still in college. I got a summer research position at the Wirthlin Group in the Washington suburbs. Frank Luntz had gone to work there, and he put in a good word for me. Dr. Richard Wirthlin was the legendary pollster to President Reagan. As senior advisor, he'd helped to shape Reagan's message going all the way back to California. He'd been Reagan's chief strategist, political consultant, and top pollster for twenty years, from 1968 through the second term of Reagan's presidency. For all I knew, he was the one who suggested President Reagan make a campaign stop in Hammonton.

The position paid eight dollars an hour, a step down from what I'd made packing blueberries. I had calculated I could bring home $320 a week, plus maybe a little overtime. That was a lot of money to me in 1988, even with my student loan payments and the intention to go to law school. Then I got my first paycheck and, with it, the rude awakening that millions of Americans had discovered before me: Taxes can really take a bite and FICA is not my friend!

I worked on issues like how to break the gender gap and was put on a top-secret project for General Motors for what would be their Saturn vehicle. Once or twice, Dr. Wirthlin called me into his office to share his insights on this field he'd helped to define. My immediate bosses, Neil Newhouse and Bill McInturff, invited me to tag along with them to a meeting at the Republican National Committee. Masters at work! I couldn't believe my good fortune. I was in the room where it happened, albeit in the back row.

I even felt privileged to drive fifteen minutes each way, each day to retrieve a hot-off-the-press, hard copy of *The Hotline*, the nation's premier daily digest of all things politics. As soon as I got back to the office, I made copies and delivered them to each of the principals.

"The client you pitched last week is mentioned on page nine," I'd announce excitedly to one of my bosses, my yellow highlighter still in hand. "Looks like that [congressional] seat in Ohio may open up. Do you want research?"

I developed a reputation for working hard and never wearing the same outfit twice. People presumed I came from money and had a killer wardrobe, endless budget, and a personal stylist. I had none of the above. What I had was a load of generous friends the same size and a scarf collection to rival that of Dr. Deborah Birx.

Later on, at times I was dispatched abroad to Ukraine, Spain, Chile—to help teach our international clients how to use polling and other Western campaign techniques. I spent four weeks in Israel, working with the Likud party and sharing a room with Frank Luntz at Tel Aviv's Commodore Hotel. (Until I met the man I would eventually marry, that was the longest time I ever shared a room with any man.) I learned a great deal culturally, politically, and professionally from those couple of weeks in Israel, and we even met a guy named Benjamin Netanyahu, who seemed destined for bigger things.

What was true in Atco was true in Washington. My life wasn't always so easy, but it was always so good. I'd been launched by wonderful women and then helped by others along the way: men and women, teachers and mentors and friends. But if I was going to keep making progress, I could already see by then, how far I would go would depend on the generosity of others, a little bit of luck, and mostly, me.

Chapter 3

The Pollstress

I sure went to a lot of trouble *not* to practice law.

Three years at the George Washington University Law School. A clerkship in the U.S. attorney's office, where my friend Betsy Schuman and I were both assigned to the brand-new sex crimes unit in the Felony I division. A summer-associate position at a top Washington litigation firm. Four—count 'em, *four*—bar admissions, which gave me the right to call myself a lawyer in New Jersey, Pennsylvania, Maryland, and Washington, D.C. Lots of close law school friends and lifelong connections, including Shelly, Chris, Andy, Andrew, and Michael Freeman, whom I nicknamed "Dollface" as soon as he noted that I seemed to call everyone "honey."

My family was proud of me, in their usual well-of-course kind of way. *I* was satisfied. But still. As I was about to leap into my lifelong career as a lawyer, something didn't feel right. I was like all those young women who break up with their boyfriends and protest: "It's not you, it's me." In this case, it really wasn't the law. It certainly wasn't the six-figure salary I stood to earn my first few years out of law school. That was mighty enticing to a twenty-five-year-old up to her eyeballs in student loan debt.

It *was* me.

Politics was still bouncing around in my head, and I couldn't seem to shake it.

My second year in law school, I'd almost taken a full-time job in the Bush-Quayle White House, an entry-level position with the Office of Presidential Personnel. I had four interviews, got an offer, and—*juicy gossip*—learned how the Bush people were trying to hustle the Reagan holdovers out the door. I loved the idea of working for the president, and I had it all scoped out. I could transfer to the nights-and-weekends program at law school, while I spent my days in the Old Executive Office Building, three blocks from campus. But Raul advised against it, saying the job was too low-level to justify diverting from full-time law school. So in the end, I said, "No, thank you." I'd have to wait another quarter century before I'd finally get my White House security badge—and a Secret Service nickname to boot.

I gave the law one last chance, clerking right after graduation for Judge Richard A. Levie of the D.C. Superior Court, a self-described liberal, a Reagan appointee, and a terrific mentor. It was fascinating seeing the court system from the inside. I coauthored what they told me was, at the time, the longest civil case opinion in D.C. Superior Court history, 213 pages, in a massive asbestos dispute. But ultimately I glanced into the mirror, gazed into the future, and did what I knew I had to do: I withdrew my acceptance of a full-time offer from the litigation firm where I'd been a summer associate. The law and me, we were just too awkward a match.

Typically lawyers were expected to "be seen" from early morning until late at night. Many of the successful female lawyers who'd made it to partners in the late 1980s and early 1990s seemed to have delayed or forgone marriage and/or children, some by choice, others through circumstance. I didn't know when I might be ready for that, but I didn't want to rule it out. And then there was the question of passion. To me, politics seemed to stir more of it.

So instead of toiling as a first-year associate in a law firm and cashing in on a big payday, I went to work for my friend Frank Luntz, who by then had been let go by Dick Wirthlin and gone off to start his own survey-research firm. Frank was the one who'd first opened my eyes to the inside world of politics. Now he was welcoming me into his own chosen corner of that sprawling field. We worked on Rudy Giuliani's first race for mayor of New York City, the one he lost to City Clerk David Dinkins. We were hired to help stop First Lady Hillary Clinton's proposed takeover of the nation's healthcare system, and we did. We also got busy on something called the Contract with America, a groundbreaking effort by Republicans in Congress to distill their conservative principles into a few clear points. That campaign was a smashing success, proving Frank's almost religious belief in the power of well-chosen language. If politics was going to be a war of words, Frank and his client (and soon to be Speaker of the House) Newt Gingrich believed, Republicans might as well win.

Frank seemed to trust me and like having me around. When he couldn't make a meeting, I stepped in for him. When a reporter couldn't get Frank on the phone, I'd dish up a quote or two. From our polls and our focus groups, we had access to valuable data, and part of our business model was sharing it. As time went on, Frank seemed to step back a little and give me more frontline responsibility. Part of it was sheer busyness and part of it was his trust in me, but it got me thinking, "How would I do this if I were out on my own?"

AS I BEGAN to learn the many secret passages of political Washington, I had an awesome ally at my side in Raul Fernandez.

My young prodigy of a boyfriend was prescient about the coming dot-com boom. With $40,000, some of it mine, he started his own company, Proxima. In Spanish, *proxima* means "next," the name of a company Steve Jobs had started. That little start-up would eventually become a top global provider of e-business services and an early partner to Fortune 500 companies like MCI and AOL. But in those early days, Raul was no dot-com bazillionaire. We shared a Welsh Corgi named Jesse. We'd push Raul's stick-shift Toyota or his used Nissan 300 ZX up the incline and splurge on a bucket of chicken and biscuits and a couple of milk shakes. I would handwrite the weekly checks for Raul's handful of employees and we dreamed of what might be.

Raul and I truly adored and enjoyed each other. Michaela went to work for him, first living with me in Washington, then to NYC, and then eventually moving to Italy with his company. To those who knew us well, marriage seemed imminent. But our road was sometimes rocky. We broke up and got back together a couple of times. Both of us were busy and could be awfully headstrong. When he was ready, I wasn't. When I was ready, he wasn't. Eventually we pulled the plug on our epic relationship and went our separate ways. I never regretted a day I spent with Raul. We parted with sadness and gratitude, he grew his tech empire and I got Jesse the Corgi. I would feel pride and pleasure in the years ahead watching Raul become a wildly successful entrepreneur, sports executive, philanthropist, husband, and father, as I went off in search of my own new adventures.

THERE COMES A time for some people, and that time came for me— the time I knew I was ready to make my professional move. I could just feel it. I'd worked hard. I'd teamed up with excellent people. I'd had my share of luck. I was ready to fly, without getting my wings clipped or soaring too close to the sun. For me, that time came in 1995, when I was twenty-eight years old. I was young for such a momentous decision, but I'd always believed in leaps of faith. I decided to leave the comfort and credibility of the Frank Luntz cocoon and fly off on my own.

Though I had tech prodigy Raul as my role model, twenty-eight is still awfully young to start your own company, especially in a world as old, male, and entrenched as the one I was hoping to reach the top of. But I'd always been impatient, for as long as I could remember, and I wasn't about to put the brakes on now.

"*the polling company, inc.,*" I would call my new firm.

That's no typo, as I had to explain to the print shop clerk who took the order for my first box of business cards. Small letters. No capitals. We would be the company without pretense or pomposity, and we could tackle almost anything. We'd underpromise and overdeliver. Do you like how I was already saying *we*? As if I had a massive staff behind me. At that point, I had a summer intern named Simone and a full-time staffer named Kim. Plus, I just kind of liked the way those small letters looked. To me, they were young and modern and cool. No caps wasn't such a hipster cliché in the mid-1990s.

The old warhorses of Republican polling didn't exactly lay out the welcome mat for the skinny, young, blond woman who was suddenly elbowing her way into their field. I think some people snickered in their certainty. But I worked hard to establish a roster of clients and a reputation in the industry. Some of the clients liked that I was a woman and could explain to businesses how they could reach female consumers and tell Republican politicians what it took to close the gender gap. Being young and hungry meant I had lots of time to travel and learn more about Americans where they lived. I pitched myself to potential clients as a fresh alternative—someone who would charge less and be more present in meetings and on the road than all those brand-name pollsters who somehow analyzed every inch of America from comfortable corner offices in Alexandria, Virginia, or midtown Manhattan. I'm sorry, but that claim was always a con job, no matter how the old boys tried to explain it to the clueless clients who hired them.

"We don't trust her numbers," one in particular would sneer about me. They hadn't *seen* my numbers. But I had *their* number. They weren't so impressive or insightful. Years later, an opposition researcher would take me to lunch and say to me, "I've never encountered one person so universally gossiped about." *Let them curse the darkness,* I thought. *I'm on the 6 a.m. to Seattle.* But it did sting.

I never bothered my family with any of this. Those same strong women were busy enjoying my cousins' babies (Ron and Renee's Alexa and Astin, and Jay and Angel's Giovanna and Jimmy), minding Grandmom's health and their own. The Beltway game of mowing people down and occasionally moving them out put me in an entirely new league now, something I'm not sure they would have completely understood. But from the loving and sturdy women who had raised me, I knew exactly how to respond: keep showing up and hold my head high. Outwork, outfox, outsmart, and outclass them.

MY MALE COMPETITORS defined themselves as *political* pollsters, working the Republican side of the street. There was a whole other group who serviced Democrats. I took a broader approach. I preferred to think of myself as a cultural anthropologist, digging out hidden truths no one had even thought to look for. That could mean working with a political candidate, a corporation, an advocacy organization, or a do-good group. Regardless of the turf or the industry, the truth-seeking techniques were the same. It all came down to three things: the science and art of survey research. The patience to listen and keep an open mind, which I had inside me, along with an abiding curiosity, from growing up in such a noisy home. I also possessed the third thing, the analytical skills to interpret the results. The critical thinking I'd learned in law school was a big help with that. There's nothing you can't discover about the true feelings of Americans if you survey the right people and listen to what they say. Don't judge them. Just let them talk. Then it's up to you to apply their authentic opinions to the issues at hand. Mentors and colleagues like J. Patrick Rooney, Len Sanderson, Arthur Mason, Grover Norquist, Karen Kerrigan, and Pat Pizzella opened doors and took a chance on me. I learned quickly to accept hearing the word *no* more often than I said it. Sure, there was hierarchy and misogyny, but there was even more opportunity—and who knew if it *would* "knock twice." I knew I would face rejection. I could not control others' reactions, but I could control my own input and integrity. High risk, high reward. Patience and perseverance. Courage over fear. I learned the hard way that in business there is plenty of room for passion but very little for emotion, and to not confuse the two. Noting that our skills do not always meet our ambition or others' expectations, a wise judicial clerk named Charlotte told me, "If you can't always be good, always be nice." There was something to that.

The Republican pollsters and consultants who filled all the seats on the gravy train did me a huge favor. They could make a living from doing just politics, but I was forced to branch out and do nonpolitical work for corporations, associations, and nonprofits. While my competitors focused only on what "likely voters" were thinking and doing that off-year election cycle, I was learning about the other half of the country, too: how Americans spent their time, their money, what their aspirations, expectations, and frustrations were. Years later, my firm was one of three invited to pitch on a substantial project for *Better Homes & Gardens*, then one of the most-read, widely circulated magazines in the country.

In the workplace, sometimes you're on and sometimes you are less "on." Sometimes you're off. I'd experienced plenty of each over the course of my career. That day in a skyscraper in Manhattan, Monica Watson and I were on. Our audience was attentive, inquisitive, and collaborative. When it was time to leave, I was already thinking about a creative thank-you package to restate our commitment and to remind them of our presentation. Then I noticed that the bigwig who was the ultimate decision-maker on this project was staring at me. Not at my face, or my chest, or—this being Manhattan—at my purse or shoes. He was staring at my belly. I was in my third trimester, pregnant with twins.

"Well, obviously, soon you will be out of commission, so who will be servicing our project?" he asked. "Who will be the key contacts?"

"You can't ask her that," objected his female colleague, an older, accomplished woman whose generation was among the first to navigate such things.

"No, it's okay," I quickly interjected. "I don't mind if he asks me that."

I did mind, actually. It is fair to ask who would be the day-to-day contact on a project. It is fair to inquire about cost, experience, competitive advantage, vision, deliverables, and the like. What's not fair is the selectivity of who gets asked which questions. The implication, of course, was that new motherhood would rob me of adequate time to fulfill the contract terms. So I continued.

"I don't mind if he asks me that, so long as he asks the men who are competing for this contract how often they golf, gamble, play video games, watch sports, frequent bars and restaurants, and carry on clandestine affairs or similar activities that divert their time and attention from 'servicing' your project."

That was my competition. Now this guy saw his competition as a couple of newborns.

The decision-maker responded with a stunned look. What else was he going to say? Ultimately, Jefrey Pollock, a Democrat, and a former colleague with whom I'd shared an office at Luntz Research (along with Ron Dermer, former Israeli ambassador to the United States), was awarded the project. Jefrey is both an excellent pollster and my friend. Maybe his presentation or prices was better. Maybe he was secretly expert in housekeeping and gardening. Maybe it was something else.

Soon, some other major clients were liking what they heard and signed with me. The acting commissioner of Major League Baseball, Bud Selig, wanted my help attracting fans and navigating novel issues. At Martha Stewart Living Omnimedia, the eponymous founder and her team demanded smart, strategic results from a coterie of consultants, and I was thrilled to be one of them. There was Harlem Success Academy (later renamed "Success Academy Charter Schools"), the brainchild of Democrat official Eva Moskowitz. I told my growing team we weren't curing cancer, but we really could do good in the world by helping groups like these charter school pioneers who were offering children in failing schools a second lease on learning. ABC News. *Ladies' Home Journal.* Lifetime Television. Various food, beverage, and service companies. It was enriching work that dropped me right into the middle of apolitical America. In strip malls, outside stadiums and movie theaters, in apartment buildings and parking lots, I developed a keen sense of what people thought, including far from the cities and coasts, and became skilled in asking the right questions.

My law degree came in unexpectedly handy, competing for business and being out in the field. It gave me a credential that the other pollsters didn't have, and, yes, that mattered in hypercompetitive Washington, especially for someone young and different.

New York, Miami, Los Angeles, Boston, Chicago, Silicon Valley—most other major American metropolises seek, reward, elevate, and celebrate youth. Young people have energy! Young people have creativity! Young people work cheaply and constantly! In Washington, seniority is supreme. Maybe it comes from the way power is doled out in Congress. Hang around long enough and they'll probably make you a chairman of a subcommittee. Bald heads and gray heads seemed to have the most power and authority.

The unofficial slogan of Washington should probably be "Wait your turn." It wasn't at all clear to me that "my turn" would ever come naturally. I felt like it had to be nudged . . . or shoved. In politics, inertia is the most powerful physical force unless and until overtaken by friction. I'd remain respectful, nearly deferential, would shut up and listen, and find a way to politely be the friction.

SUCCESS DIDN'T COME overnight for me, but my plan was already unfolding in the ways that I hoped it would. It did have one noticeable drawback, though. All I seemed to do was work.

My office at 1220 Connecticut Avenue, just off Dupont Circle, and not far from the White House, was a gorgeous loft that once housed fashion designers and would later become a nightclub. On Saturdays, I would run a few miles, clean my condo, do what I had to do, then go into the office with my corgi and work, work, work. I'd walk around the corner to St. Matthew's Cathedral for Saturday night Mass, then come back and work till 9 p.m. That's about the time of day when the neighborhood transformed into what reminded me of the lively European nightclub zones I had visited during my sophomore year at Oxford. But for me now, those Saturday nights weren't so different from the other six nights of the week. All my days and nights were the same. I worked. I visited with old friends from home and school. I drove up to Atco to see the Golden Girls and my cousins and their new babies whenever I could. But I was building a business and establishing myself and traveling all over for work, and that meant I was crazy busy most of the time. I couldn't complain. It was the life I had chosen, the life I loved. My strategy was working. My client list was multiplying. Talented men and women wanted to work with me. My competitors were noticing. And without even realizing it, I was also becoming famous, at least by Washington standards.

Which is definitely better than infamous.

I still had a lot to learn about how to fight for myself, believe in myself, and assert myself. That much became clear when I took a surprising call in my office one afternoon. On the other end was a representative from a professional speaking agency. He said I had been requested by name, along with a male pollster who worked for Democrats, to address the annual meeting of a major financial association. Each of us would speak for twenty minutes, then take questions together for twenty minutes. It would be at the Mayflower Hotel, just a few blocks from my office.

"Sure," I said. *Why not?*

"Do you have an agent we should contact?" the guy from the speakers' bureau asked. "What is your speaking fee?"

Right there, I froze.

I'd made speeches regularly but not for money. Sure, I'd studied "free speech" in law school as protected under the First Amendment. But lately, "free speech" meant, "[If you don't have a speaking budget], call Kellyanne." It was about to happen again, and this time, I had no one but myself to blame.

Someone had literally just asked me to name my price, to tell my value, and I was hesitating like a zero. I knew I was on the verge of undercutting my worth. Even when I didn't have to, I was about to sell myself short again.

I was *this* close to prattling, "Sorry. It's okay. You don't need to pay me. I'm just up the street. You've invited me for lunch. That's plenty."

Instead, I reached for Meg Ryan's line from the iconic Katz's Deli scene in the movie *When Harry Met Sally*.

"I'll have what he's having."

"Sorry? What?"

"You said Mark and I would be doing the same thing, and you already talked to him, and he agreed to it, so—I'll have what he's having."

"Well, Mark has asked for $3,500 net. Would that be acceptable?"

I suppressed a squeal, feigned standoffishness, and responded curtly in some pseudo-snotty accent, "That will be fine."

I hung up the phone in disbelief and fell to the floor. *Thirty-five hundred dollars to walk down the street and charm a crowd with polling data?* I was clearly a pushover in need of a makeover. But at least I was learning the game.

Chapter 4

The Pundettes

Gail Evans flew up from Atlanta to have breakfast with me. She was the vice president for talent and booking at CNN, the highest-ranking woman at the network. Joining us that morning in the elegant dining room at the Four Seasons Hotel in Georgetown was Tom Hannon, who oversaw CNN's political coverage in their D.C. bureau.

This was January 1996. I'd had my own polling company for a grand total of seven months by then. Gail got right to the point.

"You know you do very well on our network. We'd like to offer you a contract to be a regular political analyst on CNN."

Get paid for going on television? I think the first word out of my mouth was "*What?*"

I'd been on TV a bit over the previous year and a half. It began one day that Frank Luntz didn't show up. The booker called our office in a panic, and I rushed over. I plopped into the chair. The director counted us in. The host did his open and then turned to me.

"What does your data show?"

I didn't think I was ready for that moment. But I *was* ready for that moment.

I started talking. My facts and figures landed where they were supposed to. I had a few snappy lines of analysis. I wasn't nervous at all. If I could keep my wits about me at our raucous dinner table in Atco, how hard could a TV studio be? Soon I was getting calls from other shows and networks.

My time at CNN was magical and important for my career. I got tons of air time to cover everything from caucuses to conventions, primaries to political rallies.

The year after my CNN gig, Fox chief Roger Ailes invited me to audition with different people, including Democrat NPR reporter Juan Williams. I enjoyed the sparring segments. Ailes made me an offer in his office at the News Corp headquarters. I told him I was flattered, but I loved my work as a pollster, was about to take on my first presidential race (former vice president Dan Quayle), and needed to stay available to appear on all networks.

Declining an offer from the legendary Ailes was not something done often. I'd struggled with the decision, yet I wasn't sure I wanted or would be good at a full-time TV job.

By then, my office was already being flooded with handwritten letters and calls. (This was pre-email.) Everything from marriage proposals to death threats to "your hair is a disaster" to "how can I hire your company." I especially liked those "hire your company" calls. Somebody was watching this stuff. And not just one or two somebodies. Clearly these cable news channels were powerful, and they all had at least two things in common:

They all had twenty-four hours a day to fill. And they all needed people to fill it.

People like me.

ONE DAY IT struck me. Being a regular presence on television provided a one-on-one audience with anyone who was watching. In her living room. On his office TV. In an airport or at the gym. A chance to share my views and insights. A chance for all those people to get to know me. A chance for them to decide for themselves. No one could intimidate me or interrupt me or stand between me and the camera. No one could turn me into something I wasn't. It was a direct and pure kind of communication, even though lots of people had lots of reasons to hate TV. Now it was just me and you and whoever else was watching. And you could decide: Do you like what you are hearing? Do I seem to make sense? Do I provide compelling evidence to support my arguments? Am I someone you'd like to hear more from?

Do you have any idea how important a competitive advantage that can be in the world?

I was hearing directly from all kinds of people. Directly from congressmen. Directly from senators. Directly from political candidates. Directly from speaking bureaus. Directly from book publishers. Directly from businesspeople who might want to supplement their outside research team.

"Hey, I saw you on CNN," their emails and phones message would say. "Can you give me a call?"

These were people, many of them I'd have never been able to reach on the phone in my pre-TV days. But once they felt like they knew me from their own living rooms, they were suddenly wanting to talk to me. I recognized immediately: *This isn't just good for my ego. It could be very good for business, too.*

Though I was never nervous appearing in front of the camera, I still had plenty to learn. Stop talking with my hands. Give the hair and makeup artists more than ten minutes to apply those tricks of the trade that make us all look prettier and better rested. Thankfully, I had an honest critic who wasn't scared to mention them: my childhood friend Michaela, who came to live with me for a year in D.C. The people who knew me longest and loved me deepest—forever friends and closest relatives—could be the most frank.

"Why do you look angry on TV?" Michaela said to me early in my TV journey.

"I don't look angry," I shot back reflexively.

"You do," she assured me. "In real life, you're so funny. You're always laughing. You're cracking people up."

I went back and looked at myself on VHS tape, which was the only way we had of doing that then. And I had to admit it: Michaela was right.

"What were you thinking at that moment on the air?" she asked me.

"I was thinking of being serious," I said. "I was thinking of being taken seriously."

"People already take you seriously," Michaela said, probably too polite to tell me that what I really should have been focused on was my awful hair. "That's why they keep having you on."

This came from somebody who loved me unconditionally and would never be jealous. Michaela was always going to root for me. And she was giving me constructive criticism. "You don't seem like yourself on TV," she said.

"A lot of people don't seem like themselves," I said. "And you're right. I hate that. I want to be exactly who I am."

"Then be you," Michaela told me. "You is enough."

You is enough. I've reflected on and reminded myself of that so many times since, and shared it with other women and girls, including my own daughters. Ladies, how many times do we feel like "less-than"? Or apologize even though we did or said nothing wrong? Pass it on: "'Being you' is enough!"

I WASN'T THE only young woman in Washington or New York who was developing a growing presence on cable TV, not even the only young female Republican. Now that CNN, Fox, MSNBC, CNBC, Bloomberg TV, and others were in the game, we seemed to be everywhere. Young. Lively. Stylish. Opinionated. Thin. TV is a visual medium, and it's always had its rigid prejudices. But beyond whatever physical attributes they had, here was the good part: Almost all these women had a lot to say.

There was Laura Ingraham, who'd clerked for Supreme Court justice Clarence Thomas. There was lawyer Barbara Olson, the chief investigative counsel for the House Government Reform and Oversight Committee, who was married to Washington power lawyer and later U.S. solicitor general Theodore Olson. (Sadly, we would lose courageous Barbara when she was murdered on her early-morning flight, American Airlines 77, on 9/11.) There was April Lassiter, then policy advisor to House Majority Whip Tom DeLay, who was our own Fox-ready Joan Jett. When April wasn't denouncing Democrats on *Hannity & Colmes,* she was playing and singing in the bar band "Joe," fronted by a Florida Republican congressman named Joe Scarborough.

"I have no patience for your wink-and-nod politicization," she sang. "I have no interest in your femi-Nazi actualization."

There was Ann Coulter, also an attorney, who had worked for U.S. senator Spencer Abraham of Michigan and became the outrage-provoking "bomb thrower" of the group. There were a few others. And there was me.

I was the legally trained data expert and businesswoman of the group. As a professional pollster appearing on CNN and then on other networks, I wasn't interested in screaming on television or delivering personal insults, an occasional counterpunch or earned dig notwithstanding. I could call on actual facts to support my arguments. Survey results. Focus group illustrations. When I said, "The American people think . . ." I could back it up with fresh data, facts, and figures. I'd just been inside the heads of hundreds, sometimes thousands, of them. And as a lawyer, I knew how to marshal evidence into coherent arguments. I wasn't as interested in pissing people off for the sugar high, even as some would invite it by throwing the first punch. The businesswoman in me and the adult version of the toddler who longed for a daddy liked building bridges, not destroying them.

On TV, I was often paired with Democrats—men as frequently as women, and more than a few members of the media (occupying the "Democrat" seat). I tried to make my points with passion and professionalism without attacking my sparring partners personally . . . and still be me. In fact, I liked many of the people I was paired against. Celinda Lake. Douglas Schoen. Peter Fenn. Howard Fineman. Hilary Rosen. Many of them I respected professionally and enjoyed personally. Some of them just happened to be tragically, hopelessly, politically wrong. And I was happy to show them how with a big smile on my face.

TV gave me an unexpected taste of fame; my little business furnished the fulfillment. I still boarded those 6 a.m. flights to "flyover country" to pitch a new client or to the West Coast for a lunch speech and a thousand-dollar fee about what women really want. "How's it playing in Peoria?" the old saying goes. I'd hop on a prop plane to discern precisely that.

There were even more things to learn. When you go on TV to express your opinions, a thousand opinions flow. People will comment on how you look more than what you say, and it won't always be flattering. I lacked some of the natural beauty and the Ivy League degrees of other commentators. I was a first-generation college and law school graduate and politico. When people saw me, I hoped they would say "Wow, who is that? She sounds really smart." And maybe they would also say "She's not bad-looking, either. I'd like to know who that woman is." That is part of why I also had talk radio appearances in my repertoire. That forum forces the listener to focus on substance, not whether I was having another bad hair day, and offers long-form interviewing.

"Where do you get that stuff?" my college friend Mary-Ellen asked me one day when I dropped by to see her and her newborn in Concord, New Hampshire, in early 2000 during a first-look focus group in the "First in the Nation" primary state. "We can't stop laughing when you quote *The Brady Bunch* or *Golden Girls* episodes on TV." Who needs to be in class with Harvard professors Laurence Tribe or Alan Dershowitz if you can quote Greg and Marcia Brady or Sophia, Blanche, Rose, and Dorothy?

I was lucky to be there at the right moment, just as the news channels were growing and the Clinton scandals were exploding and a heightened interest in politics was spreading across the land. Before you knew it, major newspapers and national magazines were running long takeouts on the *pundettes*. Pundettes, that's what they came to call us, this new tribe of skinny, young, (mostly) blond, conservative women who seemed to have suddenly stomped their way into the center of the fast-changing arena of TV news.

For those of us caught in this media tornedo, the daily challenge was managing to still sound smart and focused and real as the craziness swirled around. Magazines photographed and profiled us. (Hanging with John F. Kennedy Jr. for the second issue of his business brainchild, *George* magazine, was cool.) Some of it got a little ridiculous, even in the conservative media, as when a truly ugly male (inside and out) at *The Weekly Standard* branded us "a new class of Washington-bred cigar-and-martini bimbos." Really? I never smoked cigars. And I could handle, like, half a martini. Sometimes I got a kick out of the whole thing and played snarkily along. I can't deny retorts like *thankfully*, "my broad mind and small waist have not switched places."

My self-deprecation was not self-deprivation. I was keeping it real—and keeping the mouthy mean boys and girls in check.

When it came to the rise of the conservative women on television, ample credit goes to Bill Maher, the comedian and talk show host whose programs *Politically Incorrect* on ABC and *Real Time* on HBO regularly featured men and women of different opinions. Bill seemed to fancy us for our energy, our preparation, and what we had to say. That's what made us fixtures on *Politically Incorrect*, which was just then moving to Los Angeles and ABC. This was big. The show was on right before *Nightline*. It had selfish benefits, too. For me as a small business-woman, getting a free, first-class ticket to Los Angeles and a nice hotel room was golden. Once American 77, the morning flight from Dulles, landed at LAX, I didn't whoop it up on Rodeo Drive or seek out celebrities at the usual haunts. I packed my schedule with business meetings and client lunches instead. I'd get back to the hotel, grab a quick nap and a shower, then arrive at the studio in plenty of time for a spirited back-and-forth with the host and his other guests. Then I'd take the red-eye back to Washington or I'd stay over and fit in a few more meetings the next day.

Bill Maher was great to us. He thought we were smart. He liked the fact that we came with something to say. We held our own against liberal lemmings or Hollywood honchos. And we weren't only spouting the predictable Republican Party line. Just to be clear: I didn't know what the party line was most of the time. No one was telling me what to say on any of these shows. That was up to me. It wasn't like today, when too many in Washington repeat the talking points from one party or the other or both and fear giving airtime to the other half of the country, the one that disagrees with them. It wasn't like that at all. We had to think for ourselves, and on our feet. We had to craft our own arguments and make our own bones.

I KNOW MY clients and potential clients in the polling business were paying attention, and there wasn't much my frustrated competitors, who ran the gamut between never being invited on TV or going on once and never being invited back on, could do about it.

Oh, the sniping from the Old Boys Network (and the New Boys Network) endured. It always would. If anything, as I got bigger and my media presence continued to rise, the grumbling grew louder and more intense. My jealous male competitors—and a few females—made a sport of trashing the educated, creative young woman who had invaded their turf. They spread the same types of old rumors and insinuations women have endured for ages. I won't repeat much more of their garbage, but you can well imagine. Now multiply by ten.

"Oh, yeah, she's a nice person," I heard one of them say dismissively. "We wanted her to join our firm a while ago, but we really don't know how she's doing on her own. Maybe she's trying to prove herself. Maybe she got in a fight with Frank. But we're not worried in the least about her. She isn't on our level at all."

Foolish and shortsighted. Because day after day, there I was, talking directly to and often for America through the magic of television. It delivered opportunities. Soon it would even deliver love.

Chapter 5

For Better or for Worse

I'd been in business for four years by the time George T. Conway III blipped across my radar screen. He'd seen me on TV and then on the cover of *Capital Style,* a shiny D.C. magazine running a story about "Kellyanne Fitzpatrick and the Pundettes." George had picked up a free copy on the Metroliner between New York and Washington. That's when he asked his pal Ann Coulter, who was not on the cover but was featured in the article, to make an introduction.

Looking back, this was unlike George. He was shy in a sweet and unassuming way. He could have easily tossed that magazine aside in favor of poring over a much thicker and heady legal brief. Marriage wasn't on my mind. My dating life was more theoretical than real. The only going steady I'd done lately was with *the polling company* and my four toddler godchildren, Alexa, Astin, Giovanna, and Jimmy, in South Jersey. Friends and colleagues had been trying to fix me up with people. But I had zero interest in dating anyone.

"What's wrong with him?" a friend would ask each time I rebuffed another potential suitor.

"Nothing, probably," I'd shrug. "It's me, not him."

I just didn't see the point of another round of Q-and-A with a stranger over dinner and me stuck in my work clothes for the seventeenth consecutive hour.

Not all dates were disasters. Some were better than others. I did follow up with the nephrologist whom I'd dragged to a minor-league baseball game and client dinner in Trenton, albeit a year later.

"Kellyanne, wow, it's so nice to hear from you!" the good doctor exclaimed after his office pulled him out of an appointment. "I . . ."

"I'm sorry I never called, uh, for like a year or year and a half. It's definitely me, not you, but look, my grandmother has been ailing, and now they tell me her kidneys are failing. I'm driving up from Washington. What can we do for her?"

Fred Thompson's gift for storytelling and fill-the-room personality is memorable. A few months of flirtatious dinners, deep conversation, and uncontrollable laughter with the actor-turned-senator-from-Tennessee had its roots in an interview I'd given to the *New York Post*. Asked about future presidential candidates, I separated true "presidential timber" from the "woodchips." I mentioned Thompson, who was divorced and a rising star in the Republican Party. I told the paper he had the makings of the total presidential package except for one thing: He lacked a First Lady.

Soon after my quote appeared, I was seated at a big annual black-tie dinner at the Washington Hilton. A waiter slipped me a handwritten note. It said, "Kellyanne—I saw your quote in the *New York Post* about what I'm lacking. Are you available? Fred."

"I'm mortified, if that counts," I said sheepishly when the senator wandered over later that night, and I agreed to go to dinner.

Where I come from, thirty-two is past the average age for marriage and motherhood. Way past. When my cousin Renee got married in my second week of law school, she turned and threw her bouquet directly at me. *Hell no.* I threw it right back at her and received instead a rare rebuke from Grandmom Antoinette, who must have put Renee up to it. Ten years later, I still felt no urgency to find a soul mate and settle down, whomever and whatever that might eventually look like for me. I was happy with the life I had made for myself. My business was still growing. I was constantly on TV. I had a wonderful family. It just didn't include a husband or children and I loved waking up every day, running, walking Jesse, hanging out with old and new friends, working, pitching new clients, working some more, going on TV, returning to South Jersey regularly so as not to miss out on the godchildren and elders. Also flying around the country collecting the opinions, ideas, and demands of a diverse collection of Americans, then sharing all that with the people making decisions on their behalf. Dating just didn't seem worth the trouble, especially since my professional and social interactions provided so many opportunities to engage with different people, minus the small talk, the bio exchanges, and the "now we're on a date" contrivance.

Meeting for drinks or dinner in the buffer zone of a larger group sometimes allowed me to size up potential suitors without risk of rejection by either of us. "Dating on the cheap," a friend of mine liked to call it, and it had nothing to do with money.

"I want to set you up with my friend George," Ann Coulter announced one night after we both exited the Washington set of Geraldo Rivera's CNBC talk show. "We just came back from skiing in Austria," Ann added casually, flashing a photo of beautiful people in front of a stunning snow-covered mountain. She suggested maybe we could all go skiing together.

Pass. I had broken my jaw skiing (sliding headfirst into a boulder) on a bunny hill in New Jersey. With Michaela behind me, screaming "slow down!" Never again. Plus, I absolutely hate the cold.

"He's a lawyer . . ."

Pass. I was a self-hating, fully recovered lawyer. Why double the misery?

". . . in New York."

Pass. New York always felt chaotic and overwhelming to me. And a little lonely. Whenever I had business there, I took the train or shuttle flight up and back the same day. It was a running joke among my friends that I never stayed long enough in Manhattan to buy a bagel, let alone a pair of shoes.

"He's loaded," Ann said, delivering what she assumed would be the irresistible coup de grâce.

Pass.

Oh, dear. I'd finally ended it once and for all with a newly minted, new-media dot-com multi-multi-multi-millionaire. The happiest times I'd had with Raul were when he and I were younger, sitting on the banks of the Potomac or stealing away to West Virginia for the weekend.

Plus, I was making my own good coin by then.

"You know what?" I told Coulter. "I'm sure George is a really nice guy, and we can definitely put our heads together and find someone for him. It's not him. It's me, I assure you."

That phrase again.

I had no intention of budging. Had Ann Coulter's relentless powers of persuasion finally met their match? It was looking that way for sure.

Ann waited a few months, then tried again, inviting me to a cocktail party she was hosting at her apartment at the famed Kennedy-Warren apartment complex in Washington. Her boyfriend at the time worked for Senator Joe Biden of Delaware and would be there, along with some others. George would come to town, and we would meet in the small crowd. No big deal, not a date. Just a few of Ann's friends, drinking and mingling and enjoying each other's casual company.

I agreed to go, then didn't show up. It was snowing that night in Washington, and after having dinner with three girlfriends at Tahoga in Georgetown (all of whom would later be bridesmaids in mine and George's wedding), one of them was afraid to drive on the icy roads. So I navigated her back and got home late. Too late for cocktails at Ann's place. I did call George the next morning to apologize. I asked if he had breakfast or lunch plans, but he was headed back to New York, no doubt convinced I was rude or a prude.

And that was that with George. It would take another nineteen months for the two of us to meet. Weeks after our near-miss nondate, he began dodging subpoenas in the Linda Tripp–Monica Lewinsky episode of the Whitewater investigation. Ironically, it turned out that we were both working a bit for the same cause and against the same president, William Jefferson Clinton. I was on TV daily discussing sexual harassment, censure, and, of course, impeachment, taking my law degree out for another spin. The *Wall Street Journal* published an op-ed I wrote about what to expect from plaintiff Paula Jones and defendant Bill Clinton. George was one of three conservative lawyers known in right-wing circles as "the elves," who were moonlighting pro bono for Jones. Paula was the former Arkansas state employee who in 1991 had been summoned to a room at the Excelsior Hotel in Little Rock, Arkansas, to see then-governor Clinton and who was now suing him in his personal capacity for sexual harassment, and with a little help from "the elves" and her attorney, she prevailed. The U.S. Supreme Court ruled unanimously that she could continue her lawsuit. Clinton coughed up $850,000 (in 1998 value) and later lied under oath. From sources he would never reveal (not publicly, anyway), George had obtained Linda Tripp's audiotapes of phone conversations with her friend, a White House intern, Monica Lewinsky, who confided details of an Oval Office affair with President Clinton. George shared the damning evidence with *Newsweek*'s Michael Isikoff, and when the magazine's editors refused to run the exposé, George gave a blogger named Matt Drudge the gift of a lifetime. George wrote the brief. Ann wrote the book. Literally.

That scoop placed Drudge on the major media map and Clinton on trial in the Senate.

IT WAS INTRIGUE at first sight when I finally met George Thomas Conway III on a Saturday afternoon in Quogue, New York, a beautiful hamlet in the Hamptons. It was the summer of 1999. George had rented a home on Dune Road for the month of August, and Coulter invited me to stay over. I didn't think that was such a good idea. But I agreed to rent a car and drive from New York City, where I'd been overnight for work, and stay for a few hours before heading to Philly, where I was booked to appear early the next morning on the local ABC affiliate. I was not staying at this man's house in the Hamptons. Not even with mutual friend Ann playing matchmaker or chaperone.

George was quiet in a mysterious "I've got something to tell you, but I'll wait" kind of way. Our conversation was easy but guarded. I learned he was the only child of an electrical engineer father who worked for the defense contractor Raytheon, and an organic chemist mother who emigrated from the Philippines. George grew up in Marlborough, Massachusetts, a working-class suburb of Boston. Like me, he was valedictorian of his high school class. Unlike me, he graduated magna cum laude with a biochemistry degree from Harvard at age twenty, and from Yale Law School at twenty-three. There he made law review and was president of the campus Federalist Society. A year out of law school, after he and his friend Bob Giuffra clerked for Judge Ralph K. Winter on the U.S. Second Circuit Court of Appeals, he joined powerhouse law firm Wachtell Lipton Rosen & Katz and by thirty was a partner in the firm's litigation department. It was clear from the get-go that he was generous to a fault, a gentleman who footed the bill for the proverbial party even if he wasn't the life of it. Not unlike my own path, George's route to success was circuitous and very much a modern American Dream, riddled with college and law school debt (each of us had paid ours off by the time we'd met) and punctuated by opportunities and lucky breaks.

I was reserved. He kept us busy. George drove me in his Corvette to a polo match in nearby Bridgehampton. As a house guest for even a few hours that day, I'd brought enough food to last them the rest of August. Grandmom Antoinette would have been proud. I left as planned late that afternoon, but the chase already seemed to be on. He kept angling to come down from New York to see me in Washington, trying to lure me out with hard-to-get reservations at some fancy French restaurant in Georgetown or an invitation to some A-list social event.

The problem was, I really did prefer to be at home on the weekends in my sweats, hanging out with Jesse the Corgi and my no-fail pals, Ben & Jerry. I spent my work weeks flying around the country and eating at fancy restaurants with clients. The treat for me was *not* having to do that. But I knew George was trying to make a good impression and being creative about it. Then he hit on something that was far more likely to work. He emailed to say he had two tickets to the American League Division Series. Now he was talking my language. I was finally in. We watched the New York Yankees dismantle the Boston Red Sox. Nothing heavy, just a fun day in the Bronx with my new friend George.

I'm a total sports fanatic, going all the way back to my scraped-knees days with cousin Jay in Atco. I was the tomboy who played football on the front lawn with the neighborhood boys, went to Eagles games at the Vet, and Phillies games with my father, Scott, and Christine. I was glued to the World Series every October and knew each of the U.S. Olympic hockey players' names before they delivered the "Miracle on Ice." I broke my nose playing field hockey in college and gave up on golf after two uninspiring lessons, when my client, friend, and golfer Rich Marcus noted it was more of a game than a sport. When George told me that he happened to have tickets for the National League Division Series as well, I ditched Ben & Jerry and headed back to New York on the spot.

When we saw the New York Mets play the Atlanta Braves with John Rocker pitching in the epic National League Championship Series of 1999, Matt Drudge and Ann Coulter joined us. Then the Yankees advanced, and all of a sudden George had tickets for the American League Championship Series. And then all of a sudden he had tickets for the World Series. George and the Yankees were both on a winning streak.

Our courtship was fun and easygoing. We really had a ball. We could talk about anything and everything. Sports. Our different backgrounds. Our shared politics. Places we'd traveled. People we knew in Washington and New York. We were on the same page politically and religiously. George was a solid conservative-libertarian, and he had recently reclaimed his Catholic faith. We never argued, not even about sports. We adopted each other's teams. I became a Yankees fan, and he cheered for my beloved Philadelphia Eagles. He joined the cult of Pembroke Welsh Corgi worshippers, too. George even braved the insanely gluttonous Thanksgiving Day meal with my extended South Jersey family and managed to find Atco on a map. He bought my four-legged Jesse a Donovan McNabb NFL jersey and a novel snack, pigs' ears. Clearly, he knew how to get my attention.

Spending more time with George meant spending more time in New York City. I was surprised when I noticed myself falling in love with both of them.

"What's up with this George?" my friend Betsy asked me a few months and ten professional sporting events into our budding romance. "He seems to be around a lot. Do you like him?"

"Do I *like* him?" I repeated out loud. I was as interested in the answer as Betsy was. "I find that his near-constant presence does not annoy the hell out of me."

"Oh my God, Kels!" she exclaimed. "For the rest of us, that's head over heels." Now this was getting serious. Our Bronx-to-Beltway fairy tale had officially begun.

George surprised me with tickets to Barbados aboard the Concorde. At breakfast one morning, he made note of an elderly couple seated near us. They'd sat there quietly through the meal, saying almost nothing to each other.

"That's so sad," George said. He asked me if I thought the couple had run out of things to say after all these years or was it that they just didn't like each other very much anymore?

"Probably a little bit of both," I answered reflexively.

By now, I could really see the essential sweetness of George Conway.

One day we were at a friend's house for a get-together and George, handsome in his lavender shirt and purple tie, caught my eye and winked at me. There was something just so charming and intimate about that simple gesture. When we went to brunch later that weekend, he mentioned a couple he knew and said of them, "You know, he doesn't adore her anymore. He doesn't treat her nicely with respect in front of other people. There's no adoring. You have to adore, have to cherish."

I liked that, and I never forgot it.

On October 14, 2000, George tied a diamond ring around Jesse the Corgi's neck and sent her to find me. It was after midnight because George realized when he got to my house in Virginia that it was Friday the thirteenth. So he waited to pop the question.

I said yes.

The entire next day we stayed at the house while I finished polling analyses. It was two weeks before the 2000 presidential election between George W. Bush and Al Gore. I was typing with the engagement ring that Betsy helped him select newly glinting on my finger. I was all in, but could not silence the self-doubting, self-denying voice in my head.

"Are you sure, George?" The man I loved was willing and eager to commit himself to me, and even at my age (thirty-three) and my stage (financially independent homeowner and business owner), I was self-sabotaging and giving him an escape hatch.

A LITTLE MORE than five months later, on April 28, 2001, we had an amazing wedding, with five priests on the altar (including "Uncle Father Joe," Monsignor Joseph DiMauro, the closest thing to a brother the four South Jersey Golden Girls ever had) at the Cathedral Basilica of Saints Peter and Paul. It's the mother church of the Catholic Archdiocese of Philadelphia, a domed Palladian affair built between 1846 and 1864. We chose Philadelphia because of its location between New York and Washington and right across the Benjamin Franklin Bridge from South Jersey. I'll say this much: None of our 360 guests would go home hungry.

My wedding dress was Aunt MiMi's gift to me. We had browsed at Vera Wang, Kleinfeld, and a couple of the other bridal emporia in

New York City. But we ended up at the Bridal Garden in Marlton, New Jersey, and I'm so glad we did. My white dress was off-the-rack and off-the-shoulder, skinny up top with a sparkly bodice, full and flowing below. I had lace, elbow-length gloves, and a simple, white veil. And it all meant more to me because it came from Aunt MiMi.

On the ride to the cathedral, my mother and father and I had a quiet moment together in the limousine. Both my parents were basking in my joy, and it made me happy to see them so happy . . . *together.* They walked side by side down the cathedral's center aisle, the first time they'd taken so many steps together in thirty-five years.

I walked myself down the aisle.

Ann Coulter did one of the readings, as did my law school friend Shelly Werge Allen. George and I each had a friend from college do a reading; mine was E. J. Collins, whose initials stand for Epiphany Joelle, and George's was Vicky Gorman Jacoby, whose cousin by marriage in Little Rock, Mary Jacoby, wrote the *Capitol File* cover story magazine that encouraged George to ask Ann about me. (Mary's husband is Glenn Simpson of Fusion GPS and discredited Steele Dossier fame.)

If you wanted to follow the arc of my first thirty-four years, all you had to do was glance up and down the pews. There were friends from childhood, friends from college and law school, friends from Washington and New York. There were relatives, near and nearer. Our four-day-old goddaughter, Abigail, traveled six hours in a rented Winnebago from New Hampshire with her champ of a mother, my college friend Mary-Ellen, Mary-Ellen's husband, parents, sisters, and sweet nineteen-month-old toddler, Emily. All the Petrongolos were there, and that's a lot of Petrongolos. Judge Levie, whom I clerked for right out of law school, came, too. I had a knockout lineup of bridesmaids from every chapter of my life: Christine Massarelli (K–12), Michaela Petrongolo (high school), Deirdre Mastrangelo and Maureen Blum (college), Angel Coia (my cousin Jay's wife), Betsy Schuman (law school), and Rachel Pearson (D.C.). My matron of honor was my cousin Renee. These women didn't just love me. They were a part of my DNA.

George's best man was Bob Giuffra, his classmate from Yale Law School and Judge Winter co-clerk. The Supreme Court litigator (and almost federal appellate judge) Miguel Estrada was a groomsman. So were Harvard classmate John Tormey II, Jerome Marcus, and Richard

Porter. Along with George, those last two had been the undercover Clinton impeachment "elves," three conservative attorneys who fed damaging and embarrassing evidence to independent counsel Ken Starr. The other groomsmen were my cousin Jay, my cousin Ron (Renee's husband), and my half-brother, Scott. And we didn't neglect the younger generation. We had two junior bridesmaids, the beautiful Alexa and Astin, who were ten years old. They wore matching white dresses with long, white gloves and floral tiaras, and carried bouquets of pink and white roses. My godson Jimmy and George's godson Jake were ring bearers, and precious Giovanna was our flower girl.

Yes, it was an over-the-top wedding. There's no other way to describe it. And George, who at that time did not like to be on the periphery of attention, let alone in the center of it, probably would have been happy to elope. But the way I looked at it, it may be the one time in your life when so many people you love are gathered together for a happy reason. And they sure did come. It was a big occasion for us and a big occasion for so many of them. The reception upped the bar even higher. It was in the Crystal Tea Room at the historic Wanamaker Building, across from Philadelphia City Hall. George and I missed the two hours of cocktails, caviar, escargot, Alaskan king crab legs, and other passed hors d'oeuvres while we zoomed around the city being photographed at iconic Philly locales, including, of course, the famous Rocky steps at the Philadelphia Museum of Art, where I'd taken my final "single girl" run that morning. Then everyone sat for an elegantly served dinner of sea bass and filet mignon with an array of side dishes I can't even remember anymore. That was followed by a Viennese dessert selection, an ice cream bar for the kiddies, and a six-and-a-half-foot-tall wedding cake created and assembled by famed New York baker-creator Sylvia Weinstock.

In between dances, George stood to welcome everyone. He thanked his family and my family and all the guests who came. Then I got up and said a few words. For once, just a few.

"Until I met George, forever just seemed like a very long time. Now I wonder if it's long enough. With George I can do absolutely anything or absolutely nothing and be equally happy."

Then the music cranked up. The dancing really got going. I kicked off my shoes and even dragged George onto the dance floor. We had two wedding songs: "Jersey Girl" by Bruce Springsteen and "Grow Old with

Me," from John Lennon's later years. We spoke to every single guest. All of it was loads of fun.

When the party was finally over, we headed back to the Marriott hotel, where we had reserved the honeymoon suite. The suite had a living room, a large dining area, a small kitchen, and two bedrooms. George and I took one of the bedrooms. But we weren't alone. My mother was in the other bedroom with Aunt Susie, her childhood friend, who'd been the maid of honor at my mom's wedding and who'd joined Donna Mortellite and Billy DiMeo as participants in our ceremony by bringing the gifts to the altar (the Offertory). Uncle Rocky and Aunt Joan also stopped by. Oh, and Aunt Rita, Aunt MiMi, and Aunt Angie stayed in the suite with us. "George and the Golden Girls" sounded like a cover band, but it was a fitting introduction to our new life.

At 2 a.m., George and I could hear the women in the other room, talking and laughing and reliving the whole special evening, while they tallied the cash from all the wedding envelopes our many relatives and old friends had slipped to us.

"I thought it would just be us," George said with a sigh before he reached over to turn off the light.

"Welcome to your new life," I told him. "When you married me, you married my whole family."

It was a joke. Sort of.

Soon we were off to Italy for our honeymoon. George had never been to Italy before. We took a detour to Milan to surprise Michaela, who was working there for my ex, Raul. I think Michaela was even more surprised when I insisted she spend a few days with us touring Italy.

"It's your honeymoon," she protested. "Don't you want to—?"

"*Nah*," I told her with a smile. "I've been vacationing with you my whole life. George is the new kid on the block," I joked. And that's how Michaela ended up, for real, as part of our honeymoon. "Forever is a long time," I reminded her. "He's got plenty of time with me." But it was George who pulled the real honeymoon surprise.

It was only after we got to Rome that I learned he had arranged for us to meet Pope John Paul II. And not just meet the pope. We were there as *sposi novelli*, newlyweds, and would receive a special papal blessing. I could hardly believe it. We'd be meeting the pope *in* Italy *and* be blessed by him! Thankfully, I had something to wear. George had secretly enlisted the help of my mother and my uncle Joe, the priest in our family. Uncle Joe had friends in the diocese, who had friends at the Vatican. He knew the drill. And my mom helped George pack my gown into a separate suitcase, which George hauled uncomplainingly all the way from home. I was genuinely shocked by the planning and stealth of all involved.

Pope John Paul couldn't have been nicer. And I couldn't have been more excited. I felt like a kid meeting Mickey Mouse. And of course, because my world is a very small place, a Fox News producer and her new husband were also there. The pope delivered such a beautiful blessing. George and I were both thrilled to receive it.

Our marriage was off to a promising start.

Chapter 6

Cheerful Chaos

George and I would have to commute. What choice did we have? The firm was in midtown Manhattan. My company was in Washington. We knew plenty of couples who lived in two cities. Some even bounced between New York and Los Angeles. Now, *that* was a grind! How hard could New York and Washington be?

I still had my bachelorette house in suburban Virginia. A year earlier, I'd traded up from my pre-George condo in Alexandria to a home in Vienna, in a new development called the Carrington. I was driving around one day with my Shelly when we stopped to see the model. I liked it so much, I made an offer the next day, and knowing I cannot design, draw, or decorate anything, I asked if I could buy some of the furnishings. That's where I would stay all week, trying to get my work done so George and I could have our weekends together in his city or mine, steal a three-day weekend when we could. Good-night phone calls aren't the same as good-night kisses, and there was far too much working on trains and planes. But you do what you must to make it work, and we did. When we were together, we were fully present. No extended time on our phones or computers, no separate TVs in separate rooms or one of us at the golf course for eight hours like so many couples I'd witnessed.

We had a nice, new place in New York City. George had given up the townhouse basement he'd rented for ten years on 78th and Lexington. Together we bought a condo in a brand-new high-rise on First Avenue between 47th and 48th Streets, across from the United Nations. It wasn't even finished when we put down the deposit. We picked the unit from a videotape and a construction-site tour.

Trump World Tower, the building was called. It was super-luxurious and super-tall, at the time the tallest residential building in the world. And it was built, you guessed it, by Donald Trump. You couldn't get much more New York than that.

I read in the *New York Post* that our new neighbors included Bill Gates, Sophia Loren, and Naomi Campbell. In the lobby, I eyeballed Harrison Ford and superstar New York Yankees shortstop Derek Jeter, who lived a few floors above us and was kind whenever I encountered him. His teammate Hideki Matsui soon moved in, too. *Batter up!* From our two-bedroom, two-and-a-half-bath place on the eightieth floor, we could see all the way to the Bronx.

The truth is, George made enough money for both of us, and I really didn't *have* to work. But I wanted to, and I saw no reason to stop. I was constantly inspired by the people I met, and I liked having a way of supporting myself. The women who'd raised me had always drilled home the importance of that, since they'd learned it the hard way. One day, George's best man from the wedding, Bob, rang up my new husband and offered some unsolicited marital advice.

I was trying to pull out of George what Bob had said to him, since it seemed like it hurt his feelings. Bob tried to persuade George to have me quit my career. Instead of ordering me to shut down my company, George shut *Bob* down. If I wanted to work, he told his friend, that was okay with him.

We spent the first three years of our marriage footloose and child-free, working hard but also getting to know each other's cities and seeing the world. I learned to love Manhattan by exploring it like a tourist. I'd pick Broadway shows and go by myself, meet George for dinner at new restaurants, connect with old friends, and talk to strangers in parks and coffee shops. Yes, you *can* do that in New York City, and people don't automatically think you're crazy.

On Mother's Day 2004, George and I invited family members to Mama Ventura in Berlin, New Jersey (hometown of ABC's Kelly Ripa).

George stood to acknowledge all the moms at the table: my mom, his mom, my aunts, my cousins, Monsignor Joe's mom. And then George announced me as the newest mom (to-be) in the family: Twins were coming sometime in October. Everyone erupted in tears and joy.

I loved being pregnant. I didn't love the nurse's assistant performing a sonogram on me and blurting out, "Oh, a perfect family in one big belly!" without noticing the "do not tell patient" note in big letters on my chart. George and I were over the moon preparing for our son and our daughter. Maureen and Cathleen hosted a grandbaby shower for my mother.

On Saturday, October 16, 2004, with George by my side, I walked from our apartment to Fox News Channel. Clearly we hadn't planned our birthing schedule around the presidential election, eighteen days away. After we chatted with Dog the Bounty Hunter and family in the greenroom and I sparred on set with Democrat Robert Zimmerman, George and I left the studio and went directly to NYU Medical Center. Zimmerman still loves to take credit for throwing me into labor.

My mom and Aunt Rita rushed to New York for the big event. George stayed with me in the hospital room, complaining about how uncomfortable his chair was. *Ummmmm, I'm over here, dude, having gained 40 percent of my body weight so I can give birth to your babies.* But the kids were in no hurry. That night, the couple who'd courted at Yankees Stadium was now watching the Yankees destroy the Red Sox 17–6 to take a 3–0 lead in the ALCS. The Yanks were one game away from another World Series, and we were about to add two new fans to Yankee Nation.

After a very long night of labor, my life changed forever. Two babies arrived the next morning five minutes apart: George Anthony (named for Grandmom Antoinette and immediately known to all of us as Georgie) and Claudia Marie (named for Aunt MiMi, who had died suddenly two years earlier). That night, the Red Sox won. The next night, the Red Sox won. The night after that, the Red Sox won. Suddenly the ALCS was tied, 3–3. The first time newborn Georgie spit up it was on his Yankees bib.

"What have we done?" I asked the father of my children. "These kids are good-luck charms . . . *for the Sox*," who hadn't won a World Series since 1918.

Trained as he was as a corporate litigator, George already had a strategy in mind. He insisted that he and I attend Game 7 of the ALCS that Wednesday. Attend in person. George assured me: "That's the only way to keep the Red Sox curse alive."

It didn't matter that we could see Yankee Stadium from our window. It didn't matter that we had a TV. Seventy-two hours into breastfeeding newborn twins, I was walking with my new dad of a husband to Grand Central Terminal, boarding a packed number 4 train to Yankee Stadium for a rainy Game 7 of the ALCS. And you know what was even worse? Boston won anyway, 10–3, and went on to win the World Series against the St. Louis Cardinals, hardly breaking a sweat.

IT WAS JUST about then that the realization finally hit me, we were in the ninth inning: *We need to pick a city to live in. Commuting with the twins was easier when they were in utero than in car seats. Which will it be? George's New York. Or my Washington?*

To my surprise, George floated the idea that we could all move down to Washington and make D.C. our home. "I could take a job in George W. Bush's administration," he said to me.

"George, do it if you want to," I told him, fully realizing it could mean giving up his partnership and the city he had called home for twenty years. "But in the five years I've known you, you've only spoken ill of three people, and two of them were George W. Bush." Like many disappointed conservatives and libertarians, George was upset with some of the decisions in the first term of the Bush presidency. The move-to-D.C. gambit was more a passing consideration than a concrete plan. "Let's all live in New York," I offered.

New York wasn't exactly where I'd imagined raising children. But I'd picked up a few clients in the city—Liz Claiborne, *New York* magazine—and I'd definitely grown more comfortable there. George had a great job in Manhattan. We had a beautiful apartment and kid-friendly neighborhood. I could do most of my work remotely, with trips to Washington and America's heartland as needed—and be there for Georgie and Claudia.

I wasn't ready to sell the house in Virginia. I still had to spend some time with my clients and employees in Washington. When you're a mom with a job and two infants, I discovered, you can't just grab the kids, throw on a business suit, and catch a shuttle flight to D.C. But what these kids lacked in backyards, I told myself, they made up for in access to Broadway shows, a diverse preschool steps away from the UN, and wild taxi rides.

I didn't want to hire nannies, at least not yet. I wasn't used to that. With two bedrooms, two adults, and two babies, where would we put them, anyway? My mom and Aunt Rita were still going strong, as was married Aunt Angie, and there was nothing any of them loved more than coming up from South Jersey to "help out" along with Aunts Jean, Josie, Cookie, Honey, and Annemarie as elders with wisdom, loving on my own children. This also included my father, who loved to step up and pitch in with the kids as well. We were blessed to have them, and it was always a production whenever they were there.

When I couldn't juggle Washington from New York, Mom and Aunt Rita would haul me and the babies to Washington. Aunt Rita drove. My mom took the front passenger seat. The twins were in the second row, car seats facing backward. I was right behind them with Jesse the Corgi, who by then was in a doggie wheelchair due to her myelopathy and our refusal to give up on her. *Poor Jesse!* From my command post in the back of Aunt Rita's van, I could check my laptop, shuffle my papers, help Aunt Rita with directions, feed and play with the twins, and try to keep Jesse calm while I jumped on and off my conference calls.

Sometimes we'd have to pull over at a rest stop. My mom would slip one of the kids a bottle. Jesse and her wheelchair would get a quick walk-and-roll. And I'd have fifteen minutes of roadside quiet for a phone call. But more often, I'd say to Aunt Rita at 1:59 p.m. somewhere south of Wilmington, Delaware, "I know someone's going to be screaming. I know someone's going to be barking, I know someone's going to be pooping. But this call is at two p.m." Then I'd get on the phone and create a parallel universe where I am Sigourney Weaver in *Working Girl*, in full command and control.

It's been said that "women's work is never done." To me, these trips kinda proved it. I'm sure George was working hard in his office, in peace and quiet, the half-eaten sushi lunch and Starbucks cups on his desk, speaking in multisyllabic words, sporting a silk Ferragamo tie sans baby vomit.

We'd unload everyone at my house in Vienna. I'd run into the district and put out whatever fires were burning there. We'd stay as long as we had to before piling everyone back into the minivan for the return ride north.

One day I said to Aunt Rita: "George and I want to upgrade this minivan."

"No, no, Kibbs," she came right back at me. "Don't do that. I'm fine. I know where all the gears are. I'm comfortable with it. Do not get me one of those fancy things with the electronic keyboards and all the beeps."

"Okay," I said, "but I want to get you airbags. By federal safety standards, all the new models have airbags."

Aunt Rita shot me a withering look that seemed to say, *don't you know anything?*

"Honey," she said, patting her belly and chest, "I have my own airbags. I got built-in airbags right here. Let's go."

For some reason, my mom and Aunt Rita, and professional caterers Aunt GiGi and Uncle Eddie, didn't seem to believe there was food available in New York City. Why else would they insist on packing it into every nook and cranny in our vehicles? Milk and eggs. Homemade ravioli and meatballs in trays bigger than the twins. "Family packs" of cereal ("they were on sale, honey"). George tried to put his foot down about this after one of our visits to Atco. You can imagine how far that got.

"Kellyanne," he said to me in his most serious, I-mean-business tone, "today is the last day we transport food. Uncooked food. Cooked food. Leftover food. Ingredients for food. Dog food. It's the last time we're going to transport any of it. We're not doing it anymore."

They didn't listen to George any more than they'd listened to me when I said sarcastically, "Mom, breaking news: They sell organic milk in New York City now. It just arrived last week." And why should it stop with food? The next time the ladies were ready to drive us back to New York City, Aunt Angie announced she'd bought us a tree. "It'll look great in your apartment," she said.

It *was* a beautiful and generous gift, a fake ficus in a real pot with real dirt. She'd bought it in South Jersey since, you know, there are no plant stores in New York. In Aunt Angie's mind, we would load this leafy monstrosity along with the sauce jars, the babies, the car seats, the dog, the doggie wheelchair, Aunt Rita, my mother, my binders of polling data, and me into her minivan: next stop, First Avenue and 47th Street.

I knew that wouldn't work, so I did the only thing I could think of. I rented a stretch limousine. And all of us piled in—joined now by an eight-foot fake ficus. Even before we reached the Lincoln Tunnel, I'd already paid more to transport the tree than it cost!

You should have seen the horde of tourists hurrying over to Trump World Tower as the limo pulled up, all straining for a better view. They could tell this was no normal drop-off. They readied their cameras. What celebrity was about to emerge?

But when the limo finally opened and it wasn't Derek Jeter or Donald Trump, a profound disappointment swept across First Avenue.

The Conways and their ficus tree were home again.

SOMETIME AFTER WE moved in, there was a revolt at Trump World Tower, the kind of revolt you might expect from wealthy New Yorkers who had time on their hands and were quick to feel aggrieved. In this case, the board of the condominium association was at war with the man who had developed the building, Donald Trump.

The specific issues were mind-numbingly arcane. They had to do with a tax abatement and Trump's fee for getting it and a bunch of other stuff all the way down to a door that was too hard to open because of unequal air pressure between the lobby and the street. What's important is that both sides were dug in, each accusing the other of corruption and mismanagement. Some board members loathed Trump so much, they were threatening to take his name off the building. As things got even hotter, Trump reacted exactly like you might expect. He sent an aggressive young lawyer to the next meeting of the condo board. It was March 2006. The lawyer's name was Michael Cohen.

Cohen, an attorney at the firm Phillips Nizer, was there to represent his client. But as the board meeting was called to order in the basement of Holy Family Catholic Church (our regular weekend place of worship), Cohen came out like a pit bull. He denied the board's many allegations. He singled out board members and pointed his finger at them. He even accused the board of taking kickbacks from a landscaper. The young lawyer really, really overperformed. And standing in the back of the room, speaking up only occasionally but taking everything in, was the man everyone was arguing about, Donald Trump.

By the time the meeting was over, several of the sitting members were off the board. And it wouldn't be much longer before the lawyer Michael Cohen had a new job: executive vice president and special counsel to Donald J. Trump.

What almost no one knew was that, working behind the scenes, advising Trump and Cohen, was George Conway. He and Trump didn't know each other previously, though George's firm had done some legal work for the developer years earlier. But as the battle inside the building raged, George had offered to be helpful and Trump had readily agreed, happy to get some sage advice from the Wachtell Lipton partner who lived on the eightieth floor.

After the meeting in the church basement, George got a call in his office from Donald Trump. "Hey, George, terrific job, really great," Trump said. "We really did it. I appreciate all your help." Later that afternoon, Trump's executive, Sonja Talesnik, said Mr. Trump wanted George to join the condo board.

George thanked her for asking but firmly declined. "I would never do something like that," he said. "But my wife might."

I was in Virginia as all this went down, getting the house there ready to sell. We were full-fledged New Yorkers by then. It seemed like time.

"Why would I want to be on the condo board?" I asked George when he phoned to warn me that Sonja might call.

"You should do it," he said. "You're good at that stuff." George was the behind-the-scenes guy, so insistent on his privacy he wouldn't even send his picture to the Harvard alumni bound book.

A busy mom, company owner, wife, and television pundit—I guess I wasn't busy enough already. I agreed to join the board. When I showed up at my first board meeting, it wasn't in the church basement anymore. With Donald Trump back in control, we met in a large conference room in Trump Tower.

I got there a little early. I had my binder with me, all tagged and marked. I had a few questions I wanted to ask and a few comments to make. I was standing at the table with the Diet Cokes and snacks when Trump walked in.

I didn't expect him to be there. I asked someone, "Does he attend all the condo board meetings?"

"Oh, yeah," I was told. "He's very involved."

In fact, Trump seemed to know everything that was going on. He had facts and figures and history to share. He didn't use any notes at all.

I would stay on the board for the next seven years, as long as we owned our condo. It was on that condo board that I would get my first up-close look at Donald Trump, the way he operated and the kind of person he is.

"Hey," I'd hear his voice calling out when I showed up early for another board meeting. "Who do I hear out there? Is that you, Kellyanne? Come on in."

That's how he was the first day I met him. That's how he was the last day I worked for him.

BY NEW YORK standards, our apartment was spacious, and I've already mentioned the killer views. But there's a limit to how many human beings can be stuffed into a two-bedroom apartment, even one as plush and generously proportioned as ours, and we were about to discover where that limit was.

Just before the twins turned three, George and I got some surprising news: We were having another baby. George was forty-four. I was forty-one. We'd just assumed our child count had topped out at two. We weren't expecting to be expecting, but we were.

On Monday, March 10, 2008, eight long days after our third child was due, my belly and I were walking on the treadmill in the condo gym. "Breaking News" flashed on the TV. It wasn't the arrival of my long-delayed baby. Not yet. It was that New York governor Eliot Spitzer was ensnared in a scandal involving a hooker at Washington's Mayflower Hotel. What was it with New York's Democrat governors and their sex scandals? Spitzer had been governor for only thirteen months. He'd won by a legitimate landslide, with 69 percent of the vote. Now this! Duty called me. TV duty. I jumped in the shower, threw on my TV suit, and, without trying to button the jacket, made live appearances on NY1 News and Larry Kudlow's show on CNBC, feeling like I could deliver at any second now, both the baby *and* the news. It was more than seconds. It was a few hours. But later that night, I was in full labor at Mount Sinai Hospital.

"It's a boy!" the doctor proclaimed. George and I smiled at each other and got ready for a life with Christopher.

"I mean, uh, 'it's a girl!'" the doctor corrected. I looked over my still-bulbous belly, squinting. "What?!" Hold the baby up, please.

A beautiful baby girl who resembled her big brother (from the waist up) was looking back at us. "That's a girl," I supplied sarcastically. "We have that make and model at home."

"I'm sorry, we had all boys born overnight. She's the first girl."

Charlotte Rita (named for Aunt Rita) was born at four o'clock the following day. On the TV, I could see that dozens of camera crews were camped outside Spitzer's East Side apartment, just ten blocks from the hospital. "They should cover Charlotte, not Spitzer," I told George. "She's far more classy, pure, and beautiful." That wasn't much of a contest, I recognized. We'd be replacing a liberal male governor with a conservative baby girl.

Excellent trade!

Two parents. Two toddlers and an infant. Mom and Aunt Rita still coming and going from South Jersey. George's busy law practice in Manhattan. My growing company in Washington. Something finally had to give. The Conways were about to confront a life-changing decision that millions of American families had faced before.

We moved to the suburbs.

We found a house just across the George Washington Bridge on a quiet street in Alpine, New Jersey. It was close enough to Manhattan for George to commute easily. All the kids could have their own bedrooms. There'd be room for an army of visiting relatives, and no one would have to crash on the living room floor, though I couldn't rule that out entirely since so many of our cousins had such fond memories of the ancient sleepovers of yore. We would be that house where kids' friends and friends' kids would congregate, recreate, satiate. We sold my bachelorette house in Virginia, meaning that for the first time in twenty-one years, I had no home in the Washington, D.C., area. We decided to hang on to the New York condo at least for a while, meaning I'd keep running into Donald Trump at the meetings of the condo board.

And apparently, we weren't done having babies. In the spring of 2009, barely a year after Charlotte had expanded our child count to three, I discovered I was pregnant again. As was becoming my habit, baby number four would arrive fashionably late. Her mother has the same habit, so we can't fault the newborn.

Halloween was on a Saturday that year. When the trick-or-treating began, the little pumpkin was already two days late. I waddled around the neighborhood with George and the kids, bobbing for apples and taking a breather at our neighbors', the Abramsons. It was Sunday night when I finally yelled in a panic, "George, don't panic. My water broke. We need to go. Now."

Instead of *not* panicking, George and I careened around like two people who had no idea that this was coming and didn't have months (and three other children) to properly prepare. We hopped into the car and hightailed it to New York City, leaving my mom with our three little ones.

I looked at George, clutched my belly, and said as calmly as I could, "Honey, I want them all born in New York City, but if you're really worried about crossing the bridge in all this traffic on a Sunday night, we can consider a local hospital on the Jersey side."

George didn't respond directly. "Are you okay?" he asked. "How are the two of you doing?"

"Fine . . . Fine . . . Okay . . . *Wait! There it is!*"

"*The baby?*"

"*No,* the city." We'd just rolled past the "Welcome to New York" sign on the Manhattan side of the bridge. "Whether it's right here or at the hospital, this baby will be born in New York City!"

"Dear God, don't say that," George begged.

We made it to the hospital in time. Barely.

As it happened, the Yankees were in another World Series, against the Philadelphia Phillies this time. Only baby number three had the good manners to be born during spring training and far from an Election Day. Clearly these doctors were paying more attention to the TVs in the delivery room than they were to me. I'm still surprised George didn't try to make me attend the game.

At Citizens Bank Park.

In Philadelphia.

A doctor I'd never met before introduced himself and without examining me, told me that the baby would probably come the next morning. I politely fact-checked him. "My water broke. I've had the other three children naturally, and I'm forty-two years old. Isn't this baby coming sooner?"

The doctor assured me everything was under control.

He must have been referring to the Yankees game because our child was about to enter this world on her own timeline.

Just a few hours later, George and I were still discussing names when a baby began to arrive—literally—with no doctor in the "delivery" room. When we both saw what was happening, George ran into the hallway, searching for help. A woman ran back in with him. Thank goodness she happened to be a midwife. She rushed in, and a baby girl rushed out five seconds later, very much on her own terms.

It was her brother Georgie, in consultation with Claudia (they'd just turned five), who named her Vanessa Elizabeth. Vanessa, he had learned, means butterfly in Greek. "Butterflies are dainty and pretty, Mommy, like the baby," the son-with-three-sisters declared. Since I'd just had what could fairly be called a "drive-by delivery," we were itching to supersize our demands and break free. We brought our new bundle home the following morning, Election Day. The doctor, who'd finally shown up, readily agreed. George drove me and our newborn daughter to the county seat near our new home so I could vote for Chris Christie over Jon Corzine for governor of New Jersey.

For the second consecutive year, we had replaced a liberal male governor with a conservative baby girl. Our electoral strategy was unconventional but successful.

Things were going our way.

Part II

Boys' Town

Chapter 7

Poll Vault

I was proud that America had elected its first black president, even though I disagreed with Barack Obama on nearly everything. I still appreciated the significance of his victory. That said, I didn't intend to sit quietly on the sidelines as the Obama-Biden administration instituted policies I knew were damaging to the country I loved. As the 2010 midterms were just revving up, I was hired by the chairman of the House Republican Conference, Mike Pence of Indiana, who was in charge of the House Republican Retreat that January in Baltimore. Pence actually invited President Obama to come and speak. A lot of Republicans were furious that a sitting Democrat president was asked to address the Republican gathering.

President Obama had finished his speech and was mingling with guests when he made his way to where I was standing. I was respectful, but without belaboring the problems with government-run healthcare, I showed him my family Christmas card from the previous month. I pointed out my newborn fourth child, Vanessa, cradled in her brother's arms, and whose bald head almost blended into our milky-white living room couch. The president got a huge belly laugh from that. I told him he seemed like a wonderful father. Months after the retreat, Obama went on to pass Obamacare, and the midterm election turned into a referendum on that and turned disastrous for his party. The grassroots were up in arms and the "TEA" (Taxed Enough Already) Party was born. My firm was picking up clients at a fast pace, and that November, Democrats got a thorough "shellacking" at the polls, to quote Obama's memorable phrasing following the 2010 midterms.

Following that resounding defeat, a direct result of the country's dissatisfaction with the Obama presidency, 2012 was shaping up to be a big one. I had been doing polling on and off for years for Newt Gingrich and his group American Solutions for Winning the Future. Fifteen years after Frank and I first helped with the Contract with America, I signed up as a pollster for Newt's 2012 presidential campaign. It would be my second presidential campaign. I'd worked on Dan Quayle's 2000 presidential campaign. And Newt was one of the front-runners, if not the only one, to challenge Barack Obama. After Newt won the South Carolina primary, I advised him to go to Florida, a winner-take-all state, and take his message straight to the Villages and the Interstate 4 corridor. But Mitt Romney would ultimately prevail, backed by negative ads, establishment politicians, consultants, and donors.

Later that cycle, George and I attended an event at New York's Union League Club, hosted by Home Depot cofounder Ken Langone and his wife, Elaine. Langone and his wife were philanthropists and our friends. He had been a client of George's firm as he successfully beat back specious and outrageous allegations by then–Attorney General Eliot Spitzer.

The room at the Union League Club was filled with impressive people, including an executive from Univision and former and future Hillary Clinton voter Lloyd Blankfein, of Goldman Sachs. Earlier that day the Supreme Court had upheld Obamacare in a ruling authored by Chief Justice John Roberts. Romney spent most of his speech railing against the ruling. "Today's decision is a gift for you," I told him. "You've been stuck in neutral with conservatives who think Romneycare in Massachusetts paved the way for Obamacare. This [opinion] could be great for you with women. Women are the chief healthcare officers of their families. We control two of every three healthcare dollars spent in this country. We are a majority the healthcare consumers and a majority of the healthcare providers."

"You know what my secret weapon with women is?" he asked me.

He answered his own question with one word: "Ann." His wife of forty-three years and the mother of his five grown sons.

ONE SATURDAY AFTERNOON in March 2013, I flew to Palm Beach to speak at the annual conference of the Club for Growth. The activist free-market group was then at the forefront of the continuing battle against Obamacare. Mitt Romney, who'd lost to Barack Obama four months earlier, was the night speaker. The tension in the room was thick with a displeased crowd. To diffuse it, the organizers handed me a card with a question for Romney about what direction the party should follow from here. I asked my own question instead. "What you did in 2010 was smart," I said. "After losing to John McCain in the primary, you went all around the country helping candidates raise money for the midterm election. Are you still going to be involved?" Romney's response was serviceable, yet not memorable.

Another speaker that day was Joe Scarborough, the former Florida congressman who cohosts MSNBC's *Morning Joe*. Scarborough was reliving his glory days in Congress, recalling how he supposedly stood up bravely to Newt's excesses. After he finished, a woman asked a question from the back of the room.

She introduced herself as Rebekah Mercer from New York. She immediately unloaded on Scarborough, wondering aloud, "why you are even here. Not only are you trashing Newt Gingrich, who had the Contract with America that helped you win in 1994, but this week on your show you referred to Ted Cruz, who is a guest here and a United States senator, as a, quote, 'carnival barker.' Many of us in this room helped support him over the establishment, handpicked lieutenant governor of Texas." I forget how Scarborough answered, but Mercer's question shifted the entire tone of the room. I walked over to her and introduced myself. We had met before but this time I meant business, literally.

Rebekah told me she had four children, too, roughly the same ages as mine. I knew that her father, hedge fund executive Bob Mercer, was a major Republican donor, and she too had gotten deeply involved. The family had a reputation for being hands-on givers, who wrote large checks but also insisted on seeing results. They'd been part of the Koch Brothers network, helping elect Rand Paul in Kentucky (against a Mitch McConnell favorite), Marco Rubio in Florida (against Republican governor Charlie Crist, who left the party even before primary day), and now, in Texas, the insurgent Republican Cruz. But the Romney-for-president campaign had been such an unexpected and unmitigated disaster, it had clearly left many donors around the country somewhere between disillusioned and disgusted.

The Romney consultants had confidently predicted victory over the incumbent Barack Obama. Why lower expectations when you can see a blowout? Stuart Stevens, the chief strategist, and others had been saying things were looking up—and also saying whatever else it took to keep the dollars flowing in. "Fly to the Fleet Center in Boston," the big donors were told as Election Day neared, "and watch Mitt make history."

The history being made that night certainly wasn't the kind the well-heeled guests had bargained for! Worst "victory party" ever. At the Fleet Center, the highly vaunted and ironically named "ORCA" data program failed like a beached whale. The Democrats kept the White House.

With an army of private jets idling at Logan International Airport and Hanscom Field, their owners stood in glum silence as the depressing results came in: Obama had carried every single swing state except for North Carolina and had romped to victory in the Electoral College, 332 to 206. For all their strategic brilliance and self-aggrandizing overreach, Stuart Stevens and his firm managed to bill more than $8 million to the campaign. I've heard of success fees, but in the Republican consultancy, to the losers also go the spoils. A collection of nonwizard of Ozzes were behind the screen, weird, disconnected characters who confuse mystery with misogyny.

For years I'd refer to this as "staff infection," a disease in the Republican Party where candidates often lose but consultants always win. The cure was elusive, but suddenly many donors felt as the grassroots did: If the definition of insanity is doing the same thing over and over again and expecting a different result, we need to have our heads examined.

Rebekah asked me to speak to a former Goldman Sachs investment banker and Hollywood producer who was her political advisor. He was a strange dude, gruff, unkempt, prone to sweeping historical assertions and bold declarations about the current state of politics, though I didn't have the impression he'd been a political operative for long, if at all. Steve Bannon was his name, and his main political credential, other than advising the Mercers, was being a "cofounder" of Breitbart.com, in which the Mercers had an ownership interest. I think we'd met once before at the Conservative Political Action Conference, or CPAC.

Left to his own devices, I don't think Steve would have sought me out. But Rebekah had asked him to speak with me.

I could only imagine Steve's response. "Oh, yeah, Kellyanne. One hundred percent. She's the best. Love her. Epic. Yeah. Great girl. Let's build a war room, a command center." Then he had to deal with me. And he did. Yet our arranged marriage got off to a promising start.

"Hey," Bannon was soon telling me, "the Mercers want to do a project with you in Iowa. Rebekah's hoping to get in early and do something different."

I designed a focus group of Iowa voters, exploring what was on their minds as the first-in-the-nation Iowa caucuses were just coming into view. No one could say who the candidates would be way off in 2016, but it was never too early to probe what the voters were thinking.

As the time grew near, I asked Bob and Rebekah if they'd like to watch the focus groups live. It was probable that the Mercer money had paid for dozens of focus groups, but it was less clear that anyone had ever bothered to invite them to watch.

"There's nothing like it," I told them. "It's always fascinating if you care what real people think. They can surprise you sometimes."

I was delighted, if not a little nervous, that Bob and Rebekah Mercer flew from Las Vegas to Des Moines with Steve Bannon and their very smart tech guy, Matthew Michelsen, and a couple of other people. I was already in the back of the viewing room when they arrived.

"Jeez," Bannon said on his way in the door. "Rebekah's four kids were on the plane."

"Aw, that's so sweet," I said. "Are they coming to the focus groups?"

"God, I hope not," he mumbled, looking aghast at the very idea. Classic Bannon: He's not a take-your-kids-to-work kinda guy.

The Mercers were generous and solicitous. It was obvious their motivation was rooted in love of country. They never once asked for access, or an ambassadorship or anything of that ilk. I treated their money like it was my money. But they let me do my polls and my focus groups, and they listened thoughtfully to advice about how the free-market, center-right movement needed to reframe how people talk about the economy or Obamacare. Those in the C-suite tend to talk to present economic issues as if they were at Wharton Business School. As I had learned from talking to people in quantitative and qualitative research, I explained that the economy means different things to different people: For some, it's taxes and regulations. For others, it's the ability to pay for gas and groceries or make an auto, mortgage, or student-loan payment. From the farmer to the pharmacist, where one stands on the issues has much to do with where they sit. The task was to ensure we had a better message, a message that would keep Republicans from ending up on the losing end of another presidential race. The Mercers appreciated the fact that I wasn't telling them the same old shit and blowing the same old smoke.

The Mercers were listening, but the new boys' network still wasn't.

"WHAT DO YOU mean, they left?"

They must have been in the men's room or outside the building for a smoke, I thought. Maybe they were placing the obligatory four-minute call to the three kids their wives had spent all day (week/month/year) caring for while the men were on the road yet again. But there was no way they had just *left*.

They had been rude and difficult since we had started the first focus groups of female voters the previous day in Richmond and then Virginia Beach on behalf of Republican Ken Cuccinelli's gubernatorial campaign. It's typical of these guys to give the girl the focus group and keep the polling for themselves. They barely looked up from their papers, let alone said hello, had no comments to the discussion guides or our ideas for reordering the ads to be tested. They were there to order lunch, plan their drinks and dinner on the client's dime, and suffer through a few hours watching me engage in conversation with other stupid women (aka swing voters). Instead they were behind a one-way mirror under the pretense of "learning" from these female swing voters, only to make fun of how they looked and what they said. And we wonder why the Republican Party had a gender gap for so long? These were the big dogs, the "top-shelf" pollsters and admen and consultants who were hired by dozens and dozens of candidates, usually based on the fact they had been previously hired by dozens and dozens of candidates. Their "winning records" included senators going for their fifth terms, wondering if they would receive 78 percent or just 76 percent of the vote that year. They failed most spectacularly at the presidential level. The Cuccinelli consultants were also the consultants for Bob Dole in 1996, John McCain in 2008, Mitt Romney in 2012, and Jeb Bush in 2016. George W. Bush hired someone else and won two terms. You see the pattern.

What I didn't see that night in Fairfax, Virginia, following the third focus group discussion, was *them*. Eager to discuss the key takeaways of the two-plus-hour conversation I had just led with thirteen suburban women on the fence about whether to support Terry McAuliffe or Ken Cuccinelli in the governor's race, I bounded back to the viewing room to debrief and strategize. The seats were empty. Everyone else was gone. They had literally ghosted their own focus group. The guys who had ignored and insulted the women in the focus group were doing the same to the woman who'd managed it.

The Guys on the Republican Gravy Train rushed out of focus groups for a second night to have drinks and dinner on the client's dime while their wives tucked in their kids. My husband's wife tucked in our kids by FaceTime that night because I was trying to help the consultants understand women. I dutifully filed a twenty-page report, laughed when the Cuccinelli consultants predicted their client would lose by double digits and he came within less than three points of winning, and since I was the one listening carefully and respectfully to those smart, capable engaging women in the focus groups, I was also the one, years later, to develop a "secret sauce" to beat a woman for president and help lead Donald Trump in the Oval Office.

Chapter 8

Tower of Babble

An active mind never rests, and that certainly applied to Donald J. Trump. My mother, a huge fan, kept me apprised of his latest moves. With someone like him, a new year was always going to include new possibilities.

Possibilities like running for governor of New York.

And so it was on January 9, 2014, that I was invited—more like *summoned*—to the twenty-fifth floor of Trump Tower by Michael Cohen and Sam Nunberg, Trump's hard-charging young lawyer and his equally hard-charging young political aide, respectively. You already know how Cohen arrived. Nunberg was a protégé of Republican operative Roger Stone, former business partner of Paul Manafort. With Stone, Cohen, and Nunberg whispering in his ear, Trump's tight political circle wasn't like anyone else's, any more than Trump was like any other budding politician.

This was round two of political consulting for Trump and me. In addition to the informal conversations we'd had over the years about this or that, he'd commissioned my firm to conduct a poll in 2011 with an eye toward possibly challenging Barack Obama's presidential reelection the following year. "Everyone knows who you are, many people like

and admire you, but very few think you'd actually run for president,"
I reported at the time. "President Obama is vulnerable, some of his
support has softened, but he is also formidable for reelection. He has
advantages enjoyed by most incumbents, and intangibles unique to him."
I think he genuinely respected me for sharing my best assessment of
the current reality between an unannounced candidate and a historic
president—good, bad, or in between. A lot of other Republican pollsters,
he realized, would happily tell him anything he wanted to hear—they
did then, and still do to this day.

And now we were off together on another round.

This would be my first time in the same room with Trump *and* his
family. Flanking him at the large conference table that day were wife
Melania and his adult children. The Trump children had prominent
and expanding roles in the family business, including on *The Apprentice*,
where they had assumed many of the tasks once performed by nonfamily
executives.

Also at the long table that day and lining the conference room's
four walls was a small army from various corners of the New York
State Republican Party. County chairmen. State committeemen. An
upstate sheriff. A bunch of other people who were somehow connected
to state Republican politics, just not the state party chairman, Edward
Cox, who had his own candidate lined up to run for governor. But I was
most struck by the presence of Melania and the kids. As far as I knew,
they had been fairly apolitical. But this was business—family business—
so here they were.

Winning the governorship of New York was going to be a challenge for any Republican, even one named Donald Trump. I conducted
a poll for Citizens United that said precisely that. In the 2010 governor's
race, Democrat Andrew Cuomo had crushed Republican Carl Paladino,
a wealthy Buffalo businessman, by nearly 30 percentage points. And
Cuomo, who had been the attorney general and whose father had been
governor, was already up and running for a second term. He had high poll
numbers and $33 million in his campaign fund. Could Donald Trump
realistically challenge him? Plus, I couldn't help but think, standing there
in the famous tower from which he ran his international empire, *why
would Trump want to?*

Everyone was already settled in when I arrived. I was fidgeting with the large glass door when I heard that distinctive voice calling out: "Oh, wow! We have a TV star here. What do you think, Kellyanne?"

Trump, the true TV star, marveled at the large, supportive turnout. "They've come from all over the state," he noted, no small feat given the icy conditions. He noted Melania's presence. "My wife is my best pollster," he said. "She's almost as good as Kellyanne. My wife always says that a lot of people don't think I'm really going to run for anything, and the minute I announce I'm going to run, my poll numbers will go through the roof."

That's certainly possible, I thought. That would end speculation that he is teasing people, that this is a publicity stunt.

Several of the visiting New York politicos spoke up, saying he was the only imaginable Republican who could give Cuomo a good run and that all of them would be there to support him. Trump listened carefully, but it was Ivanka who seemed to crystallize her father's thinking, going bigger and bolder than Albany.

She had said that if he was going to run for governor, he might as well just go ahead and run for president.

It was clear that this was not the first time she'd suggested it or her father had considered it, but in a room of politicos it was newsy.

"Thank you, Ivanka," he said. "I'm not sure I need to be governor to be president. I think I can wait. We'll see what happens. I'm sure I'll be at the top of the polls in terms of my name recognition."

He had clearly thought about this.

"Why run for governor?" he asked rhetorically. "Because if I win, wouldn't I be disappointing a lot of people who would be working hard for me because I would have to leave within a year and start running for president?"

SO COULD DONALD Trump be elected governor if he ran against Andrew Cuomo that November? The polls showed a steep climb.

"One thing is clear," I said. "If New York State Republicans run a normal Republican for governor, that candidate will almost certainly be defeated. Only a distinctive, transformative figure has a chance. Institutions that become sclerotic and out of touch lean on transformative figures to reset with the public. The Catholic Church has Pope Francis. The British monarchy has Prince William and Princess Kate. Each of them is not everyone's cup of tea, but clearly they were different enough to signify change to each of those sclerotic institutions. Perhaps the New York Republican Party can use a Donald Trump to shake things up."

It still wouldn't be easy, I cautioned. New York State would still be more than 2-to-1 Democratic. Andrew Cuomo would still have $33 million in the bank—and he'd surely raise millions more before November. But was Donald Trump the "transformative figure" who could beat him? It wasn't impossible, I said. But I still wondered why he would bother.

I didn't leave that meeting convinced Trump would or should run for governor. I think he was leaning against it by the end. I left the meeting more aware that Donald Trump, after decades of dancing around the idea of running for high public office, wasn't just playing anymore. He was serious, and his eye was on the prize.

The big prize.

The other thing I saw firsthand that day was how involved the Trump family was in all facets of the business, including this latest possibility: politics. Trump had done a great job bringing his wife and children into the conversation from the start. Like any good dealmaker and negotiator, he was waiting for the right time to make his move. He was assembling the allies he would need when he made it. He was gaining the support of his spouse and children and benefiting from their insights and advice. And he was getting ready to strike when the time arrived.

In all of this, Melania Trump's role stood out.

She never hogged the floor. But I could see she was providing her husband with sensible and well-grounded political and nonpolitical advice, as she would again countless times in the future. Perhaps the most important thing she imparted was that if he decided to run, he must be prepared to win and then to govern.

She intuited what many of the professionals missed: that New Yorkers and Americans craved something different, someone who had relevant, attractive experience but not necessarily in politics. The election of Obama had proved that. For the past fifteen years, Melania had seen firsthand how people related to her husband. You couldn't bottle it or buy it or reproduce it. That quality doesn't really have a name. Charisma, some people call it, but it's more than that. It's an almost magnetic connection that brings people toward you and makes them want to listen to what you say, believe in you, and follow you. Few people are born with it. Donald J. Trump was.

OVER THE NEXT couple of months, Trump started looking and sounding more and more like a candidate. He seemed to be treating the prospect seriously, and from everything I could see, he was.

"The Republicans can absolutely win the gubernatorial election coming up," Trump said. "I would make New York State one of the great energy capitals of the world, and I would cut everybody's taxes in half. And it would be easy."

But that was about as far as it went.

On March 14, Trump went on Twitter and made it official: "While I won't be running for Governor of New York State, a race I would have won, I have much bigger plans in mind—stay tuned, will happen!"

This time Donald Trump wasn't teasing. He was serious.

Chapter 9

Mixed Messages

So, what would Republicans do and say and stand for at the presidential level following the Mitt Romney debacle? He and his band of advisors blew it in 2012, even as Republicans racked up big gains in 2010 and 2014. Donors had drunk the consultant Kool-Aid and seemed sour. What was the best message for beating Hillary Clinton in 2016? And who was the best messenger? She wasn't the Democrats' official nominee yet, but *come on.* Even President Obama had snubbed his vice president of eight years, career politician Joe Biden, who had run for president twice before, for the woman he had defeated in the primaries. America made history by electing the first African American man to the presidency; now they could make history by electing the first woman. The majority of voters are women. Everything was so wired for her this time, even Hillary would have trouble blowing it.

After Romney lost to Obama, which happened after McCain lost to Obama, the same Republican geniuses who had missed the TEA Party and would later miss the MAGA movement ordered a head-to-toe "autopsy." The time had come, party chairman Reince Priebus told reporters at Washington's National Press Club, to put the "cards on the table, faceup."

And what did those cards say? "We must recruit more candidates who come from minority communities." *Excellent idea,* I thought. And their theory was that Republicans should come out firmly for "comprehensive immigration reform."

To me, all this thoroughly missed the point. Of course the party should reach out to a diversity of voters, indeed all Americans, some way other than translating into Spanish a crappy ad in English so that we now had two crappy ads and no new voters. I'm the one who'd given the Winning Asian American Voters presentation to House Republicans representing California (when there were far more of them) way back in 1997 and had told Major League Baseball they should engage more Hispanic women, often moms involved with the community, as active fans. But the party still needed the strong, clear, coherent *conservative* message that had made us all Republicans in the first place. Not a bunch of pandering "outreach" blather and PC mushiness as an excuse for why Republicans had lost back-to-back presidential elections.

The immigration reversal was especially wrongheaded, I was convinced. And soon I had the polling to prove it. In July 2014, I took a deep dive into immigration, how Americans really feel about the topic, absent all the preconceived notions and shopworn clichés.

Our data showed that a majority of voters, 52 percent, considered immigration a top-three issue in the next presidential race. Many viewed it through an economic lens. For years the issue had been dominated by the question, "What's fair to illegal immigrants?" Now many Americans were also asking, "What's fair to *us*?"

The American worker. Those looking for work. Those stuck in low-wage jobs. Those who watched their wealth and jobs be shipped overseas or who could not compete with someone willing to work for eight dollars an hour under the table. Blighted storefronts, shuttered factories, their pain was real.

If the Republican Party wanted to connect with America, we needed to talk honestly about the pressures people faced in their lives, about what kept them up at night.

I'd chafed when I heard high-minded politicians pretend to protect and help prosper the men, women, and children who had come here illegally by including them in rhetoric and ignoring them in reality. They failed to encourage or educate them about coming to America legally, as 33 million had, which excluded them from a chance at the full fruits Americans enjoy.

"The time appears ripe," I wrote in my poll report, "for a national immigration conversation. There is a new open-mindedness to populist approaches, regardless of partisan or ideological preferences."

As the data made clear, my survey report stated, people were ready for a policy that put "AMERICA FIRST."

Sixty percent disapproved of how Obama was handling the issue, but neither party was seen as especially credible, suggesting a substantial political opportunity for a candidate ready to take a more populist approach. Not nativist. Not elitist. People wanted action, not just talk, on immigration. And they wanted it soon.

And who might be the right candidate to deliver that message?

BACK IN 2005, I wrote a book with Democratic pollster Celinda Lake. The book was called *What Women Really Want*. We'd hoped the snappy title would seduce men into thinking it was a book about sex and buy it only to be disappointed that a bunch of pollsters were talking about different kinds of figures. From our two different perspectives, Celinda and I wrestled with the question of the female public policy "wish list," noting both large shifts and small trendlets that were affecting—and being affected by—women. Now here we were, nine years and two failed Republican presidential campaigns later, and I kept finding myself repeating the key points from that book.

Maybe someone would listen this time.

This was down-to-earth stuff. "What do women want? Well, what do they do every month? They fill the gas tank, go to the grocery store, pay the mortgage and car loan. They don't get an abortion every month. We need to speak to women on what they do."

I started to develop, in addition to demographic and attitudinal analysis, a way of looking at politics situationally, trying to reflect not some theory but what was really happening in people's lives. I presented our findings everywhere I could—to members of Congress, in Manhattan skyscrapers, at Lincoln Day dinners, in small and large boardrooms. "To attract someone politically," I kept saying, "you must first understand them culturally."

I talked about "the Three Faces of Eve," three women of the same age who lived thirty miles apart, in the same media market and congressional district, but who could not be more different. The forty-seven-year-old female executive with a six-figure income, postgraduate degree, who has never married or had children but is likely to be spoiling someone else's kid and helping the elders in her life navigate paperwork and problems. The forty-seven-year-old part-time volunteer part-time worker who is about to be a first-time grandmother. And the once rare but increasingly common forty-seven-year-old "young mom" with one kid in kindergarten and one on the way, who might have more in common with a twenty-seven-year-old in the same exact situation than those other two "Eves" her same age.

Age, race, and geography—polling's traditional categories—don't begin to explain fully who these women are, let alone what these women want. "'Stage' is replacing 'age' as a key factor," I proclaimed. "Women are increasingly mixing up the sequence of the '4 Ms'—marriage, motherhood, mortgages, and mutual funds—and some are deciding they don't need all four." I saw women as prolific and self-directed, not pigeonholed and stereotyped. Feminism? No. Facts. I've been saying ever since.

One other thing: Except for the hardened partisans, for female voters, strident ideological debates long on shouting and short on results are almost always a turnoff. Women want practical solutions to the problems that affect them and their families/loved ones. Call it the politics of pragmatism. Women want leaders who are measured and solutions that feel real.

"The party that fears change and represents the status quo will be unacceptable to the majority of women voters," I told the Republican congressmen. "The party that provides meaningful, workable alternatives will have the advantage among women voters."

To me, that sounded like good news for my party.

THE 2014 MIDTERMS were kind to the Republicans, just as the 2010 midterms had been. Halfway through Obama's first term, Republicans added 63 seats to their House majority and another 9 seats in the Senate. And now Obama had gotten another "shellacking" halfway through his second term. Yes, he won two presidential elections for himself. But during his tenure, the Democrat Party would bleed support, ending up with a net loss of 1,042 state and federal posts, including dozens of congressional seats, hundreds of state legislative seats, and a dozen governorships. For the Democrats, this foretold peril for the presidential election of 2016.

No matter who the president is, American voters seem to enjoy slapping him halfway through his term. *Checks and balances,* they call that in the civics books.

As all this was unfolding, more than a dozen Republicans were already getting ready to run for president. The upbeat news from the midterms, Hillary's perceived weaknesses, the usual restlessness of American voters—all of it had Republicans smelling victory in the air. And all of it was great for my company, especially since we'd been so active in the fights over healthcare and the sluggish economy. I was busier than I'd ever been before. Looking after my husband and our four growing children. Running back and forth between my office in Washington and our house in New Jersey, though less and less often in Aunt Rita's van. That was tough enough with two babies and a corgi. Once the numbers had doubled to four kids and two corgis (Bonnie and Skipper), we hit some kind of I-95 tipping point.

We kept our condo at Trump World Tower for five years after moving to the New Jersey suburbs, and I kept my seat on the condo board. Renting the condo would have been wise and lucrative, but instead we offered it to family and friends and enjoyed taking the kids overnight to the city, where they were born to soak in Broadway shows, museums, parks, dining, and other quintessential experiences of The City That Never Sleeps.

Alpine and Atco share a state—New Jersey—but are far apart geographically and otherwise. Alpine's "city" is New York, while Atco's is Philly. The South Jersey of my childhood featured small houses set on many acres. In our part of northern New Jersey, the opposite was true. There our family found community, and our children some of their lifelong friends. The same is true for me. The kids had normal suburban lives: the local public school, playdates and playgrounds, birthday parties, activities, Saturdays of soccer and softball, Sundays of Mass and Sunday school.

My collection of cherished friends grew. Andrea, Allison, Maryana, Christine, Laurie, Amber, DiDi, Anna, Marlena, Karen, Sharon, Angela, Yvonne, Amy, Agnes, Alexandra, Maria, Marleen—to name a few. We all became mommies together, loving and nurturing our children, each other's children, and looking out for each other, too. I will always be grateful for these women and pray for their safety and success. As was the case with childhood and college friends, we made memories. We climbed mountains. Some of us have grown closer. Some of us have grown apart. Not because of politics. I rarely raised politics in conversation, even as many of them did. (Their husbands certainly did.) My friends who loved Trump loved me first. My friends who did not love Trump loved me anyway. That's a beautiful thing and how life should be.

One afternoon, while I was on my way to pick up my kids at elementary school, my phone rang. It was Trump lawyer Michael Cohen. Michael said that his boss was psyched about speaking at CPAC, the Conservative Political Action Conference, outside Washington in early February and wanted to make sure he did well in that year's CPAC presidential straw poll, which he must have known my company was running that year.

Michael conveyed to me that "Mr. Trump" needed to come in first in the CPAC straw poll. It sounded like a goal, not a demand. At least, I hoped.

I told him that Mr. Trump should connect with those that attend CPAC, like all the other candidates do.

He repeated himself. Mr. Trump needed to come in first.

I had always gotten along with Cohen and liked him personally. He wasn't the first or last to call me specifically about this CPAC straw poll, but I made clear to anyone trying to bully me into what I took as a suggestion to cook the books, I was not for sale. I wasn't going to be cowed or wowed by any candidate or consultant into compromising my honest polling. As is often the case with Trump people who obsess over "pleasing the boss," it was unclear whether Cohen was speaking those specific words at Trump's direction or on his own.

If anything, Trump's speech at CPAC 2015 was his strongest one yet. He was certainly hinting broadly.

"Washington is totally broken, and it's not going to get fixed unless we put the right person in that top position," he told the packed room of conservative activists. "It's just not going to happen. I'm not a politician, thank goodness. Politicians are all talk, no action. I've dealt with them all my life."

Donald J. Trump for President was hiding in plain sight. Trump ticked off a long list of issues, including his support for tougher sanctions against Iran, his opposition to Common Core education standards, and his backing for infrastructure repair. He really lit into Obama on the fight against the Islamic State. The second-term president, he said, "doesn't know what he's doing" in the fight against terrorism.

"If I decide to run and win, nobody would be tougher than Donald Trump," he said of ISIS. "I would hit them so hard and so fast that they wouldn't know what happened. I would find a general. Remember the old days of these great generals? General MacArthur is spinning in his grave when he sees what we did. So, you gotta hit them hard, gotta hit them firm."

The crowd ate it up.

Trump won the room but it was Rand Paul who won the 2015 CPAC straw poll with 26 percent. Scott Walker came in second with 21, Ted Cruz and Ben Carson were neck-and-neck just shy of 12 percent. These CPAC crowds tended to be younger and more libertarian in those days, and Rand Paul's father, Ron Paul, had also performed well there. And down in eighth place with 3.5 percent of the CPAC straw poll vote was Donald Trump.

It didn't take long for a self-described Trump confidante to ring me: These weren't the results Mr. Trump was expecting.

"They are *exactly* the results *I* was expecting," I said. "Nobody thinks he is serious or that he will actually run. They like him but think he's playing with them. Until he runs, we will never know how much support Donald Trump has. Run—get him to run—and then we'll talk."

Chapter 10

Kellyanne 2.0

Looking toward 2016, I was worried about a repeat of 2008 and 2012, the recidivist Republican tendency to turn the nomination into a coronation of whoever had cornered the market on the silly "he can win!" claim or as a consolation prize for the runner-up from the previous primary. To avoid that, we needed to elevate and elect someone who was more than just the next in line. I already had a candidate in mind, someone who checked a lot of boxes for the conservative movement, who had showed his chops challenging Obama administration policies, and could also be a strong antidote after the defeats of McCain and Romney.

I had been Mike Pence's pollster and political advisor for five years by then, getting to know him and his wife, Karen, when he was a congressman from the second district of Indiana. I was part of his team when he won the governorship in 2012. Phil Cox, then the executive director of the RGA, commented to Mike Pence that my polling data and numbers were the only ones that were right in that race. I liked Mike a lot. If he had decided to join the 2016 presidential race, his campaign would have been run out of Indianapolis, and I would have had a seat at the big-boys' table, rubbing my elbows against the elbows of the campaign's other top decision-makers, not tossed into the mezzanine section as the girl who could tell us what the other girls were thinking.

I was part of a small but significant meeting with Mike and Karen Pence at the governor's residence on North Meridian Street on April 7, 2014. It had been clear for years that Pence harbored presidential ambitions, but that day he mostly listened. Mike Pence would describe himself as a conservative but not in a bad mood about it—this seemed to me a great way of explaining policy while engaging the electorate. I made the case for how and why Mike could compete for the nomination: His clear-eyed conservatism and connection to evangelical Christians. His midwestern decency. His defense of Israel, the unborn, the Second Amendment. His willingness to stand firm against big-spending presidents while in Congress, opposing programs from Obama's government-run health insurance and Cash for Clunkers to Bush's Medicare Part D and Wall Street bailout. Pence had spent six of his twelve years in Congress on the Foreign Affairs Committee, and had risen to the number three spot in leadership. As governor, he'd cut taxes by 5 percent for individuals and businesses in his first hundred days, negotiated a great deal with Japan, had the highest net new manufacturing gains in the Midwest, repealed the Common Core curriculum, expanded technical and vocational educational opportunities, and was the only governor to negotiate a waiver for his state on Obamacare. I also made a case for him if he wanted to run for reelection as governor of Indiana. Pence would ultimately decide to do exactly that, staying the course and staying out of presidential politics.

With Mike Pence out of the race and the other candidates gathering around, who would I back in 2016? I had conducted small projects for Rand Paul and Ben Carson. Maybe a couple of others I can't remember, there were so many of them eyeing the race that year. I surveyed voters as they tried to make their decisions and helped them figure out what sorts of campaigns they should run. But I didn't want to keep dancing on the periphery. Thankfully, I'd been getting overtures.

It wasn't ideology that would answer the question for me. All the candidates I would consider helping were right-leaning Republicans, card-carrying conservatives itching for a crack at Hillary. Personality also wasn't my biggest consideration. Temperamentally, the field of candidates could hardly be more distinct. Ted Cruz's hard-driving brainpower. Chris Christie's in-your-face Jersey style and get-it-done practicality. Rand Paul's outsider restlessness. Scott Walker's understated victories over a leftist mob trashing the Wisconsin capitol building in Madison and trying to remove him from office.

The fact is that I lacked the luxury to go too far afield. In the end, it came down to geography. I needed to work from home or close to home, which was really just another way of saying "I'm the mom." Motherhood often reduces professional opportunities even as it improves nearly everything else exponentially.

I couldn't get up and leave my family to go help some candidate and his family. I had to either bring them with me or stay home with them. That's what it means to be the mom. Not the dad. The mom. The male consultants are never so constrained, at least one of Romney's chief strategists didnt seem to be in charge of anything other than his bulging bank account and house plant. If I was going to do anything big in this election—something more than interacting with the candidate in daily conference calls or receiving information secondhand—I needed to be close to home. Other than Hillary's sprawling campaign headquarters in Brooklyn, who might be in New York?

LIKE ALL THINGS presidential, my journey started in Iowa, home of the first-in-the-nation presidential caucuses. I was invited to Des Moines to speak at the Iowa Freedom Summit. This packed, one-day event was hosted by veteran political operative David Bossie's group Citizens United, best known for the 2010 U.S. Supreme Court decision that ruled corporations and unions have a First Amendment right to spend money in federal elections. A huge victory that still has the blue party red-faced. This year's summit drew nearly two dozen high-profile conservatives to downtown's Hoyt Sherman Place. I knew it would be a great place to say hi to some of the potential 2016 candidates and watch them perform on their feet. Donald Trump was there. So were Carly Fiorina, Ted Cruz, Ben Carson, Rick Perry, Rick Santorum, Chris Christie, Mike Huckabee, Newt Gingrich, and Sarah Palin. The summit was a safe space, especially with two no-shows, Jeb Bush and Mitt Romney.

One cool thing: My son, George, flew out to Des Moines with me. Even at ten, Georgie was starting to get a kick out of politics, and he seemed to have a knack for it, chatting up would-be presidents without seeming intimidated by any of them. They enjoyed him, too, playing a backstage version of "Are you smarter than a fourth grader?" (My son won.)

In my luncheon speech, I urged the 1,200 conservative activists to do what I was doing when it came to this year's Republican candidates: "Don't be corralled into choosing too early. Make them earn it. Help them learn it. And remember, *you* are the prize." And I warned them: Do not fall for the pernicious and popular concept of *electability,* the notion that certain candidates "will never be elected" so we shouldn't even bother supporting them, no matter how great they are.

What a recipe for decades of mediocrity!

"Don't fall for it," I implored the Iowans, withholding the "again."

AS THE WEEKS rolled on, the potential candidates were all making their early moves. In March 2015, I met Corey Lewandowski for breakfast at Manhattan's über-elegant Peninsula hotel, near Trump Tower. At forty-one, he was a distinct figure in Republican politics, a native of gritty Lowell, Massachusetts, and a knock-around guy I found it easy relating to. Corey had worked for a couple of congressmen, run several campaigns, graduated from the New Hampshire police academy, served as a seasonal marine patrol officer trainee, lobbied for New England seafood producers, and run for local office more than once. Now he was working for Donald Trump. The two of them had met the previous April at a political event in New Hampshire. Trump saw something in Corey's energy and drive.

Corey jumped right into the purpose of our breakfast: whether I would hop aboard the nascent, not-yet-announced Trump campaign.

"I really wish you'd join us," he said. "Mr. Trump is very fond of you. Thinks you're smart and tough."

"I love the guy, and I think he's onto something," I said of Trump. "Either Americans are serious about what they've been telling pollsters like me for decades—or they're not. They've been saying, 'We want a candidate who has a ton of experience but has never been in politics.' I always thought, *Who is that? Who could that be?* Well, maybe it turns out it's someone like Donald Trump, pre-verified as a successful businessman who's earned his fame and fortune despite Washington, not because of it."

"He's serious," Corey said.

I told him the same thing I had said about the CPAC straw poll: Hypotheticals don't count. "You'll never know what people really think about Donald Trump as a candidate until Donald Trump is a candidate. Because people think he's just talking. They think he's got too much to lose. Too much to sacrifice. Too much to give up to do this nonsense. Run for office? Why would he do that? He's Donald Trump. He owns stuff. He makes money. He's got it all. Why would he do that?"

"I'm telling you, he's doing it," Corey said. "Wherever we go, there's a crowd. The media's following him everywhere. All those other people who say they're running, they don't have that. Not even close." Also, Trump had staying power, Corey said. "He's got the money to keep going. You're not gonna believe the number of people that want to be part of this thing."

As Corey grabbed the check, I agreed to kick this up a notch. It was time to visit Donald Trump.

IT DIDN'T TAKE long. When I got up to the twenty-sixth floor of Trump Tower, there were four people in the room: Corey, Michael Cohen, Trump, and me. In practical detail, I shared with the New York businessman my take on some of the challenges and opportunities that were now ahead of him—and what he had to watch out for. "The supposed experts will always say you aren't electable," I told him. "The media and donors ask, 'who can win?' The voters ask, 'who can lead?'"

This was all Kellyanne 101, the 2016 edition, lessons I had learned from decades around national politics and from working, learning, and living among those whom Trump brilliantly referred to as "the forgotten men and women" of America.

I told him what I thought was the right way to court the media . . . *some* of the media. "Every successful nominee," I said, "needs to have two reporters who are blatantly for him every day, and four or five reporters who are *secretly* for him. It's no substitute for being among the people, and won't overtake how many media want to destroy you, but it will help. Give you something to cite and fight for."

I told him how to answer whenever someone says, "You're not raising any money."

"Just say, 'Why would I raise money? I've raised money through my business my whole life. I have the money. I'm here to make sure *you* have money, the money you need to pay your bills, provide for your family, enjoy your life, retire someday.' Even if you never spend a penny of your own money, you need an answer to that question."

And what about the Democrat in the White House? Even though Barack Obama was term-limited and couldn't run again, I said, he will still loom over the race to replace him.

"The way you run," I said, "is you go after Obama on China like you do each Monday on *Fox & Friends*. You want to hit him on policy. You want to hit him on Obamacare. You want to hit him on 'you-can-keep-your-plan, you-can-keep-your-doctor.' One of the biggest lies a president has told the country in the past forty years."

Trump looked intrigued. "Tell me more," he said.

"You want to point out that this month is the five-year anniversary of Obamacare," I said. "March twenty-third, 2010. Five years, and we still have twenty-one million uninsured Americans and six million people paying three billion dollars in penalties to avoid this wonderful thing."

"Go on," Donald Trump said again.

"Well," I continued, "women are the chief healthcare officers of their families. We control two of every three healthcare dollars spent in this country. We are most of the consumers and most of the healthcare providers."

"How many women can we get?" he asked. "Can we really beat Hillary with women? Can we win them?"

"You can definitely tread water there," I said. "You can get Romney-level numbers and run up your totals among married women, white women, rural, and non-college-educated women. You may very well appeal to Independent women because they look at you and look at themselves as nonpolitical. But here's the deal. Don't play the Hillary game and think that women only care about abortion. That Hispanics only care about immigration. That seniors only care about Medicare. Americans are not single-issue thinkers, so we are not single-issue voters."

He still seemed to be listening.

"Thirty years in doing this, I never once heard the phrase 'men's issues.' What is this 'women's issues,' it's just a euphemism for abortion. They just presume only men can think, talk, vote, and solve every other issue like foreign policy and the economy."

"Wow," he said. "That's good."

When people say, "Donald Trump doesn't listen," that's wrong. Maybe he doesn't take their advice, but he's listening and absorbing, trust me. The man rarely takes notes. He doesn't forget anything, even when you'd wish he would. And he gives you instant feedback, telling you immediately how he feels about whatever it is you've just said. And then he returns to it later.

Trump listened to women just as intently as he did to men, if not more so. He understands how to communicate and market and sell and close the deal.

We kept talking. Then I brought up Hillary's emails and her famous "blue wall" and the eighteen states and the District of Columbia that the Democrats had won consistently in presidential elections going all the way back to Bill Clinton in 1992. A lot of the pundits were saying that this blue wall gave the former First Lady such a built-in advantage now, she might be impossible for any Republican to beat.

"The blue wall is real," I said to Trump. "There are states the Democrats will win no matter what the Republicans do and no matter how terrible Hillary is. That's a fact. But those states alone are not enough to win the Electoral College."

I had thought about this for a very long time. I'd been deliberating and discussing it and trying to make sense of it. George had heard me talk about it so often, he would repeat pieces of it to me as I plodded and plotted.

"It just means that you—or whoever the Republican nominee turns out to be—is going to have to hit even harder in the states that are still in play," I told Trump in the office that day. "We must expand the map."

"It'll be me," he said, not an ounce of doubt in his voice. "The nominee? It'll be me."

Part III

My Turn

Chapter 11

Kid Power

It started innocently enough.

On May 8, a Friday, George and I were both planning to attend a Federalist Society lunch at the Morris Museum in Morristown, New Jersey. They had a special speaker that day, U.S. Supreme Court justice Antonin Scalia. Under the theory that three Conways are better than two—and because we thought it might be educational—I asked our eldest daughter, Claudia, if she might like to come along before we left for South Carolina together.

"Leave school early?" she asked. "Sure."

Claudia was a little shy but just about as poised as a ten-year-old could reasonably be, sharing a table with an esteemed Supreme Court justice. She listened politely while Justice Scalia fielded predictable and mostly hypothetical questions from the attendees who came over to the table, keeping the guest-of-honor so busy he barely could enjoy his lunch. Claudia even seemed to pay attention while he gave his speech, slamming the political culture of Washington, Congress in particular, whose members, he said, "get elected by doing nothing."

When the speech part was done, the audience was invited to submit questions on index cards. Claudia began scribbling away. After addressing abortion and the Affordable Care Act (aka Obamacare) and the Commerce Clause, Scalia took one last question.

It was Claudia's.

"Both my parents are lawyers," the not-so-anonymous index card read. "I'd like to know if I should follow in their footsteps or find a happier, more fulfilling profession."

Once the laughter died down, Scalia joked about the "loaded question" before offering a hopeful response. "You know," he said, "I don't think there is any profession more fulfilling than the law for someone who loves the law. The reason not to go into the law is not because it's not fulfilling. It's because you don't like the work. And a lot of people don't like the work."

I'm not 100 percent sure that Claudia was convinced.

Before he left that day, the seventy-nine-year-old jurist signed copies of his latest book, *Reading Law: The Interpretation of Legal Texts,* which I don't believe is on the fourth-grade reading list in many schools. But he posed for only one photo, with our ten-year-old daughter. Sadly, Justice Scalia would die nine months later. We cherish that index card, and the photo of two smart, savvy, confident people, Scalia (Nino) and Claudia (*mi nina*), whom I will always love.

CLAUDIA'S UNIQUE WEEKEND was just starting. She joined me that same afternoon as we flew to Greenville, South Carolina, where I was scheduled to speak the following morning at the South Carolina Freedom Summit, a national gathering of grassroots conservatives. Claudia's twin brother, George, had come with me to the Iowa Freedom Summit in January. Now it was her turn for a trip with mom.

I'm afraid our mother-daughter excursion got off to a bit of a bumpy start. Our flight took off from New Jersey, circled D.C., and returned to New Jersey with mechanical problems. The next flight was delayed three hours. It was nearly midnight by the time we finally got to the hotel in Greenville. But none of this seemed to dull Claudia's excitement. When we woke up Saturday morning, she raced through her room-service breakfast and immediately began reviewing her fashion choices for the day.

"Mom, should I wear these shoes? Should I wear this dress?" My tween daughter considered every possible combination she had jammed into her small roller bag. Me? I made do with a bright pink cotton cap-sleeve dress, sure to stand out amid the buttoned-up grays and khakis of the nearly all-male speaker lineup.

Claudia and I took our suitcases to the event venue so we could fly straight home. Sunday was Mother's Day, and my mom and Aunt Rita were already waiting back in Alpine with George, Vanessa, Charlotte, and Georgie for our annual family celebration.

Like the Iowa edition had been, the South Carolina Freedom Summit was hosted by Citizens United, this time with Congressman Jeff Duncan. The event, at the Peace Center downtown, also featured office-holders, declared candidates for the Republican presidential nomination, and others who were flirting with the idea but not going steady yet, including Donald Trump. Claudia was excited to shake hands, receive hugs, and collect photographs from many of these national political figures, including not-yet-presidential-candidates like Marsha Black-burn and Tim Scott. Some of them, I discovered, hadn't even met each other yet.

In the hallway that day, I introduced Senator Marco Rubio and Don-ald Trump. It surprised me that the senator from Florida and the New York businessman had never met. Rubio lived in West Miami, about an hour by car from Trump's Palm Beach estate-club, Mar-a-Lago. I pulled out my phone and took a picture of the two of them, which I later tweeted out.

"Senator Rubio," I volunteered, "if you'd like to take Jeanette for a nice Mother's Day brunch tomorrow, you should go to the Doral, and Mr. Trump will be happy to pick up the check for the two of you!"

Trump shook his head playfully, pointing at me.

"This one," he said. "She's always bargaining, always talking. Yeah, take your wife. Take the kids. Have a good time."

I'd been joking, but I think Trump meant it.

David Bossie introduced me to the crowd. As I had in Iowa, I urged the audience in South Carolina to make the candidates work for their support and warned against the fiction of electability, blaming that concept for destroying the chances of too many good underdog candidates up and down the ballot. Eighteen months before Election Day 2016, I was already unloading on Hillary Clinton. "Of course, America is ready for a woman as president, just not *that* woman," I said. "And I'm just not afraid of a person who's the second-most-popular person in a two-person household."

That went over well in this room.

I think the guys were reluctant to hit Hillary. They didn't want to look like sexist bullies. But I'd studied her for decades, knew the weaknesses, and wasn't the least bit hesitant. I was trying out my zingers for the long season ahead.

After my speech, Claudia and I had our picture taken with Donald Trump. I reminded them both that when Claudia and her twin brother, Georgie, were born, they went straight from NYU Medical Center to our apartment in Trump World Tower.

He got pulled away to say hello to some of the other summiteers. But fifteen minutes later, I heard a familiar voice from across the noisy room.

"Hey, Kel, you girls want a ride back to New York? Come on, fly with us!"

"Oh, yeah!" I said, giving Claudia a gentle nudge. "Honey, go get your bag. Hurry, before he walks out the door!"

"Mom," she protested, "I still haven't gotten a picture with Carly Fiorina or Ben Carson!"

"We'll invite them over for coffee sometime. Let's go!"

After our nerve-racking journey the night before, no way was I missing our chance to hitch a ride home on Donald Trump's private jet. We climbed into a waiting SUV with Trump in the middle row and Claudia and me behind him in the backseat.

"You know, I never thought you were going to say yes," Trump said to me.

"Would you prefer we not come?" I asked.

"No, glad you did. But people usually don't say yes."

"Well, they are fools."

I might have been one of those people earlier in my career, too worried about imposing with a confident yes. "Oh, that's okay," I could easily have answered. "There probably isn't enough room. I'm fine. That commercial flight we tried to take down here, the one that kept malfunctioning, that was fun!"

I was so glad I'd gained enough confidence and wisdom over the years to send a different message to my daughter that day: *Buckle up, kid! We're going for a ride!*

Hope Hicks, who worked for the Trump Organization, was on board, as were Sam Nunberg and a few others. Claudia and I sat in captain chairs to the right and front of Mr. Trump's spot in the center of the aircraft. On the wall was a video screen the full width of the plane, a full-sized movie screen.

Trump said we would be making a stopover before heading to New York. He wanted to check out a golf course he was renovating in Sterling, Virginia. Once we got to the club, I ducked into the ladies' room while Trump showed Claudia the pro shop. When I came out, the two of them had morphed into Daddy Warbucks and Little Orphan Annie.

"Pick anything you want, honey," Trump was urging my daughter, a shopaholic-in-training even at ten.

A couple of years later, I would pull Jeff Bezos aside at a party and ask him in a hushed, somber tone if his company, Amazon, kept a secret blacklist of people they would never, ever deliver to, like international scam artists and drug traffickers.

"We do," a serious-looking Bezos assured me.

"I need you to add a name," I said, in my best "Counselor to the President" voice. One of the world's richest men leaned in so I could whisper it. "Claudia Marie Conway. She's twelve and a half. Get her on that 'blacklist,' please. Cease all deliveries. Alphabetically, she'll go right after Chapo, El."

Bezos's joyful, full-bodied laughter filled the air.

When I caught up with my daughter in the golf shop, her new friend Donald was urging her on mercilessly. "You have siblings? What about Mother's Day tomorrow?"

Cradled in her little arms, Claudia already had a Trump International Golf Club logo shirt and a golf hat with pink Swarovski crystals. She looked up at me expectantly, hoping I would keep my mouth shut and quietly bless her Kardashian-level shopping spree.

"That'll be enough," I told her. "That's plenty."

"What about the other kids?" Trump jumped in. Apparently, I was killing his buzz, too.

"Well, they're not here," I said. "This is *her* special day. I bought them something in South Carolina."

Trump treated all of us to lunch at the club while he went off to tend to "golf course stuff." I spent part of the afternoon getting to know Hope Hicks. Claudia and I explored the grounds in a golf cart before we all headed back to the jet.

"Do you like Elton John?" Trump asked soon after takeoff.

"I love him," I gushed. "George and I went to his sixtieth birthday concert at Madison Square Garden. Amazing."

With an Elton John concert on the wide-screen, we had a smooth flight back to New York.

I WAS WALKING by myself down a hallway in the United States Senate when I heard an urgent set of footsteps on the marble floor behind me.

I turned around. It was Senator Ted Cruz of Texas. He wanted to know if I'd be willing to fly down to Texas for a couple of days to strategize with him and his brain trust, who were trying to figure out exactly where Cruz's assertive conservative message might fit in the large Republican field.

"Sure," I told him. "I'll come."

A couple of days before my trip, I got a call from Jeff Roe, the senator's main political architect.

"Let me get this right," Jeff said to me. "You're gonna come down to Houston and join this long-planned strategy session about Ted running for president because . . . *his wife said it would be a good idea?*"

"No," I said calmly, "Heidi wasn't involved at all. Ted asked me to come. We talked in the Capitol. I ran into him in the Senate."

"You ran into him in the Senate?"

"I was in the hallway," I said, "going from a meeting to a presentation, and he stopped me and said, 'Do you think you could come? I'd like you to give your perspective.'"

"Hmmm," Jeff responded. "We already have a pollster. But we don't have a lot of women. You should come."

"Listen, Jeff," I told him. "If it's a problem, my kids would be very happy for me to skip it."

I went to Texas. We had some good conversations. I shared my perspective with Ted and his team. Heidi Cruz, a Goldman Sachs executive, offered important insight and asked the right questions. The Mercer family, I knew, had been strong Cruz backers, and it was after the strategy session in Houston that Rebekah reached out to me. She said she was launching a super PAC, Keep the Promise I, to support Ted Cruz's presidential campaign. These Political Action Committees can raise unlimited amounts of money and promote candidates, so long as the groups' activities are not coordinated with the official campaign.

"Do you want to run it?" Rebekah asked me in person and in private. She had donated $10 million and had pledges for another $20 million. We'd have a year to spend the money—or however long Cruz stayed in the race.

There were some things I really admired about Ted Cruz, even beyond his principled brand of conservatism. His brain and his courage, mainly. He'd never been scared to confront the Republican establishment when he thought they'd lost their way. He wasn't just *outside* the Washington club. He was one of the rare Republican senators who were utterly fearless in taking them on.

I was always open to working with Rebekah and her father. The entire family was brilliant and lacking in ego. They'd always given me latitude. I gave them honest advice. And while the Cruz campaign remained in Houston, the Mercers were in New York, so that's where the super PAC would be based.

Being intimately involved with a super PAC provides an entirely different perspective on the ins and outs and ups and downs of political candidates and campaigns.

Under super PAC rules, I would be legally prohibited from coordinating in any way with Ted Cruz, Jeff Roe, or anyone else at the Cruz campaign. If I went to work for the Cruz-backing super PAC, I wouldn't even be allowed to speak with any of them. Rebekah and I would be spending the money as *we* saw fit.

And we would do it from New York.

NOW I HAD a choice to make, within the clear constraints of my own family geography.

What should I do? Should I sign on as the Trump campaign pollster? Or should I join Rebekah Mercer at the Ted Cruz super PAC?

The journey with Trump would certainly be a fun one. He'd proven that in one short trip from South Carolina to New York. Like I told Corey at breakfast, "I love the guy," and his campaign was looking more real by the day. No way Donald Trump would run just for the sake of losing. He was a winner. And this long-awaited campaign of his, if that's what it was, would be run out of Trump Tower, Fifth Avenue and 57th Street, New York, New York.

So Trump-for-president also passed my geography test. The headquarters was a thirty-minute ride from Alpine. George already went into the city every day.

Being a mom and all, yes, that mattered. A lot.

Well, I chose the Cruz super PAC. For now. In part to learn the ins and outs of super PACS and for one other reason. Much as I enjoyed, respected, and believed in Donald Trump, I also had some doubts about what exactly my job would be as his campaign pollster.

My strong suspicion? I would never do a single poll.

Trump might just rely on the public polls and the Drudge Report and some random online survey and whatever some friend of his said in a phone call at eleven o'clock last night. I knew what Trump would say to me when I suggested, "Let's do a poll."

"My poll is right here, honey," he'd say, tapping the side of his head. "My eyes and my ears. My sixth sense. I'm my own poll."

The predictable grumbles from the usual mean boys would follow. "She's not really a pollster. . . . She's just flying around the country with him, being his talking head. . . ."

I told Corey. "You know, for now," I said, "I'm going to wait. If Trump's gonna do polls, if you need someone else to go on TV and explain this election, go after Hillary, let's see what happens. We'll keep talking. It's a long campaign. We'll figure it out."

Chapter 12

Primarily Trump

I was running a super PAC supporting Ted Cruz, and I kept running into Donald Trump. Spearheading a super PAC was a lot different from being on a campaign. We had a small team, outside consultants and vendors, daily calls and regular strategy sessions, but it freed me from the constant "need to be seen" and the layers of decision-making and daily chores. Just me. Turning up at any events I wanted to. Going on TV when I felt like it. More time for George and the kids. More creative freedom in the messaging and voter outreach.

I was at the Venetian hotel in Las Vegas for the Republican debate on December 15, 2015, the night Trump fully dismantled the tightly wound Jeb Bush, a target he'd softened up three months earlier at the Reagan Presidential Library debate in Simi Valley, California. Their conflict had been brewing since summer, when Trump started jabbing the former Florida governor on immigration, saying Bush had gone wobbly because of his wife Columba's Mexican heritage. Now it was Bush's turn.

"To subject my wife into the middle of a raucous political conversation was completely inappropriate, and I hope you apologize for that, Donald," Bush declared. He announced that Columba was sitting right there in the audience. Trump should tell her directly that he was sorry.

"No, I won't do that because I've said nothing wrong," Trump shot back, to which Bush said ... *nothing*. He simply let the matter drop.

Right at the key moment, the latest Bush to run for president had blinked. Score one for Trump. Round two was brutal in its simplicity. Trump had become embroiled in what the media described as his "Muslim ban," something Jeb termed "unhinged." Now moderator Wolf Blitzer was asking Jeb to defend his use of that term.

"If we're going to ban all Muslims, how are we going to get them to be part of a coalition to destroy ISIS?" Jeb demanded, before taking another swing at Trump. "He's a chaos candidate. He would be a chaos president."

Trump didn't bludgeon back, his usual instinct. His weapon this time was the scalpel of dismissiveness. "Jeb doesn't really believe I am unhinged," Trump said, more in sadness than in anger. "He said that very simply because he has failed in his campaign. It has been a total disaster. Nobody cares."

That stung. Jeb Bush had entered the race as the Republican front-runner a full year earlier with piles of money to burn (and burn the money his consultants did). Now he was fourth or fifth in the polls—and slipping even further behind. He looked like he'd just been hit by the Trump Train, and Trump didn't even have to raise his voice.

In the post-debate spin room at the Venetian, I went on a couple of radio shows and lived up to my reputations as "Sally Soundbite" by furnishing quotes to a few print and TV reporters. Trump was surrounded and followed by far the largest media contingent at the hotel. They were fascinated; he was the front-runner. Corey Lewandowski came over to me.

"What, are you in *Star Trek* now?" I said to him.

He had a shiny pin on the lapel of his sport coat. I noticed body guys Keith Schiller and Johnny McEntee also had them.

"No, no," he said. "We have to have our own pin with the Secret Service because so many people want to get around our guy."

That certainly wasn't an issue for most of these candidates, who were still struggling to draw modest crowds or to catch the attention of reporters in that room.

That's when Trump noticed me there. "Hey, Kel," he called out, motioning for me.

He was standing with elegant Melania Trump on the other side of the rope line, beaming about his performance on the stage. "Come over here," he said. He asked one of the Secret Service agents to escort me.

As he and I stood there talking, Mark Halperin, no doubt grabbing content for his Bloomberg show or his HBO show *The Circus,* caught my eye:

"Can I come over the rope?" Mark asked.

"No, but your microphone can."

"So what did you think?" Trump asked me.

"You took away Jeb's exclamation point," I said with a smile, referencing his campaign's *Jeb!* logo. "He's down to just the three letters now."

ALL ALONG, I kept running my company and talking on television and keeping up with my other clients and polling, of course. A group of donors hired me to do a nationwide poll of Republican primary and caucus voters and statewide surveys in the early states. There was a sense that divided loyalties and backing different candidates could ultimately fracture the party and hand Hillary a victory. So they wanted to gather more intel.

When all the survey data were compiled, and analyzed I made a dinner presentation to a heady room of D.C. bigwigs. They included supporters of Jeb Bush, Marco Rubio, Chris Christie, Scott Walker, Ben Carson, John Kasich, Carly Fiorina, Rick Perry, Ted Cruz—almost anyone with an *R* . . . other than Donald Trump.

My own polling data left little doubt: Trump was gaining momentum with voters and also improving his image. His high negatives were increasingly being offset with "specific positive recall": equally high positives. The balance was tipping his way, even as "Mr. Undecided" was still highest in the polls. As I laid that out, I couldn't help but notice some frowns and uncomfortable rustling in the room. The minute I finished my presentation, one of the organizer's representatives rushed over to me. Steam wasn't emanating from his ears, but it might as well have been.

"You showed Trump in the top three in all those different categories and you described him as the candidate with the most intrigue, the most recent movement," he said.

"Yes . . ." I answered.

"You embarrassed us," the man interrupted. "That is *not* what we paid for."

Isn't it, though? I thought to myself in the shower the next morning, reflecting on how rude and presumptuous he'd been. These donors and other D.C. types had all paid it forward for years, reflexively supporting nominees like McCain and Romney, never bothering to get to know how the other 99 percent live, breaking promises on core GOP issues such as taxes and foreign entanglements and recommending friends of friends to the federal judiciary, only to have them be disappointments and disasters. You made him. You did this. Trump was coming on strong, and some people were having trouble getting used to it.

I KEPT SEEING Trump, and he kept seeing me. And he kept seeing me on television. It was the same old story all over again. There I was, twenty years after I'd started communicating with people on TV, and I was still communicating with people on TV, including the front-runner for the Republican nomination for president, who watched a lot of TV.

Whoever the undercutters were, they didn't know how to get me off TV. Every time I ran into Trump, he would say, "I saw you the other day. You were saying . . ." And then he'd quote something I'd said on CNN or Fox or one of the morning shows or the Sunday shows. At this point, he even tweeted at me to congratulate me after a good segment on *Meet the Press.*

"I hadn't really thought of it that way," he told me on more than a few occasions.

In those live TV appearances, I was frequently asked about Trump and his candidacy. On a few occasions I was critical of him, calling to mind some of the small businesses that were forced out after casinos and related development had mushroomed in Atlantic City. At the same time, I was very up front with what I had seen and lived. For thousands of people who resided on or near the sixty-mile corridor between Atlantic City and Philadelphia, including my own mother, fresh employment and opportunity were available at casinos run by successful businessmen like Steve Wynn and Donald Trump. People knew that I knew Trump and I had done work for him over the years. As he kept rising in the polls and the actual voting grew near, hitting illegal immigration, hitting U.S. trade policy, hitting America's troubled relationships with its allies and enemies, Trump was the news of the day every day.

"Give the man his due," I'd say. "He's taking issues that were minor, low, single-digit issues like trade and immigration. He's giving them top platform, top billing, and he's sticking with them. Usually, people in politics are afraid to do that. They keep saying, 'Oh, jobs and the economy are number one.' Of course they're number one. They're always going to be number one or close to it. But what are you going to say about jobs and the economy that's compelling and persuasive and different from what everyone else is saying? It all sounds the same. Trump sounds different . . . and real."

IT WAS OPEN primary season—literally. People started voting, and the inevitable happened. Most of the candidates in the large Republican field came up short. It is very difficult to keep raising money for a campaign that is seen as going nowhere. And one by one, the candidates began pulling out.

Mike Huckabee, Rand Paul, and Rick Santorum all exited the race after poor showings in Iowa, which Cruz won, barely edging out Donald Trump and Marco Rubio. Scott Walker, Bobby Jindal, Lindsey Graham, George Pataki, and a mob of others never even made it that far. Chris Christie and Carly Fiorina suspended their efforts after coming up short in the February 9 New Hampshire primary, which Trump won with 35 percent (a win he'd predicted for himself way back before he was even a candidate), more than doubling John Kasich's second-place finish. Jeb Bush, the long-faded front-runner, was out on February 20, having failed to secure a single delegate in the South Carolina primary (he spent more than $150 million and collected four delegates in all), promptly enriching consultants who'd failed him and endorsing Ted Cruz, who'd survived him—*anyone* but Trump.

The tiniest things, Trump kept discovering, could get under his opponents' skin. Look at how devastating his nicknames were. It was amazing to behold how a schoolyard slight could bring a grown man to his knees. Talk about giving someone else power over you! The moment you lose your cool and get angry about being called Little Marco or Lyin' Ted or Low-Energy Jeb—voters see the vulnerability and Trump keeps you as a target. The American people understood. If a third-grade taunt could rattle you, what chance would you have against China, Russia, ISIS, or Al Qaeda?

As Trump remained the man to beat, several of the others kept their noses in the air, refusing to "stoop" by responding to his latest Twitter taunts or debate-stage disses. A few tried to beat Trump at his own combativeness, dishing up sporadic attacks on the man who'd been torturing them. But they could never get the tone right, the cocky, New York-y humor that Trump knew how to wrap around his needles. You can't just be vulgar and vile. Even Marco Rubio seemed to take leave of his good senses and go places he had never gone before.

Rubio had already called Trump a "con man" seeking to perpetrate "the biggest scam in American political history." He attacked the New Yorker for his "failed" businesses, his "fraudulent" real estate courses, and his supposed lack of policy proposals. Some of this, I could tell, came directly from Rubio, but most of it I perceived could be pinned on his flailing band of political henchmen and surrogates who, sadly, were some younger Republican members of Congress. They beclowned themselves on national TV, ridiculing Trump's "small hands" and "spray tan."

What seemed good for a few cheap laughs was bad for business. Voters knew that the challenges facing the nation were too enormous to allow the end of the Republican primary contest to devolve into a palooza of personal insults. I thought at the time that (as I had thought about Trump plenty of times, too) this was totally beneath a sitting United States senator and a person I knew to be a genuine American success story, smart, a nice guy who wanted to be president. I'd fought tears at the Republican National Convention in 2012, listening to Senator Marco Rubio laud his father, a Cuban immigrant who had been a bartender. *My father stood behind that bar, so one day his son could stand behind this podium."*

It was a double blow for Rubio. He was now the establishment candidate who had the backing of D.C. politicians and donors bent on "stopping Trump!" Where that had helped Romney in 2012, it was toxic if not fatal to a presidential candidate in an election year driven by the grassroots. (He'd go on to lose his own home state of Florida to Trump on March 15.) The original field of seventeen candidates had rapidly whittled down to three. John Kasich and Ted Cruz were now the only live Republicans still dreaming of wresting the party nomination away from Donald Trump. Dreaming was right. For weeks their aides and advisors had been insisting that, once the field thinned out, a winning coalition of never-Trump Republicans would coalesce around one of them.

The Republican primary voters seemed poised, for the first time since General Eisenhower, to choose a nominee who had no prior elective experience. Eisenhower had been a military hero. I conducted one last series of statewide surveys for the Cruz super PAC, a look ahead at the packed schedule of primary contest that still remained. The data showed that the senator from Texas could not beat Donald Trump, even in deep red states like Nebraska, where Trump had just rallied thousands of people. Trump was a true juggernaut. When I presented that data on Saturday afternoon, April 30, I did it by phone from my room at Shutters on the Beach hotel in Santa Monica, California, the final day of that year's NFL draft on the muted TV in the background (QB Carson Wentz was drafted by the Philadelphia Eagles).

The night before, I'd been on *Real Time with Bill Maher* opposite Rob Reiner and the *New York Times* reporter—and author of *This Town* and a first-timer on the show—Mark Leibovich. It was George and my fifteenth wedding anniversary, so he flew out with me. Later I would see this as an early indicator of George's growing fascination with the increasingly potent Donald Trump, which was all anyone wanted to talk about. We reflected on our own interactions with Trump and how much we'd enjoyed living in his building.

Cruz and Kasich both gave up the ghost the first week in May. Finally, the 2016 Republican presidential nomination fully belonged to Donald Trump.

A lot of people still found that shocking, but really, Trump had been hiding in plain sight as the top seed for almost a year. Trump had been at the top of the heap since the fall of 2015, a couple of months after his campaign began with the famous escalator ride down to the Trump Tower lobby. The successful businessman, first-time candidate, and political outsider (like most Americans) proved in bold color that inertia is the most powerful physical force in politics until taken over by friction. Trump was part friction, part kinetic energy.

He'd generated by far the most excitement. He'd drawn by far the largest crowds. He'd gotten by far the most media coverage. He was crack cocaine for the cable news channels and network broadcasts. They were addicted to the ratings that his name, face, and voice always seemed to bring to them. They were literally unable to pull away from Donald Trump.

Now he had the biggest, shiniest GOP prize there was: the all-important Republican delegates.

This raised some practical questions for Rebekah Mercer and for me: With Cruz out of the running, what should happen with the pro-Cruz super PAC we'd nursed from conception? Its purpose for being no longer existed, and that raised an additional question for Rebekah and her family: How should the Mercers target their political involvement and their potentially massive financial support for the rest of 2016?

It also raised a parallel question for me: How should *I* spend the rest of *my* year?

We all headed up to Trump Tower for lunch to discuss it.

Chapter 13

On Board

By *we all* I mean Rebekah Mercer, Steve Bannon, a friend of Rebekah's named Janet Boris, and me.

Janet, a successful businesswoman, was also friendly with the candidate's thirty-four-year-old daughter, Ivanka Trump. Mom of three, including an infant. Fashion brand owner. Trump Organization executive. *Apprentice* cast member. A graduate of boarding school and then, like her father, the Wharton School of the University of Pennsylvania. She'd been closely involved in her father's campaign from the very start, suggesting a run for president back when most of the people in the room had come to discuss a Trump campaign for governor of New York. Also present: Ivanka's thirty-five-year-old husband, Jared Kushner. The son of a wealthy real estate developer, Jared hailed from a family of Democrats who had made the "first donation" to future liberal U.S. senator Cory Booker when he ran for Newark City Council. Jared wasn't your typical presidential campaign architect. He had little (okay, no) previous experience in national politics and didn't know many people in the field. A Harvard College graduate who also had a joint law and business degree from New York University, he worked for his father's real estate company and puttered with his upscale salmon-colored *New York Observer* weekly newspaper, though lately his father-in-law's campaign was taking up more and more of his time. Well-groomed and unfailingly polite, he rarely revealed what he was thinking and spoke in what I would call a whisper voice.

Corey Lewandowski, the campaign manager, joined us, too. I sat between Corey and Jared and talked nonstop. Bannon sat between Rebekah and Janet and said very little we could hear, or needed to hear. We helped ourselves to a buffet lunch in the glass-enclosed twenty-fifth-floor Trump Tower conference room and ate while we talked.

The seven of us kicked around the current state of the general election race, and how to form, fund, and run a super PAC. Also, the question of the moment: how to beat Hillary Clinton and win the presidency. But to me, the most interesting part of the conversation came as our lunch was winding down and we were standing up to leave. That's when Jared drew me into a sidebar, which I would soon discover was one of his favorite forms of communication when other people were in the room. It was private but not private. He could (slightly) raise his voice or (ever so slightly) lower it, depending on what he wanted others to hear, or assume.

"Do you have any thoughts on the vice presidential pick?" he asked me.

Corey, I noticed, was still seated at the table and listening.

I was so ready for this moment and glad he asked.

"For VP," I said, "instead of *who,* the question should be *what.* Come up with a job description."

Jared nodded, and I continued.

"Republicans keep making the same mistake," I said. "It's bad enough that the nomination for the top of the ticket has usually been a coronation or a consolation prize for the person who lost to the person who lost to the person who won. But for VP, someone somewhere assembles a list of names, which everyone promptly picks apart and plays the parlor game of who's up and who's down. Before that happens, why not arrive at the most important criteria, including those skills, attributes, and experience that are the nonnegotiable 'must-haves' and the negotiable 'nice-to-haves' for Mr. Trump's number two?"

I had rehearsed bits like this in speeches and pitches, in planes, trains, and automobiles, with George and Jesse as my audience the decade before and lately with Bonnie and Skipper.

Jared immediately mentioned two names. Newt Gingrich and Chris Christie. Both men are friends of mine, incredibly talented and accomplished leaders who have defied impossible political odds to rise to the pinnacles of power. They are visionaries with little fear and loads of ideas who were actively helping Trump when other Republicans were still mumbling and stumbling. Both men had been mentioned publicly as possible Trump vice presidents, along with several other Republicans who had run against Trump in the primaries and a few business leaders. The behind-the-scenes jockeying had begun; no one was saying "no."

But I didn't linger on the *who*. Not yet. I stayed focused on the *what*. "I'd find someone with congressional/Washington experience," I offered, "but not decades of it. If they've run a state, all the better."

Then I drilled down a little more. "Beating Hillary demands busting through the Democrats' 'blue wall,'" I said. "So focus on people who represent states in the upper Midwest and Rust Belt. Michigan. Ohio. Wisconsin. Iowa. Pennsylvania. Indiana. Or leap over to the Nevada–Colorado–New Mexico–Arizona corridor, where Democrats have been more competitive in recent years."

"I like it," Jared said. "Makes sense."

I had no idea if he was just being polite—he seemed awfully polite in this first face-to-face encounter—and was only humoring me. Or maybe his unblinking eyes really were opened by my way of looking it. As far as I could remember, we had never met before. I had never been to a Cory Booker fundraiser.

"Who, then?" he asked.

So much for exploring the *what*. He still wanted my input on *who*. I ticked off some names and job titles.

The governors of Ohio, Wisconsin, and Michigan.

Senator Rob Portman of Ohio.

"My personal favorite, though, is Mike Pence, governor of Indiana. I'm biased," I admitted, "because I've been his pollster in the House and as governor for years."

"Pence," Jared said with a nod. I took it to be a favorable nod.

"Pence satisfies the criteria we've already discussed," I said. "But there's more. He is trusted and respected by religious conservatives. He is pro-Israel, pro-life, pro–Second Amendment. The conservative bona fides are there. He worked in Washington yet never became Washington, even though he was in Congress for twelve years. He took on tough assignments. Ten years on Judiciary. Six years on Foreign Affairs. He voted against major policies of both Bush and Obama. That took guts. Now he's governor of a state where school choice and charters have expanded, manufacturing is up and taxes are down, and he is the only governor in the country to get a waiver on Obamacare to make way for his own state's healthcare plan. He didn't just want to replace Obamacare. He came up with something better."

Jared was still with me. But more than pitching a single candidate, I wanted to help him think big-picture about the crucial choice his father-in-law would soon have to make. Other than the decision to run, it would be the most important choice Trump had made so far.

"Mr. Trump actually has more options than Republican nominees usually do," I said. "Lately, the conservative base of the party has been so demoralized about the top of the ticket, there's been pressure to choose a running mate who could reduce suspicion and generate excitement. Dole with Kemp. McCain with Palin. Romney with Ryan."

As we spoke, I happened to glance through the glass partition separating the conference room from the office foyer, where suddenly, there was Donald Trump.

I didn't realize he was in the building. As far as I knew, he was on one of his six-stop campaign benders that day, flying around the country to packed houses and hungry TV cameras. But there was Trump in full, fresh off his stunning march to the Republican nomination, speaking and gesticulating and posing for pictures with an entranced group of visitors.

"Don't worry about the excitement part," I assured Jared, motioning to Trump and the giddy group delighting in his storytelling. "We have *alllll* the excitement we could possibly need."

Then, as if to prove it, Trump glanced through the glass and, ten seconds later, burst into the conference room. "Hello," he said, gently embracing his daughter and looking around the table. "How are you?" Then he turned toward me and added, "Oh, look who's here, superstar! Are you gonna help us? I hear you're helping us?"

"I'd be honored to, sir," I said. "We had a really great talk at lunch about setting up super PACs and—"

"We don't need that stuff," he jumped in.

"—and we've been talking about VP."

That topic, he seemed interested in. "So who do you like best of all?" he asked me, as everyone else in the room just let us banter.

"Well," I said, "I think you should be looking at Governor Pence or Governor [Scott] Walker in Wisconsin . . . Rob Portman in Ohio . . ."

"Yeah," Trump said noncommittally. "I think they're on our list. What do you think of Newt? What do you think of Chris Christie?"

Before I could answer, he looked to his right, barely acknowledged Bannon, but immediately engaged Rebekah, whom he had previously described as tough and smart. "This one," he said, motioning back at me. "I don't know if you noticed, but so funny. This one's working for Cruz." He'd either forgotten that Rebekah and her family had funded the Cruz super PAC or he never knew. "At the same time she's working for Ted Cruz, I'm watching her on TV, and they're asking her who will win the Republican nomination, and she says, 'Well, it looks like Trump. It's gonna be Trump! Sometimes he's surging. But all the time he just keeps fighting.' And they ask her, 'Can anybody beat him?' And there's Kelly-anne, working for Ted Cruz and saying, 'Nope. I don't see anybody at this point able to beat Donald Trump.'"

He laughed out loud at that, then turned back to me.

"Did Cruz get mad at you for saying that? Did he fire you?"

"No, sir," I answered. "He didn't fire me."

"Isn't that funny?" Trump said.

BEFORE ANYTHING ELSE could happen, Corey Lewandowski was shown the door.

Trump's gritty first campaign manager always had his detractors. People outside the self-important consultants' club who dare to challenge them, let alone beat them, incur a special type of venom. Corey could be abrasive, but he was unquestionably loyal to Donald Trump and had been by his side through the multistate primary-and-caucus campaign en route to the nomination. But on the morning of June 20, 2016, during a meeting with the nominee and his adult children, Corey heard those two dreaded, Trump-branded words: "You're fired!"

With Corey gone, much of his day-to-day authority ended up in the hands of Paul Manafort, a veteran operative from elections past who happened to have an apartment in Trump Tower. Manafort would later tell me over lunch at Michael's restaurant, making clear that he had already known Donald Trump and that Tom Barrack was a mutual friend of theirs, and he had not been brought on to the campaign through a Roger Stone connection. This was an intriguing aside to me, since when I was an intern for Jack Kemp I knew that Black, Manafort, Stone, and Kelly was the hottest business in town. Now holding the title of campaign chairman, Manafort turned his attention to assembling delegates. He had helped to manage Gerald Ford's 1976 delegate fight against Ronald Reagan, then played a similar role for Reagan in 1980, and also worked for George Bush in 1988 and Bob Dole in 1996. Though he'd been largely out of U.S. politics since then, catering to Soviet bloc oligarchs and other international clients, Manafort had somehow convinced Jared and others that he was an up-to-the-minute expert in modern delegate corralling and that "free" would not come at a huge cost.

It took a little while to formalize my own official hiring by the Trump-for-president campaign, even as I was in regular contact with the big guy for months by then. But on Friday, July 1, seventeen days before the Republican convention, someone at the campaign gave the story to reporter Maggie Haberman of the *New York Times*.

"Donald J. Trump is adding two women to his team on his presidential efforts for the general election, a shift for a campaign whose upper echelons have been dominated by men. Kellyanne Conway, a veteran pollster and strategist with deep working ties to Mr. Trump, will come on as a senior advisor to the campaign chairman, Paul Manafort, as well as a member of the expanding polling team led by the pollster Tony Fabrizio."

Wrote Maggie: "She is often consulted by House and Senate candidates, and she has carved out a niche for her mining of data related to female voters." The reporter noted that Karen Giorno, who had worked for Trump in Florida, would be coming on board as a senior political advisor. "The moves also reflect an effort by Mr. Trump to try to improve his standing among female voters in a general election featuring the first female Democratic presidential nominee."

Yes, I was hired. And the job was fine, for now. And I didn't have to give up my other clients . . . for now. That was certainly something I could do, hoping my portfolio and reach might expand in a structure with less hierarchy and less hubris than most general election campaigns.

At the very least, I could suggest some of the things that Trump found compelling a year earlier, when we first discussed running against Hillary Clinton. The Romney and McCain teams had ignored the reasonable advice and strategic ideas and lost. It was certainly worth a try.

That afternoon, I taped an appearance on *The O'Reilly Factor* at the Fox News Channel. As usual, I left my phone in the greenroom. Believe me, you do not want your cell phone going off, even on vibrate, during an interview with Bill O'Reilly. When I got out of the studio, I noticed a missed call from Governor Mike Pence.

I didn't have to wonder long what he was calling about. Just as I stepped onto the Sixth Avenue sidewalk, my phone rang again.

Pence and his wife, Karen, along with their older daughter, Charlotte, were on their way to the airport in Indianapolis. Pence said they were flying to New Jersey for a sit-down at the Trump National Golf Club Bedminster.

"What can you tell me, KAC?"

By that point, the Indiana governor had been mentioned in the media as a possible running mate, along with several others, including Christie, Gingrich, Senator Jeff Sessions, Senator Bob Corker, and even General Mike Flynn. Some names may have been leaked and others were just wild guesses by reporters hoping to get lucky. But Trump and Pence didn't really know each other. They'd met just once or twice. They'd had a meal together at the Capital Grille in Indianapolis when Trump flew in for a fundraiser. But that was about it for face-to-face quality time. And though I'd vouched for Pence with Trump and laid out for Jared all the reasons I thought he made sense as a running mate, I also knew that personal chemistry in a selection like this one is an essential criterion.

Could the buttoned-down Rust Belt evangelical governor really be a match for the freewheeling, thrice-married New York businessman and reality TV star? Pence was clearly interested in being Trump's vice president or else he wouldn't be flying to New Jersey with his wife and daughter. I fired back with that very point when a few "Pence people" called me, perturbed that this "charade" had gotten this far. "I see what's in it for Trump," one remarked, "but what's in it for Pence?" The truth was that all of us were going to find out very soon. Trump still had some time to make a decision but not a lot.

Speaking a mile a minute, I told Mike Pence what I had told Jared:

that he was a conservative but not an ideologue, someone who could work with others, a practical leader who believed in accomplishing things. He had been in Washington but was never captured by it.

"So what are you saying . . . I'm boring?" Pence interrupted with a hearty laugh.

"No," I assured him. "You are steady. Sea level."

"You've got this all figured out, KAC," Pence noted, partly glib and partly grateful.

"Not really," I assured him. "That's up to you."

I knew this much: No matter what advice Donald Trump was getting from me or anyone, he would never choose a running mate he didn't like. And the final decision would be his and his alone.

"I know the Trumps are looking forward to hosting Karen and you," I said. "Wait until you spend time with Melania. She's gold." I knew that Pence, as shrewd a politician as he was, would immediately recognize that. "Karen and you will really like her."

The Pences landed in New Jersey later that Friday night. The two couples had dinner. It was then that Donald Trump discovered that their daughter, Charlotte, had accompanied them on the trip. "Invite her to breakfast tomorrow," he insisted.

At breakfast, Trump asked Charlotte Pence about the youth vote, for example, what do young people talk about, what is on their minds. Classic Trump. Then the two men headed to the renowned and exquisite fields of green in Bedminster. The men talked. The women talked. The couples talked. Trump and Pence got in a quick round of golf. And the media got nothing of any value. The get-together was "warm and friendly." It was a "getting to know you thing, a chance for both of them to connect." Phony inside information from aides who didn't have a clue. The presence of Karen Pence, the analysts noted, was probably a positive sign that the Pences were comfortable with the prospect of the Republican governor joining the ticket. Then again, Trump campaign chairman Paul Manafort, who had been handling much of the vice presidential search, wasn't at Bedminster. That couldn't be a good sign, could it? Clearly the press had no idea.

No one who knew anything was leaking. No one who was leaking knew anything.

*   *   *

ON WEDNESDAY NIGHT, July 13, five days before the convention began, Trump called Indiana from California and offered Pence the job. Pence accepted immediately. On Friday morning at eleven, Trump made it official on Twitter: "I am pleased to announce that I have chosen Governor Mike Pence as my Vice Presidential running mate. News conference tomorrow at 11:00 A.M." That afternoon the Pences, Trumps, Manafort, Pence advisors Marty Obst and Nick Ayers, I, and some others retreated to the Trump penthouse. It was there that Trump asked Pence to tell him more about the Healthy Indiana Plan and the trade deal Indiana had made with Japan. I piped in with what had been the most popular Pence policy during the campaign and through his tenure: expanding technical and vocational educational opportunities. Not everyone is college material, and that should be celebrated and accommodated. Graduating with a high school diploma and a skills certificate meant that Hoosiers—and indeed Americans—could support themselves say, as a welder, carpenter, hairdresser, or mechanic. Both Trump and Pence had been engaging and elevating the "forgotten man and woman" and the dignity of work for all.

Trump had done his homework. The VP pick was made with deliberation and intention.

The normally reserved Pence sounded thrilled to be on board. "My family and I couldn't be more honored to have the opportunity to run with and serve with the next president of the United States," he told reporters in New York the next morning, with many Trumps and Pences on the stage. Nick Ayers made sure he was next to Pence in Indiana when the call from Trump came in, and next to Paul Manafort in Manhattan that morning, projecting a "we're the two men in charge here" aura to the assembled media. The rest of us sat up front and watched more history unfold. The adult Trump kids and spouses approached us afterward.

Ivanka, holding Jared's hand, singled me out and chatted me up. Mark Halperin alighted from the media scrum and asked me afterward what Ivanka said, to which I remarked, "I'll never tell, but I hope she did not look at my feet." In the rush and madness of getting out of the house, I'd left my heels in the car that George and the kids were in. They were all driving, with my heels, to a party at the Long Island home of Bob Mercer, where I would soon join them. I was stuck in flip-flops at this August event.

"As long as she knows your name, don't worry about your footwear," Halperin remarked.

In the past two weeks, I'd come on board and days later Pence came on board. Now it was feeling more fun and more familiar. I was the only major political consultant Trump and Pence had in common. Each of them had been asking me about the other, and the pairing really happened. My decades-long track record of being a spectacularly unsuccessful matchmaker had finally produced a supercouple. The Washington boys' (and by then girls') network never saw it coming, and they couldn't stop it, either. This could get really fun and frantic really fast. And somehow or another, I knew, I would be in the middle of it all.

A few weeks later, before the Democrat National Convention, I was at CNN. I witnessed heated words and raised voices between Neera Tanden and Van Jones, where Jones was taking her to task over Hillary's having chosen Tim Kaine over people of color who either were, or should've been, considered for the vice presidential slot.

WHAT I'D SUSPECTED a year earlier about being Trump's pollster—not much polling involved—was true in the early days of the campaign. But Manafort had changed that, deploying another old friend, Tony Fabrizio, to be the campaign's *lead* pollster.

I wondered: In this case, did *lead* rhyme with *need* . . . or with *head*?

Four other polling firms, including mine, were added to the stable. We were assigned different swing states and conducted a battery of focus groups, too.

I had encountered Fabrizio throughout my career. Days into the formation of my new company in July 1995, he made me a huge offer to join his firm. Six figures. Company car. Equity. As many of the focus groups that I wanted. ("I've done it so long, I'm cynical," Fabrizio bragged to me. "I just want to punch the people in the face when they say something stupid.") I listened to the lucrative pitch over dinner and a few meetings at his Alexandria, Virginia, offices, once with his then-wife, Mychel. I was flattered but said no, bearing boxes of Italian pastries as I declared, "I want to fly on my own, Tony. No hard feelings. I'll see you on the field." Just a year later I heard he was spreading vicious rumors about me at the Republican National Convention in San Diego. I was there as a CNN political analyst;

Tony was one of nominee Bob Dole's pollsters. Dole had just selected my former boss, Jack Kemp, as his running mate. Fabrizio worked overtime to try to squeeze out the competition, and with me he got a little too close and way too nasty in so attempting. None of what his loud mouth said was true. All of it was ugly, mean, and meant to harass and embarrass me. I stood my ground and stayed in San Diego. I learned a rough lesson that I've reflected on throughout my career and life: Often the truth will set you free, but too often the truth may not be enough, or be revealed fast enough.

Jared called me on July 2, welcoming me aboard. "How much does polling cost?" he asked.

"That depends on a few things," I answered, and quickly laid out the four factors that determine a survey's cost.

"Well," he said, "why don't you tell me a couple of different versions—the top shelf, a medium version, and more of a bare minimum—of polling for the rest of the campaign. Throw in some focus groups."

Polling veterans Brett Loyd, Kevin Quinley, and Karen Smith spent the weekend helping me assemble the three-tiered proposal. I emailed it to Jared on the Fourth of July. I didn't realize it yet, but that was the day before FBI director James Comey's press conference announcing that Hillary Clinton would not be prosecuted for her emails. My proposal came in at half the price the campaign had been paying Fabrizio, whom Trump himself did not care for much and later asked me to fire.

"I saw the proposal," Jared said. "It looks solid. What would your fee be?"

"My fee?" I asked.

"How do you get paid?"

"My fee is in there. That covers everything."

Jared quickly noted that this was exactly why he had called me. They were paying too much and getting too little. I took that opening to offer one more tidbit: no more national polls.

They are meaningless. We need to turn blue and purple states red and win enough electoral votes, not popularity contests. Media would continue to conduct national polls and miss Trump's elevation and eventual election. We would go where the undecided voters who would decide the election lived, polling them in statewide surveys and microtargeting voters through consumer data and digital.

Surely Trump had his own way of surveying American voters. He watched many hours of television, knew what played with his rally crowds, and talked to his business friends at night on the phone, mostly ignoring the public polls that showed Hillary Clinton beating him. It wasn't exactly polling science, it was more art than science. But it was Trump's way of keeping his finger on the pulse of America, and it had served him well in business, television, and now in politics.

Part of my job was to help connect with the grassroots, and to convince swing voters that eight years after they took a chance and made history with the first African American president they could take a chance and make history with another political outsider, the first non-politician businessman to reach the Oval. Part of that involved advising Manafort on creative ways of attracting the support of women, Independents, suburban voters, and such. I drew up a detailed strategy on how the Trump campaign could speak to female voters with resonance and respect, about the things that either kept them up at night or kept them motivated, without alienating the guys. We women should not be talked to from the waist down only (read abortion and "reproductive rights"). Those who want our votes should speak to us from the waist up, which is where our eyes, ears, hearts, and brains are. Ladies, we are not a monolith or a "special interest group." We are 52 percent of the electorate. We decide who the president is.

Though my job title was *senior advisor and pollster*, Donald Trump was never a stickler for job titles. He kept calling me, asking questions, seeking advice, floating ideas. My experience with him, going all the way back to the Trump World Tower condo board, had taught me that he was not shy about disagreeing or even dismissing an idea, but he was almost always willing to listen. I think he valued my frankness. I certainly valued his openness. Lucky for me, he was more focused on making history than hewing to hierarchy.

I noticed another thing about Donald Trump: He abhors obsequiousness. Sure, he loves flattery, but too much bores him and means he hadn't learned anything. Say something meaningful, consequential. His campaign motto was "Make America Great Again," not "Isn't Trump Great Again?" I vowed to myself to keep speaking up accordingly, delivering my counsel forcefully yet respectfully, keeping faith with those Americans who kept showing up at Trump rallies by the thousands every day.

Chapter 14

Running It

It was not quite six weeks after I'd officially joined the Trump campaign that Donald Trump asked me to run it. I was elated and reluctant. For me, it was a moment of great self-worth but also self-doubt.

Typical!

If I'd had any reservations about being Donald Trump's campaign manager, they were set aside by my husband once I confided in him what had happened. When I got home after my mind-blowing meeting that August 12 and told George everything, first he said how proud he was of me and what a great presidential campaign manager I would make. Then he mentioned how little sense my follow-up made. Why keep it quiet? Why not lock in the good news? He was right, but now I'd just have to wait for the big announcement.

I had received my very own "art of the deal" from the big guy himself. I was the one—the "You're Hired" winner—in The Campaign Apprentice. The world's most famous real estate executive had handed me the keys to the castle.

I was out of clichés but filled with excitement.

"You can do this," my partner of seventeen years said to me, "and he can win with you."

But soon my mind was racing.

Maybe Trump will forget it, I thought. *Maybe he didn't mean it. Maybe he was just being polite. Maybe he'd been caught in the heat of the moment, railing against the current campaign management, the polls, the naysayers, the critics, and the cable news chatterboxes who were absolutely, positively, indubitably sure about their latest furrowed-brow, pursed-lips prediction. Maybe Trump is testing me. Would I leak the incredible news? Would I make this about me and not him? And, oh my God, could we actually defeat the Queen Bee herself when a majority of the electorate are women?*

He called me the next day and every day after that and spoke to me as if the deal were already done. That was saying something, since we all know in real estate you get a three-day right of rescission. Since he was already treating me like the campaign manager, I immediately started acting like it. It quickly became obvious he had listened to everything I had said, including my polite but nonnegotiable request to authorize a few big things strategically and tactically: that I'd have direct access to the candidate, that we'd go boldly right into the blue wall, that we'd smoke out Hillary from hiding behind the "I'm not Trump" wink, and that we'd examine data more situationally, given how many Americans who did not seem like Trump voters were apparently Trump voters.

He also remembered my fourth request: to install someone else in the "campaign C-suite." He settled on Steve Bannon, the Breitbart news guy who had little campaign experience.

Bannon's first order of business was informing Manafort that he'd become a liability. In two days, Manafort was officially gone. Jared, who had hired him, also fired him. On Wednesday, August 17, Donald Trump announced the campaign shakeup earlier than we had planned when he shared it with a *Wall Street Journal* reporter, Monica Langley, aboard his campaign plane. Hours later, I walked into the Trump Tower lobby on my way to a meeting with the candidate and business leaders. I was greeted by a media swarm I was not expecting.

"Two or three things we've all learned about Donald Trump," I told the reporters who were waiting in the lobby as the twelve-week home-stretch began. "Number one is, don't underestimate him. Number two, you know he exceeds expectations. And number three, he also exceeds the metrics that are usually at play, meaning he overperformed many of his polling averages in the primaries and the caucuses."

I'd been hiding in plain sight all along, just like future president Donald Trump had been. For someone who loves to talk, I had spent years and years listening. Among the things I learned was that Americans have an essential wisdom. They have thought through these complicated policies that Washington wrestles with, but there's a difference: Sometimes the people have more courage and deeper convictions and a greater urgency to find solutions, even when those are lacking among their elected officials. Even though very few people saw Donald Trump coming, perhaps more of us should have. After all, voters for years had been frustrated with their lack of upward economic mobility, access to opportunity, and prosperity. They resented that, while their own job security and access to benefits like quality health insurance or retirement plans was imperiled, there were no term limits on career politicians whose public service positions have made them millionaires and whose pensions and health care are top shelf and beyond the reach of many of their constituents they "represent."

Now it was up to me to perform.

Trump and I had known of each other for years, but not with a regular rhythm. This was totally different. I knew he had faith in me and got a kick out of me ("whoa, you really gave it to that guy on TV"). He knew I wouldn't take advantage of him, and I would always tell him the truth. I'd hoped he would return the favor. He also recognized something else. I had a micro-connection and shared background with many of the people he was talking to, the voters who rallied around him. They were hardworking Americans who hadn't always gotten a fair shake or a free pass, yet they'd worked hard, paid their dues, and tried to do the best they could. And they sometimes surprised themselves in how far they had come.

I knew and loved those people. Those people knew and loved him. They had put their faith in him. Now, he put his faith in me.

THE FIRST THING I wanted to do after becoming campaign manager was to shut up. Publicly. I wanted to say no to the 24/7 cable TV bookers. And skip the network morning programs and Sunday shows and work behind the scenes, away from the cameras and out of public view.

Donald Trump was having none of that. "Get out there and tell them how we are gonna win this," he told me. "How we can do well with women and the blue wall and everything." Clearly my idea of being a quiet worker bee in simple clothes and street makeup as campaign manager was going to have to be sandwiched between the 6–9 a.m. and prime-time TV circuits.

It was only after I was formally appointed that Alisyn Camerota of CNN informed me live on-air that I was the first woman ever to manage a Republican presidential campaign. Susan Estrich (Michael Dukakis), Mary Beth Cahill (John Kerry), and my pal Donna Brazile (Al Gore) had all been campaign managers for Democrat presidential nominees. I hadn't really thought of it. Donald Trump had not mentioned my gender when he promoted me. Yet if we won, I'd be the first woman from either party ever to manage a *winning* presidential campaign.

As much fun as it was, it didn't seem wise for me to spend every day on Trump Force One, the nickname predictably applied to the campaign plane, a familiar blue-and-gold Boeing 757 with red trim and TRUMP emblazoned on the fuselage in gold capital letters. I thought I would be better off at Trump Tower, where I could work on strategy, manage the staff, maximize my TV and radio time, and connect with the donors and grassroots leaders who were flooding us with calls. I wanted to speak to our state directors, reach out to leaders of the conservative movement, cull through polling and focus group data, crunch RNC voter scores with RNC Chief of Staff Katie Walsh, and keep sussing out the best states and counties for Trump and Pence to visit next—oh, and deal with the 1,001 crises that erupted every single day.

It was always something. Trump's freshest tweet that had reporters in a tizzy. The latest insult from Camp Clinton or the Democratic National Committee. Internal arguments over how to frame immigration, trade, taxes, policing, China, Iran, Israel. Some serial adulterer current or former Republican elected official declaring his independence from his party's nominee because "that tape!" . . . an endless stream of other issues.

Bannon and I quickly brought in David Bossie, another parent of four. Dave knew street-level, knife-fight politics better than almost anyone and was the one who had introduced Donald Trump to both Corey Lewandowski and Don McGahn, the lawyer to the campaign who would later become Trump's first White House counsel.

Another important reason to stay close to the office was that someone had to actually manage the expanding staff. I couldn't picture Kushner or Bannon looking young people in the eye and asking them what
they worked on, what else they needed to function and succeed, if they'd
slept or eaten in a while . . .

Boris Epshteyn, Alexa Henning, Steven Cheung, Ashton Adams,
Michael Abboud, Ashley Mocarski, Bryan Lanza, Jessica Ditto, Brian
Jack, Robert Gabriel, Daniel Gelbinovich, Johnny McEntee, Cassidy
Dumbauld, A. J. Delgado, Jeff DeWit, Tom Joannou, Peter Navarro,
Andy Surabian, Kaelan Dorr, Laura Nasim, Tom Tsaveras, and mar-
quee names like Anthony Scaramucci, Bill Stepien, Eli Miller, Steven
Mnuchin, Jason Miller, Don McGahn, Chris Christie . . . The younger
staffers were hungry, hardworking, eager, and energetic . . . and now they
had a work environment where they could perform. I was very impressed
with the data and digital operation, led by Brad Parscale. Our campaign
was investing heavily in social media and online ads (Google, Facebook)
while Hillary's campaign was flooding the airwaves with traditional
and expensive ads. From June to November 2016, our campaign spent
$144 million on this online presence, microtargeting voters for fundrais-
ing and electoral engagement. We had close to 6 million such online ads,
compared to Hillary's 66,000! She was running the Bill Clinton 1996 or
even Hillary Clinton 2008 primary and we were leveraging the fact that
more Americans used and trusted online sources, by literally going where
they were.

As I promised Trump, we also tried to recapture some of the fun
from the days of the primary campaign, when the candidate and just a
handful of staffers were jetting around, barnstorming the country. That
also turned out to be a phenomenal winning strategy. Where a typical
campaign day for Hillary would include a fundraiser or a phone call or
some dripping-with-sarcasm speech delivered in front of a safe audience,
Trump would jet into multiple cities a day, hosting big rallies, holding
press conferences, and smartly furnishing print and TV interviews to
members of the local press. In those final, crucial months, this was one of
the most undercovered and undervalued assets of the Trump campaign.
A Trump stop in a city near you would be previewed ahead of time,
covered as it was happening, and reflected upon after the fact, giving
us two to three days of outstanding and mostly objective coverage. We

might have been underresourced, understaffed, underestimated, and the underdog, but Hillary seemed like no competition for the way Trump was recasting modern campaigning.

Though Jared and Ivanka hadn't been involved in my promotion, and I do believe it took them by surprise, they were embracing, not resisting, it. Maybe they thought I brought something to the campaign. I knew the power they wielded. But each of them was quite complimentary and collaborative in those early days, and I was perfectly eager to work with them. We all shared a goal: getting Donald Trump elected president. We were, as the press liked to point out, an unconventional team. There was no denying that. Yet truly a team.

Things started to come together almost immediately. Trump's energy was noticeably stronger, and it was soon accompanied by an equal measure of discipline, and of course his trademark moxie. Before he went out on the road, we spoke to each other from the landline in Trump Tower about what the morning shows were saying and what the candidate and campaign needed to accomplish that day. On August 17, the same day that my promotion was announced, we met with Sheldon and Miriam Adelson. Some people look at the Adelsons and say "More money, please," but they looked at Donald Trump and said "More humility, please." On August 19, two days after that meeting, Trump went somewhere he had never gone before, and I don't mean Charlotte, North Carolina, the actual location. What made the trip memorable was that he stood up that day and expressed regret for some of the rough language he had used during the campaign. He didn't specify exactly which words he was referring to. In fact, there were plenty to choose from. But there he was, sounding genuinely contrite.

"Sometimes," he told the crowd, "in the heat of debate and speaking on a multitude of issues, you don't choose the right words or you say the wrong thing. I have done that, and I regret it, particularly where it may have caused personal pain. Too much is at stake for us to be consumed with these issues."

Trump was famous for rarely apologizing. But now he was expressing regret and making promises. "One thing I can promise you is this," Trump said. "I will always tell you the truth."

It was just the kind of opening that voters on the fence needed to hear from him. And it was brilliantly delivered.

It wasn't a single-shot deal. We all worked together to help nervous voters get comfortable with Trump. And of course, Trump himself was comfortable with all voters. Days into my tenure, Trump postponed a couple of campaigning events to join Pence in helping flood victims in Louisiana, while President Obama stayed on vacation and presidential hopeful Hillary Clinton stayed on the fundraising circuit. He went to Mexico and spoke side by side with that country's president, Enrique Peña Nieto, an invitation that had been extended to both campaigns. To Jared's credit, he took this on and arranged for the special trip. That was especially important, as it showed that Trump could interact reasonably well alongside a foreign leader despite their plain disagreements. It was part of our conscious effort to get voters used to the idea of *President* Trump. In classic Trump style, from Mexico to Arizona to deliver a rally speech about immigration.

When you are unbound by convention, and you feel like you have nothing to lose, that's when can make yourself ready to win. By the end of August, we were growing more convinced that winning was a real possibility.

THERE ARE TWO ways to win a hard-fought election. You can do well, and your opponent can screw up. It's best when both of those happen.

Hillary Clinton's single worst stretch on the campaign trail was the first full week of September. Labor Day was the fifth, and that's when the fun began. I joined Trump and Pence that day in the swing state of Ohio. George drove me to the airport and recommended I wear a prettier dress. It was exhilarating being out of the office and soaking up the love of the crowds. Clinton and her running mate, Tim Kaine, were already in the state.

"So, what's Crooked Hillary doing today?" Trump asked me.

I pointed to the huge TV on his plane, where a smiling Hillary Clinton was holding forth with some reporters. "Today is the first day they invited press onto her campaign plane. They have a bunch of stops," I said. "She and Tim Kaine plan to have a big interview with ABC."

He didn't like the sound of that. "What?" he said. "Why don't they ask us to do that?"

"They did, I'm told, and somebody in the campaign said no."

"Who?"

"I don't know. But ABC offered. The interview was going to be on *Good Morning America, World News Tonight,* and local affiliates." Trump was a media master, star of his own top-rated TV show, and he had a pretty good idea of how many millions of viewers he might reach with a wall-to-wall lineup of ABC shows like that, even if he'd sent me to appear on *The View* instead of him. He also knew he was a natural in the medium of TV. In contrast, many politicians sounded like they had marbles in their mouth or failed at faking authenticity.

I could see the wheels already turning in Trump's head. "Clinton and Kaine side by side look like empty-nesters going to couple's counseling," I chuckled. "Pence and you would be fantastic in that setting."

Trump didn't need to be persuaded. "Let's do it," he said. A quick call to ABC put the Trump and Pence sit-down back on. Why give Hillary a free ride like that? Also, ABC understood without us even saying it: They'd get much better ratings with Trump.

We agreed to meet anchor David Muir and his ABC crew at Trump's final stop of the day, the Canfield Fairgrounds, in Mahoning County outside Youngstown. The candidates weren't scheduled to speak there, just pass through quickly, sign a few autographs, shake a few hands, pose for a few selfies with local Republican officials, and move on. But Ohio's largest county fair sounded like a lovely backdrop for a Trump-and-Pence interview on an 86-degree afternoon.

As our SUV neared the fairgrounds, the crowds got larger and larger. And larger and larger. Trump hats, Trumps shirts, Trump signs *everywhere.* Since no one knew exactly when the candidate was coming, many in the crowd had been waiting for hours. I couldn't believe what I saw. Neither could the Secret Service, who had swept the area for a fair, not a full-blown Trump rally.

Trump and Pence did their quick fairgrounds pass-through, with the Secret Service limiting and abbreviating their visit. They sat for the ABC interview, not on that lovely hill, which now was a security risk, but inside a building on the grounds. Muir mentioned that Hillary was campaigning close by, just an hour away, then asked a lot of questions about the upcoming debates and Mexico and immigrants. Trump answered them all. Then he had the opportunity to sell himself to the audience that would be watching at home. "The single greatest asset I have, according to the people that know me, is my temperament," he said with a bright smile and a shrug. It was perfect.

No one in the crowd complained about waiting around. I'm sure they would have loved to have heard one of Trump's two-hour rally speeches. But just laying eyes on him and even just knowing they were at the fair at the same time he was, that was exciting enough for an early September afternoon.

"What did you think of *that*, Kel?" Trump asked me when we all climbed back into the car.

"I think you can't lose, sir, at least not in Ohio. The only Ohioan not there was John Kasich," I joked. "Your support is impossible to measure. Polls will underestimate the intensity, the sheer enthusiasm of it." Muir and his female producer hitched a ride back to New York with us on Trump Force One. The fare was Big Macs and McDonald's French fries. The conversation was relaxed and respectful.

This new energy was obvious. The next day, he and Hillary were both set to appear at NBC's Commander-in-Chief Forum at the Intrepid Sea, Air & Space Museum in New York City. When we arrived, I quietly left the hold room for a few minutes and, as I turned the corner, ran smack into Hillary Clinton, Huma Abedin, and a Clinton campaign contingent. I smiled and said hello but was met with zero response except for a soon-to-be-familiar look on Hillary's face. Her look said, *Can you believe this? The indignity of sharing a stage with Donald Trump!* I was back in the hold room within minutes, chuckling to myself and thinking how small she seemed in that moment. I didn't see a commander in chief and, apparently, neither did the people who watched the Commander-in-Chief Forum. Hillary was defensive about her mishandling of classified information in emails. But when NBC's Matt Lauer quizzed Trump, he had none of Clinton's stiffness. In front of an audience full of veterans and active military personnel, he looked like a natural-born leader.

Clinton's week wasn't close to over. In fact, the worst was yet to come. Two days after the *Intrepid*, on September 9, after Hillary had a long weekend in the not-so-swing state of New York while Donald Trump was campaigning in Florida, an unsmiling Hillary showed up at a private, high-dollar fundraiser in New York City, where she referred to Donald Trump's supporters as a "basket of deplorables" and also called them "irredeemable." She wasn't off script. She was reading (as usual) from notes. She'd said it before, in an Israeli TV interview, and she meant it. She was in safe, good company, insulting millions of Americans in front of a wealthy audience at Cipriani in Manhattan, some of whom erupted in laughter. If it hadn't blown up in her face this time, I am sure Hillary would have slung the slurs again.

I called Trump from home the minute the quote got out, courtesy of a BuzzFeed reporter's tweet. "Hillary just placed the industrial Midwest and Rust Belt right in your hands," I said. "She told half of the country they are beneath her."

Trump listened intently. He knew she had stepped in it but hung back to watch the fallout. Apart from the obvious elitism, Hillary's words insulted millions of people who otherwise might have considered voting for her. The woman first and best known for her husband lacked his people skills.

Talk about a tough week: Thirty-six hours later, Clinton collapsed near her waiting vehicle following a 9/11 Memorial service at Ground Zero that Trump and she had both attended. Later, we learned that she had pneumonia and yet went on with her schedule at Ground Zero and then made sure the press knew she was visiting her grandchildren.

"Geez!" he said to me. "Did you see that? She folded like an accordion."

Sometimes Trump needed to be protected from his own competitive exuberance, which usually served him well. This was one of those times.

"No, no, no," I implored him. "We're not touching that except to say we hope she is well. We are off social media and off the Sunday shows for 9/11. People saw for themselves what happened. This will get plenty of coverage without us saying a word." And, of course, it did.

The closer Trump got to Election Day, the more we realized what it would take to win beyond his daily diet of rallies, tweets, and TV interviews. When Hillary Clinton was shooting herself in the foot, he tried not to get in the way. When she was ignoring Michigan and Wisconsin, he hightailed it there for a rally or two.

Over at Hillary HQ, the intersection of ignorance (about the country's needs) and arrogance (about her inevitable win) was no match for the swagger and hunger of the Trump campaign. We were scrappy and happy. Trump had formed a connective tissue with millions of Americans who kept packing stadiums, amphitheaters, halls, and forums.

Something was happening here.

TRUMP CALLED AND asked me to join a midmorning meeting in his residence with Prime Minister Benjamin Netanyahu, twenty-eight years after Frank Luntz and I had first met him in Israel. I thought I could get a quick run in. About a mile and half from my house, I tripped and fell. Bruised hands and bloody knees. I called George to pick me up, bandaged myself, chose a long dress to cover most of the damage, and made my way to Trump Tower. Jared and his father, Charles Kushner, had joined the meeting. I sat there for more than an hour and never moved. After everyone stood up and the two would-be world leaders snapped a photo, Trump brushed by me and leaned into my ear. "Did you hurt yourself?"

"No, sir," I answered quickly, looking out the floor-to-ceiling window onto the city below.

"Are you okay?"

"I'm fine, sir. Thank you."

"Did you injure yourself exercising?"

"Yes. I'm fine, sir."

"That's why I never bother."

Chapter 15

Risking It

T he look on Hope Hicks's face that afternoon made clear something was wrong. Terribly wrong. I was on the twenty-fifth floor of Trump Tower with Chris Christie, Reince Priebus, Steve Bannon, Jeff Sessions, Dave Bossie, and others, prepping Donald Trump for the second presidential debate, to be held two days later in St. Louis. A Trump loyalist and one of the original campaign staffers wise beyond her years, Hope would not have interrupted the session without good cause. One by one, she pulled each of us out of the conference room and into the atrium to review an email she had just received from *Washington Post* reporter David Fahrenthold. I went first.

The reporter claimed he had gotten a tip a few hours earlier on that Friday, October 7, a month and a day before the election. I'm not so sure I buy his timeline, since, just as we were driving to the first debate eleven days earlier, he had tried to contact Trump for a comment about a charity event dealing with his foundation years earlier. Now, eleven days later, according to Fahrenthold, an unnamed source asked him whether he would be interested in checking out a video of Trump recorded by an NBC show called *Access Hollywood*. As the *Post* later reported, "Fahrenthold didn't hesitate." Of course he didn't hesitate. For months it seemed clear he had been working overtime to keep Trump out of the

White House. After reviewing the contents of the video, Fahrenthold contacted Hope.

Hope was steely and had seen and survived a lot. Her shaken demeanor was a powerful tell. With so much scurrying and worrying afoot, Trump must have wondered if he'd be the last to know. He could see us through the glass. Then he wondered out loud: "What's going on?"

As Trump was reviewing the email, we received an audio file and turned the volume up so everyone could hear. The content was shocking, including to Trump and certainly to me. To say the least, it was hard to hear and instantly problematic.

After hearing it, Trump looked genuinely confused.

I was, too. *Access Hollywood?* I knew Trump's daily schedule, upside down and backward. He hadn't done a sit-down interview with Billy Bush, certainly not since I'd joined the campaign. I could imagine in the earliest minutes of hearing the audio was that *someone* had overheard a conversation and recorded it. We'd been hearing stories and rumors that there was a tape of Trump saying the N-word during one of the *Apprentice* episodes, a word I have never heard from him. (Trump denied that and to date no tape has ever emerged, yet videos of Joe Biden saying that word have in Senate hearings.) This Billy Bush tape came out of nowhere and really threw us. It took a few minutes to realize this was an eleven-year-old recording. Over a decade earlier! That explained a little, but I knew it wouldn't make the situation any less explosive. The media who had aided and abetted Trump's ascent to the Republican presidential nomination were increasingly nervous that their Frankenstein monster might escape their grip and march all the way into the Oval Office.

He had no memory, he said, of the off-handed, off-air conversation eleven years earlier. Plus, he added, it didn't *sound* like him. "I don't speak like that," he said. "That's not me. 'Furniture shopping'?"

It was clearly his voice, but so many questions remained. Who, what, where, when, how, and certainly, why? Those of us closest to him, literally at that moment, were in a state of disbelief. We had so many questions and so too would the whole world. The words spilling forth on the eleven-year-old tape were vulgar and vile. I certainly couldn't square them with the brilliant, fun-loving, respectful man who had been the first Republican to elevate a woman to the top spot of his campaign. No one could say for certain what the net effect of this "October surprise" would be, but it had to be dealt with immediately.

Reince Priebus pronounced himself *in shock*. "How do you even *doooo* this?" he asked, staring at the words of the email and shaking his head. I hoped he meant the question philosophically, not literally, since I was sitting right next to him. The head of the Republican Party appeared to have one foot slipping off the Trump Train. He wasn't alone. The media, the Democrats, donors, half the Republican Party, and scores of philandering, boorish, Olympic-level recidivist misogynists and adulterers at home and abroad suspended self-awareness and demanded Trump fold up his campaign and exit the race. After much back-and-forth and ups and downs that evening, and with his daughter Ivanka standing stoically nearby, Trump made his first visit to the Trump Tower campaign TV studio on the fifth floor that night and put out a ninety-second video in the early hours of Saturday morning. He addressed the matter directly. He wasn't denying anything except the presumptive negative intent his critics ascribed to those words.

"I never said I'm a perfect person nor pretended to be someone that I'm not," he said. "I've said some things that I regret and the words released today on this more-than-a-decade-old video are one of them. . . . I said it, I was wrong, and I apologize."

This was one step past the "regret" rally speech in North Carolina back in August. This time he apologized for something specific.

The fallout continued. The fault lines that cracked open after the tape was released could not have been easily predicted. For example, some women who I would have expected to demand that he be dragged and quartered shrugged their shoulders and accepted his characterization of "locker room talk," harmless banter lacking any intent to ever harm anyone. Others who had seen him through the rough-and-tumble primary season and loathed the idea of a Hillary Clinton presidency suddenly demanded his immediate withdrawal. For others, his explanation of a years-old, off-script aside with another celebrity was sufficient. Neither he nor they pretended he was a perfect person incapable of saying outrageous things. No one ever accused him of being part of the "religious right." His conservative base accepted him, knowing that his lifestyle was not exactly theirs. Some of the undecided fence-sitting voters would now be forced to decide between their distrust of Hillary and their disgust at

Trump. As Trump himself said that weekend, and more than a few times since: Had Mike Pence been caught saying something like that, he would have been toast for sure.

THE MORNING OF October 8, just hours after Trump's video had aired, George drove me from our home in Alpine to Trump Tower. He was unequivocal in his support of Trump and of me. I did not know what I'd face in the penthouse of Trump Tower that morning, but I was certain a media scrum would be planted outside, waiting to see if Trump would drop out and who would be the next Republican to denounce him. The cameras caught all of us arriving, Reince Priebus looking sheepish, Governor Christie in a Mets pullover, and Rudy Giuliani in a track suit. When I got out of George's car, NBC's Ali Vitali shouted at me, asking if Trump was dropping out. I tried to look as confident as possible as I walked inside in high heels and a black leather jacket. I flipped my hair and gave her a perfunctory "NO!" before heading up to the penthouse.

I'd spent the morning on the phone with Mike and Karen Pence, who were at the governor's residence in Indiana, and now I had the vice presidential nominee's statement for Trump to review. Just four days earlier, Pence had turned in an outstanding performance in the VP debate against Senator Tim Kaine, who repeatedly interrupted the female Asian moderator and whose prevarication was no match for Pence's preparation. Speaker of the House Paul Ryan had condemned Donald Trump the night before and disinvited Trump from a Ryan event in Wisconsin that day, though Pence made clear to me that he had also declined to go as "Plan B." From the minute the *Access Hollywood* story broke, I knew that the most important X and Y factors for Trump's short-term political survival were named Mike Pence and Melania Trump.

I handed Pence's statement to Trump: "As a husband and a father, I was offended by the words and actions described by Donald Trump in the eleven-year-old video released yesterday. . . . I do not condone his remarks and cannot defend them. I am grateful that he has expressed remorse and apologized to the American people."

Trump read it and shook his head. "Whoa, that's rough!" he said.

"That's best we are going to get," I answered. "I think you should say thank you and let him issue it."

Priebus told Trump he had two choices: Drop out now and let someone else run, or stay on the ticket and lose by the widest margin in presidential history. Priebus reflected the pusillanimity of many prominent Republicans. Bannon said Trump would still 100 percent win and Trump kind of scoffed at the obsequious *rah-rah*. Jeff Sessions said we should calm down and see how it all played out. Giuliani said there had been times in his life that he wished he'd behaved differently and apologized and made amends and this was one of those times for his friend "Donald." Reince announced he was catching a train back to D.C. with Sessions.

Although Trump listened to me and respected me and the other women on the campaign and White House staff, he didn't fear us. Fear was reserved for one individual: Melania.

For him, facing her was the hardest part of the whole ordeal. He cares about what she thinks, and for good reason. She has great people instincts and is a voracious consumer of media: TV, print, social. He also loves his wife and knows that being in her good graces beats being in the proverbial doghouse. After going over the first draft of a statement I prepared for her, she offered edits and recommended it be stronger.

"Make it tougher," she said.

"The words my husband used are unacceptable and offensive to me," the final draft read. "This does not represent the man that I know. He has the heart and mind of a leader. I hope people will accept his apology, as I have, and focus on the important issues facing our nation and the world." Melania gave people an out. She was in it to win it. As she told me, people always wanted a piece of Donald Trump, physically and otherwise, men and women both. Her public support for her husband seemed thoroughly genuine to me. For the campaign, it was huge.

We remained at Trump Tower all day and all night, monitoring the fallout and preparing for the St. Louis debate the next day. Trump resisted suggestions that he host a rally or provide an interview to a network anchor. But he spontaneously went down the elevator through the atrium, where a hungry press awaited, to greet his unfailing supporters who were standing out on Fifth Avenue.

Late in the evening, Trump and I walked out of his twenty-sixth-floor office and headed to the twenty-fourth floor in Trump Tower. That's where he switches elevators to go from the commercial side to the residential side of the building. He motioned for the Secret Service agents to wait by the next set of elevators, in full view but out of earshot. We were alone, and he turned to me, both of us inching toward the corner of the small landing.

The guy who never gives up had seen reports that the party could force him off the ticket or hold a vote to expel him. Heading that off must have seemed face-savingly attractive.

"Should I get out [of the race]?" he asked me.

He needed to have this conversation with a woman other than his wife or his daughter. I didn't know if he was testing me or testing himself. My answer was more clinical than emotional. "You actually can't," I said, "unless you want to forfeit and throw the whole damn thing to Hillary."

"What do you mean, I *can't*?"

"It's too late to print new ballots," I explained. "Early voting has already started in some places. Do what you want. I know you don't like to lose, but I also know you don't like to quit."

"Will I lose? Will we lose? Can we still win?"

"Maybe," I said honestly. "And maybe not. People love to complain about what offends them. But they vote according to what affects them. This will play out in unforeseen ways."

There was a beat of silence, while we both considered our thoughts. Finally, I spoke. "You know that ever since Labor Day in Ohio, I've been convinced you will win. This crap, this tape—certainly doesn't help. What you said is disgusting. It's reprehensible."

Trump nodded.

"What were you really thinking when you talked to Billy Bush?" I asked him, flipping through a mental catalog of the countless times I'd been alone with him and never felt uncomfortable, put upon, threatened, or propositioned. I truly wanted to know.

"That's locker room talk," he said, repeating his media line. "I don't remember even saying it. Billy Bush . . ."

"Mr. Trump, one last thing," I said, reminding him of a private conversation we'd shared in the earliest hours of reckoning with the video. "Hillary stood by a man for decades who didn't *say* these types of things. He *did* these types of things. She suffered and stayed so that she could be president one day. You said it, but he did it. He was president for eight years. Eight years! And you're just going to hand this to her?"

"What about Melania?" he asked me.

"What about her? She made clear today how she felt about your statement through her statement," I said. "And she made clear how she felt about you, and you staying in this race. We're still here. I mean, who's tougher than her?"

He nodded. "You're right, honey, she's tough. You're tough. This is tough. We're all tough." Clearly spent, he sighed a long sigh and said, "Good night."

"I'll see you tomorrow," I told him and then, as a final, affirming note: "We're going to St. Louis."

The battle was still on, and we were still in it.

He wasn't quitting. His wife wasn't quitting. Pence wasn't quitting. The tens of millions of Americans counting on his presidency to replace their obscurity with opportunity, their plight with prosperity—they weren't quitting. Neither was I.

I PUT OUT word that I'd be skipping the Sunday shows. So did Chris Christie. So did everyone else anywhere near the top of the Trump campaign, except for Rudy Giuliani, appeared on, or was quoted on, all the major shows. It was dangerous to stand between Rudy and a live camera.

Trump would be speaking just hours later in front of a worldwide audience at the St. Louis debate. Why step on that or, worse, have him be forced to answer for something one of us said on a show that morning?

One important expression of support did come quickly. "GOP mega-donors Robert and Rebekah Mercer stand by Trump," said the headline in the *Washington Post*. The Mercers declared themselves "completely indifferent to Mr. Trump's locker room braggadocio" and said the hypocritical media "resolutely looked away" as former president Bill Clinton was accused of multiple sexual indiscretions. "We have a country to save and there is only one person who can save it," the statement said. "We, and Americans across the country and around the world, stand steadfastly behind Donald J. Trump."

Unfortunately, but not completely surprisingly, much of the early reaction went the other way, and not just from Democrats and finger-waggers in the media. A long list of Republican officeholders were quick to walk away from the party's nominee. New Hampshire senator Kelly Ayotte said she wouldn't vote for Trump anymore. (She would lose her reelection bid a month later.) Alabama governor Robert Bentley said the same thing.

(He'd resign in disgrace months later after a sex scandal. *President* Trump and I watched his televised perp walk in the Oval Office dining room.)

"I'm out," announced Utah congressman Jason Chaffetz. "I can no longer in good conscience endorse this person for president." (He would practically trip over people to shake President Trump's hand at the address to the joint session of Congress months later.)

The hits kept coming. "Donald Trump should step aside and allow our party to replace him," agreed a Republican congresswoman. "If Donald Trump wishes to defeat Hillary Clinton, he should do the only thing that will allow us to do so—step aside," said a Republican senator.

Rumors were already swirling that I was going to quit. The morning of the debate, I walked past a blaring TV as we were about to make our way to the airport, and I heard one of the talking heads mention that Trump's female campaign manager, a devout Catholic and mother of four, was thinking about resigning from the campaign. Really? I hadn't said that to anyone. I hadn't even hinted it. This was the media's favorite trick: present fake facts, or no facts at all, and have people who cannot possibly know the facts discuss them. I couldn't bear to hand the nation over to Hillary Clinton. Plus, my husband, George, insisted that we stand by *our* man.

I climbed into the SUV with both Trumps and Bannon. I asked Melania if she could take a photo of her husband and me so I could post that we were on our way to St. Louis.

AS EXPECTED, THE debate was peppered with references to the *Access Hollywood* tape. The anchors and Hillary Clinton kept it alive during the ninety minutes. What's more, four of the best-known "Bill Clinton accusers" were seated in the debate hall. They had held a press conference beforehand, pointing out that it was Hillary Clinton who did not "as a woman stick up for other women," choosing instead to insult the accusers or insinuate that they weren't credible. Yet it was Hillary Clinton and her allies in 2015 who demanded that reporters not use thirteen adjectives to describe her, including "polarizing, calculating, disingenuous, insincere, ambitious, entitled." (They might have thought to add "sore loser.")

Apparently those adjectives were "coded sexism."

The debate got under way with Hillary Clinton accusing Trump of peddling the "racist lie" that Barack Obama wasn't born in America.

Trump said Clinton had "hate in her heart" for saying half of his sup-porters were in the "basket of deplorables." The two of them interrupted each other constantly. He referred to her as "the Devil" and promised he'd order the Justice Department to probe her private email server. She said he lived "in an alternate reality," charging that "Donald always takes care of Donald and people like Donald."

Moderator Anderson Cooper did bring up Billy Bush, who is the grandnephew and nephew of the former Bush presidents, and the hot mic, arguably manipulating what Trump had said: "You bragged that you com-mitted sexual assault," Cooper stated, asking Trump if he understood the implications of that. Trump rejected the characterization entirely. "I didn't say that at all. I don't think you understood what was said. This was locker room talk. Certainly, I'm not proud of it. But this is locker room talk."

At the end of this ninety-minute back-and-forth, the obsessive ques-tions about *Access Hollywood* continued in the spin room. Some media, resembling high school freshmen, gleefully repeated the P-word as part of their "official questioning"; others whined that the presence of the Bill Clinton accusers was a cheap shot since a spouse should not be judged for another spouse's actions (more on that later, folks). I reminded them that the accusers were there because of how *Hillary* Clinton had treated them. "Believe all women" was hardly her ethos or theirs back then.

It turned out that the spin room that night was *key*. "I don't think we would have made it" to victory after the *Access Hollywood* tape, Steve Bannon would say to *The Atlantic* later, "without Kellyanne."

We certainly couldn't have made it without Donald Trump's wife.

The typically reserved Melania Trump was fully present on this. First, she stood by her husband and accompanied him to the debate. Next, she pulled a major boss move by wearing a certain Gucci blouse that night. Third, days later, Hope and I helped arrange a crucial interview with CNN's Anderson Cooper in the living room of their penthouse apart-ment, questioning the credibility of some of the women coming out of the woodwork, which included a woman who had had forty-two minutes of time on Anderson Cooper's show the night before and about which I challenged him, regarding the veracity of her claims decades earlier on an airplane. When it came to her husband's presidential ambition, Melania had again made it clear: She was in it to win it.

*   *   *

THE NEXT TWO weeks were crucial.

I went with Trump to Gettysburg, Pennsylvania, on Saturday, October 22, for a major policy speech outlining what he would do in his first one hundred days as president. We had crafted the speech carefully. I waited in the SUV with campaign advisor Stephen Miller and Rudy Giuliani. Trump joined us extra late and in a fit of pique.

"Now I'm losing all these women," he bellowed as soon as he got in. "I just saw a focus group on the *Today* show. And it's because of all these false accusers."

"It doesn't help that you fat-shamed Miss Universe," I said, referring to a passing comment he'd made almost twenty years earlier that had gotten a revival since Hillary brought it up at the end of the last debate. I attempted to explain to Trump-the-businessman why women were reacting to the Alicia Machado matter: "We women spend billions a year to try to lose weight and look good, and the next year we do it all over again."

"No, it is not," he shot back. "It's that stupid tape and all these people and the media having them on their shows, letting them say whatever they want."

Rudy chimed in and agreed. "Actually, she is right, Donald, listen to her. That is it." He was snapping back at me as the SUV raced toward the airport but was looking out the windshield. "I think I'll be *your* pollster, 'KellyannePolls,'" he said to me, using my Twitter handle as my nickname. We kept bickering the entire way up to the airport and up the stairs of the plane.

"You are making gains nearly everywhere," I told him. "Her floor and her ceiling are close together. You won that debate in Las Vegas the other night." That was debate number 3 (George came), the final one.

"Yeah," he agreed. "All they do is attack. I used to get the best press of anyone."

"Well, sir," I said. "Now you want to be the leader of the free world, so the standards are different. The threshold is higher."

I think he got that, not that he liked it. "You know," he said, "I had a great life." He turned and faced me and continued. "I have a really good life in real estate and TV, and I'm very successful. I can just go back to that if this doesn't work out."

We were in the cabin of the plane by then, still standing. Now my voice got louder.

"No, you can't," I told him. "Your life is great and theirs isn't." As I spoke, I enunciated each syllable and motioned outside the plane. "What about the people who stood in the rain for four hours to see you? They are counting on you to make their lives better. And you know what? You and I are going to argue for the next seventeen days because I know you're going to win, and you're acting like you're going to lose."

WHY DID I want to win so badly? Because I believed in my candidate. Because I loved my country. Because I feared the future policies of our opponent. Because I am competitive by nature. Because forgotten man and woman was not a slogan or a sound bite—it wasn't even a strategy, it was real people facing real challenges and losses. But also because I am a Jersey girl from a broken family in a tiny town outside Camden, and for my entire life the people who loved me most wanted me to succeed and said I could do something—anything! But they did not always know how to get me to the next steps, and the people who could have helped guide me to those next steps didn't love me and didn't want me to succeed.

Some friends and colleagues, TV makeup artists and technicians, drivers and doormen—and more than a few strangers on the street— whispered that they did not like Donald Trump but they liked me, who had always treated them with respect and genuine interest. Plenty of them ended up voting for Trump.

Some people thought that since Hillary had it in the bag, Trump wasn't a real threat to anyone. Neither was I. They would compliment me, quote a TV appearance nearly verbatim, and then crinkle their nose with a knowing look of pity and relief. The campaign was hopeless and hapless, they thought. No way could Donald Trump be president. Nothing at all to worry about.

I have a living, breathing, video catalog of what I saw in the race: I appeared on every show imaginable. *Meet the Press, Face the Nation, Good Morning America, CBS This Morning,* and the *Today* show. MSNBC (including a forty-six-minute interview with Rachel Maddow), CNBC, CNN, HBO's *Real Time with Bill Maher* ... five, six times a day some days. It took up about 5 to

10 percent of my workday but the dividends to the campaign and the value to Trump himself, who loved it, were much higher. Particularly on *Morning Joe,* where I was handed ample uninterrupted airtime. A sampling:

In mid-October, the week after *Access Hollywood*:

- "I predict that we will win. I said that last week before all this happened. For all the articles last week, 'The path is nonexistent,' we have a couple different paths to 270," the number of electoral votes required for victory.

The week before the vote:

- "So we are pushing into blue states. Look, if you try to apply conventional political wisdom to Donald Trump, you lose every time. The idea that, well, Michigan and Wisconsin have been elusive to Republican candidates: He's just different; his message on trade and illegal immigration and jobs and patriotism, it's just a different message and it's just a different messenger, and we see it resonating in Pennsylvania, where I will be with Melania Trump for a speech."

When asked about Pennsylvania being "fool's gold" for the Republican Party in past decades, I said *not this time*:

- "In part, it's the Trump message. We see that this message is now resonating in other parts of 'P-A.' It's really the axis of jobs, trade, illegal immigration, and a lot of patriotism. We will be in Hershey, P-A, tomorrow night. There will be twelve to fifteen thousand people there. Folks feel like they are part of a movement. In P-A we have seen some gains in nonpresidential years, and I'm a student of the 2010 and 2014 elections. My point is, if you can get a messenger who can tap into those 2010, 2014 messages, you can increase turnout and part of that messaging was Obamacare."

And there I was again the day before the election on *Morning Joe*:

- "We are now talking about flipping blue states. We now have six different routes to 270."

A *Washington Post* correspondent, Philip Bump, wrote: "There is no possible way Donald Trump's team actually believes this is their path to 270." In his "analysis," he predicted we were likely to lose Texas, Georgia, and Arizona, and "almost probable, he'll lose Utah" to independent candidate Evan McMullin. Or, as another *Post* writer said, "Donald Trump's chances of winning are approaching zero."

Speaking of zeroes, he still has a job.

WHEN THE POLLS opened on election morning, every mainstream media anchor, talking head, and political reporter was busy preparing for the long-predicted, inevitable outcome.

Madame President.

The polls supported it. Almost everyone believed it. It was as much a foregone conclusion as there ever is in politics. All across the media, the scripts and stories had been prewritten, with "TK" notations for numbers, percentages, and the exact Electoral College breakdown. (Old-time newspaper slang for *to come.*)

While Donald Trump and Mike Pence had worked overtime to eke out a win, presumptive members of presumptive president Hillary Clinton's presumptive cabinet were already house-shopping in D.C. (I would actually tour one of those a few months later when an embarrassed almost-secretary was looking to unload.)

The professional prognosticators were uniformly confident. I had noticed they'd stopped paying attention to the Trump rallies. They were too busy repeating and retweeting each other's snark. They traded and scrutinized the same old moldy data. They weren't talking to enough real voters to detect the rumbling groundswells.

The voters were out there. They were happy to talk if anyone had bothered to ask. But the media and their pollsters never deeply examine that which and whom they deeply disdain.

They were the faces of the forgotten America, determined to vote for something and someone different.

They were about to be heard and seen.

Chapter 16

Winning It

As Election Day arrived officially at midnight, we were still on Trump Force One, heading to Grand Rapids, Michigan, for one last rally, our fifth and final of the day. Ronna Romney McDaniel had told us time and again that Michigan was trending Trump and that a few more candidate visits and digital and TV ads could break a twenty-eight-year drought for Republican presidential nominees and seal the deal.

I looked at my phone and saw a text from Robby Mook, Hillary's campaign manager. Robby presented their plan for Election Night. If Mr. Trump were to win, Secretary Clinton would phone him within five minutes of the race's being called by the Associated Press. And if Hillary were to win, they would wait five minutes after the AP call for Trump to acknowledge his loss before she claimed victory and addressed her supporters at New York's Javits Center and around the world.

The implications were obvious. They were preparing to win.

As we flew back to New York from Grand Rapids, I found myself sitting across from Jared Kushner, sharing an extra-long blanket, adjacent to Mr. Trump. Jared was sleeping. I was trying to, but couldn't stop reflecting on everything. Sitting in the dark with a bag of Vienna Fingers in one hand and a bag of Cheetos in the other, I said to myself, "This son of a gun had better win. My diet's gone to crap."

That morning's *New York Times* gave Donald Trump a 9 percent chance of winning Michigan. Other media outlets offered similarly bleak predictions across the entire electoral map. Maybe they should have paid more attention to what I said over and over on *Morning Joe* and other shows, and not just humored me and our hopeless cause.

As was their custom, the political and media cognoscenti had been too focused on "electability" and national polls, which we'd stopped doing months earlier in favor of statewide surveys in the true battlegrounds. The fight was not for 51 percent across the country. The fight was for 270 in the Electoral College. There were several possible combinations of states that could get us there, and those were all different from the single path I'd noted when I assumed the campaign management role. I'd made this exact point on the phone to executives, anchors, and reporters at ABC News, along with Dave Bossie and Brad Parscale, on a call that Sunday, November 6, from my office in Trump Tower. Brad Parscale, the campaign's digital director, kept repeating a common and eerily prophetic claim: "I don't know politics."

"We've been focusing on sixty-four counties, and now we're closer to thirty-six," I said.

Jonathan Karl, ABC's chief White House correspondent, implored: "Can you send me that list of sixty-four?"

"Sure," I told him. "I'll send it on Wednesday. After we win."

The public polls all said this was fantasy. ABC's own "chief political analyst" (since let go) didn't even bother to hop onto the call. But as they had done all along, those polls focused way too much on Trump and not enough on his underwhelming, underperforming opponent. Clinton's electoral firewall had faded to faint blue. I felt bullish. The strength and enthusiasm of Trump supporters had increased, not abated. As reporters would look across a screaming, packed crowd of thousands of rallygoers, they literally see that and turn to me and ask "But will they vote?" So they stood in the rain or the sweltering sun for hours just to be where he is and join this movement but they aren't going to vote? That made no sense.

The media weren't buying it and were setting up for our loss. But I liked the phone calls I was receiving from the folks out in the field and early poll results, even as the TVs in the distance were bragging that George H. W. Bush had voted for Clinton, George W. Bush left a blank for president on his ballot, and both McCain and Romney had not voted for Trump.

Really, the media condescension was fine with me. I was already smiling inside at the thought of proving all of them wrong.

Our supporters assembled in a large ballroom at the New York Hilton. The Trump family, the campaign leadership team, and various friends and hangers-on hunkered down at Trump Tower for what we all knew would be a very long night. Once we had something to talk about, we'd all go over to the Hilton.

I called Mr. Trump after 7 p.m. "Time to come down. Things are happening."

"What do you see? Where is everyone?" he asked.

"I'm in the bullpen on the fourteenth floor," I told him. "Was just in the data room on the fifth floor. [Bill] Stepien has some promising numbers and early returns."

Members of the Trump family started filing in. The seventy-year-old improbable candidate was the first. He showed up on the fourteenth floor. We walked past a mountain of just-delivered pizza boxes, looked up at the TV screens, and started poring over a stack of printouts. George, who was there with me, snapped dozens and dozens of photos for posterity before Trump and I made our way to the fifth floor.

The concrete and mostly windowless space on the fifth floor had been transformed several times over the course of the campaign. First it was home to a handful of staffers and the occasional visitor. Media came to conduct interviews, but mostly to gawk and squawk about their perceived lack of seriousness compared to Battleship Hillary at her Brooklyn headquarters. Later that area housed the makeshift TV studio and became somewhat of a warehouse and shrine to the countless pieces of mail and gifts Americans had sent.

That night, a small, easy-to-miss room behind closed doors to the side of the main conference table was the central nervous system. Stepien, Bannon, Bossie, Hope Hicks, Jared Kushner, and others were assembled. Stepien ran through some of the knowns and unknowns. Cautious optimism filled the air. The most cautious was Donald Trump.

Waiting on the returns to come in was like watching a nineteen-hour Grand Slam tennis tournament. It was intense. It was exhausting. It was impossible to turn away even for a moment. It was also a study in human psychology, as the commentators, so sure they knew what was going to happen, were slowly forced to explain as the contrary evidence trickled in. They dodged, delayed, deflected, and resisted as long as they possibly could.

7:05 p.m. Eastern: Three early-closing states were called by the Associated Press. Trump grabbed Indiana and Kentucky. Clinton snagged Vermont. No surprises there. Vermont had voted Democratic in every presidential election since 1988. Republicans had won Kentucky every time since 1996. Red-state Indiana was, of course, Mike Pence's home.

10:39 p.m.: Trump took Ohio. A big win. The first swing state to be declared for us. We'd led in the polls there, but Team Hillary had pushed hard in the late going. It was one they were really hoping for. Oh, and voters in Ohio had correctly picked the winner in every single presidential race since 1964.

10:53 p.m.: That path to victory I'd been talking about? It suddenly grew much clearer. We secured another swing state, veteran consultant Susie Wiles being the key, and we took Florida and its 29 electoral votes.

11:14 p.m.: North Carolina was declared for Trump. Another blow to Clinton, who had been up in all the polls there and who, along with her high-profile surrogates, had made some last-minute campaign stops in the state. Now the Clintonians had to hope and pray for Pennsylvania, Michigan, and Wisconsin.

11:56 p.m.: Trump prevailed in Utah. Which means Philip Bump and others who predicted a third-place finish for Trump there lost big-league.

12:06 a.m.: Trump won Iowa. The core four I had talked about every day on TV—Iowa, Ohio, North Carolina, and Florida—indeed went Trump's way. Hillary's path to victory kept narrowing as ours began to resemble a boulevard.

1:35 a.m.: *Yes!* We had reached my so-called reach state. We kicked a vital brick out of Hillary's firewall. Pennsylvania. That state was so key to Clinton's victory, she'd held a rally in Philadelphia with Barack Obama and Bruce Springsteen that past Monday night. Before that was superstar couple Jay-Z and Beyoncé. Folks liked a free concert more than they liked Hillary Clinton, but it was doubtful anyone on her team would admit that to her. We were tantalizingly close to victory now. Pennsylvania got us to 264 electoral votes. Just six to go. And we were ahead in Wisconsin, ahead in Michigan, ahead in Arizona. None of those states had been called yet, but any one of them would put us over 270.

2:07 a.m.: Clinton campaign chairman John Podesta came out to the podium to address the sparse crowd across town at the Javits Center. He said Clinton would not appear in front of her supporters that night, which was a strong tell right there. Podesta conceded nothing: "Let's get these votes counted and let's bring this home," he declared. But his words sounded hollow.

Earlier in the night, a small group of aides and advisors joined Trump and his family in their Trump Tower penthouse. The air was thick with promise. A buzz had been building all night, alongside a shocked and saddened media and the improving numbers for a man long dismissed by the "experts" who had replaced facts and figures with "hopes and prayers" (Okay, bias and groupthink). Donald Trump was the last one among us to accept his victory. This man had made deals, destroyed deals, walked away from deals. The three-day rescission period is a staple of real estate. He knew it was never over until it was over. What if someone could snatch it away in the coming days or hours? John Podesta tried to.

There were two speeches prepared for that night. But up in the residence, on the large dining table centered in a grand space looking out over the city synonymous with Donald Trump, only the victory speech was pulled up on a laptop for Trump's final edits. Many chimed in with ideas and words. But as was his custom, Trump Sharpied it up and sharpened it up. This was really happening. The next president of the United States was standing right there.

2:30 a.m.: For the first time in thirty-two years, a Republican captured Wisconsin's 10 electoral votes. By then it hardly mattered that razor-thin Michigan wouldn't be called for Trump until November 28, the first time a Republican would carry the state in twenty-eight years. Hillary Clinton's three-state firewall was already rubble on the ground.

We were all backstage at the Hilton by the time Wisconsin, where Trump had been down by 24 points in August, was declared for Trump. Jason Miller, the campaign's communication director, flashed his phone at me with tears in his eyes.

"The AP just called it!" he exclaimed.

"Which state?" I asked.

"The whole thing!"

Everyone was getting the news at once. Expectation was turning into reality, which was turning into euphoria. A thunderous chorus of cheers came from just beyond the divider inside the ballroom. I didn't hear my phone, but Chris Christie's twenty-three-year-old son, Andrew, saw it flashing in my right hand.

"Kellyanne!" he said. "Someone is calling you."

It was Huma Abedin, Hillary's closest aide and confidante and vice chair of her presidential campaign. Huma certainly had expected to speak with me this evening, though she never in her wildest dreams imagined she'd be the one making the concession call.

Huma was having a rough week, and she was more courteous than curt as she told me that she had her candidate on the line.

Trump and his family were in the corner, just a few feet away. I walked the phone toward them. "Be quiet, everyone!" I shrieked, needing to make our euphoria official, as I handed Trump my phone.

"Hillary wants to speak with you," I said. "Congratulations, Mr. President-elect."

Thinking those words and saying them were two very difference experiences. We had defied the odds, denied the critics. Life changed in a flash.

The instant the phone was out of my hand and into Donald Trump's, Don Jr. picked me up and twirled me in the air. We could overhear his father graciously complimenting his Democratic opponent, telling the former First Lady of Arkansas, First Lady of the United States, U.S. senator, secretary of state, and now twice-failed presidential candidate what a great campaign she had run. He said he hoped he could rely on her to help in the days and months ahead.

I turned to Mike Pence, the new vice president–elect. "Make sure she actually concedes," I told him. I wasn't totally joking.

AS PRESIDENT-ELECT TRUMP took the stage at the Hilton, the triumphal theme song from the movie *Air Force One* blared through the hall. The crowd shouted, "USA! USA!" He was flanked onstage by his youngest son, Barron, and his partner for the next four years, Mike Pence.

"I've just received a call from Secretary Clinton," Trump said. "She congratulated us—it's about *us*—on our victory, and I congratulated her and her family on a very, very hard-fought campaign." Trump could hardly have been more gracious. "Now it is time for America to bind the wounds of division. I pledge to every citizen of our land that I will be president for all Americans."

I stood onstage in my bright red Alexander McQueen dress between Chris Christie and Steve Bannon, soaking it all in, so proud of what we had accomplished. Trump singled out our amazing campaign team. "Kellyanne and Chris and Rudy and Steve and David," he said. "We have got tremendously talented people up here, and I want to tell you, it's been very, very special."

For him and for us.

He described the previous eighteen months in terms larger than politics. Here's how he put it, with a first line I'd repeated often myself: "As I have said from the beginning, ours was not a campaign but rather an incredible and great movement made up of millions of hardworking men and women who love their country and want a better, brighter future for themselves and for their family."

He was right, I thought, to turn the focus outward on the people who had really delivered us here. As he spoke, I cast my eyes across a sea of hopeful faces. These people had endured scorn, cynicism, and ostracism from family, friends, and colleagues, as well as the so-called cognoscenti. They didn't look like deplorables to me. They looked like patriotic Americans who wanted something better for the nation they loved.

Was it improbable? Maybe. Was it impossible? No way. Together we had proven that.

With clenched-teeth understatement, the *New York Times* described Trump's victory as "a surprise outcome." The geniuses there had started the day giving Trump a 9 percent chance of winning Michigan and a 28 percent chance of winning overall. As it turned out, he was the first Republican to win Michigan since 1988. It would take a while for the numbers to settle. But by the time all the votes were counted, the Trump-Pence ticket would win 306 electoral votes, 100 more than that inevitable president Mitt Romney from four years earlier. Trump-Pence had won 31 of the 50 states, 2,600 counties, and would flip 200 counties that voted for Obama in 2012. Breathtaking in size and scope.

TRUMP WAS BARELY off the stage when the high fives and congratulations began raining down on me. People were rushing over—people I knew, people I didn't—shaking my hand and hugging me. Without me, they kept saying—and still do say—that Trump would not have been elected president. That was debatable, I knew. But here's what was not in doubt: Without George Conway, I never would have been able to be Donald Trump's campaign manager, not the way I was in those critical final months. George stood by my side as I stood by Trump's side, providing love, support, and shelter from the social media mob. He had insisted I grab the promotion to campaign manager. He had scolded me when I gave Trump an out after he did promote me. He pushed me to take my shot and expressed confidence in my competence. "You're the best political mind" was a common refrain. He was there for me every step of the way. He pitched in more with the kids. He visited Trump Tower many nights after work. Driving with me between home and the campaign. Discussing critical moments like the *Access Hollywood* tape and debate prep. In his Trump MAGA cap (black, not red), he was first at Trump Tower for hours and then in the stunned audience at the Hilton, with tears streaming down his face. His voice was loud and clear, shouting above the din.

"She did it! She did it! She did it!"

Trump and his family decamped quickly to his Fifth Avenue penthouse to field congratulatory calls from leaders around the world. I stayed back at the Hilton. If he was still awake and the media were still working, what chance did I have of sleeping that night? I'd be lucky to even get out of the hotel. At 4:30 a.m., he was still blowing up my phone. I missed one call, and now he was trying again. Before I said *hello,* my husband, George, still beaming and still wearing that cap, and Jay Connaughton, a digital and ad consultant on the team, both leaned in to snap photos of my caller ID.

"I just got off the phone with the guy from Egypt," Trump began.

"President Sisi . . ." I supplied.

Even at seventy, Trump's energy was the stuff of legend. Being able to jump into the rapids midstream had served both of us well through the fall campaign, confident that our secret sauce could vanquish Hillary Clinton no matter what the polls and pundits were predicting. Silencing the critics and negating the naysayers never felt so good. History was made, and it wasn't Hillary Clinton making it.

I told Trump I had just wrapped up a string of impromptu interviews with the shell-shocked media, including John Heilemann, in jeans and a puffer jacket, thinking the night was already over hours earlier. They were still shaken, I said, not just by his victory but also by the gracious tone he'd set in his speech to his ecstatic supporters and his stunned global audience. Ducking into a quiet corner of the hotel lobby, away from the reporters and victory party stragglers still eager to buttonhole me, I assured Trump that I would handle the round robin of ten TV interviews scheduled to begin at 6 a.m. I would get to the studio inside Trump Tower at 5:30, I said. I'd be talking. He'd be watching. Neither one of us would be sleeping.

"You have to be press secretary," Trump declared.

I was caught off guard by that. White House press secretary is one of the most coveted posts under any president. Massive international media exposure. A box seat to history in the making. A fine launch into the next chapter of life.

I politely deflected. "We'll discuss it later," I said.

"You'd be so good at that," Trump pressed.

I'd be a terrible press secretary, I thought to myself, gently shaking my head.

My deflection was no deal breaker to the world-famous dealmaker.

To Trump, even a solid *no* was just the sound of the door swinging open for negotiation, and negotiating was his favorite sport, next to golf. He boasted an impressive handicap in both games.

Contrary to his flattering assertion, I did not share Trump's appraisal of my skills in that regard. In my view, I was often on message but also off script, because there was no script. I also didn't want to reflexively slide into the communications (or scheduling) jobs that women often filled, especially given the trust and authority he'd already invested in me in a management and leadership role.

As Trump had just said in his victory speech, "This political stuff is nasty, and it's tough." Foxholes weren't my natural habitat. Fielding questions from the press corps in the White House Briefing Room held zero appeal to me, no matter how prestigious the title or large the fame. As a pollster, I'd spent my entire career asking the questions and listening to the answers—not the other way around. If a CEO or politician wanted to know how a product or a platform would play in Peoria, I was the one who eagerly hopped on a plane to go find out, then connected the dots for them, with the voice of the people, not my own voice, leading the analysis.

Trump tried again, dangling a different plum this time. "Okay, director of communications," he offered.

Did we really have to discuss this at 4:45 in the morning after Election Night? I needed to find some concealer and mascara to face the cameras and tell the world what just happened.

Still no.

Just as we were about to hang up, he surprised me again. What he said sounded more like a statement than a question, presuming a given I wasn't sure I could give, not even to the soon-to-be leader of the free world.

"You're coming with us to Washington, right?"

I paused, not knowing the answer myself.

"Mr. President-elect," I said, savoring his new title, "congratulations again. We'll talk about all of this in the days to come."

*   *   *

I HAD SIXTY minutes to catch my breath. Not enough time to sleep. If I tried to nap at that point, what shape would I be in for the ten morning-show hits? It wouldn't be pretty, I promise you that. The best I could do was to grab a few minutes of quiet in the Hilton hotel room that had been reserved for George and me.

I knew we had a lot to think about, important choices to weigh as a family, and we were going to need some space to do that. One decision at a time, please. Up in the hotel room, I changed into a sleeveless, all-leather black dress for the morning shows, my first predawn fashion choice as I officially represented the president-elect of the United States.

The kids were back at home in Alpine. We'd told them they could stay up late to watch the results come in, with an added bonus of again witnessing history. But I had no idea how late they'd lasted. I couldn't imagine them really keeping their eyes open until 2:30 to hear the race called or, even later, to watch Trump's victory speech or catch Mom on the stage or Dad in the crowd. We'd have to sit down later and review the mighty sacrifices we had made as a family, sacrifices that now seemed to have paid off. And then start thinking about: What was coming next?

The head at one of their schools fired off a nastygram about Trump's victory. One of those over-the-top, clueless screeds about the end of the world. Trauma counselors and comfort pets would be available, as they were after *tragedies* like 9/11 or when, God forbid, a young classmate perishes. A sprawling campus where tuition for two exceeded the average national income and yet students are cosseted, were worried about finding a "safe space" from the hours-old Trump-Pence presidency. Clearly he was not going to consider that a mom in the school had just helped change the arc of history, but might he consider how much of a lie Hillary's career had been?

Hillary did not concede publicly until 11:50 that next morning, a sobering moment when she and her running mate, Tim Kaine, walked into the grand ballroom of the New Yorker hotel. Many of her supporters, the ones in her campaign and the ones in the political press corps, would never concede. Hillary herself would later claw back her own concession, spending months and years trafficking in conspiracy theories and blaming everyone and everything else for her loss.

But that morning, she opened on a gracious note.

She began with boilerplate concession language, the kind losing politicians have been delivering for decades. "Last night," she said, "I congratulated Donald Trump and offered to work with him on behalf of our country. I hope that he will be a successful president for all Americans. This is not the outcome we wanted, or we worked so hard for, and I am sorry we did not win this election for the values we share and the vision we hold for our country. But I feel pride and gratitude for this wonderful campaign."

But that wasn't the interesting part. The interesting part came later in her remarks. That's when she revealed the depth of her personal disappointment and her painful sense that she had let down the women and girls of America.

"I know we have still not shattered that highest and hardest glass ceiling," she said. "But someday, someone will and hopefully sooner than we might think right now. And to all the little girls who are watching this, never doubt that you are valuable and powerful and deserving of every chance and opportunity in the world to pursue and achieve your own dreams."

There was no arguing with that sentiment, as far as it went. I had followed a similar upward path of my own. But Hillary Clinton still did not seem to grasp how poor a vessel for that noble idea she was, or that millions of hopeful women had carefully considered her candidacy and then voted for Donald Trump. Thanks to the efforts we'd made, the gender gap was far narrower than any of the pundits had expected it to be. And ran up the totals among men, white suburban voters, rural voters, and the working class. The first would-be female POTUS carried women over Donald Trump by roughly the same percentage Barack Obama had carried them over Mitt Romney and his secret-weapon wife four years earlier. We held our own among married women, white women, women with less than a college degree, moms, and seniors.

Hillary's political career was over.

Her concession was short-lived because she immediately launched into a game of name, blame, and shame those whom she held responsible for her own loss.

She had a hard time facing a simple fact: America *was* ready for its first female president—just not this one.

*   *   *

THE REST OF my day was a deluge of congratulatory calls, texts, emails, notes, and flower arrangements—and even more flowery language. The stacks of job offers also began pouring in. Television networks, publishers, and Fortune 500 companies were promising titles, contracts, and partnerships. I could create any new business I wanted to. I could sign on with major firms. I was looking at what could potentially be an eight-figure income. Or maybe a government salary and a seat at any table of power in Washington that I chose.

It was all so overwhelming. I couldn't think seriously about any of it. Not yet. But some things were slowly sinking in.

Throughout my career, a seat at the table was never freely given. I was willing to earn it, but a fair opportunity to have a fair opportunity was sometimes withheld. Donald Trump saw what I could do. He saw me differently. He understood what I could do for him and what we could do together. He had no use for the "prominent" Republican consulting class, which he had detested for decades (a feeling my husband shared), believing that their ranks were populated by too many insatiable grifters and serial losers. It was no surprise that nearly all of them had missed his rise and stayed obsessed over his social media and cable TV appearances instead of recognizing the nerve he was touching in people across America. If you're on Twitter talking to yourself, you are missing an opportunity to understand the frustrations and feelings of millions of people who feel forgotten—*abandoned*—by their own leaders.

Trump the businessman had survived and thrived in the ubercompetitive meritocracies of New York City real estate, network TV, and the Republican presidential primaries. Now he had taken it onto the big stage and also triumphed there, while the walking RICO violation of the Republican consultancy greased each other on their never-ending gravy train, too afraid to adapt to a party, to a country whose daily needs were different than the privileged planets they inhabited, and to an electorate they had long ago stopped listening to and couldn't hope to understand. They didn't speak the language. They didn't reflect the aspirations. They may well have felt, like Hillary did, that tens of millions of

Americans were nothing more than deplorable and irredeemable. With blighted storefronts, hollowed-out factories, imbalanced trade deals, a rising China, a nuclear-capable Iran, a military of depleted resources and morale, veterans dying waiting for care, and a creeping government take-over of our education and healthcare systems, men and women across this country watched their jobs, wealth, and pride be shipped overseas. Many thought that when their economic wherewithal declined, so too had their freedom. Yet not their hope. For the establishment Republi-cans, the country had changed behind their backs and right in front of their eyes, and they didn't have a clue.

Many Americans wept and cheered at Donald Trump's election. Their lives were about to change now, and mine was, too, though I didn't quite know how yet.

For much of my career, the proverbial glass ceiling seemed more like Plexiglas. My hard head had banged against it again and again. Now I had just become the first woman to manage a winning presidential cam-paign, breaking through a true glass ceiling, a barrier that had stood since the dawn of modern American politics. And it was Donald Trump who'd placed me there. Trump had become the first elected president never to have held political office or a military position—another entry for the history books. Much of America had finally found its wish fulfillment, having told pollsters like me for years that they craved a candidate who "has a ton of experience but isn't a politician." And standing by Trump's side through those crucial, grueling final months of campaigning, and standing with him that night on the Hilton stage, was my ally and client of many years, Governor Mike Pence, now the vice president–elect.

I would still have to figure out what all that meant. But I knew this much already: I was literally living the dream.

Part IV

White House Mess

Chapter 17

Three's a Crowd

The Trump-Pence presidential transition office in Trump Tower was set up like the campaign headquarters, which was only appropriate. We'd turned the battleship in a few short months, and Trump had stunned the world with this victory.

With no rest for the weary (a category that notably excluded Trump, who never lacked for energy), a government would need to be formed in even less time. Identifying potential cabinet secretaries. Staffing hundreds of federal agencies. Drafting executive orders the new president would want to issue on day one, or week one, reversing some of the more egregious excesses of the Obama years. Receiving calls and even a stray visit from world leaders, who knew—*they just knew it!*—that Trump was going to beat the former secretary of state . . . or swore they did.

I had a beautiful corner office with a balcony that overlooked Fifth Avenue. It had been briefly occupied, until his messy departure, by former campaign chairman Paul Manafort. Whatever else might be said of Manafort, he never slummed. There were two TVs mounted on the wall, but I never switched on either of them. In the first week after the election, the news was mostly an endless loop of anti-Trump rants, interrupted by other commentators agreeing how awful Trump was and how the rest of us, who had fooled and flummoxed them, didn't know what we were doing.

Frankly, I didn't need the distraction. And we had a team of talented young men and women who consumed media in all forms and shared content and concerns continuously.

Three men quickly secured places for themselves at the top of the Trump transition on their way to the top spots in the Trump White House: Jared Kushner, Steve Bannon, and Reince Priebus. The president's son-in-law, the former campaign CEO, and the Republican Party chairman each had his own unique claim to authority and his own personality quirks. Jared was quiet and opaque. Bannon was disheveled and explosive. Reince was the Washington insider's Washington insider. For some reason, these three distinct individuals decided they could share one brain.

Their way of doing this began with Bannon and Reince declaring themselves co-CEOs of the Office of the Chief Executive for the incoming Trump administration. As they saw it, and as the president-elect himself would explain it, they would be coequals sharing power and decision-making as Trump's closest advisors and gatekeepers, Reince as White House chief of staff and Bannon as "chief strategist." Jared wouldn't need a fancy title. He had the family connection, unfettered access, and unchecked power.

Their plan didn't require U.S. Senate confirmation.

Less than a week after the election, Bannon and Priebus dropped by my office for some friendly chitchat and also to get something settled right away.

Me.

They were keen to know if I intended on joining the new administration, what role I would play, what my title might be and—most important of all—what all of that might mean for *them*.

I told them I wasn't eyeing *any* job, because I didn't expect to be hanging around. I think that took both of them by surprise.

"*Fuck, girl, c'mon,*" Bannon said. "You gotta do this."

"The president really wants you to do this," Priebus urged.

"Listen, Kellyanne," Bannon said. "So here's what you do. Get up early. Just do the morning shows starting at six, seven a.m. and leave by three."

"Get to work three hours before you? No thanks," I shot back. There was no way I would leave any office at 3 p.m., much less an office in the West Wing of the White House. "And," I reminded Bannon, "I've got four kids. I am their mother. Two of your three ex-wives are raising your three daughters."

Bannon just smiled, quickly checking the math in his own head.

I offered that the better role for me might be to stay outside the administration and build an external political superstructure to advance Trump's agenda beyond the Beltway. David Plouffe had taken on a role like that after he managed Barack Obama's successful 2008 campaign. David Axelrod went "inside" and later they would switch.

"Something like that might make sense," I said.

We weren't going to resolve this in one drop-by meeting in the transition office. Actually, I wasn't going to resolve it at all by talking to Steve Bannon and Reince Priebus. This was a topic for me and the president-elect and a topic for me and the rest of the Conway family.

Whatever I did next—inside the government, outside the government, or at home in Alpine, New Jersey—I wanted it to count. I wanted it to have an impact. I wanted it to deliver meaningful results, for the people of America and for George, and above all for Georgie, Claudia, Charlotte, and Vanessa. And I didn't want to spend my days on TV anymore. I'd been on TV constantly for months and it had served its purpose.

That last part, preferring to stay off television, was something few in Washington or New York could ever understand. Most people in politics and the media would kill for TV time. They all want more, not less of it.

Been there, done that, and I learned a key lesson along the way: The people who step in front of a White House camera are often conveying a major decision and not helping make one. If I was going to the White House, I wanted to have some influence once I got there so I could help accomplish things, not just deliver ten-minute morning hits about the things other people had done. Little did I know Donald Trump intended to empower me with both.

THE MALE EGOS surrounding me took off on a magic carpet ride of self-importance long before we were ready to leave for Washington. To them, the transition office in Trump Tower was like a starter White

House, a safe place for an early test drive of their agendas. The Bannon, Kushner, and Priebus factions didn't know each other well beforehand or hold each other in especially high esteem. Having been thrown together only months before, in the service of an underdog campaign, their unlikely alliance, if left unchecked and undefined, wasn't bound to serve the president well or for long.

Bannon had already finagled his way into landing $9 million in project fees from the cash-strapped Trump campaign for Cambridge Analytica, a British-based political data company that he had a financial stake in (and that would eventually collapse and be investigated). For now, he showed up at every meeting, weighed in on every potential cabinet choice and personnel decision, and made clear in meetings and in furtive phone calls with media that his agenda was President Trump's agenda.

Priebus shape-shifted himself into a Trump acolyte and supplicant just about the time Hillary Clinton was calling to concede the election. The longest-serving national chairman in Republican Party history, he had pulled out all the stops in 2012 and confidently projected the victory of Mitt Romney and his running mate, Paul Ryan, also a close friend and fellow Wisconsinite to Priebus. Yet Priebus never saw Trump-the-front-runner coming, never wanted him to be the nominee, and told Trump on October 8 to get out of the race or risk a historically embarrassing loss. Days before the election, members of his staff told high-ranking people at NBC News and Fox News that the Republican National Committee had done all it could, but that President Hillary was inevitable.

Reince Priebus and Steve Bannon were proving once and for all that being a fixture in Washington does not position anyone to fix Washington. Jared had had no problem with my title "campaign manager" until after Trump won. The candidate himself had offered me that role and title, one that was repeated countless times in print, radio, and television stories and rolled off the lips of millions of relieved Trump supporters. The old saying is that victories have many fathers, but in this case, it certainly had one eager, ambitious son-in-law. Jared got busy with a new campaign—revisionist history—as he completely realigned his own memory about who had thought what and did what when. He began a buzz that the only person who had known Trump would win was Bill Stepien. Gotcha. Bill's data had certainly been very helpful. My reserved-ness was no match for Jared's ego, but my living, breathing video catalog of how and where we'd win will last forever. I had taken the risks in saying it publicly, and also taken the criticism and derision that followed.

Jared was new to Washington. He barely knew the place, and that left him vulnerable to a whole different kind of danger: the confident assertions of people who are legitimately smart and successful but don't know what they don't know about the nation's capital.

And what about me? Though surrounded by these guys, I wasn't new to Washington. I arrived at eighteen and left twenty years later for marriage and motherhood in Manhattan. I had eyes and ears in plenty of places, friends across the aisle, and allies and acquaintances of all political stripes, secretly relieved to not have to deal with the Return of the Hillary. At first people were quiet about the passive-aggressive insults and slights hurled in my direction. Then they were increasingly candid and compassionate, viewing this childishness for what it was: something between unhelpful backbiting in a new administration with tons to tackle, and flat-out rudeness to a core confidante of the new president.

As one senator said to me, "I'm big on family, and Jared seems like a nice guy. But when you came to my state for two days several years ago to speak to donors, train grassroots activists, and make the phone bank volunteers feel special, Jared was raising money for Cory Booker and probably voting for Hillary Clinton. You've walked with us. We know who you are, and what you can do."

I had friends. In high places. On both sides of the aisle.

MOST SIGNIFICANTLY, I had little people under my roof. Georgie and Claudia had just turned twelve. Charlotte was eight and a half. Baby V, Vanessa, had been seven for all of a week. My mother and my loving circle of close friends had pitched in to help George manage our hectic household in Alpine, while I logged eighteen-hour days across the bridge in Manhattan and zigzagged around the country with Trump, stumping everywhere from convenience stores to country clubs in the quest to turn purple and blue states red. I came home regularly and grabbed whatever time I could at home and filled in the cracks with phone calls and FaceTimes to George and the kids. That said, like countless other D.C.–New York commuters who packed the express trains and shuttle flights every morning and night, there were times when I raced home like a maniac only to arrive after everyone was asleep. Even worse were the times when I had to turn right around and leave the house again before any of the kids woke up.

On God's Good Parent Report Card, did that count as "a night at home"? Not unless He was grading on a very steep curve. Clearly I had to come up with a better plan.

Most of our Thanksgivings were spent in South Jersey, and we filled our home with friends and family, but every other year we followed the tradition of watching the Macy's Thanksgiving Day parade at the home of Ted Gewerz and Claire Chappell. For me, this went all the way back to the Golden Girls and those ancient Atco Thanksgivings where we all got stuffed like turkeys before the turkey and stuffing got to the table. But after everything the kids had put up with since August—after everything they'd put up with for years!—I promised them we would spend Thanksgiving in Florida, a real family vacation for all of us.

Everyone thought that was a fabulous idea. I knew I could use some downtime, too.

Before the holiday, Mitt Romney's name was being floated as a potential secretary of state, fourth in line to the presidency. The former governor of Massachusetts and failed 2008 presidential candidate had never been a diplomat before, but his backers said his time at Bain Capital and as head of the committee organizing the 2002 Winter Olympics in Salt Lake City made him suitable for the job. Personally, I thought Romney was a terrible choice, not worth the ire among the grassroots, and I was happy to say so when reporters asked. It didn't even seem like a close call to me.

Back in May, just as Trump was nailing down the Republican nomination, *and four years after Trump had endorsed Romney*, Romney thought it would be an excellent idea to viciously attack his own party's frontrunner for president. "Here's what I know," Romney said that day. "Donald Trump is a phony, a fraud. His promises are as worthless as a degree from Trump University. He's playing members of the American public for suckers: He gets a free ride to the White House, and all we get is a lousy hat."

And now Romney wanted to be secretary of state in the Trump

administration? Are you kidding me? If he got the job, every time he went abroad representing the United States, there'd be another TV split screen of Secretary Romney at the orange screen presser, ridiculing Trump. That wasn't the only reason I opposed it. I had never seen the grassroots so up in arms.

For core Trump voters, the ones who brought the energy and passion to our win, Romney was a mushy, moderate corporate raider who had been trounced by Barack Obama. Then he said terrible things about the man he was now sucking up to for a job. To say the Trump base didn't like Romney was like saying Yankee fans didn't love the Red Sox. And, come to think of it, having spent all that time in Boston, who do you think Romney rooted for?

But the Conway Six were heading off on a mini-vacation. This debate would have to await my return. Or maybe not.

Florida was just about perfect. Warm. Relaxing. Lots of time around the pool and on the beach with the kids. Throngs of people approaching me, requesting a moment to offer congrats, furnish advice, snap a selfie. We didn't notice it at the time, but photographers recorded many of our moves and published more than one hundred pictures of me jogging, kids poolside, George and I walking on the beach as the kids rode the waves. It was eerie seeing those. Friends were calling, trying to plan a big party. I got my share of calls and texts from New York and Washington, including several daily check-ins from the president-elect, who was ninety minutes up the road at Mar-a-Lago, most of which added up to: "Take some time with your family, honey. We'll all be here when you get back."

Just as George and I and the kids were boarding the plane for the flight back north that Monday, my phone suddenly exploded with texts from reporters, and numbers I did not recognize (also reporters). All of them were asking if I had any response to Joe Scarborough. That morning, it seemed, Scarborough had gone into a sneering rant about my criticism of Mitt Romney. Donald Trump, Scarborough said, was livid with me for saying how ill-advised it would be to make perpetual underperformer Romney secretary of state.

"SOURCES: TRUMP 'FURIOUS' OVER CONWAY COMMENTS ABOUT ROMNEY," screamed the *Morning Joe* headline that one of the reporters texted to me.

"Do we have Wi-Fi?" I asked the flight attendant as we were board-ing the plane. We had a three-hour flight ahead of us.

"No," she said. "I'm sorry."

I had time for one call before the plane door shut. I dialed Trump's landline at home. As soon as he answered, I asked him point-blank, "Are you mad at me?" We'd been in touch the whole holiday. He'd never sounded mad. But first Scarborough and now the entire press corps seemed convinced that Trump was seething at me. When I asked him, Trump still didn't sound angry and repeated to me what I'd said on the Sunday shows, but he did say "Everyone is asking what *you're* going to do and you haven't said." He seemed more interested in whether *I* was joining the administration than whether Romney was.

"I have Jared on the other line," he said. "Talk to him." Jared acted like he had no idea what Scarborough or the others were talking about, saying, "I don't have time to watch the morning shows" and "You know how Joe is."

With a busy day ahead of us, I set aside the pettiness. It did not dawn on me at the time that *Time* magazine's request to photograph Bannon, Priebus, and me as part of their feature on their "Person of the Year," Donald Trump, might leave some others out of sorts.

That night brought an early-warning sign that I missed. Eliana Johnson, a reporter who was writing her first big scoop after moving from the *National Review* to *Politico*, called me that same night and said, "I hear you are being iced out of the inner circle."

"What?" I replied. "I spent the day with the president-elect and just left him twenty minutes ago, where we discussed some personnel and policy matters."

Being told the story wasn't true wasn't enough for Johnson. Report-ers often fear angering and alienating their sources, even when their focus should be on covering their subjects accurately and fairly. It was, after all, her first day with a big, new assignment. In fact, these weren't credible sources at all. She was being used as a willful and unsuspecting member of the press to shape stories and curate others' images.

I should have realized what was happening then or at least how it might easily be interpreted.

"Challenging the Boss in Public? For Kellyanne Conway, It's Part of the Job." That's what a *New York Times* headline stated on Monday morning, November 28, though the *Times* didn't seem entirely sure if this was a sign of healthy, open communication or I was walking on shaky ground.

As I told the *Times* reporters with a laugh after we landed at JFK International Airport, "When he's upset with someone, they know it."

Who could argue with that?

"It is virtually certain that Ms. Conway will remain close to Mr. Trump, whether as an influential West Wing aide or, in a move that seems more likely, as an outside advisor with guaranteed access to the president," the *Times* concluded.

That last part was true enough. At that point, I was leaning *against* joining the new Trump administration.

I COULDN'T BELIEVE how much public attention my soul-searching was getting. Lots of people seemed to have opinions, and almost no one was shy about sharing. At a "Women Rule" conference sponsored by *Politico* on December 7, I caused a genuine uproar when I was asked about my reluctance to take a job in the new administration. "My children are twelve, twelve, eight, and seven, which is a bad idea, bad idea, bad idea, bad idea for Mom going inside," I told the audience. "They have to come first, and those are very fraught ages."

People couldn't fathom my hesitance and especially the reason for it. Social media lit up immediately with a torrent of *How can she say that? That's terrible!*

Apparently, modern women aren't supposed to feel squeezed by the opposing pressure of their careers and their families, and they must never, ever suggest that they might put their families first. It is fine to recognize the challenge, just not to consider acting on it.

I also mentioned that several men interviewing for potential positions in the Trump administration had asked why I hesitated about taking a White House job. "I do politely mention to them the question isn't 'Would you take the job'—the male sitting across from me who's going to take a big job in the White House—but 'Would you want your wife to?' You really see their entire visage change. It's like, Oh, no, they wouldn't want their wife to take that job."

My openness about all this got a ton of media reaction, much of it reproachful. Some writer at *Vogue* seemed to believe that somehow I was putting the nation at risk.

"There are several troubling aspects with Conway's specific reasoning for passing on a White House job that are worth pointing out," she wrote. "While Conway has insisted that she will continue to be an informal adviser to the president-elect, by taking herself out of the running for an official role she has left Trump's administration with virtually no working mothers. Of the 17 appointments the president-elect has made so far, only four women have been tapped for high-level positions: Secretary of Transportation Elaine Chao (who has no children), Secretary of Education Betsy DeVos (whose four children are grown), Seema Verma to run Medicare and Medicaid (no kids) [N.B.: she actually had two in high school; the writer was wrong to say she had none], and U.S. Ambassador to the United Nations Nikki Haley, the only mom of kids still in school (she has two). As of yesterday, Trump also selected WWE cofounder Linda McMahon to head the Small Business Administration, but as a grandmother of six, she's well past the age of carpools and parent-teacher conferences."

It seemed to me that women should be allowed to make their own life decisions, balancing their own desires and their own responsibilities, without a lot of finger-wagging from women's magazine editors or internet scolds.

I hadn't even made my decision yet.

I HAD PROMISED Trump I would stick around at least until the inauguration on January 20, and as the days went by, the pressure on me to join the White House staff continued to ratchet up. The real peer pressure campaign to leave New Jersey and move to Washington wasn't even coming from the president-elect. It was coming from my husband.

Twenty-sixteen was a first for America, electing this unique nonpolitician as president. But it was the seventeenth consecutive autumn I had heard George Conway talk about changing his career. Shaking things up. Doing something different with his life.

"Go be a judge," I had told him. "Be a professor. . . . Be a writer."

George has a biochemistry degree from Harvard and a law degree

from Yale. He was a brilliant litigator who had made partner at a top-tier
law firm by the age of thirty. He had won a unanimous decision in a case
before the U.S. Supreme Court—one of my favorite pictures of us—on
the steps as he is holding the opinion in his hand, that had major implications for U.S. securities law. It seemed to me that George could do just
about anything. He wasn't a risk-taker by nature, but the prospect of following me into the deep end of "the Swamp" now excited him, and the
more we talked about the possibility of my working in the White House,
the more animated George became.

Soon he was bandying about the idea of joining the administration
himself. Throughout the campaign, he had been an ardent Trump supporter, and an ardent Kellyanne-my-wife supporter. We both wanted
the America that Trump envisioned. It wasn't just us. There was something electric in the air that fall for tens of millions of independents
and conservatives who had been waiting and working for this moment
to arrive. And now it would be here soon. Real change was about to
unfold, reshaping the landscape of America inside and out. Feeling part
of that was both exhilarating and empowering. It wasn't hard to see why
George was eager to dive in. And the more George talked enthusiasti-
cally about the unique moment we found ourselves in, the more I felt my
own ambivalence fade. Maybe this was *it*. Maybe going to Washington,
where George and I could both work in the administration, would be the
right move for me and finally satisfy George. We could stop the frantic
commuting and move the family to Washington.

Apart from Donald Trump, who was itching to make another deal
with me, one person whose voice resonated with me through all the noise
was Mike Pence. The vice president–elect sat down with me in the glass-
enclosed conference room on Trump Tower's twenty-fifth floor. With
the straightforward honesty, I treasured in him as an old friend, he provided the perspective I needed.

"What are you thinking?" he asked open-endedly.

"I don't think I'm coming," I told him with genuine regret. "I am
staring at a gold mine of life-changing money, and I'm inclined to run
toward it." The vice president–elect chuckled at that. I continued. "And of
course, the major reason is my children. There are so many of them, and
they're so young!" I said with exaggerated effect. "I can support you guys
and everything you do from the outside."

"Kellyanne," he said, "none of us would be here without you."

He paused a second and let that sink in. Then he continued.

"I know you. I know your heart, your family, your work. I think your path—your calling—includes a tour of duty in the West Wing."

Finally, it was time to have a secret meeting of my own.

After weeks of demurring and deferring, on December 21, I rode the elevator up to the twenty-sixth floor and met alone with the president-elect. What a journey we'd had together. What an amazing success we shared.

We'd sat together in this very same office the previous August, when he'd offered me the campaign manager's position with his unexpected "You wanna run this thing?" And look at us now.

This time I spelled out my plan to advance his agenda on the outside and give his historic presidency the legacy it deserved. He heard me out as I began to lay out the details.

"I know, I got it," he said, "the outside superstructure idea."

He sounded a little exasperated. Like the world-class negotiator he is, he already had his counteroffer ready and he knew how to sell it. "The big superstructure," he said, "is actually the White House. It's ready and waiting for us."

I had to admit he had me there.

"If I do come," I said, relenting a little, "I have five asks."

"Five?" he said, mouthing the number more than saying it.

I listed all five.

I wanted the title of assistant to the president, the highest rank for a White House staffer and on a horizontal plane with Jared, Reince, and Bannon.

I wanted walk-in privileges in the Oval Office.

I wanted direct access to the president.

I wanted to be included in key meetings and foreign and domestic trips, and also self-exclusion rights of meetings I preferred not to be in.

And I wouldn't be expected to appear regularly on TV.

And that was it.

The following day, Donald Trump would formally announce my appointment as counselor to the president.

Within the hour of making our latest deal, I would walk to George's law firm for a scheduled meeting. Yet I wouldn't be setting up an outside superstructure. I wouldn't sign the paperwork to sell my company for a large amount of money. I wouldn't join a major organization in a vaunted role, at an eye-popping salary. I knew I was giving up millions of dollars to go to the White House.

There was a lot I still didn't realize, but I would discover soon enough. How much privacy I'd be giving up. How some people who'd been cordial and collaborative before would now be gunning for me. I was naïve.

Trump shared the news with Mike Pence, who'd just walked into the office. Pence congratulated me and warmly welcomed me aboard. I received a chillier reception a few minutes later when Jared, Steve, and Reince shuffled into the office with no appointment.

They too said congratulations, but they didn't look happy at all.

"She'll be right up there with the three of you," Trump said, looking satisfied. "Counselor to the president," he repeated, his hands outstretched toward me across his massive desk.

No one said "c'mon" this time. No one called me "girl." No one said "You gotta do this."

Jared, Reince, and Steve all wore blank expressions. I can't say for certain if any of them thought of jumping out the window. But under the terms of their power-sharing arrangement, if one of them leapt, I guess the other two would have had to follow.

I wasn't worried in the least. I didn't even try to mask my Mona Lisa smile.

I'd been raised by strong women. For as long as I could remember, I'd been manhandling jealous little boys.

Chapter 18

Rude Awakening

I was walking and talking with Vice President–elect Mike Pence on the House side of the Capitol, joined by a gaggle of staffers and Secret Service agents, quickly making our way to Speaker Paul Ryan's office.

It was January 5, 2017. Hillary Clinton had been reduced to a "name, shame, and blame" tour long on recriminations and short on self-awareness. She refused to accept the election results that she had said she accepted from two months earlier. No matter. The following day, Vice President Joe Biden would certify and accept them at the U.S. Capitol, a typically perfunctory role for a vice president.

Walking and talking: That's the biathlon of official Washington, where everyone is far too busy—or thinks they are—to conduct either of those activities one at a time.

The vice president–elect and I turned a corner, and suddenly I saw the outstretched microphones and heard the clicking cameras everywhere. The press surrounded us, shouting questions, and taking photos. I'd (sort of) become accustomed to that on the campaign trail, but this was on another level entirely, feeling both excessive and premature.

I knew I'd better get used to this, cameras and reporters everywhere I went. With Inauguration Day so close, the media swarm were just making sure they weren't missing anything. They didn't even have anything urgent to ask.

Hours later, I found myself on what's commonly referred to as Pebble Beach, walking toward the front door of the West Wing of the White House. Pebble Beach is the nickname journalists use for their designated stakeout spot on the North Lawn. Just outside the entrance to the West Wing lobby and the James S. Brady Press Briefing Room, the encampment affords a pretty shot of the North Portico as a backdrop for live broadcasts, while green cabanas serve as makeshift studios for interviews where the interviewees stand and stare into a blank camera. On this gravel patch and adjoining fieldstone patio, generations of TV crews have passed their downtime on cheap lawn furniture, hopping up to grab easy sound bites from passing staffers and visitors who wish to be seen.

I said nothing on my way into the building, minding my business and adhering to the directions provided by my host. The reporters flagged me down on my way out. I stopped briefly to say I had just enjoyed a lovely lunch with Valerie Jarrett, Barack and Michelle Obama's confidante and White House senior advisor of eight years. I said she had made it clear to me that President Obama wanted a smooth transition of power and that they were there to help. It turned out I was a little naïve. While Jarrett and I were amiably chatting over lunch in the Ward Room, a very different exit strategy was being plotted in the Oval Office that day.

Obama and Vice President Joe Biden were getting briefed by Director of National Intelligence James Clapper and the directors of the FBI, CIA, and National Security Agency about Russia, including a thirty-five-page dossier from a purported Russian intelligence source whose identity was not disclosed. It would later be revealed in a curious email about that meeting that outgoing national security advisor Susan Rice sent to herself on Inauguration Day. "President Obama said he wants to be sure that, as we engage with the incoming team, we are mindful to ascertain if there is any reason that we cannot share information fully as it relates to Russia," Rice wrote.

Rumors of a bombshell "Russian dossier" had been circulating all summer, with media outlets eager but unable to confirm and publish them.

Now that I'd accepted a title in the incoming administration and the White House would be my official place of work, Pebble Beach stop-bys were about to become a regular part of my daily comings and goings. I'd said no to press secretary and communications director, but soon would be on the receiving end of a four-year presidential commission: "go out and tell them that." "Get her on TV." "Say it just like you did to me." And so, on Pebble Beach, I would find myself, time and again, under fire, in the rain, under the weather, and occasionally over the moon, depending on the news cycle.

HOPE HICKS AND I arrived at the Trump family penthouse at 8:30 a.m. the next day to accompany President-elect Trump downtown for a meeting at Condé Nast, the company that owns *The New Yorker, Vanity Fair, Bon Appétit, Wired, Glamour,* and other magazines. Our host, Anna Wintour, the grand dame of this sprawling media empire, the fashion magazine *Vogue.* Before we left, Trump's longtime friend and Inaugural Committee chairman, Tom Barrack, went over seating for the big day.

"Hope and Kellyanne, make sure you look at this," Trump instructed us. "You know where everyone should sit, who should be there. The calls are coming in. It's the hottest ticket. I want them all to be happy."

Trump 's "all" included just that, a potpourri of friends and allies from a lifetime outside politics, along with some who had supported him from the moment he and Melania rode down the escalator, and others who were suddenly scrambling to jump aboard the Trump Train to avoid being run over by it. They never saw his victory coming and had never given a dollar to help make it happen. But many in the donor class woke up on November 9, 2016, and said to themselves, "Holy shit, this guy just got elected! Let me throw some money at him!" The upcoming inaugural celebration was the perfect opportunity to do that—and *to be seen* doing that.

Anyone could give any amount of money to the 2017 Presidential Inaugural Committee, and corporations weren't excluded. Fat checks have funded inaugural balls, concerts, parades, prayer services, and other events for as long as anyone in Washington can remember, and most of those checks come from people who aren't just happy that a new president is being sworn in on January 20. They almost always want something from the new administration. Such are the swampy ways of Washington.

Suddenly people were calling and writing seven-figure checks, hoping no one would notice that the same high-flyers who'd donated to Mitt Romney in 2012 and flown to the Fleet Center in Boston for the sad results had sat on their hands in 2016, hidden their checkbooks, and gone to bed early on Election Night this time. *Surprise!* I wasn't sure what kind of access they all thought they were buying now, but I suspected a lot of them were going to feel mighty disappointed.

At the Condé Nast sit-down, twenty-five writers and editors, including Trump detractors (to put it mildly) David Remnick of *The New Yorker* and Graydon Carter of *Vanity Fair,* were seated and waiting when Anna Wintour ushered Trump, Barrack, Hope, and me into the room for an hour-plus Q-and-A. The meeting was supposed to be off the record but was promptly leaked to *Politico,* which reported that the topics included racism, hate crimes, climate change, abortion, and Vladimir Putin and Russia.

Wintour was gracious through what must have still been disbelief and disappointment. The renowned British-born editor had been the rumored favorite for the coveted ambassadorship to the United Kingdom in a President Hillary Clinton administration. And look at her now: She was stuck asking Hope and me what we planned to wear to the inaugural ball. Wintour was kind and chatty and made sure we knew she had known Melania Trump "for years." I've never had a stylist. I hadn't settled on attire for the inaugural festivities. I was wandering into a world that I wouldn't exactly call my natural habitat. At that moment I really wished someone would pop out of a pocket door with a rack of curated choices for me right out of *The Devil Wears Prada.*

Afterward, we raced back to Trump Tower, where national intelligence director Clapper and the directors of the FBI, CIA, and NSA gave Trump and Pence an intelligence briefing. Oddly, this was the first time FBI director James Comey had ever set foot in Trump Tower. He was in the middle of a ten-year term as FBI director that he clearly wanted to keep under this new, unexpected president. I wondered what had prevented Comey from coming by sooner to say hello.

The prime minister of Japan, musical artist Kanye West, and TV superstars Steve Harvey and Harvey Levin, among many others, had found their way to Trump Tower during the transition. I could only hope the FBI was more assertive about investigating crimes.

When the intelligence briefing was over and the others left, the FBI director hung back.

Trump and Comey stood aside together, the way two people might linger after a meeting to discuss their grandkids or weekend plans. I wasn't right there. So I didn't hear what they said to each other, but it was definitely more than small talk. I know Trump's version of it, which is similar to Comey's account, something about Russia and something about a dossier and something about something called "golden showers."

The discussion was, we would soon discover, a summary of a more thorough briefing President Barack Obama and Vice President Joe Biden had received from their intelligence team in the Oval Office the day before, perhaps when I was downstairs in the Navy Mess with Valerie Jarrett.

The thirty-five-page "dossier" (French for "load of crap") purportedly came from a Russian intelligence source whose identity was not disclosed. The document alleged widespread collusion between Russian intelligence and the Trump campaign, peppered with unproved salacious claims about encounters Donald Trump had supposedly engaged in on visits to Russia.

As these wild claims slowly made their way around the incoming West Wing staff, I knew one thing for certain: I hadn't seen any hints of Russian collusion in the Trump campaign, and I was the one who had managed it to its successful conclusion. I was talking to field staff in Macomb County, Michigan, and Mecklenburg County, North Carolina, not in Moscow. The only other things I learned at this point was that, as early as the previous summer, reporters had been chasing rumors of a bombshell "Steele Russian dossier," though no one had been able to confirm or to publish anything.

That week we had a huge ice storm. But it didn't stop more than one hundred people from attending a party hosted by my friends Andrea and Paul, who invite our kids on vacation each summer, and some of the girlfriends I've named throughout the book. They threw a party in Alpine to celebrate my fiftieth birthday and my going away. The Kavalers and Giuffras joined. There were college and law school friends, childhood

buddies, bridesmaids, neighbors, and cousins. And my mom. Judge Bill
Kuntz sang an incredible rendition of "God Bless America."

I dozed for just forty-five minutes to do two Sunday shows. I pre-
taped *Meet the Press* first. It was a nine-minute interview, but Chuck Todd
kept asking me the same question. It revolved around the Comey-Trump
meeting. I felt like he somehow knew more about the meeting than I
did. As I was getting up to leave the set after those nine minutes, I heard
something in my earpiece. It was Chuck's voice saying to his staff that
they had nailed it and finally gotten what they wanted.

They ended up airing only forty-five seconds of the interview,
something that had never been done to me before. Which led to a Trump
tweet: "Kellyanne Conway went to @MeetThePress this morning for an
interview with @chucktodd. Dishonest media cut out 9 of her 10 minutes. Terrible!" And a call to me from Chuck Todd.

The Obama-Comey camp's calculated bombshell was leaked,
including a misleading characterization that somehow Trump, Pence,
and their team had been briefed the same way Obama and Biden had.
This led to false information in stories, most prominently by CNN,
which later won an award, that Comey had handed Trump the two-
page summary, and by ABC's Brian Ross, who ran a hair-on-fire report
on *Good Morning America*, to which I responded live the next day on
set. Ross was taken off air by ABC later that year after additional false
reporting on the same topic.

I tried to politely inform both Anderson Cooper and Brian Ross
that the reports were wrong and that the limited information conveyed
by Comey to Trump was done so orally and that any summary had been
buried in another document and not handed to the president-elect. As I
left *Late Night with Seth Meyers* on January 10, a nervous Michael Cohen
called me, saying Bannon had just asked him if he'd ever been to Ukraine
and to show "them" his passport as proof.

Then I went directly to Trump's office on the twenty-sixth floor as
copies of the dossier were distributed to the few of us assembled there.
Trump looked up and said, "What is this?"

I found myself really doing the dirty work, explaining what a golden
shower was (honestly, I'd just learned myself). "You are the world's leading germaphobe," I offered. "This seems out of whack."

"This is all made up," Trump said. "Russia? Showers? We weren't there long, and I tell everyone who goes to Russia, they have cameras everywhere. They see everything."

There were no photos or videos, just a salacious and unverified, fact-free dossier funded by the Hillary Clinton campaign and the Democratic National Committee that the "facts-first" media and their allies in the Democrat Party used to medicate their Trump Derangement Syndrome. They were unable to accept the election results and find a way to work with President Trump to unify the nation and get things done on its collective behalf. That was the true shame.

WHILE GEORGE CONTINUED to weigh his options and the two of us began to face the logistics of moving our family to Washington, our relatives and close friends were all making plans to join the inaugural festivities. And I mean *all* of them. My aunts, all my cousins, the rest of the extended family, my father and his fourth wife. They were coming from everywhere. I was thrilled. Who better to share this milestone with than all the people I loved, while we all witnessed history and I danced with my husband and adorable children at an inaugural ball? Turning fifty would be a glorious event.

My final day in New York was the Tuesday before inauguration. George met me in his tuxedo at Trump Tower, and I changed into a white, one-shoulder cocktail dress. The president-elect had a dinner with ambassadors and big donors that night in Washington and wanted me there. *This is crazy,* I thought. *This is really happening.* George and I flew to D.C. with Trump on his private jet. Trump asked George if he knew Preet Bharara, U.S. attorney for the Southern District of New York, and what he thought of him. Governor Andrew Cuomo had been calling me and later that week visited Trump in New York City, saying that his adversary Preet was a Senator Chuck Schumer guy and needed to go. As soon as we stepped onto the tarmac in Washington, photographers started snapping pictures—not just of the president-elect but also of me.

Why do they want pictures *of me*? I wondered. An assistant and a private car were waiting for us. It all felt very surreal. At dinner, a throng of ambassadors from here to Borat's Kazakhstan formed a spontaneous line to speak with me and snap selfies. I complied but felt shy in some way.

Trump flew back to New York that night, while George and I stayed behind in the Washington rental apartment George had found and leased for me as we house-hunted for the family. I would be in D.C. on my own during the week until the kids finished their school year, when we'd all move together into our new Washington home. By then, we expected, George would have a presidential nomination to a coveted administration position, since he wanted one and the president was happy to oblige.

In the politics of Washington, with a new administration arriving, this wasn't a heavy lift at all. George was brilliant. He was a politically savvy conservative lawyer with connections and cred in the Federalist Society, a few big scalps from the Bill Clinton–Monica Lewinsky drama and subsequent impeachment, and a wife who was about to become counselor to the president. He had worked for decades in a prestigious, powerhouse law firm.

Until George and the kids got down, I would commute back to New Jersey whenever I could, and George would bring the kids for visits as often as they could. The apartment was more expensive than expansive, but it was close to work and nice enough. And really, how much time would I be spending there outside dinners alone and sleeping?

The celebrations continued. Turning fifty tasted sweet. My close friends in Washington, Shelley Hymes and Marlene Colucci, who had cofounded RightNOW with me twenty years earlier, hosted a congratulations/happy-birthday fete for me at the Four Seasons.

In recent decades, Inauguration Day has bloated into Inauguration Week. George stuck around for the cavalcade of glamorous events that would lead up to the big day, Friday, January 20, as the kids finished classes and jumped in friends' cars to join us for a historic weekend.

Wednesday was the big launch party for the news website *Axios*. It was being held at RPM Italian, the trendy restaurant Bill and Giuliana Rancic had recently opened. Bill Rancic, in this D.C. version of six-degrees-of-Kevin-Bacon-separation, happened to be the first winner of Trump's hit TV show, *The Apprentice*, while his wife hosted the celebrity-focused *Live from the Red Carpet* and *Fashion Police*. The media elite turned out in force, from Wolf Blitzer to Bob Woodward, who came up to talk with us and appeared delighted as George gushed about the *Washington Post* associate editor's storied career. The party boasted more than a scattering of sports, television, and corporate boldface names. It was all very heady for mom-of-four me, who didn't get out all that often at night. According to news reports, Joe and Jill were there, Vice President and Doctor Biden. I hadn't noticed.

Later Wednesday night, when we met up with Trump at the Library of Congress for a gathering of friends, allies, and patrons, watching George interact with the president-elect reminded me of when the kids first saw Mickey Mouse. He was excited beyond all reason, and it was charming to watch.

After fifteen years of marriage and four children, there was something special about George and me being able to share this unexpected chapter of our lives. Just as his support during the insane past few months had made such a difference, sharing the excitement and anticipation for the Trump presidency eased any misgivings I had about making such a huge life change for the six of us. I knew our two corgis, Bonnie and Skipper, would be happy anywhere.

The next night, George and I arrived at what promised to be the height of pre-inaugural glamour, a candlelight dinner at D.C.'s historic Union Station attended by a who's who of Washington and honored guests from around the world. There's a photograph of George and me on the red carpet that would end up in files of every media organization on earth, to be used anytime they ran an article about the two of us. George is standing off to my side, holding the fur wrap he'd bought for me a few years earlier, and grinning proudly. I am striding as if into battle, yet still with a smile on my face. Once inside, we were greeted by throngs of joyful people from across the country and seated for dinner in the Beaux Arts main hall with friends from Alpine, the Donnellys and Minnetians. Cindy Adams from the *New York Post* joined us. George and I were both grinning at all the pomp and circumstance—and, just as much, at each other.

What wasn't there to like? How could I have known that a buzzkill was waiting for me off to the side?

That would be Reince Priebus, who hastily ushered me into a corner to pass along some unsettling news: "The president is going to sign the paperwork for you," he said in as hushed a tone as he could manage above the din of the party. "Starting Monday, you get a Secret Service detail."

A Secret Service detail? "Why?" I asked. That protection, I knew, was generally assigned to presidents, vice presidents, and their families, and cabinet members or others in the line of succession to the presidency. I didn't check any of those boxes.

"Because you're a target," Priebus said flatly.

Now, that was alarming.

"If there's something I need to know . . ." I said anxiously. "I'll be separated from my kids for a while. Does the Secret Service think these crazy people who vomit venom online would actually—"

"You are famous now," Reince interrupted. "People see you and recognize you and may approach you. I get protection automatically as chief of staff. The family gets it automatically, and now you're getting it, too." Reince was genuinely concerned for me and felt good that he had the position and authority to help keep me safe. I appreciated that.

As the public face of Trump's fall campaign, personal insults had become standard fare for me, punctuated by the occasional nutjob threatening much worse. I'd attributed much of it to "social media muscle," the phony courage that emboldens otherwise weak people to hurl anonymous invective at total strangers alongside their best friend, the keyboard. There was even a sub-diagnosis, Trump Derangement Syndrome. Its sufferers had taken solace in knowing that Donald Trump would never get far, the charade of his candidacy destined to lie in ashes on November 8 with the historic election of Hillary Clinton, America's first female president. Trump's election shocked and embarrassed them and spawned a new obsession and narcissism among many people straight out of the *DSM-5* who sought personal revenge, not national unity. Donald Trump wouldn't be fading from view. He would be in the White House, on their social media feeds, and in their faces for at least the next four years.

Did that drive some deranged people mad enough to graduate from snide remarks about my "skinny ass," my "lying face," and my "evil boyfriend Donald Trump" into the realm of physical violence? I didn't know, and I certainly wasn't eager to find out.

I knew I'd have to think about the implications of that. I kept hearing about new ways my life was going to change. Here, I suppose, was another one. I tried to put it out of my mind for now as I made my way back into the elegant hall, where the main-course dishes were now on the tables and the man who would soon be the forty-fifth president of the United States had begun his remarks.

"I see my Kellyanne," he said in that booming voice of his. "Come here. Get up here."

No!

I tried to demur and then tried to get the elegant and smiling First Lady in waiting to join me, but Trump insisted that I walk in his direction so he could pull me up on the stage. "She's been so great," he told the crowd as I stood at his side. "Wow! There is no den she will not go into. When my men are petrified to go on a certain network, I say, 'Kellyanne, would you do it?' 'Absolutely, no problem.' Then she gets on, and she just destroys them. So, anyway, thank you, baby. Thank you."

Amid the applause, I could almost hear self-righteous people watching from home, shrieking. "'Baby'! . . . He calls her 'baby' and 'honey' and 'my Kellyanne.' . . . How demeaning. How disrespectful. How dare he!'"

How ridiculous, I'd say. Donald J. Trump had elevated and empowered me to the top of his campaign, helping me crack glass ceilings that had never even been dinged before. Angry feminists can bitch all day long in their pink hats and yoga pants. Talk is cheap. They should have at least once in their lives a "girl boss" as generous, respectful, engaging, and empowering as Donald Trump was to me and my other female colleagues. Same for the men behaving badly who were about to be my White House colleagues and those on the outside who will never be anyone's White House colleagues.

Trump's gratitude and effusiveness were genuine. So were George's. He was emotional when I returned to the table. It was hard to know who was prouder of me, my boss or my husband. No matter. I was blessed on both counts, and those are fundamentally different relationships. Trump's public show of faith in me and fondness for me would no doubt irk some thin-skinned troublemakers jockeying for their own favor within the administration. But I didn't care. I didn't need to be in anyone's circle to get to the president. I had my own direct line.

INAUGURATION DAY DAWNED in Washington beneath an overcast winter sky. I woke early for a round of morning interviews on the National Mall, followed by a memorable golf cart ride to breakfast at Blair House and Mass with the Trump family at St. John's Episcopal

Church, on Lafayette Square, before the swearing-in ceremony at the U.S. Capitol at noon.

Fifty felt fantastic.

I am one of those people who is always cold. While George plans ski trips, I call myself the "summer parent" and laugh about wearing sweaters and socks to the beach. So, I was confident that the Gucci ensemble I had purchased for Inauguration Day, a beautiful red, white, and blue military-style coat, would shield me from the elements. No one saw the long-sleeve dress beneath it that day because I was so cold. I had hand warmers in my pockets as a backup, and I put on a red hat and gloves at the last second because I knew that, no matter the forecast, I would be freezing.

"It's Trump revolutionary wear," I joked to reporters who asked me about my outfit. My three daughters would echo the patriotic theme in their gorgeous hand-made inaugural ball gowns later that night— Claudia in blue, Charlotte in white, and Vanessa in red. Their brother, George, was handsome in his tux.

My coat would instantly become a meme, sparking an internet and media snarkfest that compared me to Barbie, Paddington Bear, and nut-cracker soldiers. "Sorry to offend the black-stretch-pants-wearing women of America with a little color," I sarcastically said later in an interview with Michael Wolff, who was profiling me for *The Hollywood Reporter*. "I apologize to everybody out there who no longer wears anything that zips, buttons or snaps for having a little class on an Inauguration Day."

For all the criticism, I would read later that the coat was the bestseller in its category that quarter. Days later, when General James Mattis was sworn in as defense secretary at the Pentagon, I approached to congratulate him and he remarked, "I really loved your coat at the inauguration."

Four-star fashion sense!

One thing was becoming clear, even before the president put his left hand on his family Bible and raised his right hand to take the oath of office and spoke to the nation in his inaugural address: The bitterness of defeat and the defeated wasn't going to segue gracefully into some "country-over-party" call for bipartisanship. But you can't say he didn't try.

I sat for the inaugural address with Hope Hicks, Steve Bannon, and Dan Scavino, the new president's social media director, who had worked with Trump for decades. Just before Trump began to speak, I gazed across the massive crowd on the Capitol lawn, spread as far as I could see. I'm no expert on crowd size. I wouldn't pretend to offer any kind of estimate. I just knew that the Capitol Police and other agencies had prepared for 700,000 to 800,000 based on past experience and, not surprisingly, that Trump had predicted "an unbelievable, perhaps record-setting turnout" for the inauguration.

His succinct and moving words from the steps of the Capitol promised an end to the "American carnage" of rusted-out factories, broken schools, and mothers and children trapped in poverty. Trump decried the drugs, gangs, and crime that "have stolen too many lives and robbed our country of so much unrealized potential." He spoke eloquently of the hopeful alternatives to that. "We share one heart, one home, and one glorious destiny," he declared, arguing for a new national unity. "The oath of office I take today is an oath of allegiance to all Americans."

What the spectators on the Mall cheered as a message of promise, patriotism, and unity, media commentators and pundits couldn't wait to deride as a bleak and dark message with ominous undertones of nationalism. Every new president identifies problems he wishes to solve, challenges he wishes to confront, hopes and promises he wishes to unlock. But the grumbling on this day could have just easily been prewritten months earlier with a fill-in-the-blanks form. Haters hate, and lots of them hated Donald Trump. The critics' complaint was not really the message. It was the messenger. Fifteen minutes after Trump became the forty-fifth president, a *Washington Post* headline blared, "The campaign to impeach President Trump has begun."

Senator Roy Blunt from Missouri and his wife, Abby, had generously given me one of the toughest tickets to score that day, to the inaugural luncheon at the Capitol. I was seated with future Trump nemesis and Sinophile congressman Eric Swalwell and former Speaker of the House John Boehner. Just as I was leaving the Capitol to go to the White House and dive straight into work, I spotted two familiar faces. The Clintons, Bill and Hillary, were crossing in front of me, heading out a side portico. Hillary was limping. She looked at me and just kept walking with the usual scowl on her face. I kept walking, too, with the usual smile on my face, mouthing "thanks for playing, Hillary" to myself until I heard an unmistakable, raspy voice.

"Young lady!"

This being my fiftieth birthday, former president Bill Clinton had me at "young lady." I stopped and smiled.

"Young lady," he said, "you did a really great job," referring to the presidential campaign that had just crushed his wife's greatest ambition. "It was something to watch. Congratulations!"

"Well, thank you very much, Mr. President," I said.

Pointing at my coat, he added, "And I love your outfit."

"Thank you for a second time," I said. "Would . . . would you ever consider helping us on big topics?" I'm still not sure if the counselor to the president or the Golden Girls' progeny from Atco asked that question. But I blurted it out and was glad I did.

The forty-second president supplied a name and number for me to call: Tina Flournoy, who took my call but never connected President Clinton to me or that shared work I'd mentioned. Four years later to the day, Flournoy became the embattled chief of staff to embattled vice president Kamala Harris. She should place a distress call to one of us.

AFTER THE INAUGURAL Parade, I walked into the Oval Office and, for the first time ever, saw President Trump sitting exactly where he belonged. He stretched his arms out wide in that signature, expansive gesture that he uses when he's punctuating the air.

"Look at this place, Kel! Do you believe it?"

"It's incredible," I agreed. "I love seeing you there behind the Resolute Desk, Mr. President."

That was also the first time I got to call him "Mr. President."

Staffers were bustling about—or in the case of Steve Bannon, standing like a spring break bar bouncer—wanting to be there when the press was allowed in.

That would lead to the media's first mistake of the new administration. Within the first minutes of the Trump presidency, Zeke Miller of *Time* magazine falsely tweeted that a bust of Martin Luther King Jr. had been removed from the Oval Office; it was too incendiary a claim to bother fact-checking. Later Zeke would quietly apologize and, as with any of the myriad mistakes by the media, we would just all need to move on.

Priebus, meanwhile, was making sure he was in every shot.

I headed upstairs to see my office and think about how I wanted to arrange it. I already knew that my revolutionary coat deserved a place of honor as a reminder of my unique fiftieth birthday and as an homage to the self-absorbed social media mob so easily triggered by anything Kellyanne. That red coat would hang in my office for the next four years.

We were a floor above the Oval Office, and I called our suite the Cool Kids Corridor because it ended up being me, the White House counsel Don McGahn (and later Pat Cipollone), Gary Cohn (later Larry Kudlow), Dina Powell (later Johnny DeStefano), and Ivanka Trump. Ivanka didn't come up right away. She had the luxury of figuring out what she wanted to do and being with her kids, who were one, three, and six at the time, getting them all set up in school and so forth.

I had a view of the Washington Monument and a vestibule for my team. My office had a true if-these-walls-could-talk lineage. It had belonged to Valerie Jarrett (Obama), Karl Rove (Bush 43), and Hillary Clinton (President Clinton, thankfully the only one). The sprawling East Wing suites reserved for first ladies were not enough for Hillary. She also needed a piece of prime West Wing real estate, since her goal was not FLOTUS-type work on children's literacy or healthy living, but the presidency itself.

The downstairs offices were about a third the size, but a man cave for the cavemen, who measured influence in inches. The fewer inches between them and the president, the more powerful they felt.

I had sunlight, a view, and peace and quiet so I would be able to get some work done. And, I would learn, it would only take me about twelve seconds to run downstairs to the Oval in three-inch heels.

Chapter 19

Alternative Hacks

On Saturday, my mom hosted a huge birthday brunch for me at the JW Marriott two blocks from the White House. My kids, my relatives, my friends and their kids. My college and law school friends. My friends from childhood, my friends from Alpine, my friends from New York and Washington, seven of my eight godchildren. Outside, the "Women's March" was taking place, with all their hats and posters. They marched for women's independence—but we were the ones truly celebrating it. We couldn't even get out of the hotel.

We already had many executive orders, had prepared things the president wanted to do on day one. We were getting cabinet members confirmed. Trump wanted to get to work right away, and we were all expected to work through the weekend. I was supposed to be at the White House, but I texted the deputy chief of staff for operations: *I can't get near it. I'm sorry.*

And that's when Sean Spicer held his press conference about the largest Inauguration crowd ever. Period. Reince got his guy into the job everyone had been pushing me to take, the position I did everything I possibly could to avoid. White House press secretary was Sean Spicer's dream job, not mine. He also got an additional big job, White House Communications Director.

Sean had spent the previous six years as communications director of the Republican National Committee, working for Reince Priebus. Energetic, combative, steeped in the ways of Washington, Sean got credit for creating an RNC rapid-response team. Well, he didn't have to wait long to show his stuff. The day after the inauguration, he marched into the White House Briefing Room, stood behind the podium, and complained that the media had purposely underestimated the size of Trump's inaugural crowd. The president's swearing-in, he said, had drawn the "largest audience to ever witness an inauguration, period—both in person and around the globe."

Sean got downright defensive and a bit unmoored from the facts, citing Metro ridership numbers that turned out to be wrong. Some of the media images, he said, had been cropped to make the crowds look smaller. Grass covers also made the event appear more sparsely attended than it was. Then he stormed out of the Briefing Room, refusing to answer questions, which is what seemed to have a lot of the reporters steaming.

It was an unforced error, and now I would be expected to clean it up. One day on the job, and I was already doing what I didn't want to do—going on TV to clear up or clean up other people's messes!

THE NEXT MORNING, I woke up early to do three Sunday shows live from Pebble Beach. CBS's *Face the Nation*. ABC's *This Week*. NBC's *Meet the Press*.

I wasn't as rested or prepared as I'd like to have been, given the consecutive late nights that week, and the dozens of guests in town for whom I felt grateful and responsible. Sprinkle in some late-night friends-and-family drama the night before, kids nervous that they would return to New Jersey that day without me, and a crappy hair-and-makeup job that morning and who knows what might happen.

The president called me on my way over.

"Oh," he asked, "did I say happy birthday to you?"

"You did, Mr. President. Two days ago."

"What a weekend! You had a whole weekend of it. I loved your outfit, too. I love that coat."

"Thank you, Mr. President."

I said I expected to be asked on the shows that morning about Sean's inaugural crowd claims. "I know what he was trying to say," I told the president, "but it was just wrong. He was making the point that in 2016, the full inaugural audience goes far beyond who is physically present on the National Mall. If you look at alternative information and additional facts, it is true that, this time, many more people were watching on their phones, tablets, and computers, which was not as much of an option before—as opposed to physically being on the Mall. I think that's what he may have been trying to say. But that's not the way it came out and he hasn't called me."

The Trump crowd was different. Everyone knew that. These weren't wealthy Romney donors jetting into Boston for Election Night in 2012 or well-heeled Obama supporters making a celebratory Washington weekend of it at his inauguration in 2008 or 2012. These were regular, working Americans. They weren't going to leave their jobs and families and drive to the nation's capital and rent expensive hotel rooms on a full-priced weekend to cheer the man they'd helped elect, much as they might have loved being there in person. But they were still part of the inaugural *audience.* Streaming live on their cell phones. Watching on their tablets and desktops and rec room TVs, whether from thirty or three thousand miles away.

I didn't need to say any of that to Trump. He knew it intuitively. He had helped to define that giant swath of America. He had given those people their voices back and had truly empowered them. Anyone who doubted their appreciation and enthusiasm for what they'd accomplished together had never stood for four hours in an airplane hangar or an open field in some noncoastal county far from New York, Los Angeles, or Washington, waiting for a Trump rally to begin. This was a man who had attracted crowds like no one ever had before and also knew how to count them.

"A lot of people were watching," I told Trump, "beyond the people who were physically on the Mall."

THERE'S A BIG difference between me going on a Sunday show from Pebble Beach and the White House press secretary speaking from behind the podium in the Briefing Room. It's not a distinction that most civilians would think about. But the difference can be summed up in one word.

Personnel.

The White House press office has dozens of staffers research-ing, writing, and contributing, with lawyers and senior officials buzz-ing around, preparing thick binders and spending hours rehearsing the press secretary before he or she steps foot in the Briefing Room. So do the TV anchors who grill those press secretaries. They too have massive staffs, producers speaking into their earpieces, and writers filling tele-prompters and note cards with carefully vetted words. When the system works—and it normally does—every word that is uttered from the Brief-ing Room podium has been checked by ten people six ways to Sunday. That morning, the only person who talked to me before my interview was the president of the United States.

Forty hours into the Trump administration, I had not a single staff member assisting me or a single page of professional research. Talk about being out on a limb by myself! No one was preparing me, accompanying me, or warning me. The sharks smelled Spicer's blood, but mine would do just as well.

It's strange how alone you can be while you are appearing in front of millions of people on national TV.

None of this was new to me. I'd done thousands of television interviews. But I had never done any in an official capacity from the White House's "Pebble Beach," with no notes in front of me and no net beneath me.

All told, I did thirty-eight minutes of live television that morning, standing in the cold, staring into a blank camera with no ability to see the interviewers, let alone interact with them. Two of the interviews, on CBS with John Dickerson and ABC with George Stephanopoulos, went per-fectly well. Routine bantering between a couple of network TV anchors and a senior advisor to the president. In more than twenty minutes of those two interviews I covered a lot of ground. But all the risks of a live, national encounter like this one came together as I faced a faceless Chuck Todd for an interview with *Meet the Press*. Staring into a blank camera with no notes, no net, no binder, no assistants, and very little sleep, the first person to go on the Sunday shows representing the Trump presidency, two words slipped out that would immediately become leg-endary to the TDS-addled crowd.

It started with me rattling off a list of what was ahead for the first week of the Trump administration.

I talked about the president's plan for healthcare, how he had signed an executive order to limit Obamacare's individual mandate. I previewed Trump's first trip as president. He was going to the House Republican retreat that week in Philadelphia. I gave some details about the president's first head-of-state visit, with British prime minister Theresa May. I took aim at the entertainer Madonna, asking why she had decided to address that weekend's anti-Trump Women's March, where she said she'd thought about "blowing up the White House" but, as I put it, "couldn't be bothered to support women by maybe stopping by a local shelter and writing a check."

As I expected, the other two show hosts asked about Spicer's crowd claims. I knew I didn't want to get bogged down in a back-and-forth on crowd size.

I wasn't much of a "crowd-size person," I said. Presidents are judged by their records on peace and prosperity, I pointed out, not on the turn-outs for their inaugural events. They're judged on the domestic economy and our country's international standing. And anyway, crowd sizes are notoriously hard to pinpoint, I added, and of little interest to most people. So far, so good. But Chuck Todd could not leave it there and shift to policy. He had already violated what I had said previously, that the Trump White House and mainstream media were going to have joint custody of the nation for the next four to eight years and we should find a responsible way to co-parent.

"Why did the president send out his press secretary, who is not just a spokesperson for Donald Trump?" Chuck began. "He also serves as the spokesperson for all of America at times. He speaks for all of the country at times. Why put him out there for the very first time in front of that podium to utter a provable falsehood? It's a small thing, but the first time he confronts the public, it's a falsehood?"

Chuck was waving his hand for emphasis, although I could not see that. He was already revved up. I tried to lower the temperature immediately.

"Chuck," I said, "if we're going to keep referring to our press secretary in those types of terms, we are going to have to rethink our relationship here. I want to have a great, open relationship with our press. But look what happened the day before, talking about falsehoods. We allowed the press to come into the Oval Office and witness President Trump signing executive orders. And, of course, the Senate had just confirmed General Mattis and General [John F.] Kelly to their two posts. And we allowed the press in. And what happened almost immediately? A falsehood is told about removing the bust of Martin Luther King Jr. from the office. That's just flat-out false."

"And it was corrected immediately."

"But Chuck, why was it? Why was it said in the first place? Because everyone is so presumptively negative."

"I don't know," he said.

"No, no, no, that reporter was writing on behalf of the press pool. That falsehood got spread three thousand times [on Twitter] before it was corrected. And it's still out there."

"But that's no excuse, and you still did not answer the question."

"I did answer your questions. Yes, I did."

Things were getting testy.

"You did not answer the question," Chuck said. "Why did the president ask the White House press secretary to come out in front of the podium for the first time and utter a falsehood? Why did he do that? It undermines the entire credibility of the entire White House press office on day one."

"No, it doesn't," I said. "Don't be so overly dramatic about it, Chuck. You're saying it's a falsehood, and Sean Spicer, our press secretary, gave"— pause and stumble—"alternative . . . facts to that. But the point remains that there—"

Without realizing it, I had merged *alternative information* and *additional facts*. What I was trying to say is what I had said to Donald Trump on the phone just before the interviews: that what Sean said was wrong, what he meant to say was reasonable—working from alternative *information,* explaining that the spread of streaming devices had vastly expanded the inaugural audience regardless of exactly how many people were standing outside on the Mall, even though a lot of people were.

Alternative information and additional facts came out as alternative facts, that was a mistake. I had never said that phrase before, I had never thought about it, and I hadn't thought much of it at the moment either, knowing there was no malicious intent behind it. It was a misstatement.

Moments later Chuck laughed. I couldn't see him in the blank camera, but I could hear him mocking me in my earpiece.

"You can laugh at me all you want," I shot back, "but I'm very glad—"

"I'm not laughing. I am just befuddled."

"But you are," I said, "and I think it's actually symbolic of the way we're treated by the press. The way that you just laughed at me is very representative of the way we're treated by the press. I'll just ignore it. I'm a bigger person than that. I'm a kind and gracious person." Even though weeks earlier he had aired a tiny portion of our full interview and weeks before that said that I was bragging or showing off because I had kept on my Twitter bio "we won."

Then it dawned on me: As goes the new Trump White House, reporters had little interest to "get the story." Their new mission was to "get the president."

I should have realized then and there that there would be *zero* interest in the types of facts, figures, problems, and solutions I'd addressed in interviews with the same anchors and reporters hundreds of times.

ALTERNATIVE FACTS WAS an unintentional slip of the tongue, with no malice or forethought and no strategy to fool the public who was watching. Yet the avalanche of outrage was swift and, frankly, nutty. I was being accused, convicted, sentenced for a crime I had not committed.

Could I have spoken more clearly? Yes, like 99 percent of people on TV and in life.

Did I use the perfect words? No, like 99 percent of people on TV and in life.

Intent matters. Had I intended to deceive anyone or in any way to lie? Absolutely, positively not. And the real crime was how quickly and shamelessly people who knew better would lie about me lying.

"Alternative facts," as the hesitation and tongue-twisting show, was never intended to deceive anyone. It was corrected "quickly and often," the stock defense of left-wing celebrities and Democrats when they *intentionally* say something foolish or outrageous, for example, about rape, race, or the Holocaust. That had also been Chuck Todd's automatic defense of Zeke Miller's misstatement about the MLK bust being removed from the Oval. "He corrected it immediately!" Well, so had I. But as with all things in the Trump presidency, presumptive negativity kicked in and the new president's mindless detractors distorted it all, replacing my guileless intention with their sinister interpretation and never letting it rest.

Let's face it: The two words that shocked and outraged the media, their fellow Democrats and so many others were not "alternative facts." The two words were "President Trump."

Our critics quickly became the Orwellian liars, knowing full well that I had misspoken and that I wasn't trying to manipulate the minds of a nation in broad daylight.

The irony about "alternative facts" is that the lemmings who have spun it for their own petty and political purposes are the ones trafficking in blatant falsehood. The same media themselves who often say things like two things can be true at same time which also sounds like alternative facts. 1+3, 2+2, 4+0 all equal 4. Again, "alternative facts" was a misstatement made without malice. It was an innocent mistake that lasted two and a half seconds. The "Russian collusion!" lie, which lasted for two and a half years, intended to change the view of the American people toward their president and the legitimacy of his election. Everyone lied; no one apologized.

When I spoke to George afterward, he shrugged and assured me it was no big deal. But those two words dominated the coverage by a hungry media that issues its retractions quietly and rarely apologizes for its many and more serious transgressions.

THAT AFTERNOON, PRESIDENT Trump and Vice President Pence presided over a formal ceremony to swear in two dozen senior White House aides, including me.

Since none of us needed to be confirmed by the Senate, there was no reason to wait. Cabinet secretaries and their top deputies were in an entirely different category. Their swear-ins could take weeks or months or longer or never happen at all, depending on the ever-shifting whims of the United States Senate.

My mom, George, and our four children were with me in the East Room for that special event. So were the spouses, kids, and other loved ones of the other top White House aides. It's easy to think of people who work in government as nameless, faceless public officials. But that happy afternoon reminded everyone that all these jobs are held by human beings and all of us have outside lives.

Before we got started, Mike Pence whispered to me, "You took the bark off of Chuck Todd this morning."

I took my place in the reserved seats in the front row alongside Kushner, Bannon, and Priebus.

Trump seemed like he was settling in. He held up a note he said Barack Obama had left behind for him. "It was really very nice of him to do that," Trump said. "And we won't even tell the press what's in that letter." The president had already set up meetings, he said, with the Canadian prime minister and the Mexican president. "We're going to start renegotiating on NAFTA, on immigration, and on security at the border," Trump told the intimate crowd. "And Mexico has been terrific, actually."

It was Pence who administered the oath of office.

After the ceremony, my family checked out my new office and then left for New Jersey to begin our new normal. They got home late that night, and George opened an envelope waiting in the pile of mail on the table.

There was white powder inside.

Maybe Reince knew more than he was saying when he told me my family and I would be given Secret Service protection. My detail was starting in the morning. Suddenly the idea of it didn't seem so excessive.

The white powder turned out to be nothing, just someone's sick idea of a statement or a joke. But it still took us hours to learn that, and those hours were chilling.

That was my home, where my young children and elderly mother would remain until the end of the school year, when they would all move down to Washington.

As I drifted off to sleep late that night, the Alternative Hacks were busy pumping out more venom, writing screaming headlines, and dusting off their copies of *1984*. Yet I had bigger concerns: I couldn't help but worry what this new life of mine was really going to mean for all the people I loved.

Chapter 20

Men Behaving Badly

One of the people who'd been interviewed during the transition for the White House communications job, the job I had already declined, was a seasoned TV producer who had covered major moments and shaped stories across five presidencies. For some reason, he was required to interview with Jared Kushner, who had no experience for such a position and isn't known for his communications prowess. Toward the end of the meeting, Jared mentioned to him, unprompted, that "Kellyanne won't be that involved. She won't be involved much and won't be on Marine One or Air Force One." The exclusions from the transition followed me into the White House.

Now, six days into the Trump presidency, I had embarked on my first trip with the president—on Marine One and Air Force One—and we flew to Philadelphia for the House Republican Retreat. It would be my first of many, many trips on Marine One and Air Force One, and Jared's first Republican retreat. I was sitting on the couch outside the presidential dining room on Air Force One, eating a Twix bar, when Jared came and sat down next to me. He said, also unprompted and unnecessarily (definitely not eating a Twix bar), "I think it's been harder for you on television because you don't have an enemy now," he said. "You know, you had Hillary, but it's much harder to message governing."

I responded, a bit off guard. "We have lots of enemies to fight, Jared," I assured him. "They are always going to hit us. They weren't expecting us, and the administration will try to make change quickly. And for the record, being on TV is always hard. That's why so few of us do it, and even fewer of us do it well." He swallowed hard but did not blink.

Once we got to the retreat, I mingled with members of Congress, and toward the end of the speech, I headed to the ladies' room. A line of congressional spouses was stopping me, taking selfies next to the paper towel holder, until a female Secret Service agent came running in to retrieve me, saying the motorcade was leaving.

That week, I was in the Oval Office with the president to discuss the nomination of a Supreme Court justice. Also in the meeting were White House counsel Don McGahn; Mitch McConnell, the Senate majority leader, who in 2016 had wisely delayed a vote on Obama nominee Merrick Garland; Chuck Schumer, the Senate Democratic leader; Senate Judiciary Committee chairman Chuck Grassley, and ranking Judiciary member Dianne Feinstein.

Schumer brought up his idea that Trump should renominate Garland. Trump looked at him skeptically and then asked what I thought. "I don't think much of it, sir," I said, before turning to Schumer: "Respectfully, Senator, why would he do that?"

"It would heal the nation," Schumer replied.

"Isn't he pro-choice? Is there a pro-life judge you could support?"

The meeting didn't go much further after Schumer's pipe dream fell flat in the room, though that wouldn't be the last time I heard from Senator Schumer. He'd call me in the summer of 2017, asking how we could work together, telling me, "You're one of the reasonable ones."

THREE WEEKS INTO the Trump administration, I was a lightning rod again—and for the dumbest imaginable reason. It all started when Nordstrom abruptly stopped selling the Ivanka Trump fashion brand. It was disappointing to me that the high-end department store chain bowed to pressure from a few loud activists who couldn't even stand the existence of the first daughter's affordable line of clothing and accessories for young, professional women.

Yes, everything was political now, including Ivanka's dresses, jewelry, shoes, and handbags.

On the morning of February 9, I made an off-the-cuff remark on *Fox & Friends,* standing up for the suddenly canceled Ivanka and her clothes. "It's a wonderful line," I said. "I own some of it. I'm going to give a free commercial here: Go buy it today, everybody. You can find it online."

Really, I was just trying to be nice. I wasn't part of some secret marketing program. Ivanka certainly didn't need me to shill for her clothes. But a storm of accusations erupted immediately, including a barrage of claims from Trump critics that I had violated federal ethics rules against endorsing commercial products. I was wrong to have done that, but the malice assigned to me made it seem like the only proper punishment would be the electric chair.

Then Sean Spicer walked into the Briefing Room and told the press I had been "counseled" about my comment on Fox. Almost as soon as that word was out of the press secretary's mouth, President Trump summoned him to the Oval Office and, as I sat there quietly, proceeded to rip him a new one.

"What did you just say?" Trump thundered. "'*Counseled*'?' Like she's a baby. She's been 'counseled'? What does that mean? Who told you to say that?"

Spicer named someone in the White House counsel's office.

"Well, I want to meet him," Trump said. The poor guy soon arrived.

"Why would you say that?" Trump demanded.

"Well, uh, it's a violation," he stammered.

"No," Trump roared. "Why would you tell the press secretary to say that in the briefing? We don't say things like that! She didn't mean that!"

The irony was that I had been standing up for Ivanka in a similar way to how I had tried to explain (but not defend) Spicer and his wild claims about the inauguration crowd.

I went on Fox again that night and told anchor Martha MacCallum, "The president was very gracious and understanding." Then I added that I had *not* been counseled, despite whatever may have been said in the Briefing Room. "I'm the one who does the counseling around here." I also noted how understanding and gracious President Trump had been amidst my flub and "hoped" aloud that working women would have a boss like that at some point in their careers.

"MOUTH LIKE AN effin' machine gun."

That was Donald Trump's latest phrase for me.

He never gave me an official nickname. Thank goodness, I should probably add. I didn't need to join the lineup with Crooked Hillary, Low-Energy Jeb, Lyin' Ted, Little Marco, and Mini Mike Bloomberg. And the way he used his memorable phrase for me—to the rest of the staff, to his old friends from New York and Florida—he clearly intended it as a compliment. But a few people who heard him say it one time too many started to chafe. They were somewhere between petrified to go on TV and pathetic at appearing on it. And so some of them pounced and twisted the president's praise into a passive-aggressive putdown that usually came down to some version of "she's good on TV, but . . ."

They saw me in meetings on the opioid crisis, the Trans-Pacific Partnership, the Supreme Court opening, veterans, immigration, and Obamacare during those early months. They knew better but weren't better. You can't be a good communicator for the president's policies unless you know the policies first. Clearly some of them didn't want another senior advisor to the president who had his ear and respect. They wanted a White House spokesmodel . . . and a mop-up woman.

They really should have been grateful, not scornful, that I was still willing to go on TV and run interference for all these men behaving badly. I was there smoothing things out for everyone from Michael Flynn, Jeff Sessions, and James Comey to Paul Manafort and Jared himself, whose sit-down with a Russian lawyer during the campaign and meeting with a troubled bank during the Trump transition were already under scrutiny as the administration began. And I would happily but honestly do the same thing for Donald Trump, whose Twitter habit and general disdain for "the way things were always done" meant I'd almost certainly have plenty of explaining to do on his behalf when I felt it appropriate. Many times, including in those early months, I refrained from saying everything I was asked to say.

One day, my staff said the president needed me to come to the Oval Office. I took a folder with a list of things I wanted to discuss with him.

"Did you like my tweet?" he asked.

"It took me twelve seconds to get here. Did I miss it?"

He told me the tweet was from earlier that morning. "Yes, I saw it," I said. "It's not in my top one thousand favorites."

"Rupert liked it," he said, referring to media mogul Rupert Murdoch.

"Well," I answered, "Rupert is great, and if I'm ever an eighty-nine-year-old Australian male billionaire, I might like it, too, but I'm not and I don't." Trump needs to tweet like we need to eat. It's all about making better choices. Sometimes I eat a kale salad. Other times my girls and I polish off the brownies. If we do it right, it all balances out.

I always tried to show him that his highest-performing tweets were the ones of substance, breaking news announcements, or when he was telling America what he was doing that day or what he wanted Americans to do. So much of Trump's connection to the American people was built on the unfiltered nature of his communication, via Twitter and other means. To me it was all just part of the conventional nature of Donald Trump the candidate and now Donald Trump the president. On balance, it seemed like a good deal: So early in his presidency, when other new presidents might have been tentative or restrained, he was raring for action and doing an excellent job of being Trump.

Bannon and Kushner started out as buddy-buddies, leaving a preternaturally paranoid Priebus on the outside. Then the alliance shifted to Bannon and Priebus, who must have calculated there was safety in numbers and that their two-thirds would be an even match for one presidential son-in-law. Overall, the buffoonish attempt at one-upmanship led to the jockeying and leaking that plagued the White House and essentially wasted part of the first precious months of a four-year term, to say nothing of the incessant investigations and slew of subpoenas that were raining down on our new White House.

REINCE PRIEBUS WAS the longest-serving chairman of the Republican National Committee and was Donald Trump's handpicked first White House chief of staff. Yet the president's grassroots supporters were still somewhat suspicious of him. As such a longtime Washington insider, he was certainly an unusual choice. He did bring comfort to Senate Majority Leader Mitch McConnell and Speaker of the House Paul

Ryan, who were going to interface with the brand-new president on a regular basis. And, of course, he had told Trump to get out of the race after *Access Hollywood*. But if Trump was on his way to the White House, Reince was certainly going to try to follow him there. Literally. Reince's own chief of staff at the RNC, Katie Walsh, helped him secure that job, as she had at the RNC.

"Reinnnnncccce," as Trump called him, liked to present himself as "just a guy from Kenosha," his wholesome Wisconsin hometown, but he operated more like Edward Scissorhands. As soon as he took over as chief of staff, I knew a knife or two had my name on it. To be fair, it wasn't an easy job Reince was handed. He had Trump family members to placate. He had a headstrong boss, whose effectiveness was partly a function of his own stubbornness. He had a party establishment that, despite Trump's stunning victory, still had plenty of grumblers and mumblers. And he had Jared, Bannon, and me and others also reporting directly to the president. In those first chaotic months, he was navigating nepotism, subpoenas, investigations, and a president he was constantly trying to manage and mollify.

Reince is thoroughly conservative but not remotely MAGA. That distinction became hard to ignore with the Conservative Political Action Conference on the schedule for February 24.

"CPAC is always huge," I reminded Reince. "I hope you will allow a number of people throughout the administration to speak. You should consider going, Reince. I've committed to a prime-time interview with Sean Hannity and a separate sit-down the following day with Mercedes Schlapp."

"That's 'cause you love the crazies, Kellyanne, and they love you," he said. I flashbacked to Reince and me standing next to a screaming crowd of supporters at an airport hangar in North Carolina in late October. I was signing autographs, taking selfies, and chatting up the crowd, while the chairman of the Republican National Committee was hiding behind me. Later he would tell me how amazed he was at how much I loved to be among the people.

"What? Who's 'crazy'?" I asked him now, stupefied that he still didn't get it. "These are the backbone of the movement, many young people, somewhat skeptical of the party actually, but they *love* Trump." Reince relented and spent an hour onstage at CPAC with Steve Bannon.

Naturally, they went together. *The Odd Couple.* Oscar Madison and Felix Unger. One Jared short of a throuple. No one remembers what they said.

Reince mostly stayed out of my way as chief of staff, in part because he had installed half the RNC into the West Wing and in part because I was never a subject of the subpoenas and investigations he was forced to confront. I was surprised one afternoon to look up and see him at my office door. That was unusual.

"Listen," he told me nervously. "There's really no role for you on this trip."

"Excuse me?" I said.

"You know, we need people back here doing stuff," he finished lamely. "There's no role. It's a lot of people."

Trump was heading off on his first foreign trip as president. The itinerary was Saudi Arabia, Jerusalem, and the Vatican—the seats of Islam, Judaism, and Catholicism—and then on to the G7 meeting in Belgium. I'd mostly sworn off international trips, but the timing of this one would work for the family and me.

The pre-trip meetings and the manifests featured dozens of people, some of whom had roles ranging from dubious to duplicative. Sean Spicer, struggling in the job I had turned down, took an entire entourage with him. Romantic couples who had formed on the campaign or in the White House were magically in the manifest of "essential travelers" heading together on the overseas adventure, posing for Instagram and collecting countries.

And Reince thought *I* was redundant?

I could have raised a stink, but for what?

"Sure," I said. "No problem."

Priebus and Bannon ended up being forced to return early. Trump was pissed at them, and the Russia investigation was heating up.

NO ONE STOMPED around the White House like Steve Bannon did. And no one did less work—less *actual work*—while he was there.

How could he? He was far too busy buffing his image in the media, sowing discord among other staffers, and undermining his rivals (real and imagined) in the West Wing.

Steve made plenty of sweeping pronouncements. He pretended to possess scads of secret knowledge. He swaggered like a man who must be running everything. But the more I watched him operate, the more I came to realize how hollow his confidence was. I thought for sure he must be spending quality time in the Oval Office with the president, trading gossip or running the country or something. Then I came to realize the sad reality: The president hardly spent any time with him at all.

Trump was charmed at first, I think, by Bannon's bravado and disdain for official Washington. But it quickly became apparent: The man behind the three shirts and three phones was Oz behind the screen. With so little to back up the bluster and so few fresh ideas that could become policy, Bannon mostly kept busy trying to push the Bannon agenda on those around him—and pretending to hate the press.

"Fuck the media," he often said to me, to others, occasionally to the press, and sometimes just to himself as he walked down the hall. Yet I began to notice he was far cozier with the "fake news" press corps than he ever let on.

A reliable line of reporters stood outside his office door after the West Wing had mostly emptied for the evening, waiting for an audience with the man *Time* magazine had dubbed "The Great Manipulator." I could only imagine the version of White House reality he was peddling to them. I can guarantee you one thing: In the anecdotes he was so eagerly sharing, Steve Bannon was the shadow president, a gift that kept on giving for *Saturday Night Live*. I never heard him say whether he loved the *Time* title or hated it. My strong suspicion is he loved it. Why else would he have a framed copy on his office floor, waiting for someone who knows how to hammer a nail to display it on his wall? I knew Trump didn't love it. He quickly grew wary of aides who seemed too full of themselves.

Journalists also regularly and secretly scurried to Bannon's secret apartment in a state-of-the-art building in Rosslyn, Virginia, where he fed them Chinese food dinners and barrels of bullshit. He'd then take the White House car service from the hideaway apartment, which had a perfectly nice bedroom, to his residence at the "Breitbart Embassy" on Capitol Hill, none of which he paid for out of his own pocket.

Bannon and I had been in a few foxholes together. With Rebekah Mercer, for whom I have deep admiration and affection, we'd tried to shake up some stuck-in-the-mud Republicans and introduce fresh names to the candidate hunt. We both hated the Republican default

Working hard on
the blueberry farm
in Hammonton, NJ,
1987.

Michaela and Marina
Petrongolo and I in our
thirties.

Grandmom
Antoinette,
Grandmom Claire,
Aunt Millie, and I at
the Claridge Hotel &
Casino.

Our wedding party, April 28, 2001, Philadelphia.

The Golden Girls and Uncle Eddie.

My first Mother's Day, with twins Georgie and Claudia.

My father, his sisters, and their kids and grandkids at the twins' first birthday.

Great-aunt Rita and newborn Charlotte Rita.

The Eight Wonders of the DiNatale World: Great-grandchildren Alexa, Astin, Giovanna, Jimmy, George, Claudia, Charlotte, and just-christened Vanessa.

College friends (and tiny tots) celebrating the life of our friend Cathleen Hart. Long Island, 2010.

One of my all-time favorite snaps of the kids. Pure joy.

Rushing to see what
Santa brought!

George's fan club (my parents, his parents, GiGi, and Uncle Joe), outside the U.S. Supreme Court, following oral arguments.

Claudia, Donald Trump, and I in South Carolina ahead of hitching a ride home with Trump on his jet, 2015.

Family and friends gather for Charlotte's first Holy Communion, May 2016.

Boys' Club (and I): backstage at the first presidential debate, Hofstra University, Sep. 26, 2016. *Doug Coulter*

The spin room, following the final presidential debate, Las Vegas, Nevada, October 19, 2016.

Euphoric election! The Guiffras, Donnellys, Abramsons, and others celebrate the improbable.

An overjoyed MAGA voter and proud husband on Election Night.

‹ Recents   Edit

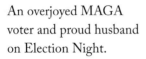

Huma Abedin

Today

2:30 AM   **Incoming Call**   2 minutes

Huma Abedin calls my phone; Hillary Clinton concedes the presidential election to Donald J. Trump. New York City, November 9, 2016.

The president-elect calls me at 4:30 a.m. ahead of my ten TV appearances discussing "what happened."

Mommy and I, January 7, 2017.

Inaugural Ball on my
fiftieth birthday, with
Claudia, January 20, 2017.

The Conway Six all smiles
at the White House garden
tour, September 2017.

The Core Four of my White House Team in 2018: Catharine Cypher, Renee Hudson, Tom Joannou, and I.

POTUS, FLOTUS, and cabinet members for a briefing on the drug crisis.

Georgie, Charlotte, and Vanessa soak in a strategy meeting about trade, in the Oval Office.

Comfort Zone: hanging with the peeps at a Trump Rally, 2018. *Official White House Photo by Shealah Craighead*

Hall of Famer Mariano Rivera, Rob Manfred, Commissioner of MLB, and others meet with President Trump in the Oval Office.

Government shutdown, 2019.

Official White House Photo by Andrea Hanks

Watching the Democrat response and coverage of President Trump's first prime-time Oval Office address. *Official White House Photo by D. Myles Cullen*

First official White House reaction to the Mueller Report, Pebble Beach, May 2019. *Official White House Photo by Andrea Hanks*

Two American heroes return to Normandy seventy-five years later, my seatmates in an Osprey, June 2019.

Georgie, Charlotte, and Vanessa ride on Air Force One for a rally in Wildwood, NJ, January 30, 2020. *Official White House Photo by Tia Dufour*

Addressing the media, White House Press Briefing Room, January 2020.

Daily
Coronavirus
Task Force
meeting in the
White House
Situation
Room, April
2020. *Official*
White House Photo
by D. Myles Cullen

POTUS, VP,
Sec. DeVos,
education
stakeholders, and
I discuss how to
safely return to
school, August
2020. *Official White*
House Photo by Delano
Scott

Vanessa and
Governor Kim
Reynolds at
Terrace Hill,
Iowa Governor's
Residence

A final ride on Marine
One with President
Trump and the First
Lady, following my
prime-time address to
the RNC Convention.

Grandma
Antoinette and
Jesse.

position on presidential nominees: Run the guy who lost to the guy who lost to the other guy. But sharing a partial perspective with someone isn't always enough to make you true allies. Now that we were in the White House, his main job seemed to be building his own fiefdom. He certainly never respected my wish to reduce my media footprint, pressing me to go on TV to showcase talents he lacked.

Several times, Bannon summoned me to his office to scold me. He had four TV screens and three mobile devices going at all times, but no computer with an official White House email, where a record would be created. Hey, hadn't Hillary gotten in trouble for that? Where the rest of us hung family pictures, he hung whiteboard lists of Trump's "promises" and a long list of personal errands he would have his White House staff manage. Bannon fancied himself the four-star general of his own makeshift war room.

"Who, who, who, what, who told you to go on TV today?" he sputtered at me one day, finally looking up from his BlackBerry.

"The president."

"Well, that's not good enough."

Was he joking? Maybe not.

"Why did you say all that stuff?" he demanded.

"Because it's true and people should hear it."

He paused, then had the audacity to say to me, "You're going to get us all in trouble."

I was going to get *him* in trouble? What an ironic premonition that was.

Bannon's tenure at the White House would last six months.

None of it could be called surprising. Early on, Ivanka Trump called from Mar-a-Lago to warn me about being associated with Bannon. That was about the time the president rescinded Bannon's self-gifted seat on the National Security Council. In the understated language of military officials at the White House, it wasn't "all that helpful having him there."

Ivanka's call was an early hint of what a short fuse he was on with the Trump family. She warned me that Steve might reach out to me for support and approval as the walls closed in on him. I was puzzled at first and noted that just the night before, Bannon had been in the Situation Room at Mar-a-Lago while the president gave an order to retaliate against Syrian president Bashar al-Assad for gassing his own people. But I thanked Ivanka for her warning. I didn't do anything dramatic and certainly did not tell anyone. Information is power. I was amassing it here and there, anywhere and everywhere.

One of Trump's biggest selling points was his refreshing lack of political experience. But the flip side of that quality was his occasional blind spots when it came to personnel decisions and political endorsements. He was often too trusting of others who lacked transparency or talent, and insufficiently skeptical of those who were pushing the wrong people as candidates for office or as colleagues in the administration. I won some of those arguments and lost some.

Trump's guilelessness left him fuming over Senator John McCain's reluctance to embrace the Republican effort to repeal Obamacare. McCain's own presidential run was a distant bad memory, given Trump's swift rise and triumph, which included winning many swing voters and swing states that McCain had not won. The two had an oft-acrimonious relationship, punctuated by some personal insults. But Trump was still baffled by McCain's refusal to take a stand as the critical vote drew near, especially since the Arizona senator had voted against the Obama administration's push to pass the Affordable Care Act.

"I don't understand these guys," Trump said to me. "They voted to repeal and replace Obamacare thirty-six times, but Obama was never going to say 'Oh, great idea. Put that on my desk. Let's repeal Obamacare.' Now I'm here. Ran on that in part . . . but we can't get their votes! Why is that? Why is McCain giving me a hard time?"

"It may be philosophical," I suggested, though I had my doubts. I wanted the president to consider the subtext. It was time for me to put my familiarity with the deep end of the swamp to good use.

"Look," I said, "there are maybe thirty, forty people max in this country right now who are Republicans who have run for president or who believe they could be president or who have been told by people, 'You should be president.' And then there are the other three hundred and thirty million of us. So, if you're one of those thirty-five people, you, at some point, recently pictured yourself sitting behind the Resolute Desk. Not only are they not here, sir, but improbably, Donald Trump is. It's going to take people a minute to process that."

Trump did, in fact, win over some of his fiercest challengers for the 2016 nomination. He ended up having good relations with Ted Cruz, Marco Rubio, and Rand Paul, to name a few. Lindsey Graham fancies himself a BFF. Mike Huckabee was a solid ally, and his daughter, Sarah Huckabee Sanders, was the best White House press secretary during Trump's tenure. Rick Perry and Ben Carson served in his cabinet. Whether elected or appointed, the smarter career pols learned early on that one of the worst things to say to President Trump was "no one's ever tried that before" or "that's not the way they do it in Washington or on Capitol Hill."

The easy and obvious retort was "Well, that's why I got elected."

PRESIDING OVER IT all, lingering at a safe distance yet constantly nudging everyone, was the duke of 1600 Pennsylvania Avenue, Jared Kushner.

Jared was shrewd and calculating. There was no subject he considered beyond his expertise. Criminal justice reform. Middle East peace. The southern and northern borders. Veterans and opioids. Big Tech and small business. If Martian attacks had come across the radar, he would have happily added them to his ever-bulging portfolio. He'd have made sure you knew he'd exiled the Martians to Uranus and insisted he did not care who got the credit for it. He misread the Constitution in one crucial respect, thinking that all power not given to the federal government was reserved to *him*. He never put it like that exactly, not in so many words. But that was how he always carried himself, secure in the knowledge that no matter how disastrous a personnel change or legislative attempt may be, he was highly unlikely to be held accountable for it.

I couldn't help but wonder if he were projecting when he stopped me in the hallway outside the Oval one day early on, "No one knows what you actually do here! They see you on the covers of magazines but don't know what you do," said the man who had posed for the cover of *Time* and *Fortune* magazines. "You're at a fucking two. We need you at a ten." I was stunned. Before I could even defend myself or explain what I was working on, he kept walking.

The economy of Jared's words did not match the enormity of his power. He could breeze in and out of any meeting he fancied, never taking a single written note. He is a man of knowing nods, quizzical looks, and sidebar inquiries.

Jared was part dreamer, part schemer, dipping in and out of discussions, adding himself at will to national security briefings and domestic and international trips, and undertaking secret, impromptu lobbying of his father-in-law in the private residence. I came to see that one problem with Jared was his floating in and out—Bannon had described Jared Kushner to the *New York Times* as "air"—but he was also *heir*, married to the president's daughter. If drop-in privileges were a gold card, Jared's was platinum. His preference for talking to the president off-campus and off-hours meant duties normally assigned to Senate-confirmed cabinet members suddenly became his, or policy processes that had been months in the making would be unilaterally scuttled with little explanation and even less emotion.

"Jared asked us to hold off." That was all the explanation required to stop a major policy initiative in its tracks.

Normally, one amasses experience before one amasses power, especially in Washington. There bald heads and gray heads reign supreme. It was attractive and persuasive to the electorate that President Trump had no Washington experience, but less charming that top members of his "brain trust" had none.

Chapter 21

How to Spot a Leaker

W ith their sprawling staffs and fragile yet bloated egos, some of the early, biggest players in the White House, including Jared, finally settled on a way to undermine my credibility with the president.

They accused me of being a leaker.

And not just a leaker—*the* leaker, as if the White House had only one.

They began by whispering to colleagues that I could not be trusted. I couldn't be allowed to attend certain meetings because of my propensity to leak. Then, sure enough, the details of those very meetings would show up in the media, even though I wasn't anywhere near the room. They fingered me as a leaker while they were whispering to *Politico*, feeding *Axios*, plying the *Post* and the *Times* with juicy little nuggets, and spilling incendiary charges or spinning incredulous tales to Michael Wolff, Josh Green, and other book authors, the exact authors the president had specifically directed staffers to avoid.

Leaking, as that's known.

People I'd known for years began calling me, dumbfounded.

"Be careful," they warned me.

"Careful of what?" I asked.

"If you're leaking, be careful," they said.

"Thanks, but I'm not leaking."

Anyone who knew me but wasn't unnerved by my access and power knew the Kellyanne-is-a-leaker gossip was ridiculous. But I kept hearing echoes of the leaker smear. One of Jared's assistants, essential on those overseas trips and himself an Olympic-grade leaker, even called my assistant when I showed up for a meeting. It was a meeting, by the way, that the invited outside participants had asked me to attend since I'd worked with them in the pre-MAGA conservative movement for decades.

The assistant wanted to make sure I didn't "leak the meeting," probably because that was one of *his* jobs. Then Jared's assistant asked: "Can Kellyanne talk about the meeting and initiative on TV?"

Yes, some days these people couldn't even decide if they wanted me speak up or shut up . . . or both!

It spilled over to anchors and book authors, some of whom repeated that I was a leaker even though they had evidence to the contrary. They did not even have my contact info, while exchanging missives with others in the White House on encrypted apps. Other reporters, including those who were Bannon regulars, would tease nervously when I was called a leaker, "Hey, why are you holding out on me?" The president, too busy to recall whether I was or was not in a particular meeting, would later seek my counsel anyway. He'd quickly fill me in on whatever I may have missed, and I would proceed to have my one-on-one audience with the chief decision-maker, whether in the West Wing, the East Wing, or on the phone.

All these attempts to diminish or discredit me: All they did was create a bigger, bolder Kellyanne. Then, one day, the president called me into the office. The Kellyanne-is-leaking talk had finally reached him.

DONALD TRUMP HATED leaks.

That alone didn't make the forty-fifth president any different from his predecessors. All presidents hate leaks. Leaks are embarrassing. Leaks are often half-true. Leaks make the president look like he isn't fully in control. Leaks are rocket fuel for the infighting and jockeying that are part of any presidential administration. When a White House starts leaking, it usually means the staffers are more focused on their own agendas and reputations than on advancing the agenda and reputation of the president.

So why was the White House so leaky? It's not that hard to understand.

For White House staffers, leaking is an easy way of sucking up to the press, and there's no denying it can be effective. How do you think Steve Bannon's mug ended up on the cover of *Time* magazine . . . because Bradley Cooper was too busy? Leaking is like paying protection money to the mob. Thankful for the leaks, reporters tend to write more flatteringly about the leakers. Leaks can also undermine your rivals. Wouldn't you rather the reporters trash *them* in print instead of you? Why not help with a few morsels of inside info? That's what motivated much of the administration's leaking, calculations far more selfish and pedestrian than some grand theory about "the people's right to know."

In Donald Trump's view, leakers were traitors and weaklings. But what exactly was he supposed to do about all the White House leaking— other than complain about it and try to smoke out the leakers? And that wasn't as easy as you might think.

Leakers can be devious, and they certainly were with Trump. The actual leakers provided the president with the names of suspected leakers, normally young men and women he did not know well and who could not walk into the Oval Office and defend themselves. Colleagues spent hours paranoidly scouring press accounts for "anonymous sources" and "background quotes," trying to match what people said in private meetings with what they must have been telling the media. This led some people to appropriate other people's private comments publicly, hoping to implicate them. With Reince in charge, little was done to the real leakers, since he had so many people spread across the West Wing protecting and advancing his image, often I believed through leaks.

The bigwigs all had their favorite reporters to leak to, and also had underlings who were ready to leak for them. Fewer fingerprints that way. What would MAGA think if they could see this, Bannon all comfy with the press at home and at the office while calling them "the enemy of the people" in front of MAGA?

One day, a sobbing midlevel staffer named Cliff Sims was confronted in the White House counsel's office for leaking. Priebus, Spicer, and Mike Dubke, who were already trying to get rid of him, relented and let him stay. But he petered out for other reasons and then wrote a book long on self-promotion and short on facts. It earned him a brutal Trump Tweet Takedown, and a lawsuit.

As the president grew more and more frustrated with the leaks,

Reince finally decided he needed to do something—or at least appear to. He announced a new rule for the entire West Wing senior staff. From now on, he decreed one bright spring day, we would all have to leave our personal cell phones in a secure location before we went to our offices.

"It's a matter of national security," Reince declared, even as we all knew it was a matter of his job security.

You can imagine how well this decree went over with the senior White House staff. I gently informed Reince that the other West Wing moms and I might need a daily reprieve akin to a smoke break around 3 p.m., the witching hour when kids bust out of school and have a list of questions, complaints, demands, and announcements for their moms. That's check-in time for children and their moms everywhere.

The chief of staff chuckled. "Can't your kids call your desk phone?"

"Does the school nurse call Sally on a desk phone? Do the kids?"

"Sally who?" Reince asked.

"Sally, your wife."

I took seriously the charge that China may have been using our personal cell phones as "microphones," but I wasn't removing from my small children's small hands their lifeline to Mom. Not while Bannon had three personal phones in his possession at all times—for babysitting his pals in the press but definitely not for child rearing. He often carried on conversations on multiple phones at once. You could hear him through his open office door.

"Just a second, just a second," he'd rasp to one of his callers while he finished a sentence with another, leaving everyone—the people on the phone calls and the random office eavesdroppers—wondering exactly who was being addressed in these mosh-pit calls.

It was right around then that the White House frenzy over leaks got personal for me.

I was attending a birthday swim party with Charlotte and Vanessa in New Jersey when a nonpolitical friend of mind sent me a link to a gossipy article. It said that I was about to be edged out of my White House job. Of course, it included "anonymous sources" and background quotes praising the phenomenal work being done by the Three Stooges. It also mentioned how frustrated they had grown with me. All I could do was smile. The rumor of my impending demise had been floated (leaked!) to select reporters by the usual suspects ever since the night Trump won the presidency and hugged me with one arm while grinning and pointing at me with the other arm on the stage at the New York Hilton, in a photo splashed across newspapers worldwide.

The article was partially right. Big personnel changes were in fact on the horizon, but the blood in the water wasn't mine.

Before that happened, however, Trump called me into the Oval Office. I was standing. He was sitting. He shot me an icy stare across the desk.

"You know," he said, "some people think you are the leaker."

"Well, Mr. President," I said. "Do you think so?"

"No," he said. "No, but people are saying that."

I knew I had to confront it directly.

"Mr. President," I said, "part of my job is to provide information to the media. That's not leaking. That's often a demand coming directly from you. Other times you do it yourself." I said that was why we sometimes affectionately referred to him as "Leaker-in-Chief."

I continued: "If you ever think I'm *a* leaker—let alone *the* leaker—I'll walk out the front door immediately. I won't even walk upstairs to get the kids' pictures off my wall."

His glare softened at that. "No, no," he said. "You are going to be here all eight years. I'm just telling you what people are saying."

Under the circumstances, I was happy to hear him say that. It was always his way of warning me what others were saying about me.

"Sir," I continued, "I spend hours on TV and on the White House driveway, speaking to the press in full view, often cleaning up the messes other people in this place make."

He half-smiled. He knew all too well how true that was. He'd seen me out there, refusing to flinch as the media fired fusillade after fusillade at me and about him. The truth was, I had learned to be unbothered by most of it, including its predictability. My audience was never the anchor or the reporter anyway. It wasn't the other people in the White House. My intended audience wasn't even the so-called audience of one, the president. Others tried to impress and flatter him through their TV appearances; I had direct access to him and didn't need to do that. My audience was always the *people*, the ones hoping they were forgotten no more. The ones whose opinions I'd been listening to for decades. The ones who had a right to access information from elected officials without paying to access a political fundraiser. The ones I had taken an oath to serve, the ones this president was here to help through his policies.

Motherhood and maturity had been clarifying for me. The commitment to my position in the White House and the commitment to my four beautiful babies were the two "big deals" in my life, not the stupid gotcha games people in Washington wanted to play.

Trump shook his head ruefully. He knew about all that. He knew about the lack of discipline on the staff and the human vacuum cleaners that White House reporters had become. He knew the damage that had already been done to his administration's crucial first one hundred days. Instead of daily proactive messaging on policy initiatives like tax and regulatory reform, infrastructure, healthcare, and border security, we were caught up in the soap opera of who was up, who was down, and who was gunning for someone else's job.

He knew I had been on the receiving end of those stories.

"We have these leaks," Trump said, stating the obvious, though now I was his ally again, not his potential target.

"Yes, we do," I agreed, noting the unconscionable public disclosures of his conversations with the leaders of Australia and Mexico, which had the set the tone for his administration right at the start. I reminded him that I hadn't been party to either conversation, nor had I seen the transcripts. Most of the leaks had been petty and personal. Tiffs and rivalries. But none was too small to become a five-alarm fire for a thirsty press still pretending they had not embarrassed themselves in missing the rise of Trump and his election to the presidency.

My credibility with the president was solid, I believed. Standing in front of his desk, I made a mental tick list of the dozens of events, statements, and situations I'd been privy to that would have made for great salacious leaks, nuggets that could have driven the news for days. They may have gotten me more money to write this book, but I'd kept all that quiet and would continue to do so. I was a trained lawyer and seasoned secret-keeper who understood the value of confidentiality. My knowledge bank included what my colleagues on the campaign and in the administration really thought of each other. I knew that this senior aide couldn't stand that senior aide. I knew which prominent officeholder had said of Jared, "That young man doesn't finish anything."

Ditto for members of the press and Congress, who would let loose on colleagues and competitors privately and then phonily "collaborate" moments later. I would hold my fire and take my shot—if and when I needed to someday. I'd also witnessed what happened when something leaked from a small group. Whoever was on the receiving end of the embarrassing information would combust, then redeploy the West Wing to do damage control. These dramas were easier than changing monetary policy or learning how to replace the Trans-Pacific Partnership (TPP).

"I'm going to light up 'Princess Ivanka,'" Bannon said menacingly one Friday evening in March after anchors from CNN and ABC were calling me to confirm that Trump had told Bannon and Priebus they couldn't go as scheduled with him to Florida that weekend. He blamed Ivanka for leaking that. The whole sad affair was "breaking news" to me, since I had actually been in a big meeting on healthcare most of the day with Speaker Ryan, other members of Congress, administration officials, and White House staff in the Eisenhower Executive Office Building (EEOB).

Doing my job, in other words.

The seats at that meeting assigned to Reince, Jared, and Steve were empty. None of them bothered to walk over to the Eisenhower Executive Office Building, where the meeting was being held. They were focused on Attorney General Sessions's recusal from the Russian investigation the night before, leaked to the media.

Some of this leaking frenzy, I told the president before I wrapped up our conversation on the topic, had a gender component. "Women spend their entire careers trying to amass power, and then struggle to keep it," I explained. "Information is power. The idea that I would just squander it to curry favor with a twentysomething reporter is foolish.

"Keep an eye out for that," I added.

As our meeting drew to a congenial close, I offered the president some useful perspective.

"You really want to know how to spot a leaker?" I asked.

He nodded.

"Follow my four-point plan."

1. Leakers get great press from the reporters they leak to. It's called returning the favor. That is clearly not me, who is a constant victim of nasty, untrue headlines.

2. Leakers try to shroud their leaking behind vitriolic attacks on the press. The more someone uses the phrases "fake news" and "enemy of the people," the more likely that person is to leak.

3. Leakers are shameless flatterers. Often, they bat their eyes in adoration just before they make the call. The thicker a supposed friend lays on the compliments, the more likely that person is to be secretly smearing you. "I don't know how you handle the media like you do," was a compliment I got often . . . from a high-ranking colleague who was texting and talking with media all day and spending too many evenings with them, too.

4. Leakers are self-aggrandizers, inevitably at the expense of the person they were ostensibly serving. They are the ones insisting off the record that they are really in charge, not the president.

Meanwhile, the granddaddy of all Washington leaking was just then getting ready to explode.

AS FAR AS I could tell, no one liked FBI director James Comey.

Dumbfounded Democrats thought his late October comments on Hillary Clinton's email had cost her the 2016 election. Now a lot of Republicans were convinced that Comey had a vendetta against Trump over claims of Russian collusion in the same race. Before Trump fired Comey on May 9, Jared had persuaded him that the move would, at worst, be a political wash—and both sides might secretly be glad the priggish FBI director was bum-rushed out the door. Bannon referred to it as the biggest mistake in modern political history.

Comey's firing provoked instant outrage, a frantic afternoon that led into a frenzied night. I'd just landed back in D.C. from a day on the road dealing with the opioid crises in New Hampshire and Maine and was headed back out early the next morning to do the same in Ohio and Michigan. But with Comey's firing making headlines, the president wanted us all on TV. I went on CNN and provided information to an eye-rolling Anderson Cooper. Whatever Anderson asked, I kept coming back to a scathing memo from Deputy Attorney General Rod Rosenstein recommending that Comey be fired. It remains one of my favorite documents of my White House tenure.

"I cannot defend the Director's handling of the conclusion of the investigation of Secretary Clinton's emails, and I do not understand his refusal to accept the nearly universal judgment that he was mistaken," Rosenstein, who had recently been overwhelmingly confirmed to the number two spot at Justice and had worked with Comey for years, wrote. "Almost everyone agrees that the director made serious mistakes. It is one of the few issues that unites people of diverse perspectives."

Comey's handling of the investigation, Rosenstein wrote, is "a textbook example of what federal prosecutors and agents are taught not to do." Rosenstein quoted half a dozen other top Justice Department officials denouncing Comey's behavior and then summed up: "The way the Director handled the conclusion of the email investigation was wrong. As a result, the FBI is unlikely to regain public and congressional trust until it has a Director who understands the gravity of the mistakes and pledges never to repeat them. Having refused to admit his errors, the Director cannot be expected to implement the necessary corrective actions."

Back in the dining room off the Oval, I sat with the president as he met with the lawyers and fielded calls. Principal Deputy Press Secretary Sarah Huckabee Sanders was on the TV, discussing the Comey firing with Fox News' Tucker Carlson. Reince walked in, stressed as usual. The president pointed to the TV.

"Reince," he said, "look at her. Listen to her. She's doing such a good job. I don't know about Spicer. I don't know."

Reince immediately put distance between himself and his longtime colleague and supposed friend. "Oh yeah," he said. "I know. Sean's gotta go to military duty soon. We'll be seeing more and more of Sarah at the briefings and all."

I jerked my head around to lock eyes with Reince. Just a little while earlier that night, the media had unfairly dissed Spicer for hiding in the bushes. But here I was, staring at the real snake in the grass.

*   *   *

IF ANYONE KNEW how to leak, it was James Comey.

Comey got a friend to put out an internal FBI memo that Comey had written. It recounted a private conversation the FBI director had with Donald Trump on February 14, Valentine's Day, less than a month after Comey's first visit to the White House and a day after the president had fired Michael Flynn as national security advisor. Trump said Flynn had lied to Mike Pence about a conversation Flynn had with Sergey Kislyak, the Russian ambassador to the United States. Got all that straight? According to Comey's memo, Trump said Flynn was a good guy and urged the FBI director to "let go" of potential criminal charges. But once the Comey memo was leaked, all hell broke loose. People started panicking. The Justice Department began to investigate. Because Attorney General Sessions had recused himself months earlier, Rosenstein appointed former FBI director Robert Mueller as special counsel to investigate.

All this was a total lie, as Mueller's drawn-out investigation would ultimately make clear. Russians didn't alter the result of the 2016 election, a fact that was confirmed by President Obama's director of national intelligence, James Clapper, and a bipartisan Senate report. The Trump campaign didn't collude with any foreign power in violation of U.S. law. Hillary Clinton lost all on her own, the same way Donald Trump had won. No investigation was going to turn any of that around. But we sure could waste a lot of time between here, there, and Trump's inevitable exoneration.

The phony Russian collusion delusion illusion would end up being a huge letdown for the president's enemies in the Democrat Party and the party's standing auxiliary, the national media. There was no *there* there, and even Mueller would eventually make that clear. There would be subpoenas and investigations, prosecutions and peripheral guilty pleas, leaks and more leaks and more leaks. The real shame is the huge diversion of time and resources from delivering for the American people. The "investigation" would end up interfering with more than 60 percent of Donald Trump's presidency but, alas, without the indictments and convictions of Trump and his family that so many had promised on cable TV.

As the Mueller investigation heated up, I was encouraged by the legal advice the other Conway was quick to dispense. Before George was tapping out tweets against the president, he was trying to help the president by furnishing memos for him, calling the investigation the "*Seinfeld* Scandal," meaning a scandal about nothing. The president ended up calling George about his memo. George's friend Bob Giuffra, who had worked on investigations and oversight for Republicans in the U.S. Senate, personally came to the Oval Office to offer Trump advice and help find him counsel.

In the meantime, we had a country to run, and had better get busy running it.

Part V

Family Values

Chapter 22

But George Doesn't Tweet

Did you know about this?" Sean Spicer asked as he bounded toward me in the East Room of the White House on June 5, while President Trump was speaking about privatizing the nation's air traffic control system.

Sean had his phone out. Twitter was open. On the screen was a tweet that was supposedly written by my husband, George.

"That's not possible," I said. "George doesn't tweet."

Yet there it was: a one-line post from @GTConway3d. The message was a little obtuse, but it was clearly taking a jab at Trump, saying that the president's tweeting was complicating efforts by the Office of the Solicitor General to defend the administration's travel ban on countries with a history of exporting terrorism. The issue was in front of the U.S. Supreme Court.

George's exact wording: "These tweets may make some ppl feel better but they certainly won't help OSG [Office of the Solicitor General] get 5 votes in SCOTUS, which is what actually matters. Sad."

"Sad"? Was that a harbinger of things to come? I tried calling George and texting him, hoping maybe his account had been hacked. No answer. And the questions were already flying around in my head. Why had George done that? Why hadn't he mentioned it to me beforehand? And was this tweet really posted by my Trump-loving, MAGA-cap-wearing husband, George Conway?

I can't emphasize enough how out of character it was for him to *be* on a public platform like Twitter, much less offering even a small critique of the president he'd always spoken so highly of, a president who also happened to be his wife's boss. Assuming this *was* from George, why not so much as a "Honey, we need to talk"? While the tweet itself was fairly mundane, the duplicity of it stung me. Of course it did. And the mere fact that George was my husband meant that his slap at the president was sure to generate attention and traction it never would have gotten otherwise.

In fact, I learned later, George was so excited about his Twitter debut that he called Bob Giuffra, to ask if Bob had seen the tweet. I don't think George got the reaction he was expecting. Bob's wife, Joyce, had volunteered on the Trump campaign, and the two of them were at the Hilton celebrating Trump's win. Bob told me in a phone call that he'd admonished George for being disrespectful to both me and my boss and told him to delete the tweet.

George did and then promptly posted another string of tweets declaring that he "VERY, VERY STRONGLY" supported the president, the Trump administration, its policies, and "of course, my wonderful wife." But then he tacked on another message to his fellow Trump supporters that seemed to double down on the criticism he was making in the first tweet: "those that support him, as I do" need to reinforce the fact that tweets have legal consequences.

Which meant that now George's tweets would have consequence.

The usual gossip boys and girls sprang into action, filing breathless dispatches about the "husband of Kellyanne Conway" and his sudden flurry of anti-Trump tweets. The president saw the story on TV that night and called me while I was in the middle of a strategy dinner about school choice, asking, "What's going on?"

I told him I didn't know exactly, but that it made no sense. I tried to hide my discomfort.

Trump knew firsthand that the media turned every little blip in his administration into a five-alarm fire. But George's tweeting, like the president's own tweeting, spoke for itself. When I did finally get George on the phone, he didn't seem the least bit chagrined about any of it. He said he was just expressing his opinion, an opinion he thought had merit. He said he didn't understand why it was such a big deal.

Our older kids certainly did. Claudia and Georgie, finishing up the sixth grade, noticed the media coverage or at least the social media coverage of the media coverage. A wise-beyond-his-years Georgie told me that "Dad shouldn't do that." When I FaceTimed the kids in Alpine that evening from Washington, Claudia instinctively sensed I was out of sorts. Still on camera with me, she walked into the master bedroom and announced sarcastically, "Nice tweet, Dad."

IN ALL OF 2016, which had been dubbed the "Year of the Tweet," George Conway had sent out a grand total of zero tweets. *Zero.* He did have a Twitter account, but he had minimal followers and never seemed the slightest bit inclined to spend the hours it would have taken to keep up a social media presence.

A zest for living life offline instead of online was one of the many things my husband of fifteen years and I had in common. We didn't have accounts on Facebook or Instagram. We shared photos of our children privately with family, almost never beyond that. The only exception was our family Christmas card—and what a comical endeavor that was every year, getting everyone to pose for one decent shot! Beginning in 2016, the media typically recycled the same photo of the six of us from a Yankees game in 2015 because there were no other good options. I have never been a social media mom, reporting on our children's latest triumphs and curating images of our perfect family tableau. George and I were of a single mind that our young family was blessed to have such a fabulous, joyful life. We had no particular need to prove it or convince anyone else.

All of that made George's motivation so perplexing to me. And then there was the timing, which was simply bizarre. He was very supportive of his wife and our president. We'd committed to D.C. as a couple. Our lives were just about to return to semi-normal.

A few days earlier, I had moved into the house we had recently purchased in D.C. on a quiet block near Embassy Row. I was sleeping on an air mattress with the windows open in the lower-level apartment to escape the smell of floors being stained and walls being painted. In mere weeks, the kids would finish school and a new adventure for the Conway Six would begin. After months of commuting back and forth from New Jersey every weekend and kissing my children good night on FaceTime, our family would be together again, starting our new life as Washingtonians.

By then, George already knew he was not going to be the next U.S. solicitor general, the job he had really had his eye on in the Trump administration. Those hopes were dashed when Trump tapped Noel Francisco, a partner from the Jones Day law firm, to be the nation's top lawyer on cases before the U.S. Supreme Court. Though mentioned here and there, George's name had never really been in the running, which did not stop the media from insisting he was being seriously considered. It wasn't a snub, and George was offered another prestigious position in the administration, assistant attorney general in charge of the Justice Department's civil division. That was a big job, too, dependent on Senate confirmation, and one George had accepted and for which he began to interview staff. Some people got George spun up because they were worried about what some senators with long memories might think about his involvement in the impeachment of Bill Clinton. Then George withdrew his name from nomination three days before his tweet. The reasons he gave were practical, not political.

His gracious no-thank-you letter mirrored all our private discussions, emphasizing that this just wasn't a good time for George or our family to have both of us in demanding federal jobs. "Kellyanne and I continue to support the president and his administration," George wrote, "and I look forward to doing so in whatever way I can from outside government."

I felt slightly guilty that our move to the nation's capital, albeit a mutual decision, meant that George's decades-long tenure with the Wachtell Lipton law firm would end. I had marveled at the first-in-class law practice established by four young lawyers who built a powerhouse law firm often regarded as top tier in the world. George was fortunate to be there. I appreciated being a Wachtell Lipton wife and felt welcome.

I resuscitated for George the prospect of being a judge, made more possible by a Republican president who'd promised to nominate constitutionalists to the federal bench and who favored educational credentials like George's. "Central casting" for the courts under President Trump included Harvard undergrad and Yale Law School. The one strike against George could be the Left's fury or fright that he might satisfy one of *their* "central casting" criterion. "Get on a [U.S.] circuit court, honey," I'd say to him, "then be the first Asian American on the Supremes."

All so sweet. So why that tweet?

My first theory about the flurry of tweets—after *evil hacker*—was *bruised heart*. It couldn't have been about Trump, whom George just confirmed he supported and had tried to help in the early weeks after Mueller was appointed special counsel. So, it must have been me. That was terrifying. Did he regret saying we'd all move to D.C. and now expect me to break my commitments and follow his new whim? Was George perturbed that I'd been getting so much attention in the news? I knew he was proud of me, but was there another, darker side to that?

Whatever he was feeling, it still seemed to be in flux. It wasn't like he was hate-tweeting every day. The first few months after the move down to Washington, he mostly spoke like a Trump supporter and kept coming to enjoyable or exclusive White House events (Fall Garden Tour, Halloween) as a guest of Donald and Melania Trump and as my plus-one. But a point had been made. An impression had been left with the media. And they were going to get to the bottom of this, even if they had to imagine half of it.

By now, the ever-thirsty, one-track media had their sights on what they presumed to be a fault line running through my family. The stories about George's initial tweets vaporized quickly in a news cycle. But our marriage became a beat for gossip columnists, content churners, and the trolls who concluded that my personal life was "news" and that reporting on it might make their own miserable lives somehow more bearable. The White House reporters were also zeroing in on that part of the story. That was especially distressing to me. The White House press corps were supposedly among the best in the business, hard-driving, hard-boiled, fact-based journalists who had clawed their way to one of the higher-profile and most demanding postings anywhere. Some of them truly were. Yet they started following George on Twitter and placed him on Google Alerts.

Where did that leave me? Still confused.

Was this just a passing eruption? Was my marriage in some genuine peril? There was no law that said husbands and wives needed to agree about everything. Certainly not in my life or my house. Some of my dearest friends, including a few of the ladies who had hosted the January 7 congratulatory celebration, were not fans of the president and had voted for Hillary. We adore each other outside of politics and have been in foxholes together and raising our children devoid of political considerations or conversations. Yet George had been an unabashed DJT and KAC supporter. I didn't want to believe it. Still, I couldn't help but feel that the issue had more to do with trust and respect and openness than it did with political analysis. But frankly, I really didn't know what I was dealing with or what, if anything, might be coming next.

My discomfort shared space with my disappointment.

For the first time since George and I had gotten serious, I was looking at the possibility that the man who had always had my back might one day stab me in it. Was that too improbable to consider? I grew angry with myself for even thinking it. *Stop it; that's unfair to George.* Every marriage has its own rhythms, I know, its high notes and lows. My husband's loyalty and respect had been a treasured constant for me, and from what I could tell already from office politics at 1600 Pennsylvania Avenue, I was going to need all the unconditional love and support I could get.

I HAD READ Trump right. Sean Spicer's days were numbered. He was gone on July 21, replaced by his principal deputy, Sarah Huckabee Sanders. Sean wasn't fired. He resigned in protest over the hiring of Anthony Scaramucci, who as the new communications director took one half of Spicer's title. The fact that Reince Priebus couldn't save Spicer, his longtime aide, and couldn't block the arrival of the freewheeling and self-confident Scaramucci certainly didn't bode well for Reince's longevity. One week later, Reince was out.

The president was taking a mulligan. Six months into his presidency, he'd ordered a do-over on his own chief of staff. In tapping John F. Kelly, a four-star U.S. Marine Corps general and a Gold Star dad, Trump was choosing a generational peer whose hiring signaled the arrival of something akin to military discipline.

General Kelly had been confirmed by the Senate as secretary of the Department of Homeland Security, 88 to 11. His confirmation marked the very start of the administration, coming on January 20, shortly after the inauguration ceremonies. General Kelly was central to helping Trump get an early jump on priorities like border security, building the wall at the U.S.-Mexico border, stopping the flow of drugs, and combating domestic terrorism. It made perfect sense that a man who had led multiple tours in Iraq and ran the U.S. Southern Command could handle this next tour of duty as White House chief of staff.

The changing of the guard in the chief's office capped an unusually frenetic two weeks—and set up another frenetic week. A few days earlier, I'd been at a small dinner in the White House residence with the president and the First Lady. The newly appointed Scaramucci and I were the only staffers there, bookending the first couple on one side of the table. On the other side were Fox News host Sean Hannity, two of the three *Fox & Friends* hosts, Ainsley Earhardt and Brian Kilmeade, and one-fifth of *The Five* cast, Kimberly Guilfoyle.

Later, the six of us, everyone but the Trumps, sat outside at Del Frisco's restaurant at City Center to continue the conversation over drinks before the Fox folks had to fly back to New York. We ran into senior advisor Stephen Miller, who joined us. When our drinks arrived, I noticed that Scaramucci had drifted away from the table. I texted him, then texted him again when the New Yorkers said they needed to leave soon, then went to see if everything was okay with Anthony.

That's when I found him huddled in a nearby corner, talking agitatedly into his phone. It was that call and his profanity-laced tirade about Steve Bannon that was quickly published in *The New Yorker* and put Scaramucci in the media bull's-eye before half the staff had even learned how to spell his name.

On Saturday morning, I was at the Jersey Shore with my family when Trump called. "Kel, can you tell Anthony I want Harvard Business School Anthony, not gutter-mouth Anthony?"

I laughed at that. I knew exactly what Trump meant. "I'll call him, Mr. President."

"Geez, that mouth," Trump said.

I'd heard those three words many times from the president but almost always applied to me, often following a TV appearance or an especially spirited meeting. But this time I was pretty sure he was referring to Scaramucci. After promising I'd call Anthony, I complimented the president on promoting General Kelly to chief and said I looked forward to working with him.

"That guy's a four-star general," Trump said. "This will be great."

He then invited me to the White House movie theater to join a small group that night viewing the new film *Dunkirk*, followed by dinner at the Trump International Hotel.

"Can you please call John Kelly and invite him to the movie tonight, him and his wife?" Trump asked.

"Sure, Mr. President."

"And you're coming, right?"

"Okay, I . . ."

"Come, the movie's great. Talk to John. Wilbur and Steve are already coming with their wives." Wilbur Ross was commerce secretary. Steven Mnuchin was Treasury secretary.

I'd prefer to be in this bathing suit and cover-up as long as possible, I thought to myself, making a sour face at the thought of putting on makeup and heels and once again leaving the family behind. But the way I heard the invitation, it was an offer I couldn't really refuse. I stopped being a brat in a bikini and tried to get about the get-together. I called the White House switchboard to contact General Kelly, who was declining most calls, since he'd just been named chief and was being deluged. After I reached him and then separately reached Scaramucci to deliver Trump's message, I finally went outside to inform the head of my Secret Service detail about the change of plans.

He said, sorry, you can't do that. They weren't staffed for a sudden move.

"What? That can't be!" I exclaimed.

"That's how it must be."

"What am I supposed to tell the president?"

"Just tell him what I told you."

I wasn't about to fight with my Secret Service detail.

The president, his new chief, my friends Louise Linton and Hilary Geary Ross and their husbands, the secretaries of the Treasury and commerce, respectively, all had a lovely time that night—without me.

I stayed down at the shore and had a great night with the kids and did a Sunday show from my house instead. *Fox News Sunday*'s Chris Wallace asked if Anthony Scaramucci and I would be reporting to the new chief.

Of course we would, I replied, almost shrugging my shoulders. To me that was a given. Neither Chris nor I could have anticipated how relevant his question was.

*   *   *

THE PERSONNEL PURGES continued the very next day. The day began with a gracious Reince Priebus introducing his successor at the daily senior staff meeting. John Kelly was sworn in as chief of staff in the Oval Office. Between that event and a previously scheduled cabinet meeting an hour later, he fired Scaramucci.

Anthony ran up to my office after the cabinet meeting he did not attend and said, "I just got fired."

"What?" I was caught completely off guard. The brand-new chief of staff had fired the communications director? Already? "Go talk to the president," I said.

"I can't," Anthony said. "Kelly said Trump signed off on it, and they are escorting me off the property."

I was sad—especially for Anthony, who was endearingly referred to as *the Mooch*. He and I had had some entertaining meals together before we were official colleagues, dropping "I get you" references from our Italian American upbringings, talking about our kids and how best to communicate the president's policies and priorities. He was smart and savvy, and I didn't find him overly vulgar. Yes, he had a mouth on him, but who was I to take offense at that?

Obviously, General/Chief Kelly looked at it differently. He assembled us in the Roosevelt Room for another senior staff meeting at 1 p.m. He announced the Scaramucci news and vowed ominously, "More changes are coming." When Kelly proclaimed he would get rid of the leakers, Steve Bannon, a serial leaker, was nodding so emphatically (and nervously), he looked like a bobblehead doll in a windstorm. The new chief said that he was closing the door to the Oval Office, because "it's like Grand Central Station in there." *Walk-in privileges? What walk-in privileges?* From now on, he said, the only people who could drop in without an appointment were Mrs. Trump, her young son, Barron, and Ivanka "as a daughter."

People had been floored by Scaramucci's hiring. Practically a New York minute later, people were floored by his firing, the sheer suddenness of his fall from a Jared and Ivanka favorite to persona non grata. Just a week before, he and I had been on the road with the president, milling around with the rallygoers, posing for selfies, and doling out autographs.

He had spent a mere eleven days as White House communications director, barreling into the Oval and barnstorming the cable TV circuit. But for Anthony, it was over before it began.

Kelly was intimidating to some but accessible to all. He sat with each of us individually to learn what we were working on and how he could be supportive. He resisted becoming a drama queen or a gossip girl. He brought order and discipline to White House decision-making.

He could also be funny in his own passive-aggressive way. In the senior staff meetings, he would go around the room and ask for updates. When particular people would say "No update, Chief!" Kelly would remark sardonically how ironic that was for someone the newspapers referred to as the "real" White House chief of staff.

I cottoned to Kelly the chief and respected Kelly the general. He and Trump forged a decent working relationship, and many in the cabinet seemed relieved to have one of their own now minding the store. Meanwhile, the Conway Six were undergoing a makeover of our own.

NOW THAT THE kids were with me in Washington and we had decided on area schools (single-sex Catholic schools), I was beginning the process of getting everyone settled. We tried to think of the summer as a time to reacclimate, renovate, and rejuvenate. I was relieved that George seemed happy with all of it and was impressed that he wanted to weigh in so heavily on the refurbishment and decoration of the house.

"It's great for entertaining," he remarked repeatedly, eyeing the spacious office just off the main entrance, soon to be his.

I experienced a range of emotions walking around the new home and sifting through the mountain of paperwork tied to the kids' new schools, new doctors, and new activities. Elation. Trepidation. That feeling of a fresh, promising "new car smell" in a city I'd loved since I'd arrived for college thirty-two years earlier, while also praying that my kids, too, would grow to love the city and all it had to offer. I was wistful listening to each of them describe how he or she wanted to arrange and furnish their new rooms and which friends from "home" had already promised to visit.

But what if my kids aren't happy?

Moms ask that question all the time. This move wasn't so different,

I suppose. At the same time, it was all *very different*. There were Secret Service agents with us 24/7, selfie-seekers and well-wishers everywhere we went, and the occasional miserable lunatic telling me off in between barking at the moon.

At least George and I were in it together. United in purpose, we were also united under one roof again. That little tweeting episode felt like forever ago.

A FEW WEEKS after Kelly became chief, a group of us went to visit the president at his home in Bedminster, New Jersey, while repairs were being made to the West Wing. Kelly had said he wanted to fill up Trump's schedule, or else the president would be bored and tweet all day. I think he was joking. Now I wonder. Either way, I was grateful for an opportunity to present a progress report and a look ahead at our efforts to fight the opioid crisis.

Mrs. Trump attended, too, as she became more active on the issue, especially as it affected babies who suffered from neonatal abstinence syndrome (NAS). At that point, an astounding one hundred newborns each day—1 in 150 births—came into this world struggling to take their first breaths. They experienced painful withdrawal symptoms from mothers who had used drugs while pregnant.

The roundtable in Bedminster was sad but also inspiring and was followed by an unexpected press briefing on the topic. I sat at the long table two seats to the right of President Trump. First Lady Melania was on his left as he gave his remarks. Then came the first and only question from a reporter. "Any comment on the reports about North Korea's nuclear capabilities?"

The president's unscripted response was by far the biggest news that day.

Any aggression from North Korea, said Trump, "will be met with fire and fury like the world has never seen."

I don't know if it was the influence of having a four-star general around, but that caught a lot of people's attention.

That same month, George and I and the kids were lucky to slip in a family vacation out west, zip-lining in Big Sky country, playing tourists at Mount Rushmore and Yellowstone. The kids were still getting settled in the nation's capital. School hadn't started yet, and everyone had a blast exploring the national parks and overloading on bison.

Back at Trump Tower in New York, the president, flanked by officials Gary Cohn, Steve Mnuchin, and Elaine Chao, was focused on infrastructure. The press, however, was singularly focused on the horrible events that had unfolded in Charlottesville, Virginia, where white supremacists and other extremists clashed at a so-called Unite the Right rally.

Trump denounced hatred, bigotry, white supremacy, and evil. But as far as the media was concerned, his comment about "fine people on both sides" overshadowed everything. The president was referring to the debate over tearing down monuments to Confederate figures from the Civil War, not the actual protestors, one of whom killed another protestor with his car.

To Trump critics, his intent was always assumed, never asked. I called this "presumptive negativity." It attached to practically everything the president said or did and was on full display in the shadow of the horrible events in Charlottesville. The distortions metastasized and stuck. To this day, those five words—"fine people on both sides"—are trotted out without any regard for the context or meaning. Two years after the event, Joe Biden would mention "Charlottesville" in his announcement video for his presidential campaign, and the year after that, Vice President Pence would elegantly correct vice presidential nominee Kamala Harris when she, predictably, distorted the facts. Trump had been talking about people on both sides of the tearing-down-monuments argument. As Pence reminded Harris, "Senator Harris conveniently omitted after the president made comments about people on either side of the debate over monuments, he condemned the KKK, neo-Nazis, and white supremacists, and has done so repeatedly."

When we returned to the White House following our family's Wild West trip, I dashed into the chief of staff's suite for a meeting with Kirstjen Nielsen, the principal deputy chief of staff, and doubled over in laughter outside the door.

"Is that a wall?" I asked. "You actually built *a* wall! *The* wall!"

There now was a full floor-to-ceiling wall with four TVs on it, physically separating the chief of staff suite from Jared Kushner's office, which under John Kelly would be more isolated. "You can't even climb over that sucker," I said, laughing. "You actually built a wall along the West Wing border!"

Chapter 23

Mom Guilt

Working-mom guilt is real.

At least for me, it is: that daily feeling—and failing—of needing to give 100 percent of myself to work and 100 percent to my family. As many of us women know, that'll never add up!

And now, I felt like I was also accountable to the 330 million people I had sworn to serve. They were paying my salary, after all, and they had a right to the best I had to give. But it all added up to an awful lot of people expecting things from me, and I couldn't imagine turning my back on any of them. Not the work I had chosen. Not the people I answered to. Certainly not the people I loved. All that said, I still didn't know what to do with the constant guilt of never, ever feeling like I was giving enough of my time, my energy, and my attention to any of them.

None of this made me unique. It landed me in a club with tens of millions of other American women: the nation's working moms. I'd had one myself. My mom and her three sisters worked outside the house. They kept it classy, made it look easy. It's not. No matter how and where we working moms spend our workdays, we have the same secret calculator in a reserved corner of our minds, constantly tallying up what we *didn't* do for our children during the time we were playing breadwinner, tutor, taskmaster, housekeeper, cook, butler, driver, ATM, in-house doctor, social coordinator, and entertainer.

We constantly feel so guilty, we even feel guilty bringing up our guilt.

All the while, we are outwardly sympathizing with our spouses when they moan and groan about their long daily commutes, lack of time, or lack of sleep.

Twenty-four hours in a day never feel like enough, especially to us women. I've never once thought of trading any of the chaos of being a working mom. I was thirty-seven when I had my twins, forty-one and forty-two for my younger daughters—and I went to work in the White House on my fiftieth birthday.

Welcome to the era of mom-on-demand.

To compensate for having a work life, I was often among the first to sign up for the classroom snack list or the teacher-conference slots. I worried that the email from the principal's office would get lost amid the hundreds of others arriving in my inbox that day. I had to respond immediately and later appear in homeroom with the nut-free muffins and something healthy to drink.

I knew the bigger picture perfectly well. I'd written about it in articles and client reports: "Yes, women can have it all—just not all at the same time." I believe that was the phrase I used. And every day, I was still testing that proposition and violating my own rules.

Over the years, I had listened intently to other women talking about how they "balanced" it all. Like pretzels, too often. For me, it's always been a high-wire act without a net below . . . in the middle of an EF5 tornado. I marveled especially at the single moms who somehow managed to keep it all together and the millions who didn't have anywhere near the financial resources that George and I did. (Later in life, we relied at different times over the years on wonderful (live out) professionals like Eduardo Silva, Paige Murray, and Ottilia Joo. Their assistance to George and me and their affection for our children allowed me to be a mom who worked more than a "working mom." But I had also learned: There is no amount of disposable income, no amount of career glamour, and no amount of outside help that will ever buy a working mom a get-out-of-guilt-free pass. Instead of being harried jugglers, unshowered and braless with specks of baby vomit on our sweatshirts, moms should be viewed as the fulcrum of our national life, centering and steadying the weight on either end of a perpetual seesaw, finding equilibrium and smoothing out the bumpiness.

There's plenty of data to support this. I had even gathered some of it myself. Some years back I had conducted focus groups and polls of highly educated, highly compensated female professionals at the height of their careers who were taking "exit ramps" out of the workforce. Some left to care for elderly loved ones. Others wanted to spend a few years climbing real mountains and traveling the world. Others just felt burned out. I could relate to all of them. But one subgroup really caught my eye: the professional women who were hitting pause on their careers because their children were now tweens and teens. The Washington lawyer who couldn't get home to her kids in Virginia when a plane hit the Pentagon on 9/11. The Silicon Valley tech exec whose workdays blended together, leaving no time to be off the clock. The business owner in Atlanta who felt like she'd given so much to her company, she didn't have anything left for her kids.

The essence of their comments was that everyone expected new moms to be there for the first steps, the first words, the mundane, and the other magical milestones of infancy. But these precious babies mature and really, really need us to "be there" when they are in the difficult and sometimes dreadful years of middle school and high school. Fifteen years before a global pandemic would force millions of American women out of the workforce to stay home and help their kids navigate "virtual learning" (including, eventually, me), these professional women were voluntarily exchanging afternoons in corporate boardrooms for afternoons in teenagers' bedrooms consoling and cajoling their kids when they felt bullied, sad, vulnerable, confused, or just "less than."

I found it all very moving. Like a lot of other working moms, I believed I was mostly handling it all. Maybe not as perfectly as I wanted to, but all the scrambling, rushing, and extra effort was a living, breathing, functioning plan that maybe had a few holes in it sometime. The so-called mommy wars that pitted stay-at-home moms against working moms seemed overdramatized (even as I had absorbed some snotty asides over the years that sounded more like judgment and jealousy than compassion and curiosity).

George and I spent our weekends with the kids. We were not part of the social circuit that included lots of folks who seemed to be super busy exactly on the days and hours when the kids were home. In a brilliant study, not mine, mothers and their children were separated and asked the same, simple question: What would you like more of?

The moms all said, "Time, time, time!"

The children did not. Mostly, they wanted their moms to be "happier" and "less tired." I'd violated that dozens of times, but I'd never forgotten it.

I CERTAINLY WASN'T expecting nine-to-five when I went to work as senior counselor to the president. But at least my office was just several miles from our new home, and close to my kids' new schools. George was the one running back and forth between New York and Washington. My White House workdays started early and ended late. Having an entire weekend or holiday off—*completely* off—was rare. Bringing work home and taking calls at all hours was a given. It was hard to shake my head *no* when the caller ID popped up and it was the president.

Though my children had been the main reason I had hesitated at first to take a position in the White House, once I was there, I would end up working alongside quite a few other moms. One morning I was in an 8:30 a.m. senior staff meeting and I looked around the room. Ivanka Trump, Mercedes Schlapp, Brooke Rollins, Sarah Huckabee Sanders. Among the five of us, all of whom had the highest rank as assistants to the president, we had nineteen children: twelve daughters and seven sons, ages two to sixteen years old.

And all along, my working-mom's guilt was just as useless as it was real, as I'm sure theirs was, too. There was no remedy to the constant feelings of maternal inadequacy, not even the belief that we were doing something important for the world. If Georgie left his gym bag on the stoop, if Claudia needed a last-minute permission slip, if Charlotte's science project was still on the dining room table, if Vanessa totally forgot about Dress Like Your Favorite Hero Day, I still knew it was partly my fault and I sprang into action to make it all better.

People sometimes find it hard to believe when I say this, but it's true: President Trump was very good to the working moms in his White House. He and I never had an explicit conversation about this, but it was implicit in our workplace and our work ethic. I had long bemoaned the hypocrisy in Workplace America where the executives crowed about their "family-friendly policies," which were mentioned on pages 682 through 686 of the employee handbook and then completely ignored in the reality of life. Things were *always* busy in those offices and peers were at the ready to judge and eye-roll parents who dared to slip out for the museum field trip or the school play.

Kids really do say the darnedest things, and they say those things whenever they want to, caring not at all that Mom is in the middle of a live TV hit or a heart-to-heart with the president. I got accustomed to that in a hurry, just as I'd grown accustomed to the kids blowing up my phone at the most inconvenient times imaginable. In recent years, a few pompous or humorless colleagues or clients had responded with smirks or snorts when I whispered, hand over my phone, "It's one of my kids. I'll be right there." I could never figure out what made these powerful people so miserable, since their biggest decision of the morning had been whether to meet for breakfast at the Four Seasons or the Hay-Adams, or have their personal trainers focus on their abs or legs. My morning workout consisted of feeding and walking two adorable but lazy dogs, making sure my mom (who was living with us) was ready for the day, finding homework and shoes for four kids and getting them ready for school, and dealing a husband who would also ask what was for breakfast or where's my stuff.

But now that I was in the White House, it was hard to top this one: After Georgie and his sisters and his father came to the White House Easter Egg Roll, I got a call from Alexa Henning, who excelled at her thankless job of booking administration guests on TV. She'd heard from CNN. "People are upset over there," she said. "Apparently, your son popped out behind Jim Acosta on the South Lawn. While they were filming, he said, 'Fake news, fake news, fake news.'"

"What? That doesn't even sound like him."

I hadn't seen it happen, and Georgie was usually camera-shy. I also hadn't seen the meme of Kellyanne Conway's twelve-year-old son that was already breaking the internet. The trolls had identified Georgie through footage that day of all four kids trailing me like little ducklings. It's fair to say I was part mortified, part amused.

"It wasn't appreciated," a woman from CNN emphasized over the phone.

"Well," I said with a sigh, "I don't appreciate CNN calling me the devil or whatever it is today. He's a kid, and a talented one at that."

That first year, George and the kids not only had a chance to join in the fun on the South Lawn at the Easter Egg Roll; they also got a firsthand view of Mom pivoting between the wildly different demands of her job. Charlotte and Vanessa enjoyed the festivities and played games on the South Lawn of the White House. I took my first turn reading *God Gave Us Easter* aloud to rapt schoolchildren in the outdoor "story nook." Then, five minutes later, I was answering a reporter's terse questions about a North Korean missile test. When Ainsley Earhardt from Fox News spotted George and the kids festooned in dressy clothes off to the side waiting for me, she asked if viewers could meet my family.

George and Georgie both hung back. Charlotte buried her face in my pastel-pink Easter dress, and Vanessa waved, while Claudia smiled and fielded the questions with poise for all of us.

Ainsley must have been expecting something along the lines of "awesome!" or "super-exciting!" when she asked Claudia what she thought life in D.C. was going to be like. Not my Claudia! Claudia paused for a thoughtful moment, milking her camera time for comedic effect before offering a sardonic answer that would prove to be true in every way imaginable:

"I think it will be . . . *interesting*."

They may have been camera-shy, but Charlotte and Vanessa were at the perfect ages to participate and enjoy the festivities. They are both adventurous and appreciative. An hour later, we were standing in the East Room preparing to take a family photo with President Trump and the First Lady. My kids were at that age where they were messing around in line and getting cranky. By the time we neared the front, I was hissing: "Okay, folks, listen to me, everyone just look straight ahead, smile, say 'Thank you, Mr. President. Thank you, Mrs. Trump, Happy Easter.' And that's it. Keep it moving."

When it was our turn, the president graciously complimented me. "Wow, what a beautiful family! You were great today on *Fox and Friends*."

"Thank you, Mr. President," I answered simply, just as I had instructed my children to.

Then he spotted Claudia in front of me. "And this one, she's a comedian," he added. "She was pretty funny out there."

Oh, dear God. Why couldn't he have been watching sports or be on the phone when that part was on?

He turned his attention directly to Claudia.

"You know what, honey," he said with a smirk. "I can understand. I like New York, too. But we're all going to be here for a few years. It's going to be fun. We'll have fun."

IT WAS DEFINITELY one of the coolest perks of working in the White House, being able to bring my kids around from time to time. Dropping by to see Mom's office could easily turn into a living lesson in economic policy or international affairs. Charlotte and Vanessa got a personal tutorial from Larry Kudlow and Kevin Hassett, the president's chief economic advisors, one afternoon. Kudlow sized up the girls, who were still in their Catholic school uniforms and are often mistaken for twins, and asked, "Which one of you did I welcome into the world on my TV show?"

That would be newborn Vanessa.

Every visit to Mom's workplace brought something new, educational, and fun that I hoped the Conway children would remember forever. One day, Vanessa, Charlotte, and Georgie were quietly ushered into the Oval Office to watch the last few minutes of an important meeting between President Trump and his trade team. The confidential business had been discussed and resolved. No state secrets would be in the third-grade show-and-tell. But the president did take the opportunity to tell the kids in front of Secretary of Commerce Wilbur Ross and U.S. Trade Representative Robert Lighthizer that China was eating our lunch and that it wasn't fair for Beijing to steal our jobs, our wealth, and our technology. The kids nodded plaintively. All that talk about China eating our lunch made our next stop the Navy Mess.

Claudia was my plus-one at an event in the East Room in honor of International Women's Day. When we got there, our place cards were in the front row:

MELANIA TRUMP. KELLYANNE CONWAY. CLAUDIA CONWAY.

Afterward, Claudia stopped to admire a beautiful Steinway grand piano in the Entrance Hall.

During social functions, members of the Marine Band often play the mahogany piano, which was built in 1938. As described by the White

House Historical Association, a gold-leaf mural on the case depicts five classic American musical scenes: a New England barn dance, a cowboy strumming his guitar, the Virginia reel, a ceremonial Native American dance, and two black field hands dancing and clapping. Three of the piano's legs are gilded and carved as American eagles.

"Do you play?" the usher standing by the piano asked Claudia.

"I do," she said without elaboration. Music is, in fact, her passion.

"Well, go ahead," the usher urged.

The photograph I took of her that day playing a classical piece on a storied piano is blown up in black-and-white in our D.C. house, a beautiful reminder of the privileged and unique experiences the Conway Six enjoyed as a family during the Trump administration.

The kids also were there to watch Marine One take off from the White House lawn with Mom aboard. Georgie attended both a congressional picnic and a solar eclipse on the White House lawn with no further complaints from CNN. We sat in the president's box for performances at the Kennedy Center (I don't think Trump ever used it but I can still see Charlotte and Vanessa lip-synching the entire *Hamilton* soundtrack from the best seats in the house), bowled in the White House bowling alley, and treated many other people's children to guided tours of the East and West Wings, the Press Briefing Room, the U.S. Capitol, and the halls of Congress. The real privilege for me was being able to expose my children in a real, intimate way to the work I did and the issues I championed in the White House.

How many moms can say that?

But if you asked Georgie, it was probably the visits from sports champions he cherished the most. White House staff and their families were invited to share in the trickle-down thrill of these events. Georgie posed with Heisman Trophy winner Joe Burrow after Louisiana State University won the national championship in one of college football's greatest seasons ever. Georgie also got to be part of what long-suffering D.C. sports fans hadn't experienced in ages: two championships: the Washington Capitals (and part-owner, my ex-boyfriend Raul Fernandez) winning the Stanley Cup and the Washington Nationals winning the World Series. Before standing with President Trump and a packed crowd on the South Lawn, the Nats players passed around Georgie's baseball cap and a Sharpie in the Roosevelt Room, leaving him with one of the best baseball keepsakes of all time.

It went on and on. The private Halloween and Christmas parties for senior staff members and their children. The day Charlotte and Vanessa got to tour the president's limo, known as "The Beast," and decorate cookies in the White House with the kid-loving First Lady. A somber Memorial Day outing to Arlington National Cemetery for Charlotte, Vanessa, and me, joined by Michaela and her family.

At some of the larger, public events, I was reminded that we couldn't just be anonymous faces in the crowd anymore. While watching the Fourth of July fireworks on the Mall, I was surprised the first time two Secret Service agents materialized out of nowhere to say: "Why don't we put you in your own spot off to the side." Sometimes this is for safety concerns and other times it was so that my children and I could actually enjoy our time together without interruption or interrogation by well-meaning people.

At special moments and events like this, my working mom's guilt was no match for the experiences and emotions of those precious innocent children.

Chapter 24

—————

Family Matters

It wasn't always so much fun being the children of Kellyanne Conway.

As the president's most visible spokesperson during the campaign, I had been on TV many times a day. Now that we were in the White House, no one was a more enticing target than I was for the trolls, haters, nutjobs, and misfit attention-seekers who lived online from their basements, bathrooms, brothels, and bat caves.

The attacks aimed at me were bitter, swift, and ugly, fueled by social media muscle and the cloak of anonymity. Yet some notable members of the media took their swings, too. They had been personally distraught and professionally embarrassed by Trump's surprise win. I was the woman who had helped to put Donald Trump behind the Resolute Desk, and as far as these folks were concerned, I had to pay. That seemed to be the depth of their fevered thinking, to the extent that they were thinking at all. I wish the four youngest Conways hadn't had to witness so much of it. I wish those keyboard cowards would have had the common decency to understand that their nastiness would sometimes mean my innocent children would be drawn directly into their hive of hate.

Isn't that what the *Vogue* reporter acknowledged when she claimed I needed to join the White House because I was a working mother?

The implication was that I would represent and inspire working mothers. Where was the forbearance *now, as a working mother?*

With social media so pervasive and the internet everywhere, it's almost impossible to shield children, even very young children, from the awful way that people sometimes behave. Adjusting to a new life in Washington and making new friends in new schools was hard enough without seeing the latest cruel spoof courtesy of a playmate with YouTube, or stumbling across the lies and insults from a pack of anonymous hyenas in the comment threads.

I knew there was no way to fully insulate them from the nastiness. So I chose to acknowledge and confront it head-on whenever one (or all) of my kids felt the impact. That was the case when my daughter came to me hysterical over a comment she'd heard from a political person she recognized.

"Why does that person on TV say that nothing truthful ever comes out of your mouth?" my daughter cried. "I thought she was nice to you."

"She *was* very nice to me until President Trump won the election," I tried explaining. "Couldn't get enough of me, or what she called my 'brilliance.'" I pulled out my phone and opened my messages. "See this text from her, warning me that some of my colleagues don't have my best interest at heart? Now she's one of them." I paused. "Well, you actually know me, and I care what you think. Your opinion matters most."

"You're very honest, Mommy. And I love you," she said through her tears. One child's affection versus thousands of faceless and mindless trolls? Not a fair fight, not even close. She wins.

"Remember, honey, just because someone says something doesn't make it true."

She shook her head as if she understood, looking appeased but still wounded by the attack she couldn't begin to comprehend. I repeated a point that had quickly become a mantra for my kids and for me.

"Nobody can make you feel bad about yourself without your permission," I said. "And so far, I'm not granting it to anyone. You shouldn't, either."

Another common response from me was to "pray for all those unhappy people online who get joy in *trying* to upset others," and somehow think a repetitive, snarky post about a stranger will make their joyless, unfulfilled lives better in some way.

I told myself I was too busy for their bullshit.

Too happy to let their harassment rattle me.

But let me say this as clearly as I know how. It was true that day and every day since: Stepping over the bright, buzzing "do not enter" line and into my kids' brains and business, that was beyond the pale—and is beyond forgiveness.

PRESIDENTS HAVE ALWAYS been considered fair game in the public forum for ridicule, snarky commentary, and flat-out character assassination. Smearing our leaders is one of the privileges of democracy. Gerald Ford was routinely portrayed by comedians and the media as a clumsy, dim-witted jock in over his head. Jimmy Carter was slammed as a redneck Georgia peanut farmer filling the White House with relatives straight out of *The Beverly Hillbillies.* Ronald Reagan was dismissed as a B-level actor who was too old to be president at sixty-nine, a decade younger than Joe Biden when he was elected—and far more energetic. The Bushes and Cheneys were vilified in every kind of way ("Satan," "war criminals") until their anti-Trump comments and crusade got them lavished with later-in-life liberal media redemption.

What was different about the bile aimed at Donald Trump was the sheer viciousness and relentlessness of it all, courtesy of social media, cable news, and a whole new level of righteousness. Much of it was compliments of a new type of hit-job "reporting" by no-name bloggers and stringers, ungrounded in actual journalism, publishing "articles" that simply knit together someone else's tweets and comments, all of which were opinion in the first place.

Please, stop telling Grandma you're a "reporter"! You're a garbage recycler! Unhinged from facts, driven by preconception, and accountable to no one. Impressive.

The other difference, and this one affected both me and my children, was that a president's staffer had never been targeted like this before. I am a presidential staffer guilty of nothing, and yet they claim in their Twitter bios that I'm "a girl dad" (and a shitty one), I'm "a wife" (that poor guy).

I don't want to quote too much of it. It only encourages them. It's all still out there on the internet. What you won't see are my responses. The attacks got pretty vile pretty quickly, and I decided at the beginning that there really wasn't much point in making lunatics relevant or emboldened. I'm keeping them irrelevant.

Disagree with my politics. Go ahead and back another candidate. But many of these personal attacks had no connection to reality or the important work I was hired to do. The late-night show hosts had long since become more political and less funny anyway.

How should I have answered Jimmy Kimmel when he ripped me apart with no regard for how my kids would feel, while his own young son was having surgery? I didn't answer him. My family prayed quietly for his little boy's recovery.

The whole thing was surreal. Their invective gushed down a one-way street, and they were unwilling to show some testicular fortitude and face me and spar with me. And the irony was not lost on me. Many of the same networks, anchors, producers, bookers, and executives who could not get enough of me now could not get enough of making fun of me. Thick skulls and thin skins, much like many others in the business.

Kate McKinnon was one of the *Saturday Night Live*'s breakout stars. She was famous for her dead-on Hillary Clinton, as well as her takes on a long list of other political figures that would eventually include an elfish Jeff Sessions, a wonky Elizabeth Warren, a self-contradictory Lindsey Graham, a thoroughly lovable Ruth Bader Ginsburg, and an off-the-rails Rudy Giuliani.

When she started doing me, I joked to *The Hollywood Reporter*: "Kate McKinnon clearly sees the road to the future runs through me and not Hillary." Her messy hair and red dresses were a dead ringer. In "A Day Off with Kellyanne Conway," right before the election, with actors also playing George and each of the children, she captured me so playfully and so accurately, my cousin Jay remarked that the writers must have followed me around for a week.

After Trump won, *SNL*'s characters and caricatures turned more dark and more cruel and often less funny. I still take it all in good humor and am grateful that an incredibly talented woman who is fifteen years younger than me played me. It beats the heck out of the women who played the men in the White House.

*   *   *

WE'D HUMILIATED THE 95 percent of the media that neither wanted nor voted nor expected Donald Trump to be president, so they wished to humiliate us back. If my kids had the challenges and opportunities of me as a mom in the Trump White House, imagine being a child of Donald Trump at the same time. "This will be fun" was not the message he gave his own children about life in Washington.

When the grown-and-flown Trump kids first showed an interest in moving down to work in the West Wing, their father urged them instead to avoid "the swamp," focus on their successful careers and young families in New York, and simply enjoy his presidency as members of the first family.

If only they had listened.

I watched all this happen gradually. During the 2016 campaign, I was struck by the Trump family's devotion, energy, and ability to shift into an entirely different line of work. Ivanka was visibly pregnant with her third child while moving tables and reorganizing the Trump zone at one of the Iowa caucuses. When I was asked to rehearse one-on-one with her before she introduced her father at the Republican National Convention in Cleveland, I suggested she change just three words. She earned serious accolades for her performance on that big stage. Ivanka is a quick study, willing to learn a new craft—campaigning—and she found a way to channel her stardom to help her father's electoral chances.

Tiffany Trump is the unsung sweetheart of the Trump kids. She's naturally pleasant and a sharp conversationalist, and I've always enjoyed her company and her insights. During the campaign, Tiffany was in her senior year at her father's alma mater, the Wharton School at the University of Pennsylvania. So she wasn't as free to wander America. But you should have seen her enthusiasm for helping her father in the "reach state" of Pennsylvania. It produced one of my favorite Trump-as-dad moments. We were on the campaign plane heading to Valley Forge, where Trump and Pence were delivering healthcare speeches eight days before Election Day. It was the first day of reenrollment for Obamacare, a great opportunity for Americans to hear about alternatives to the government-run system that had forced millions to pay billions of dollars in penalties, and led insurers like UnitedHealthcare and Aetna to flee from the Obamacare exchanges. Tiffany and I and another staffer were discussing her three-day solo tour of the state, beginning that afternoon, when she helped me persuade her father to make a stop at a nearby Wawa convenience store after the speech.

"What's going on?" Trump bellowed above our nearby conversation.

"Tiffany is leaving us this afternoon to do her own stops and radio hits in Pennsylvania," I responded. "She's extended it to three days, and we are just—"

"No, no, no, honey, you don't have to do that," her protective father interrupted. "You've got school, and the LSATs and law school applications. Just focus on that. You're with us today. Three days is too much."

Tiffany insisted, Trump relented, and she was great. When it came to his children, he is a soft touch.

The older Trump brothers were champs on the trail. Don Jr. was confident, funny, and was a natural for warming up a crowd and an unflappable star on talk radio. An ardent hunter who loved being outdoors, he blended in seamlessly with middle-class Americans, even though he was a Manhattan real estate tycoon. With just hours to go until Election Day, I asked Don if he could do even more radio. "Kellyanne, I'm like an organ-grinder monkey," he responded, standing in the doorway of my office at Trump Tower. "Just throw another quarter in my mouth, and I'll keep going." He said it with a smile. He and Eric were both relentless in their focus and performance. It made a measurable and positive difference.

Don Jr. would occasionally come to my office at the campaign and apologize for a stray tweet or a comment on a radio show and say, "I'm new to this." Junior deeply cared how his conduct affected his father's chances to be president. His then wife, Vanessa Trump, joined the family for important campaign events, sometimes with the older of their five young children.

Eric was also highly engaged and effective, deftly transferring many of the skills he'd developed in his day job to the campaign, including his knowledge of data and marketing and his business chops. He made quick work of shooting down even the most seasoned pundits when challenged with the useless and wrong national media polls, many of which sounded Trump's political death knell. "Look, I went through this in the primary, where you understated my father's strength," Eric chided George Stephanopoulos over ABC's poll showing Hillary Clinton leading Donald Trump nationwide 50 percent to 38 percent, weeks before the election.

"I'm not saying they're biased, but they're just wrong," he said. "There is something new and different about my father that doesn't survey well."

Exactly!

Eric was polite but bullish—and ultimately correct. His wife, Lara, meanwhile, helped her father-in-law campaign in her home state of North Carolina and joined the "Women for Trump" bus as it rolled through towns across America. Eric and Lara were always asking what else they could do, where else they could go.

Even Hillary Clinton had to give the Trump children their due. In the second debate of 2016, when both candidates were asked to say something nice about each other, Hillary offered up: "Look, I respect his children. His children are incredibly able and devoted, and I think that says a lot about Donald. I don't agree with nearly anything else he says or does. But I do respect that and I think that is something that, as a mother and a grandmother, is very important to me."

The one who didn't publicly campaign was Jared, though he too was materially involved.

He preferred being behind the scenes, monitoring the campaign coffers and presiding over hiring and firing. He secured a $10 million personal loan from Trump to the campaign with ten days to go. Jared accompanied his father-in-law on the road, often with Bannon as his sidekick, just not up to the podium. An unfortunate and ill-advised meeting with a Russian lawyer notwithstanding, it was not until the transition and the early days of the administration that Jared's personal profile really began to rise. And you know what? He seemed to like it, especially when he was portrayed as the smart and handsome crown prince.

Apparently he thought he deserved more praise beyond the incomparable prize of his father-in-law as president.

Jared didn't have the guts to bring it up to me himself, but Ivanka told me her husband resented all the credit I got for the 2016 election win, while he "had been written out of it." He must have forgotten about the time he posed on the cover of *Forbes* magazine as "The Guy Who Won the Election," his regular communications with Rupert Murdoch and Matt Drudge to help shape coverage (including of him), or when he summoned acolyte Brad Parscale onto *60 Minutes* to claim how brilliant the two of them were in securing Trump's victory in 2016, or the . . . well, you get the point.

After Trump won, literally no one had anything like my permanent video catalog of multiple, daily TV appearances predicting Trump would win and how and where. The uninterrupted minutes of strategy. The bullish predictions. The connection with viewers who were also voters. To say nothing of the fact that when Donald Trump asked me to be his campaign manager, he was losing by double digits, especially among women. Jared had been at the campaign the whole time. But now Jared was keen to regale the world with reminders that he had been the mastermind from the beginning.

I considered all that silly, the exact opposite of what we were taught as Catholic schoolgirls, which was to be humble in success and give credit to everyone else for everything.

When Trump had asked me to be his campaign manager, I accepted and blended into the existing team. We all worked our tails off together and no one more so than Donald Trump, who of course deserves most of the credit for his win. Jared and I had gotten along fine during the campaign. The victory changed so many people because it must have shocked so many people. Our relationship wasn't a problem at first, including the day we were seated next to each other and sworn in as assistants to the president and he said that his brother, Joshua, wanted to meet me. A perfectly friendly, even familial, thing to do. So it was a huge surprise to learn later how much Jared had tried to exclude me during the transition and was then repeatedly at odds with me in the West Wing, tossing logs into my path and diminishing me to high-ranking officials not named Donald Trump. In New York, Kushner had a famous name, skyscrapers, liquid assets, and his very own newspaper. In Washington, he was the new kid on the block. His political cred was scaffolded together as a donor to Democrats and a son-in-law to a Republican president. People who knew the place or had made their bones there from scratch must have been annoying. Or was it intimidating to Jared to work with someone like me, who knew Washington and had made my bones there from scratch.

THE TRUMP FAMILY business has always been exactly that, a family business. The three eldest of his five children, Don Jr., Ivanka, and Eric, worked well and successfully together in Manhattan, home base to their father's real estate development and licensing business. They'd all gone to work there shortly after graduating from college. Trump had also created recurring roles for all three on NBC's hit show *The Apprentice*. An earlier print interview with Don Jr. had stuck with me. He noted that the Trumps had a knack for adapting to any new acquisitions and avenues that would become part of the family business. They had learned real estate and development, then TV, and now politics. After working long and hard in the 2016 campaign to help get their father elected, it seemed reasonable that they might follow him into what must have looked like Dad's latest and greatest venture.

But this was Washington, not New York, where "business as usual" means something different entirely. Governing is very different from real estate development. "You're fired!," the signature line from *The Apprentice,* is rarely echoed by voters, who keep reelecting career politicians for decades while they tell pollsters they pine for term limits.

Eric and Don Jr. soon returned to the Trump Organization in New York. Only Ivanka and Jared decided to relocate to D.C. and become advisors to the president. Ivanka spent a couple of months moving her preschool kids to the capital before moving herself into the West Wing. I admit I envied the luxury she had of easing into her job, instead of the abrupt way I'd been forced to do, while my kids, much older than hers, remained in New Jersey with their father and grandmother, finishing out the school year. The first one hundred days of any administration are absolutely critical, and everyone on his staff knew President Trump would be moving with his usual volume and velocity.

While his wife tended to the family's transition, Jared had gotten busy upping his profile. He was able to dive right in, making sure he was the person who accompanied the president-elect to the White House the day after Trump won, joining President Obama and Trump in the Oval Office in what some joked resembled photos of "Take Your Kid to Work Day."

It is without question that Jared, and especially Ivanka, are supersmart and successful. There was no doubt they came to Washington to help the country and their father, who was about to run it. Their undefined roles and unchecked power were a challenge for others inside and outside the White House, though. Early on, doors swung open on Capitol Hill, in corporate America, and with Big Tech titans. But with no clear ask or any direct nexus to the president's priorities, a lot of this came over time to feel like wheel spinning. When Jared came calling, people assumed it was with the authority and agency of the president, and most were not in a position to question or verify that. But often, then, it was noted, nothing much happened next at all.

Though General Kelly would eventually limit even Jared's and Ivanka's walking-in privileges, theirs extended far beyond the Oval Office—into the residence(s) and anywhere else the president was, including his foreign trips and his weekend meals. It didn't take long for Jared to figure out how to make two quick right turns into the president's private dining room rather than go through the Outer Oval, where Kelly's staff was now keeping closer tabs on the phone calls and foot traffic.

All the personnel changes and rules couldn't and wouldn't fully restrict the couple's access. We all knew that. There was no chief of staff, even a four-star general, who could limit that. Nor should they have. Jared and Ivanka were family. If Jared or Ivanka wanted to see or know or be involved in something, no one was going to say no. It's not that people were jealous of that access and the associated authority. They understood it. But they were sometimes dubious about how it would be used.

It didn't matter that some other staffer (or cabinet secretary) was making a well-reasoned, well-prepared presentation that the president had requested. Fortunately, the president did work the phones often enough to uncover the real deal and make up his own mind.

But it went the other way, too.

A snap of the fingers from Jared or the promise of a clandestine meeting free from leakers that nearly always leaked could mobilize multiple people to pursue a dead-end strategy for months on end. Then there was the leap-first penchant of inviting Democratic senators to dinner at the Kushner home in the Kalorama section of D.C. to discuss immigration, wall funding, criminal justice reform, or child-care tax credits. These evenings weren't only a well-intentioned nod to fostering bipartisanship, a goal I certainly supported as reasonable to advance progress for America. They also invariably meant that staffers from the White House legislative team or the Senate-confirmed cabinet who had authority and responsibility for those issues needed to play catch-up. And let's not forget that every single one of those Democrats at dinner with the Kushners in Kalorama would go on to impeach President Trump twice. Plenty of them also went after the Trump family members. Talk about biting the hands that feed you!

How much goodwill and how many good deeds did all that wine really buy?

The Kushners positioned themselves as the influential "voice of moderation" in the West Wing. That brand quickly melted as Trump went his own way and made good on his promises to be a pro-life, pro–Second Amendment leader who would build a wall at the southern border and pull the United States out of the Paris climate accord.

Ivanka quickly made her first big move and asked for my help on an issue she had championed for some time, abortion rights.

Ivanka Trump is a nice person. Brilliant and poised in her interactions and warm to staff. A good listener. A great laugh. We shared a strong working-mom bond and lived in the muddy-to-quicksand trenches together when it counted most. I was genuinely moved when Ivanka thanked me for "all you've done for my father and our family" that first week of November 2016 as she handed me a jewelry box. Hope Hicks received one, too. Inside was a dainty, custom-made, gold bracelet with a sturdy message: "#MAGA."

Ivanka Trump is willing to invest energy into her convictions. Turns out, so is her father. And that was not good news for Ivanka's abortion rights campaign. The man who had run as a pro-life candidate would now govern as a pro-life president. No, as much as I liked Ivanka, I was not going to help her help Planned Parenthood score a private audience in the Oval. Luckily Ivanka had many other ideas that were more in line with her father's beliefs, and I was always open to discuss those other areas of agreement and engagement. Years later, in October 2020, I would admire Ivanka's courage when she would show her strength and willingness to reexamine her previous views, stating, "I am pro-life, and unapologetically so."

The Kushner couple's media honeymoon wouldn't last forever. I don't think anyone expected it to. Ivanka was taking body blows from unfair, unkind, and unrelenting press coverage. The president felt his daughter's pain.

"You know," he said on more than one occasion to those of us standing there: "Here's Ivanka: Her whole life, nobody really says anything negative about her. She's brilliant. She's beautiful. She's a good person. Top of her class at Wharton. All Ivanka gets is positive press. She comes down the runway, here comes her new jewelry collection. Oh, look at her new shoe line. Oh, she's helping build this building. And then she gets here, and these people are brutal."

He wasn't wrong about that.

"I told her not to come," he said. "I told her, 'Don't come to Washington, honey. It's brutal.' She says, 'No, no. I want to help the women.' I told her the women will be fine."

He expressed similar regret and a father's protectiveness over the problems his presidency was causing Don Jr. and Eric. The father felt sympathy for his sons as they tried to run the Trump business empire in his absence, with all the controversy that inevitably meant.

"Look at Don," the president lamented to me about how his name-sake was being treated. "Don just wants to go hunting. He wants to get lost in the woods, go hunting for a couple of weeks, mind his own business. He didn't ask for any of this."

Then, of course, there was Barron, the youngest Trump child, who was ten years old when his father got elected and eleven when he moved into the White House.

In previous years, even hardened partisans like me made clear to the comics and critics that the Clinton and Obama daughters were totally off-limits. No such forbearance had been accorded to Donald and Melania Trump's tender-aged son. Barron was exposed to outrageous and sometimes scary images, like the severed head held up by unfunny, D-list comic Kathy Griffin or the stabbing of a Donald Trump look-alike in a production of Shakespeare in the Park. All along, Melania's top priority was her son. She kept him protected, though not sheltered. It's not an easy balance. And it was always clear that Melania had a natural connection with millions of us mama bears across this country who know our first priority is and always will be our children.

Chapter 25

Turning Points

Going into our first holiday season at the White House, I felt encouraged by the wins we had under our belt and the direction we were heading.

The president and the First Lady were deeply involved with the opioid crisis, now declared an official national public health emergency and a big piece of my portfolio. In the Middle East, Trump had fulfilled a promise that seven presidents had made by moving the U.S. Embassy in Israel to Jerusalem, and now he was well on his way to passing the Tax Cuts and Jobs Act, a landmark piece of economic legislation that showed the ability of our White House and administration to collaborate with Congress and get things done.

General Kelly was bringing order to the White House and making sure the president was appropriately briefed, even though gossip-beat gawkers like Annie Karni, then at *Politico*, "reported" as fact a mere two months into his tenure that Kelly's days were numbered. He'd go on to be Trump's longest-serving chief of staff. Kelly didn't seem the least bit rattled by any of it.

"How did that go, Kellyanne?" he asked me after one briefing with the president.

"Oh, fine," I said. "But you may want to check the call log to see who keeps ringing him to insist the sky is green and the grass is blue."

Adding to my good mood that December was knowing that George and I would soon be hosting a big group of relatives and friends in our new home, just a couple of miles from the White House. I loved being in a position to connect people from all over the country, including folks in my own circle of life, with the opportunity to enjoy the gorgeous decorations and unique celebrations of the nation's capital. In paying homage to two hundred years of White House tradition, First Lady Melania Trump created a winter wonderland that combined elegance and warmth in a way that was uniquely hers. Hundreds of Trump-loving volunteers helped deck the famous halls with 53 trees, 71 wreaths, and more than 12,000 ornaments. The Grand Foyer and Cross Hall evoked the snowy woods of the *Nutcracker Suite,* the balsam firs with their fairy lights reflecting off the gleaming marble floors. In the State Dining Room, a 350-pound gingerbread reproduction of the White House featured one of Melania's wreaths in each window.

True to their promise that this would be the People's House, the president and First Lady opened the doors to more than 25,000 visitors that year, hosting dozens of holiday parties and posing for hundreds of pictures nightly with staff, guests, members of Congress, the Secret Service and their families, and residence staff.

The Social Office requested my presence at the festivities daily, and I was happy to greet, converse, and take selfies with scores of visitors. My standard line to young girls who would ask me what it was like to work in the White House was "We kept the job of first female president of the United States open, and it could be *you!*"

I may have said that to my own daughters here and there, but for now, they were tweens taking in the East Wing and White House grounds, not commanders in chief in the Situation Room. My kids thoroughly enjoyed the Christmas party in the East Wing that the president and First Lady hosted for young children of senior staff. Charlotte and Vanessa made ornaments, wrote letters to military, toured the decorations, and made new friends.

Among the more special Christmas events at the White House that year was the intimate senior staff dinner hosted by the president and First Lady. Making it to that table felt like a season of *Survivor*. In normal circumstances, lasting in the West Wing for the eleven months from Inauguration Day to Christmas may seem like a given. But in this first year of the Trump administration, it was a sheer contest of will and endurance. Just eleven days into the administration, as the president sat at the Resolute Desk and I stood nearby, I told him that our days were measured in "dog time," meaning everything already felt seven times longer than it was and perhaps seven times harder than it needed to be.

George came with me to the exclusive senior staff dinner. He and I arrived in our festive best and were both excited to be there. When dinner was served, we sat next to the president and the First Lady. That year the dinner seating was assigned, in other years it was by lottery. Thankfully, no one's tweets were on the menu. Melania's understated elegance and humility belied how hard she and her team had worked to make the night incredible yet intimate.

We left the East Wing holding hands and carrying incredible gifts: a personalized leather portfolio for me, and a set of keepsake cuff links for George, embossed with the presidential seal. George had been to the White House just five weeks earlier for a kids' Halloween party, but the novelty and thrill of being a guest of the Trumps apparently had not worn off for him, whatever conflicting feelings were inside his head. I loved seeing how much he enjoyed himself on these special occasions, and I can honestly say that it was great fun that we could experience these remarkable events together.

Donald Trump is great company. Funny. Conversational. He looks you in the eye, and he doesn't drink. He is clear, sharp, and present, telling stories and remembering people, places, and things (even when I wished he wouldn't). Also, he was generous in sharing his proudest achievements with those in his orbit. That night while we were at the staff dinner, the Senate was in session on Capitol Hill, passing Trump's sweeping Tax Cuts and Jobs Act. No time off for the most powerful man in the world. He took calls throughout the evening, providing us live updates on the vote. It must have been the joyous season, because even the Washington journalists' reports were encouragingly positive.

George and I both complimented the military band that had treated us all to a private performance of holiday tunes.

It was an evening to remember. I still cherish the photo of a beaming

George and me in front of the trees and presidential seal in the Cross Hall of the East Wing. I stole a glance at my husband as we left the White House. "Wasn't that amazing?"

"Yes, really great," George agreed.

I learned later that, before the dinner began, he'd been sending photos and comments to his friend, expressing awe and appreciation of everything from the extraordinary decorations to the interesting group of guests.

"The president's a piece of work," George added, a phrase he had used many times over the years as a compliment when amused by someone.

I just smiled. I knew my husband well and took the comment at face value. I didn't detect any sarcasm beneath it. The next day, I boarded Marine One early with President Trump for a few events in New York City. Later that evening, George and I and Georgie and Claudia went to a neighbor's bat mitzvah in New Jersey. As much fun as the lavish party was, we were still talking about the previous night's dinner.

With Trump and with George, I felt like I was really hitting my stride.

A WORKING WEEKEND at Camp David in early January helped to set the table for a busy, challenging, and thrilling year ahead—busy when it came to policy, challenging when it came to politics, and thrilling when it came to football. Thankfully, the thrill came first. My beloved Philadelphia Eagles were heading to Super Bowl LII at U.S. Bank Stadium in Minneapolis, against perennial favorite the New England Patriots.

Thirteen years earlier, the two teams had faced each other in Super Bowl XXXIX. Tom Brady and the Patriots eked out a victory that time, 24–21. I'd had my twins just a few months earlier, but George and I were at the game, then flew back on a chartered Hooters Air jet from Jacksonville to Philly with a planeload of equally sad Eagles fans. The fans were sullen if not exhausted. The men perked up and paid rapt attention to the airline safety briefing presented by the women in Hooters uniforms.

The buildup to this long-awaited rematch had started two weeks earlier when George, Georgie, Claudia, and I watched from the stands as the Eagles walloped the Minnesota Vikings in the NFC Championship, 38–7. We screamed and celebrated knowing that this time the twins were old enough to come with us to the Super Bowl. Hours after we returned from Philly, I was on TV in an Eagles-green dress, dispensing with the news of the day before giving a shout-out to the team I'd cheered for in the freezing cold for decades at Franklin Field and Veterans Stadium, and now the Linc, the affectionate name fans had given Lincoln Financial Field.

"That's good for your team," Trump said to me, "but [Patriots owner] Bob Kraft is a friend."

"The Patriots are like Hillary Clinton, where they are supposed to win, and, win or lose, they resurface again," I said. "The Eagles are like you, the underestimated, scrappy underdog. Plus, you won Pennsylvania."

The excitement even crossed partisan lines. That week, I ran into Senator Chris Coons, a Democrat from Delaware, on Capitol Hill and we shared our "Iggles" anticipation.

"I hope you are riding [Minnesota] Senator Klobuchar hard about that blowout," I joked. Let's be honest, it's always more fun being on the winner's side.

In Minneapolis for the big game, George and I and the twins walked from our hotel to the stadium, when the windchill said six degrees below zero. I barely felt the cold, I was so excited. We cheered ourselves hoarse for four quarters, as every play felt like life or death. Georgie knew every player's name and position and could predict most plays before they happened. Charlotte and Vanessa were holding firm in their Philadelphia fandom, especially for Nick Foles. First in New Jersey, where they lived among Jets and Giants fans and now in Washington in Redskins country. I had waited my entire life to witness this moment.

We were part of the sheer pandemonium when the clock ran out and the Eagles finished the game on top, 41–33. We promptly bombarded our stunned friends and family with our on-the-scene photos and videos. Order and justice had settled across the football world. For the second time in sixteen months, I'd supported an underdog, one who had defied the silly screed of "you can't win" and forced a solid upset. By the time we arrived back in D.C. it was early the next morning. I only had time for a too-short power nap before heading to Cincinnati with the president and First Lady to join Senator Rob Portman and his wife, Jane, at a children's hospital doing incredible work with babies suffering from neonatal abstinence syndrome, or NAS. Let me tell you, standing next to the extraordinarily beautiful Melania Trump, after you've only slept for an hour, is the absolute last place any woman would want to find herself.

POLICIES WITH REAL-LIFE consequences for Americans—isn't that what government *should* be about? I wasn't really feeling any of that when Robert Mueller's investigation finally groaned to life. Suddenly colleagues of mine in the White House were pushing important work to the side as they were receiving subpoenas, lawyering up, and testifying.

And for what? The entire charade was based on a lie that the Trump campaign had "colluded" with Russians and that this illicit conspiracy had cost Hillary Clinton the election.

I was one of a handful of people close to the president who went thoroughly untouched by the Mueller investigation and the corollary clown show in Congress. Out of the loop? No. Out of the lion's den? Yes. As Trump himself remarked, "Well, because you don't do stupid things." Instead of lawyering up, I spoke up, amused by how easy it was to trigger the Trump Derangement Syndrome crowd.

The investigation was an outrageous waste of taxpayer dollars and in certain circumstances what felt like to me organized harassment of innocent citizens. It became an obsession of the media and the Democrats and Hillary Clinton, who was still refusing to accept the election results from 2016. Outrageously, as the investigators came up with little or nothing, these anti-Trumpers only intensified their search—desperately hoping to absolve themselves of their embarrassing miss and somehow get rid of Trump.

The president, meanwhile, was keenly focused on the midterm election, as presidents typically are, knowing that historically, the party in power often suffers grievous losses, especially true in first-term presidencies. Seasoned political pros would have kept their focus on the down-ballot races. Not Jared. He may have been a crown prince who used encrypted apps to literally talk to a crown prince but he had very limited political experience. In his infinite wisdom, he insisted on making the presidential election that was more than two and a half years away his primary focus. At the end of February 2018, more than eight months before the vital midterms, he turned to his acolyte Brad Parscale, the digital director from 2016 who'd admitted too often and too late in the 2016 election cycle, "I don't know anything about politics." Brad was named Trump's campaign manager for the 2020 reelection bid. Even though I had done the job once, I did not want or expect to do it again. Our work at the White House was meaningful and at this point consequential. Also, I believed that incumbent presidents rise and fall mostly by what they do in the White House, not on the campaign.

By historical standards, this was nine months too early to begin campaigning for reelection. The focus, as anyone with even a modicum of political insight would understand, should first have been on retaining or recapturing control of Congress. The outcome of the 2018 elections would have a huge impact on the president's agenda in the second two years of the term. If Democrats gained control of even one house of Congress, legislative progress would be harder by tenfold. Also, announcing too early tended to cannibalize donors. They'd give their maximum to Trump early and already be tapped out when his campaign would need that money later on. Who knows the real story behind the time line— was it because the subpoenas were flying?

Corey Lewandowski, fired by the kids in 2016, was back in the president's orbit, and back on the president's mind. For Jared and Brad, the only thing possibly worse than Corey and David Bossie helming the reelection campaign would have been me agreeing to it.

If they'd so much as heard a whisper that sounded like "C'mon, Kel, we did it last time, let's do it again"—they might have impaled themselves on the Washington Monument.

Conspicuously, the announcement of Brad as campaign manager included extensive quotes of praise from Eric Trump and Jared Kushner and nothing from the president, a prophecy of sorts. It was also leaked to one of Jared's preferred scribes in the print media and linked by the Drudge Report, a reliably obsequious outlet for Kushner coverage.

WITH INVESTIGATIONS AND 2020 reelection talk outpacing midterm plans, I wasn't paying much attention to my husband's Twitter account. George's worrisome flurry a year earlier seemed like ancient history. But it was around this time that George's sporadic Twitter posts began turning more critical of my boss. Now, instead of just the occasional retweet or article post, he was taking fresh shots at the man he and I had both supported for president. It was nothing outrageous at first, more like wry observations. In fact, I don't think anyone really noticed right away. Even I wasn't especially alarmed. And I hardly gave it a second thought when Jared and Ivanka proposed a Kushner-Conway couples dinner at their home. Despite the regular practice of Jared ignoring me or icing me out, I thought the dinner invitation could only be a positive sign. We discussed many things that night, including pressing legislative action, the midterms, and the president's far-off reelection. George remained quiet at the dinner, as was typical for him in these settings, shrugging when the occasional opinion was asked of him.

A week after the dinner, George typed, then deleted, a string of critical tweets. They were gone except for eagle-eyed screenshot grabbers, but then he got even busier.

Oh, no, I thought. *Here we go again.*

Without the courtesy or candor of discussing it with me, George not only increased the volume of his tweets, but also accelerated their criticism of the Trump administration. As far as I knew, my husband was still a supporter of the president—and certainly of me. He had objections to the way the president acted sometimes. Plenty of Trump's supporters did. But I was completely blindsided by the public nature of George's criticisms. That he would change his mind and his tone about Trump was odd to me. But that was more understandable than aiming the poison keyboard toward his wife of seventeen years and the mother of his four children.

And now, here was Eric Trump writing about "the utter disrespect George Conway shows towards his wife." So many other strangers and former colleagues, too, joined in the George and Kellyanne watch.

All of this was started by my tweet-free husband, who had observed the social media revolution largely from the sidelines—until something happened.

Exactly how, when, and why George shifted the weight of his daily life from its off-line moorings to a parallel online universe remains a mystery to the woman who knows him best. I said little to nothing about it publicly or privately. Yet two camps seemed to form. The first camp joined me in the silence, people who did not know what to say or how to approach the topic, even though it was clear they were eager to talk about it. The other camp spilled forth with hints, theories, ideas, and specu-lation. Boredom. Fame and attention. Career disappointment. Midlife crisis. Jealousy of me. Hatred of Trump. Regret over moving to Wash-ington. I preferred neither to speculate nor ruminate at the time. What the thirsty press covered as "news" was really noise. I tried to tune it out. Then the volume (both amount and decibels) of George's newfound pas-sion swamped any such ability.

I did recognize this much: Those weeks from mid-March to mid-April 2018 definitely marked a turning point of some kind for George. During these weeks George appeared on a podcast, which got picked up by CNN and other outlets, where he claimed that he knew by April 2017 that the White House was "a shit show in a dumpster fire." Yet after April 2017, he was still coming to the White House often and still considering an offer to join the administration. It was easier to evade conversation or confrontation when I was in D.C. alone with the kids and George was holed up in New York and New Jersey, commuting between home and the law firm. But right before my eyes, what up till then had been occasional tweets and retweets about points of law in the Mueller investigation soon broadened into other topics and started to feel like a sugar high of mockery, aimed squarely at President Trump. And, by extension, me.

In mid-April, George managed to almost crash an interview I was giving CNN's chief political correspondent, Dana Bash, on the network's Sunday show *State of the Union*. After less than ten minutes discuss-ing topical news of the FBI raid against now-former Trump attorney Michael Cohen, who would later go to prison, and James Comey's book tour, Dana abruptly changed the subject.

"I've got to ask," she said, "what's up with your husband's tweets?"

Actually, she did *not* have to ask, not on live TV, anyway. Dana and I had known each other for years, and I would never raise publicly, let alone on live TV, anything about her own personal or marital life, about which I knew plenty. I was the one the female reporters were inviting to their homes for receptions, dinners, book parties, and the like. Not for a scoop. Not for a leak. For the company, for the conversation, for the connection outside of politics. "You're the one we like," I'd heard over and over.

As a frequent guest in mixed political company, I'd been much more transparent and much more reserved in my dealings than the leaking Bannon dirigible hovering about, and the taxpayer-funded Kushner image-curation machine stationed inside and outside the White House.

Dana and I had each muscled and grinded and worked our way through our respective patriarchal professions. I like and respect her. We'd sparred on-air but had connected as moms and fellow "Jersey Girls." With two weeks to go until the 2016 election, I had finally relented and participated in a CNN feature story of me that Dana had been pitching for months. She had visited my family at home in Alpine and portrayed fairly and warmly a professional woman with four school-aged children who was trying to stop Hillary Clinton from making history by making a little of history of her own.

"Really?" I responded to her inquiry about George's Twitter habit, only half-surprised but fully disappointed. "We're now going to talk about other people's spouses and significant others just because they work at the White House or at CNN?" I asked, flashing my widest smile to mask my fury. "Are we going to do that? Because you just went there. CNN went there."

A Rubicon, I told Dana, had just been crossed.

"This ought to be fun moving forward," I promised.

That was not directed at Dana, but boy, did I hit a nerve.

Predictably, the media, who collaborate and cohabitate on Twitter, were on fire. They can never swallow their own medicine. They are aching to be household names, so why not know a little bit more about their personal lives? On the one hand, my reaction and challenge were justified: If you dish it out, be ready to eat it. On the other hand, I had less interest in some of these people and their boring lives than in almost anything else.

If the "breaking news" was that spouses sometimes disagree (duh), well, then, I wondered aloud, what about adultery (by definition, a disagreement about your spouse's sexual partners) or draining the joint bank account or hiding an alcohol, porn, or gambling problem? Shall we, everyone? Is cheating by tweeting actually a thing? When I alluded to other people's troubled relationships, I had no one in particular in mind. I had *many* people in mind. Dozens of terrified, thin-skinned people living in glass houses. How was that debauchery their "private lives" and "no one's business" and yet my husband's tweets "breaking news"? After all, these folks were, or were trying to be, public figures. They had agents. I did not. I did not ask for any of it. My fame followed, not preceded, my success.

SOMETHING ELSE I was not prepared for, and something I never would have expected he would receive or relish: the cult of George Conway.

Online encouragement and praise began to encircle my husband. To celebrities and sycophants alike, it was clear that he would be the biggest *get* of the Never Trump movement if his objections were real and they could reel him in. The recognition and hero worship did not always translate to the offline world, where most of us happily live. That spring, George and I brought three of the kids to Nationals Park for a baseball game between the Nats and the Yankees. Trump had received a small number of votes in both cities. We weren't exactly in MAGA country. Standing in the concourse during a long rain delay, dozens of D.C. residents and New Yorkers lined up to introduce themselves and snap selfies with me. People from liberal Washington and New York! My kids nudged me to get them ice cream as George was temporarily relegated to taking pictures for the Kellyanne fans who asked. After one too many, George said he'd had enough—"No more selfies!"—and left me and the kids in the crowded concourse surrounded by dozens of eager fans.

"Why would you leave us there like that?" I asked him once the kids and I had made our way through the storm to our vehicle in the parking garage and then home.

"I'm just sick of it," he said.

"Well, George, it's no big deal. People want to give a suggestion or take a photo."

"They wanted to take photos with O. J. Simpson, too," he replied to his uncharacteristically speechless wife.

This was getting serious, and not in a good way.

Chapter 26

But Trump

Screaming graphics. Alarming headlines. "Breaking news" that sounded awfully like the same breaking news from the night before. Made-for-TV-lawyers dressing up for the cameras and then dressing up wishful thinking as their evidence, spun with conviction and met with such sober head-nodding and certainty from the anchor that all the same people would do it all over again the next day, the next month, the next year. Whatever the facts might eventually say—and they weren't saying much yet—reporters were still square-jawed in their certainty that "Russian collusion" was real and had swung the Trump-Clinton election away from the candidate they'd all voted for, and who they'd all predicted with the same level of certainty would win the last time out.

Now, in the spring of 2018, media attention was heating up at the southern border. I was surprised to learn one morning, while reading the newspaper, that Attorney General Jeff Sessions had announced a new "zero-tolerance policy" that would mean arrest and criminal charges for every adult caught crossing illegally into the United States. Any children they'd brought with them would be placed in holding facilities outside the jail.

"If you don't want your child separated," Sessions declared, "then don't bring them across the border illegally."

A naturally reserved Southerner, deferential to the point of being scared of his own shadow, Sessions didn't usually talk so bluntly. And maybe *separating parents from their children* (!) wasn't the best place to start.

The outrage was swift and ferocious, and it wasn't only coming from Democrats and the media. Many of us in the White House were also blindsided and confused. The policy itself did not separate parents and children, but the result of applying the policy in some instances did. This was a classic case of someone trying to please Trump by going rogue, only to get Trump in more hot water.

An emergency meeting was called in the White House Situation Room. The urgent questions: What exactly was happening, and what should be our next moves?

Thirty hours after being in New Mexico, and then addressing hundreds of young women in Dallas and cheerfully complying with an organic line of photo seekers at Turning Point USA's Young Women's Leadership Summit, I was on *Meet the Press* that Sunday with Chuck Todd. This was damage-control time. This is what Trump meant by going into any den while others, whose actual job was to do so, wouldn't. I was unequivocal. "Nobody likes seeing babies ripped from their mothers' arms, or from their mothers' wombs, frankly," I managed to work into my response. "But we have to make sure that DHS's laws are understood through the sound bite culture that we live in."

I then reminded Chuck that we don't know what happens to those children, especially the young girls, on that journey up through Mexico. I quoted Obama's homeland security secretary, Jeh Johnson, who'd said in the summer of 2014 that unaccompanied minors at the border had been the "bane of my existence" in that job. I did not express support for the policy. How could I? Citing the Trafficking Victims Protection Reauthorization Act and the Supreme Court's *Flores* decision, I stated the obvious: We needed help from Congress and the courts to address the root problems of these massive border crossings.

I made the same case directly to the president. Many times. When the First Lady traveled to the Mexican border, she insisted on visiting with the children in the holding facilities. The cameras were not allowed to go in with her. So, the media's add-water-and-stir negativity "reported" the "facts." The round-the-clock story had rightfully been the children. But now something far more exciting was consuming the press's attention: a thirty-nine-dollar jacket by Zara that announced on the back, I REALLY DON'T CARE, DO U? The internet erupted, and suddenly everyone decided she was referencing the migrant kids in Obama's cages.

The president's secretary brought Melania's outerwear choice to his attention while the First Lady was still in transit. Lucky me, I was standing there, as was Mercedes Schlapp, our director of strategic communications. We had just concluded a meeting in the Cabinet Room where POTUS was present and were now expected in the Situation Room about this very topic.

"What is *this*?" he demanded.

"*That*," I said, "is probably the First Lady trolling the trolls."

"They're saying she doesn't care about the children," the president continued.

"They said that before she put on the jacket," I reminded him. "They said that while she was actually *with the children* at the border. They say that anyway."

I suspected I knew the intended target of her not-so-subtle message—porn people, press people, petty people, political people, really anyone who had thought they had gotten under her skin. She settled it once and for all.

AS THE RUSSIAN-COLLUSION probe dragged on, the Department of Justice indicted twelve Russians on charges of meddling in the 2016 presidential election. George spent hours tweeting about it. Quoting a *Politico* story headlined "European leaders do not think Trump is a stable genius," George twisted the knife, sarcastically writing: "What could possibly make them think that?" I didn't pay attention to those specific tweets at the time, but they were out of character for George, these small, insolent strikes. Three days later, the president and First Lady flew to Helsinki, Finland, for Trump's first summit with Vladimir Putin. Standing alongside the Russian leader for a press conference following their two-hour private conversation, Trump was asked if he believed the U.S. intelligence officials who said Russians had tried to hack the American election. Or did he believe Putin's denials? His answer seemed to side with Putin.

The next morning, Trump arrived back at the White House. Most of the staff had gone home to catch some sleep after the long flight from Finland. I hadn't gone on the trip, so I was at my desk. The president was already wide awake, as the news cycle was frothing that he agreed with Putin and took the Russian leader's word over that of his own intelligence community.

Trump, who rarely admits to misspeaking, called my desk. "I didn't say that."

"Well," I told him, "you *did* say that. I'm reading right here in the transcript. It says, 'President Putin says it's not Russia. I don't see any reason why it would be.'"

"That is not what I meant," Trump said. "I meant 'any reason it would *not* be Russia.'"

"Well, Mr. President," I said, "that's fundamentally different. Actually, it's the opposite of what you said. So, if that is the truth, you need to clarify this ASAP. If not, you might as well leave it and explain why you said it and what it means."

He had just been on Air Force One for hours with the traveling clique of senior staffers and press and communications staff. They'd all heard him speak at the press conference. They'd all seen the same media I had after he spoke.

"Meet me downstairs."

I walked into the Oval Office dining room to meet the president. We went over the current transcript and he clarified again what he said he truly meant. One by one, Trump staffers came in. John Kelly. Bill Shine, a former Fox News exec who'd been named communications director less than two weeks earlier. Now the room had twelve people trying to clean up this statement he made. Most of those people were on the trip with the president and had flown home with him for hours. Why hadn't they said anything before before? So with the president committing to issuing a clarifying statement, I took my leave.

"Bye!" I said.

My walking-*out* privileges worked, too.

*   *   *

HEADING INTO THE school year in the fall of 2018, all four Conway children were thriving. They were with me full-time in D.C. My mom had moved in with us to help with my Core Four. George was spending chunks of time in New York at the firm, where he voluntarily went from partner to an of-counsel role, spending his nights alone at our house in Alpine, New Jersey, 240 miles away from D.C. The numbers don't lie. During this time, the frequency and ferocity of his tweets accelerated. Clearly he was cheating by tweeting. I was having a hard time competing with his new fling.

I had already said publicly what I'd said privately to George: that his daily deluge of insults-by-tweet against my boss—or, as he put it sometimes, "the people in the White House"—violated our marriage vows to "love, honor, and cherish" each other. Those vows, of course, do not mean we must agree about politics or policies or even the president. In our democracy, as in our marriage, George was free to disagree, even if it meant a complete 180 from his active support for Trump-Pence–My Wife–2016 and a whiplash change in character from privately brilliant to publicly bombastic.

"Whoop-de-do, George!" I said to him. "You are one of millions of people who don't like the president. Congrats."

The usual silence.

I continued: "But you are one of one whose wife is counselor to the president. You shouldn't criticize me publicly. And when did you become so mean? That is so *not you*."

George's answers were always the same. *Trump, Trump, Trump . . .* The reflexive, obsessive, formulaic "but Trump" slur that permeated half the Congress and half the country was now dominating half the Conway couple.

On one side was my marriage and my husband. On the other was my job and my boss. George was mixing the two of them in a highly combustible manner. I was able to keep these things separate and in perspective. George should have, too, but it seemed the flood of reaction and attention he was receiving was magnetic and irresistible. And not just to George. There were the so-called Never Trumpers, roughly 5–7 percent of the actual Republican Party but 90+ percent of those "Republicans" on

CNN and MSNBC (in fact, hating Trump seemed to be the only crite-rion you needed to be invited on one of those networks).

CLAUDIA CONWAY HIT the eighth grade and blossomed. She ran for president of the middle school student body against six other girls. Clau-dia and the other top vote-getter were in a runoff election, and Claudia prevailed. My running joke was, "I'm now counselor to two presidents, and Claudia is definitely the more demanding one!!"

My other children were also successfully fitting in at their new schools. I made friends with moms like Kim, June, Laura, and Jill. Even as New Jersey felt like "home," all four kids loved walking to George-town and exploring D.C. They loved hosting friends and family, show-casing and sharing their new city and the unique trappings of their mom's job.

Meanwhile, on September 4, the Senate Judiciary Committee was beginning confirmation hearings for Brett Kavanaugh. The contentious hearings were expected to dominate the news cycle for the rest of the week, but you know about the best-laid plans. The following morning, the *New York Times* published an unsigned op-ed under the headline "I Am Part of the Resistance Inside the Trump Administration."

Here we go again, I thought as I read the latest from yet another secret source. The op-ed kicked off a new policy-free parlor game inside the Beltway: Who was Anonymous? Predictably, the media lost its col-lective mind, breathlessly and myopically asking every White House offi-cial, cabinet secretary, and even the vice president to deny, *on the record,* that he or she was Anonymous. Mainstream media and social media even had me in the mix of possibilities. And George. Or maybe it was the two of us writing together. The lonesome dum-dums' speculation on Twitter looked especially foolish. (They'd still be speculating three years later when Anonymous was revealed to be exactly that, a not-senior-level staffer in the administration.)

An entire segment on *Morning Joe* featured John Heilemann, the same guy who'd been insisting for years that Russian collusion had swung an election after he had long sworn Hillary would absolutely win: "The more you think about it," he said, "the more Kellyanne Conway makes some sense [as 'Anonymous']. She's very cagey. She's the kind of person who would find out that Mike Pence used the word *lodestar* a lot and put *lodestar* in to try to pin it on Mike Pence. If you think about the double act she's doing with her husband, trying to set herself up to be [James] Carville and [Mary] Matalin of the future, this is a good hedge against Trump failing because she would be the kind of person who would want to come out after Trump failed and say, 'You know what? I was working on the inside for the resistance all along.'"

Read that again. That convoluted passage. Your brain might hurt, but you will feel supersmart that you are not this guy.

Somehow the intrepid reporters sleuthing out "Anonymous" (who should have remained that way) found time to check in on the Kavanaugh hearings, where things looked like they would wrap up fairly quickly. He was poised for confirmation to the U.S. Supreme Court, when, on September 17, the world was introduced to a woman from California named Christine Blasey Ford. She lobbed decades-old allegations of sexual assault against Kavanaugh. That Sunday, I spoke separately with the president and Senator Lindsey Graham of the Judiciary Committee about what would happen next. Graham committed to protecting Blasey Ford's privacy, if that was important to her.

When asked about her allegations on *Fox & Friends*, and minutes later by an unusually large and raucous press gaggle on Pebble Beach as I tried to enter the main doors to the West Wing, I was clear about Blasey Ford: "She should not be insulted, and she should not be ignored."

There was no doubt Blasey Ford would have her day and her say. But where, how, and when? Senator Graham offered her privacy and convenience to testify. The FBI furnished an investigation into the allegations. Among White House and administration staff, I was ready to assume a larger public role in the Kavanaugh hearings, Part II. I was ready as a woman, as a parent, as a lawyer, and as a constitutionalist who had worked with the Federalist Society and had conferred with Donald Trump many times about Supreme Court selection. I was also ready, unbeknownst to the public, as a victim of sexual assault. This wall-to-wall coverage was not in a vacuum. This was happening against the backdrop of the "MeToo" movement, which was claiming big names in nearly every industry, including media and politics. The president agreed I should take the lead on this.

I put it this way to Gayle King, Norah O'Donnell, and John Dickerson on *CBS This Morning*: "I know there's pent-up demand for women to get their day, women who have been sexually harassed and sexually assaulted, and I personally am very aggrieved for all of them. But we cannot put decades of pent-up demand for women to feel whole on one man's shoulders. What exactly is the standard for ruining one man's life based on decades of allegations that have nothing to do with him?"

I also acknowledged that Blasey Ford's testimony was "compelling" and "very sympathetic" and that it would appear she had been "absolutely wronged by someone," but that there was no hard evidence it was Brett Kavanaugh. I was pleased she came to testify and was pleased we asked for an extended FBI background check—the seventh FBI background check of Brett Kavanaugh.

I inadvertently revealed my own personal story on CNN while I was on Jake Tapper's *State of the Union*:

"So you're always going to find somebody to try to impugn the integrity of either Kavanaugh or Ford," I said. "That is not what this is about. This is about whether this man and his impeccable judicial temperament and qualifications in twelve years on the second-highest court in this country is qualified to be on the United States Supreme Court.

"What you saw the other day, even though a lot of it was a national disgrace, what you saw the other today is a Senate Judiciary confirmation hearing. It is not a criminal or civil proceeding."

I continued: "It's not a meeting of the MeToo movement. I feel very empathetic, frankly, for victims of sexual assault and sexual harassment and rape. That . . ." I took a breath. "I'm a victim of sexual assault. I don't expect Judge Kavanaugh or Jake Tapper or [Senator] Jeff Flake or anybody to be held responsible for that. The perpetrator has to be responsible for their own conduct."

Tapper immediately said that he'd never heard me say something so personal (fact-check: true) and was so sorry that happened to me. That was decent of him. What he said next was not decent of him: "But . . . you work for a president who says that all the women who have accused him are lying."

That sentence from Jake Tapper might as well describe the whole Trump era. Trump, Trump, Trump. It is so central, so blinding, that it creeps and seeps into conversation after conversation, even one on live TV where the anchor, who has "a wife and a daughter," is seated feet away from me and where the topic is about a woman's sexual assault allegations from decades earlier against a man not named Donald Trump—and now my own unplanned disclosure. For the critics who just can't quit him, Trump must be the subject, the predicate, and the adverb of every sentence, even here, when I had blurted out such a raw and personal revelation on live national TV, saying I was sick of everything from "you look nice in that dress" to forced penetration being treated as if they were the same thing—sexual assault. "But Trump" was still the thoughtless response and presented as some sick justification for the awful things that had happened to me.

George was still asleep when I returned from CNN. I woke him and told him what had happened. What I'd said and wished I hadn't. He tried to be reassuring.

People were urging—and some were demanding—that Trump dump Kavanaugh, who had held several senior positions in the George W. Bush White House, as had his wife, Ashley. The president stood firm, asking for a full and fair hearing before the usual mob jumped to the usual conclusions. In this case, their advice was to cut and run. Judge Amy Coney Barrett of the Seventh Circuit, some said, would be a safe choice, and a good substitute, in this #MeToo climate. Her name was floated by a few internal and external advisors, along with a couple of others'. But the president was steadfast, waiting and watching the proceedings like everyone else.

I had been in Indiana to headline a fundraiser for Mike Braun for Senate. On the tarmac, Mike Brey, the Notre Dame men's basketball coach, caught up with me and asked to take a photo. After he posted the photo, I received a text from a reporter asking if I was in Indiana to meet Barrett and replace Kavanaugh. I hadn't even thought of that as a possibility, but the media was eager to see if Trump would drop Kavanaugh.

Weeks after I'd said Kavanaugh's accuser "should not be insulted" and "should not be ignored," meaning she should have her say, she did testify in public for all to see. She certainly did not avoid the limelight, and Kavanaugh could not avoid the klieg lights.

Neither, it seemed, could I. Walking back to the White House, I was again surrounded by a mob of reporters on the driveway. Peter Alexander of MSNBC followed me, insisting the president had been disrespectful in addressing the hearing testimony through a comment he'd made at a political rally the night before. "Ford has been accommodated by all," I reminded him. "She's been treated like a Fabergé egg by all of us, beginning with me and the president." In fact, she had been deified by the usual loudmouths, all of whom had no basis to know whether her decades-old claims were true. Those same people couldn't and wouldn't have cared less about my own painful experience . . . because . . . "but Trump."

Evidence of that double standard was crystal clear. The next morning, *Morning Joe* cohost Mika Brzezinski launched into a furious tirade over my unintended revelation of sexual assault. She didn't seem angry with the perpetrator. Her ire was reserved for me, the victim. I didn't ask for anyone's sympathy, so why the scorn? Does the MeToo movement or the so-called "Sisterhood" go where the law does not, deciding who deserves respect, justice, and compassion based on her politics or day job? I was shocked when I caught wind of it, because I'd known Mika to be an intelligent and compassionate person and a fellow traveler in the band of moms with daughters.

"So tell us your story," Mika railed at the camera, speaking directly to me, who wasn't watching, while the show's bleary-eyed insider audience listened in. "Who is your attacker? Who broke the law? Who hurt you? You seemed really uncomfortable when you let that slip out. Your voice got small. Your voice cracked. You had to clear your throat. You were really uncomfortable just saying 'I am a victim of sexual assault.' And, you know what, I say that as a victim of sexual assault myself. So, I want to ask, 'Why can't you be the egg, Kellyanne—the Fabergé egg—and tell your story because you say women should be heard.'"

Victims of sexual assault, of course, are under no such obligation. And I wasn't the one accusing the next associate justice of the United States Supreme Court of a crime from thirty years earlier. I hadn't planned to say anything at all, let alone place myself, as Blasey Ford did, squarely in the arena, destined to become an instant heroine for feminism, whatever that now was. I didn't confront Mika, but plenty of outraged viewers and other critics did, roundly condemning her for her blame-the-victim insensitivity.

Two more accusers came forward, led by their attorney, Michael Avenatti, whom the media turned into an instant hero. I had run into Avenatti at an after party that year. Don Lemon pushed me toward Avenatti, who had been touted by Lemon's CNN colleague Brian Stelter as a serious presidential candidate. Avenatti looked me square in the eyes, put his hand on my shoulder, leaned in, and said, "You are the best thing that ever happened to Donald Trump." I scoffed at the flattery and replied with a wink, "And you are not the worst thing that's ever happened to Donald Trump." (That was before federal authorities took seriously Avenatti's attempted extortion of Nike and theft of client money, which would lead to several felony convictions.) Still, Kavanaugh was confirmed after Senator Susan Collins delivered a one-for-the-ages address and an affirmative vote. Even so, it's hard to overstate how pitched the fever remained in the D.C. swamp.

Nearly two weeks after Justice Kavanaugh was confirmed, I was out at a Mexican restaurant with Claudia and other eighth graders as they celebrated her birthday and the birthday of another friend. As the girls were blowing out the candles, I felt someone grab and shake me from behind. I turned to see a red-faced woman pointing her finger in my face with one hand and pulling on my arm with the other. I couldn't understand her out-of-control rant but exclaimed "You're touching me" and told her to get her arm off me. She did, but just kept spitting and spinning herself into a tizzy.

Claudia bolted up.

"You're crazy!" she shouted. "Get away from my mom." Other parents had been watching, and a few rushed over.

The woman did seem crazed, like the worst of the trolls come to life. She was in my face and just inches away from my daughter. The worst crossed my mind. The police were called. Claudia's poise throughout this ordeal was remarkable and her defense of me was striking. Months later, with a court hearing imminent, Lonely Loser Liberal Lady would apologize. But this wasn't just about a physical attack on me. She had done the unforgivable: interrupted the innocence and joy of a fourteen-year-old's birthday celebration. Incredibly, it turned out that the woman lived on the same street as the Kavanaughs. She also lived on the same planet as senators like Mazie Hirono and Kamala Harris, who as Judiciary Committee members forced us to watch the tops of their heads as they read from notes other people wrote in a quest to destroy Kavanaugh's chances of being a Supreme Court justice, and to destroy Kavanaugh himself.

AHEAD OF THE midterms, the president and vice president were doing their part to be sure the America First agenda remained front and center. Even staffers like Sarah Huckabee Sanders and I were joining the president and speaking from his podium at rallies, including on election eve in three different states—Ohio, Indiana, and Missouri, all Republican victories the next day. In Georgia and Florida, Trump's endorsements in the primaries and active campaigning in the general election helped Brian Kemp and Ron DeSantis, whom Pence and I also campaigned for together, win razor-thin governor's races.

Watching the midterm returns from the East Wing of the White House, we experienced all the highs and lows. On the disappointing side, key governorships fell to the Democrats. But Republicans defied history by picking up seats in the U.S. Senate. Even so, we confirmed historical precedent by losing the House. That night, enough races were called to put the Democrats over 218 seats and back in control. We had Speaker Nancy Pelosi to look forward to again.

Tucked in a corner of the East Room toward the end of the Election Night event at the White House were two couples: Donald and Melania Trump and Nick and Jamie Ayers. I knew that wasn't by accident. Something was clearly up. Nick Ayers was Mike Pence's chief of staff, a Kushner ally and plenty ambitious. Ever since John Kelly became White House chief of staff, Jared and Ivanka had been bristling under his military-style leadership, his attempts to curb their power and access, and his refusal to look the other way when they ran into roadblocks over their security clearances. Jared, on his own, had been looking around for a possible replacement. Now it was clear: His handpicked candidate was Nick Ayers.

The Nick I knew was always discreet. So why was he discussing a possible promotion to become the president's chief of staff in plain view of the guy who already had the job, John Kelly, Kelly's wife, Karen, and the rest of us? That seemed decidedly off-script.

When I confronted Nick about it, he told me he was leaving the decision to the Lord, which I respected, even as he sure seemed to be giving the Almighty a hand by campaigning so single-mindedly for the job. The media were involved in the open speculation, and there had already been rumors that I didn't want Nick as chief, even that I had threatened to quit if he was appointed. Those rumors weren't true, and Nick knew it. I honestly hadn't given the matter much thought and was more shrugged-shouldered about it than anything. Over time, I'd learned that, sadly, it really didn't matter to me (and possibly to the president) who was chief of staff.

Nick Ayers is smart and likable. He had the makings of a good chief. He had shown a knack for popping in and out of Trump-Pence World while presiding over a wildly lucrative consulting empire. He'd helped Pence prepare for what was a very successful vice presidential debate against the outmatched Tim Kaine. But then Ayers split his time between our busy campaign in New York City and his other lucrative clients, like Governors Eric Greitens and Eric Holcomb. (I had severed ties with my clients, and the money they had contracted to pay.)

Nick had come in handy when Jared removed Chris Christie as transition chairman in favor of installing Vice President–elect Mike Pence. After the transition, Nick was around all the time, making a savvy deal to stay on the "outside" for six months before entering the White House to replace a longtime aide as Pence's chief of staff and settle into working for the far punier government salary that went with it.

While John Kelly was a generational peer of the actual president, Ayers was a generational peer (and pal) of Jared. But a few weeks later, when Kelly announced he was leaving, Nick accepted the job, then shortly after reneged, moving back to Georgia with his young family. The president would tell me later that Nick "only wanted to do it for six months, and I couldn't do that." Nick later told me that he was sure Jared wanted him to be Trump's chief of staff, but he wasn't convinced that Trump felt as strongly about it.

CHIEF OF STAFF wasn't the only shuffling going on in the wake of the disastrous midterms. Attorney General Sessions, whom Trump had totally soured on for recusing himself from the Russian collusion investigation and other strokes of genius, including his family-separation policy at the border, was shown the door, too. The president named Sessions's chief of staff, Matthew Whitaker, as acting attorney general. Critics thought it was Trump's way to finally fire Robert Mueller and end the long-running Russia investigation. They were as sure of that as they were of the existence of Russian collusion in the first place. And they were clumsily and chronically wrong about both.

With everything else happening, those same questionable news sources were insisting on referring to the Twitter-famous George Conway as "Kellyanne Conway's husband." George got his own promotion, going from 140 characters in the crowded Twittersphere to a solo platform on op-ed pages.

A reporter on the South Lawn tried to ask the president about an editorial George had penned for the *New York Times* declaring Whitaker's appointment unconstitutional. The reporter had just gotten the operative three words out of her mouth, "Kellyanne Conway's husband," before Trump interjected.

"You mean, *Mr. Kellyanne Conway*? He's trying to get publicity for himself. Why don't you do this: Why don't you ask Kellyanne that question, all right? She might know him better than me. I really don't know the guy."

That crystallized something for me, something I wasn't eager to face. But it had become impossible to ignore any longer.

I had two men in my life.

One was my husband. One was my boss, who happened to be president of the United States.

One of those men was defending me.

And it wasn't George Conway. It was Donald Trump.

The response was classic Trump. He called out someone he saw as using him for publicity. He described that person rather than say his name. He dismissed the inherent silliness of the question. Why exactly would he be asked that question about someone else's spouse? And why would he care about someone else's tweets when he thought his were "the greatest"?!

George Stephanopoulos followed the president's advice three days later on his ABC News Sunday show and asked me about George.

I noted that George was now referred to as "Kellyanne Conway's husband" far more often than he was being referred to even by his first name, for which "I'm sure the feminists are very proud of me, that I'm an independent thinker who has a strong, powerful position in this United States government, counselor to the president." I continued matter-of-factly: "I offer my advice and opinion to the president in private. I don't need to put it on the op-ed pages . . . and by the way, none of this will be litigated in newspapers, or on TV." Then I mentioned something that had struck me the few times Donald Trump had raised George with me, all in passing, all teasing me more than taunting me: "The president is never worried how it [George's behavior] affects him. He's always worried about how it affects me."

Marriage vows are not promises of loyalty or fealty to Donald Trump or to any other political figure (or nonpolitical figure). They're vows of loyalty to *each other*. I love Donald Trump, but he is my boss, that's my job, and its term is limited; marriage is totally different, far more sacred and permanent. I was thinking about what my traditional Catholic wedding vows said at the end: "What God has joined, let no man put asunder."

All day long, I was hearing "but Trump," and now I was also hearing it when I got home at night. I was not about to accept *that* as the reason my marriage was fraying and my extended family was praying. People were horrified to think George was either using me for fame, or abusing me to force me to quit. The unimpeachable fact was this: As close as I was to the president, as intensely and as long as we had worked together, for all the disappointment I had felt about some things and the gratitude I had felt about others, I had not, or would not, think or speak about him a fraction of the time George had. I didn't want to be stuck in a cable news segment in the master bedroom. In our house divided, George and Kellyanne Conway spent a good part of their days dealing with President Donald Trump: me by his side, George on his phone.

The schism was sharp.

Chapter 27

Life of the Party

Donald Trump had a circuitous path from pro-choice Manhattan billionaire to ardently, actively pro-life president. But at heart, his path was not so different from that of many Americans. A personal experience with a couple he knew had challenged his default presumptions and changed his mind.

"What happened," as he explained it, "is friends of mine, years ago, found themselves pregnant. She wanted to have the child, he preferred not to, you know, abort it. And that child today is a total superstar, a great, great child. And I saw that. And I saw other instances."

The result? Donald Trump went from cohosting an abortion rights fundraiser at New York's Plaza hotel, which he owned at the time, to becoming the most pro-life president in U.S. history.

He first shared that story with me in 2011, and it hung over our conversations about abortion ever since.

I explained to him in March 2015 how the issue could help him defeat Hillary Clinton. (Far more women, I told him, are pro-life than the feminists pretend, and they are increasingly put off by Big Abortion's big money, including half a billion a year from taxpayers.)

I showed him the polling I had done on the issue over the years. (The Democrat Party platform and most Democratic politicians are abortion extremists compared to most actual Americans, who support early intervention, not eighth-month abortion.)

Later on, when I took over as campaign manager, I talked to him about crisis pregnancy centers, adoption options, and how to reach reluctant voters with assurances about the federal judiciary.

Some people, including heavy-hitting right-to-lifers and friends from Concerned Women for America and the Susan B. Anthony List, questioned the sincerity of Trump's professed change of heart. I never did, and the rest of them all came around. It didn't hurt that two months before the election, on September 10, Trump and I (along with Melania, Steve Bannon, and David Bossie) all flew out to St. Louis for the funeral of conservative icon Phyllis Schlafly. It was on that flight that Trump agreed to sign the Susan B. Anthony List's four-point pro-life pledge, promising to appoint pro-life Supreme Court justices, defund Planned Parenthood, sign a bill banning late-term abortions, and make the Hyde Amendment permanent, which for years had prevented federal funding for abortions.

He didn't stop there.

Just as he was reaching for his Sharpie, he asked me, "Where's all the other stuff?"

"What other stuff?" I had proofread that letter and knew it by heart.

"All that stuff you tell me about Hillary, that she's extreme, that she wouldn't stop abortion in the ninth month, that abortion's okay if you know you're having a boy or a girl and don't want the boy or the girl. Let's put all that in here."

"Oh, wow," I said to him. "We can do that."

I grabbed a pen out of my bag and began writing. I still have the marked-up copy. It was an incredible moment, truly. Donald Trump had the heart and passion of a convert. His additions to that letter laid bare the harrowing realities behind Hillary Clinton's support for abortion for anyone, anytime, anywhere, which included termination up to an hour before birth and for any reason. She had admitted just that in an interview a year earlier on CBS, saying she did not support any federal limit on abortion.

"Do you think the pro-life group will be okay with that?" Trump wondered aloud.

"I think they'll be thrilled with it," I assured him.

It was such a moving moment, throwing the gauntlet at Hillary Clinton. Signed letter in hand, I said to Bannon and Bossie in my best Donald Trump voice, "I'm loving the babies, I'm saving the babies, 'Crooked,' and you're killing them!"

That letter, along with Trump's bold move as a candidate to double the number of names and publicly share his list of potential Supreme Court nominees, helped save his bid for the presidency when the *Access Hollywood* scandal broke a month later. The combination of conservative groups (my longtime clients like the Federalist Society and Heritage Foundation) and pro-life leaders like Penny Nance and Marjorie Dannenfelser (also my clients for years) stuck with him through that brief but battering storm. Had he not put out a list? Had he not signed that letter? Had he not placed Mike Pence on the ticket as his running mate? Had he not done all of that, it would have been easy for that key part of the conservative base to all say in unison: "You know what? Screw it. We're not dealing with this. We knew we couldn't trust him. We'll focus on keeping the House and Senate Republican and make sure Hillary is a one-term president."

The climax of all that came on October 19 in Las Vegas, in the final Trump-Clinton debate, when moderator Chris Wallace asked about abortion. Trump did not throw away his shot. He took it.

"Well," Trump replied coolly, "I think it's terrible. If you go with what Hillary is saying, in the ninth month, you can take the baby and rip the baby out of the womb of the mother just prior to the birth of the baby."

Trump was just revving up.

"Now, you can say that that's okay and Hillary can say that that's okay. But it's not okay with me because based on what she's saying and based on where she's going and where she's been, you can take the baby and rip the baby out of the womb in the ninth month on the final day. And that's not acceptable."

The nation let out one long, loud *Ewwww!*

I squealed and jumped up backstage in a viewing room with Bannon, Jared, his guest Matt Drudge, Hope, Scavino, and others.

Finally! That decades-in-the-making zinger! And Trump came down hard on his female opponent in the final hour of the final presidential debate, something that "lifelong pro-life" politicians had lacked the courage to do. The overly rehearsed Clinton was flummoxed and had no good response. Trump had turned the extremist tables on Hillary. She reverted to the shopworn sound bites of a movement that no longer understood or responded to a changing culture. Then Trump landed a final blow:

"And, honestly," he said, "nobody has business doing what I just said, doing that, as late as one or two or three or four days prior to birth. Nobody has that."

The shoe was now firmly on the other foot.

The unfair slandering of pro-lifers as applauding the murder of abortion doctors or angling to keep women "barefoot and pregnant" was melting into a reckoning for the abortion-on-demand crowd. They were left justifying partial-birth abortions and the sale of fetal tissue and organs from aborted babies. Sonograms meant that "out of sight, out of mind" wouldn't work anymore. Neither would "back alley." The back alley had become a place where young generations crossed between this Starbucks and that Starbucks to get a drink customized one of twelve thousand ways. The idea that illicit medical procedures might occur there in the twenty-first century was a tough sell. Once Trump got settled in the White House, his connection to the pro-life community would still occasionally be challenged. But it would never seriously wane. Month after month, year after year, it would only grow stronger and more prominent.

FOLLOW THE SCIENCE becomes *follow the politics.* People scream "Science!" when it comes to a paper mask on a five-year-old's face to prevent the spread of a global pandemic, but not when it comes to a sonogram of a five-month-old baby showing a clear image of a human life, the baby's gender, heartbeat, and limbs.

Religion and emotion do not tell the whole story. Neither do self-proclaimed feminists and prominent celebrities who claim, in elitist if not racist harkening back to the eugenicists who were the founders of Planned Parenthood, that this woman or that woman should abort their babies because "those kids would not have much of a life anyway," all the while announcing their own pregnancies from their mansions while the stick is still wet, naming their "wanted" children months before their baby bumps are evident.

At some point, the fetus beat us. Science stepped in. Sonograms are scientific evidence that there is a real life inside a womb. The "facts first" "truth-seekers" pretend they don't see a BABY waving back at them in a 4-D ultrasound photo. Radical liberal governors in recent years have expanded the time frame in which abortions can be performed in their states, eager to mollify the multimillion-dollar Big Abortion industry. But these governors are at odds with millions of their less-vocal residents. A growing number of Americans find it impossible to reconcile abortions being performed at twenty-five weeks while learning that babies born at that point or earlier are surviving and thriving. I understand why people are pro-choice, but can't imagine many or any of them think sex-selection abortion or late-term abortion or pain-capable abortion is a good idea. Yet that is the Democrat Party platform. In 1996 their platform reflected President Bill Clinton's famous albeit phony call for abortions to be "safe, legal, and rare." By 2020, the word *rare* had been long removed. Now their platform states that they believe a woman should be able to obtain a "safe and legal abortion."

I was thrilled to read that the world's most premature baby had celebrated his first birthday. He was born at roughly the halfway point in a normal pregnancy. He weighed 340 grams, less than a pound, and could fit into the palm of a hand. Since he was born at twenty-one weeks and two days, abortion advocates would call him "uterine material" or a "choice." His parents call him their son, Richard, and we should all call him a miracle. Such survivals are more common now.

The extraordinary scientific developments of the twentieth and twenty-first centuries extend to in utero intervention and medically assisted conception. Big Abortion denies all this, pretending every abortion is to save the life of the mother or because the pregnancy is a result of rape or incest. Yet Planned Parenthood's own research arm, the Guttmacher Institute, disproves this, widely citing the statistic that "less than 1 percent of all abortions are because of rape or incest," even as 99 percent of their screeds included it. "Women's issues" or "women's health" is often a euphemism for abortion in political-speak.

My personal feelings were only deepened by my work as an outside-the-box survey research professional. I was determined to get past the limited "pro-life" and "pro-choice" labels and dig deeper into the fear, frustrations, beliefs, and expectations of Americans about the one issue that fuses medicine, science, religion, morality, gender, law, and politics.

No other issue comes close.

As is always true in my business, the wording of survey questions in a poll affects the outcome. That's not a comment about bias so much as utility. The classic question, "On the issue of abortion, are you mostly pro-life or pro-choice?" is not on its face a biased question. It is a limited question, though. If the pollster allows volunteered responses like "both," "neither," or "it depends," a richer, more accurate set of responses will follow. As on many intense questions of policy and humanity, there aren't only two positions on abortion. The nuances matter.

For many Americans, where they sit on the "pro-life-to-pro-choice spectrum" depends on who is pregnant, how she got pregnant, and, most prominently, "how pregnant" she is. As science progresses, so do opinions. As the fetus developed in the public's view, the public's view about the fetus developed. In this way, easy labels like "pro-life" and "pro-choice" exclude nuances and invite noise.

Instead of this oversimplification, I went looking for how people really felt. I wanted to surface the gradation of viewpoints I'd already heard in focus groups and read in responses to open-ended survey questions. Americans were split on which label they felt more comfortable with. In most legitimate surveys, neither achieved 50 percent. So we developed a set of questions that would allow for nuance.

We started where we always did:

Do you consider yourself pro-life or pro-choice?

Pro-Life

Pro-Choice

Neither (volunteered)

Both (volunteered)

Unsure/Depends (volunteered)

Refused (volunteered)

Followed by:

Which of the following statements best describes your own position on the issue of abortion?

1. Abortion should be prohibited in all circumstances

2. Abortion should be legal only to save the life of the mother

3. Abortion should only be legal in cases of rape, incest, or to save the life of the mother

4. Abortion should be legal for any reason, but not after the first trimester, or three months of pregnancy

5. Abortion should be legal for any reason, but not after the second trimester, or six months of pregnancy

6. Abortion should be allowed at any time during a woman's pregnancy and for any reason

Unsure/Depends (volunteered, accept and record)

Refused (volunteered, accept and record)

Ironically, Americans who called themselves either "pro-life" or "pro-choice" in the conventional either/or question could gravitate to any of the first four responses in the second one, and they often did. They "live together" in that space. In fact, close to 60 percent placed their personal point of view into one of the first three positions (never allowed, allowed to save life of mother, allowed to save life of mother or in cases of rape or incest), which aligned more with pro-life views. When you added responses to the fourth position (no abortions after the first three months/first trimester), some 75 percent of the country was accounted for.

That's where most Americans were. It is not where all Democrat elected officials in D.C. were.

In fact, only 15 percent placed themselves into one of the more absolute positions, that abortion should not be allowed under any circumstances or that abortion should be allowed at any time for anyone during a normal nine-month pregnancy. Yet 100 percent of federally elected Democrats today agree with and represent only 15 percent of the electorate. Every Democrat should be asked, "Is there ANY abortion you think would be a bad idea or the 'wrong choice'?" In polls, the most common answer to "What does Roe v. Wade mean" is "I don't know." The Democrats use that ignorance, which helps them tremendously, to frame any restriction to abortion as an assault on "women's rights." Although nearly three-fourths of the electorate do not align with Democrats on the specifics of abortion, the Democrats' Roe v. Wade scare tactics works.

In the very early days of my polling company, we got a big project from pro-life clients to run focus groups about something called "partial-birth abortion." At the time, I had no idea what that was. Neither did America. In these late-term abortions, a baby descends through the birth canal feetfirst so that everything from the baby's shoulder to its feet is outside the womb. Before the head is out and the baby takes its first breath, a "doctor" punctures the head with a sharp instrument, causing the skull to collapse so it can fit through the birth canal and to save anyone the inconvenience of hearing what clearly would be a newborn baby's first cry.

"No, that doesn't exist, not in this country." But it did, and Rick Santorum, then a young Republican U.S. senator from Pennsylvania, was sponsoring legislation to outlaw it. When Santorum and others on the House floor were showing factual medical diagrams of what happens during a partial-birth abortion, C-SPAN refused to air the video.

The term and the truth of partial-birth abortion were introduced in the well of the United States Senate and by extension to the consciousness of many Americans, allowing the pro-life movement to start to shift the extremist label over to the other side. Many of the radical extremists on abortion, the practitioners and profiteers more than the much more reasonable populace, have been made to own and eat these out-of-the-mainstream positions ever since.

The Democrat Party pretends to represent all of America, but the party does not represent Americans who are pro-life. Roughly half of the country is pro-life. But today zero percent of federal elected officials in the Democrat Party are pro-life. The Republican Party has U.S. senators who are pro-life and pro-choice. In fact, the first time I learned of the name Barack Obama was when he was a state senator in Illinois and a bill was being considered in the state legislature, the Born Alive Infants Protection Act. The bill, a companion to federal legislation passed by unanimous consent in the U.S. Senate in 2002, was designed to extend legal protection to an infant born alive after a failed attempt at induced abortion. In the state senate, Obama voted *present* once and *no* twice when the bill was being considered. Obama argued that, while babies might be aborted alive, it would be a "burden" to a mother's "original decision" to assess and treat them. In other words, no standard of care would be provided to the baby despite the baby being alive. Jill Stanek, a nurse in Illinois, elevated this issue by testifying that, in the hospital where she worked, infants who survived induced-labor abortions were abandoned to die in a utility room.

The Democrat position on abortion has become so unpopular that, according to a *Washington Post* study, Democrats did not say the word *abortion* one time during their 2020 national convention, while Republicans said it thirty-one times at theirs. Imagine that.

AS SOON AS Donald Trump was sworn in as president, he was ready to put his pro-life words into action. But what exactly would that mean, beyond nominating pro-life judges to the federal courts? That part was a given. The answer was unapologetically standing with the pro-life movement and encouraging those in his administration to do so.

The Trump administration was one week old when I took a short SUV ride and also a big leap from the Oval Office to the Ellipse on the National Mall, still within view of the White House. I emerged from the black vehicle into the crisp late January day and blew warm air into my freezing hands, which held the note cards I'd prepared after chucking the draft address someone in the White House speechwriting office had kindly prepared for me.

I kept my coat on until the last possible second, slipping it off to reveal a candy-apple-red knit St. John suit as I bounded up the stairs and onto the stage. In a suit that bright, I wasn't hiding from anyone. Mike and Karen Pence, on their eighth day of this new journey, stood nearby. In fifteen minutes, Pence would make history as the first sitting vice president to address the March for Life, an annual event since 1974 protesting the *Roe v. Wade* Supreme Court decision. I was the warm-up act. Literally.

The Pences were regulars at the March for Life. Mike Pence's famous phrase, "I'm a conservative, but I'm not in a bad mood about it," seemed especially apt that morning, as tens of thousands of men, women, and children on the Mall were smiling, screaming, and sobbing with relief and hope for what I referred to in my remarks as a "new dawn" for the respect and protection of life in America.

That same week, President Trump signed an executive order reinstating the "Mexico City Policy," which holds that U.S. dollars going to international nongovernmental organizations overseas cannot be used to promote or provide abortions and sterilizations. The following week, he nominated Judge Neil Gorsuch to the U.S. Supreme Court to fill a seat previously held by the reliably pro-life Justice Antonin Scalia, who had died the previous February.

We seemed to be on a roll.

The president, vice president, and I were seated in the White House dining room talking about making good on the promise to redirect federal funding away from dripping-in-cash Planned Parenthood's abortion factories and toward qualified women's health centers that provided mammograms and a wide spectrum of other women's health services that many abortion clinics did not. I was laying out the details when the president shot me a look.

"Oh, I don't know," he said. "I think this can just backfire, you know, the women . . ."

I recognized immediately where that was coming from. He had to be hearing from some of the registered Democrats on the senior White House staff. My guess was that some of them who had voted for Hillary over him months before doubted the sincerity of his pro-life conversion.

They believed he wasn't sincere—and sincerely hoped he wasn't.

Pence and I closed ranks immediately. If he was thinking politics, we were more than ready to talk politics. We showed him state-by-state charts making clear that despite the scare tactics on the other side, in many places women's health centers outnumbered Planned Parenthood clinics by more than 20 to 1. In Senator Susan Collins's Maine, for example, there were two Planned Parenthood sites, both near Portland. They were hundreds of miles away from women living in other parts of the state, which was flush with qualified women's health centers. In fact, Planned Parenthood tended to be in urban areas, belying their message about "access" for "rural Americans" and helping them profit off a higher-than-average abortion rate among African Americans and Hispanics.

Racism, anyone?

"You know, this isn't a negative at all," Trump said finally, after hearing actual facts. "If anything, I think it could be a positive."

*   *   *

ONE YEAR LATER, Mike Pence and I weren't the only members of the administration who would make history with the throngs on the National Mall at Washington's annual March for Life. On this day, I stood in the White House Rose Garden with my son, Georgie, then thirteen, and with other invited guests and staff members. It was considerably warmer than the year before, although I was, as always, bundled up and cold. This year we got to hear a sitting president directly address the March for Life. In all of U.S. history, that had never happened before.

A satellite beamed Donald Trump's message in real time to Jumbotrons on the Mall, where more than fifty thousand pro-life activists had converged again to crusade for the sanctity of life. The crowd had at least two reasons to celebrate: Donald Trump was in the White House, and conservative Neil Gorsuch was on the Supreme Court.

Trump said he was especially "proud" and "honored" to be addressing this particular crowd. "The March for Life," he said, "is a movement born out of love. You love your families, you love your neighbors, you love our nation, and you love every child—born and unborn—because you believe every life is sacred, that every child is a precious gift from God."

He praised the marchers for offering friendship, mentorship, and "life itself" to women in need of support.

I had shivers as I stood there listening in the Rose Garden, and I knew it couldn't be the fifty-degree January weather.

Georgie, along with a few classmates we had invited, listened just as intently, aware that something special and historic was happening here as the president's words rang out in the clear, crisp air. Out on the Mall, Trump was wildly cheered by the crowd of movement leaders from across the nation, along with busloads of church groups and schoolkids, legions of families with their children in tow, and people of all ages coming together in protest and in prayer.

"Because of you, tens of thousands of Americans have been born and reached their full, God-given potential," he told the crowd. "Because of you."

Trump really sounded good up there. He was connecting. He was himself. He was passionate. He was real. Hearing him speak that day, I had no doubt the pro-life cause had a lifelong ally. In total, people on both sides of the schism are quick to note that Donald Trump is the most pro-life president in history.

Chapter 28

Death Close to Home

They were always a key part of the Trump appeal and the Trump coalition: *the forgotten men and women (and children) of America*. People whose work lives weren't what they used to be, their factories shuttered, their jobs moved to China. People who were struggling with the mortgage or the car payment. People who could never be sure how they'd pay the next hospital bill or send their kids to college. People who couldn't imagine they'd ever be able to retire.

Too many Americans had spent the past couple of decades watching their opportunities narrow and their futures shrink. It used to be that each generation could realistically expect that the next generation would be better off than this one. But for a vast array of American families, that just wasn't true anymore. And these forgotten people weren't only a slice of America. Increasingly, they *were* America.

I began to realize that these economic struggles went way beyond a lack of employment. In fact, research showed that even among people who had a job, who did not worry about losing or replacing that job, the white-knuckled angst about making ends meet was a chronic affliction. Just a generation or two before, that household may have had one job (and one car), enough to support the entire family and have a little left over for a modest family vacation most summers. Now households have two or three jobs, and even that is no longer enough. The cost of living and the cost of complying with increasingly intrusive, invasive, expensive, and expansive government mandates, regulations, taxes, and fees are diminishing the value of work rather than rewarding and dignifying it.

From the start, lifting the forgotten and marginalized, the stranded and the struggling, and bringing hope to them was a crucial part of Making America Great Again. It was a message and a set of policies that Donald Trump could deliver like no conventional politician had dared, and he was eager to do it.

Among the "forgotten" were the tens of thousands of Americans dying of drug overdoses in this country each year and the countless men and women (and, yes, children) whose lives had also been ravaged.

Under Obama and Biden, those numbers soared.

These people were suffering in hiding, their struggles often blocked from view by the fading trappings of middle-class life. Their numbers were up in the tens of millions. Their plight was both a symptom and a cause of the decline our nation had been undergoing.

The statistics told the tale. Tens of thousands of deaths. Enough prescribed painkillers to numb into a stupor every man, woman, and child in the United States around the clock for a solid month.

I knew all this from the polls I had taken and from the people I had met. Donald Trump knew it, too.

OxyContin, Vicodin, Percocet, and all their generic cousins: The miracle relief these prescription meds once provided too often cycled into a morass of depression, job loss, impoverishment, and hopelessness, pushing millions of desperate and addled Americans toward illegal drugs like heroin, cocaine, methamphetamine, and street fentanyl when they could no longer access the legal meds. As soon as I got into the White House, I began to work on realizing this goal of candidate Trump and helping him to keep his promise. I knew it was an issue I had to take on. If promoting alternatives to abortion was one side of the pro-life cause, the other side would be offering hope, help, and healing to these vulnerable people among us and fighting this raging epidemic of opioids. "Pro-life" should mean throughout one's entire life.

"What did she say to you?" I once asked candidate Trump as we'd turned to leave a campaign event in Ohio. "It looked intense."

"The drugs, everywhere we go, the drugs," he said bleakly. "She lost her boyfriend, whose mother had been in jail for drugs years ago. Can you look into this? I keep hearing it from people, really everywhere we go."

I promised I would.

Here's what I learned: Appalachia, New Hampshire, and Ohio were among the hardest hit, but the crisis was indiscriminate and unforgiving. Both supply and demand had surged over the eight years of the Obama-Biden administration, which had done precious little to curb the rise. As was detailed in a *Washington Post* investigative report titled "Fentanyl Failure," the Obama administration was caught flat-footed by the surge in fentanyl. Experts said that "despite mounting deaths and warning, the Obama administration did not take extraordinary measures to confront an extraordinary crisis." Traditionally, Democrats placed more emphasis on treatment. Republicans placed more emphasis on interdiction. Each of these measures was important. But even combined, they had left the nation with an incoherent strategy, inadequate resources, and impossible odds.

"We lost enough people to drug overdoses last year to fill every seat at Yankee Stadium," I told Trump and others once we got to the White House. "This is the equivalent of a passenger plane falling from the sky every day. If a plane was falling from the sky every day, don't you think we'd all stop and focus?"

No one disagreed that the problem was sizable and alarming.

"So, let's focus on it," I said and got to work immediately.

I was minding my business, researching and conferring with experts in the field in the opening weeks of the administration, when Jared Kushner said to me one day, steps away from the Oval Office and his office, "You know, when you go on TV and say you are working on opioids and veterans, you offend the people here who are working on opioids and veterans."

"What?" I was taken aback.

"Yeah, we're already doing that. OAI is handling it."

Jared's pet project, the Office of American Innovation, packed with his handpicked appointees, was quickly becoming the kitchen sink of the White House, now stacked with a growing pile of the seemingly random issues he had taken on: taxes, tech, veterans, the drug crisis, peace in the Mideast, potato farms in the Midwest . . .

"Oh," I replied. "Does the president know that? Because he asked me to work on those issues. We had that meeting with Johns Hopkins and the Cleveland Clinic at Mar-a-Lago about veterans. And I've been digging into the opioids crisis. I could share with the guys at OAI that—"

"It's not necessary," Kushner snapped, clearly annoyed that I hadn't obeyed the first time. "There's plenty to do around here." Was he trying to think up less impactful ways for me to contribute?

What's next? I wondered. *Will he expect me to fetch that off-the-menu chopped salad the Navy Mess makes especially for him?*

Getting in my way for sport was one thing. But he was not about to block me if I could actually help people, and I was convinced we could. Several of the counties near my hometown of Atco, I'd noticed, were experiencing sharp increases in overdoses and deaths. My own family had experienced the drug horror up close. A friend's sibling was terribly addicted and suffered overdoses, time and again. Thankfully, first responders were able to use the drug NARCAN and, each time, that friend survived. But survival did nothing to cure the dependency. Eventually the body can only take so much. He passed away, a life cut far too short by this national crisis.

Millions of families have similar stories—and worse.

New Jersey governor and longtime Trump friend Chris Christie, who had delivered an impassioned account about drugs destroying and killing one of his successful, healthy friends, had cut the ribbon on a new treatment center in the town where my parents married. It sent a strong signal of seriousness and consequence when President Trump tapped Christie to chair the bipartisan President's Commission on Combating Drug Addiction and the Opioid Crisis. Trump asked me to head the issue on behalf of him, the First Lady, and the White House. Meeting in the Cabinet Room, we heard directly from people whose lives had been wrecked or whose children had been lost through opioids. It was one of only a handful of times I was brought to tears in the White House.

A young, beautiful, dark-haired woman from a small town in South Jersey shared her story of addiction and recovery. Vanessa told us she had become dependent on prescription painkillers while recovering from a cheerleading injury in college and quickly spiraled into heroin. My heart ached as she described her mother frantically driving up and down the streets of Atlantic City, where my own mother had worked for twenty-three years, searching for her daughter as darkness fell. The familiarity of

Vanessa—small town, loving home, private schools, college, great professional opportunities, and the world at her feet—it shattered me.

When I embraced Vanessa afterward, I felt the energy and resilience
of a young woman who had overcome addiction and lived to talk about
her triumph. We both knew that not everyone was so lucky. I told her
that if others could share their stories about the "crisis next door," they
might reach a stranger or save a life. *That's real power,* I thought, and a
major initiative of the Trump administration took hold.

Saving lives was the goal. So was reducing the shame and the stigma
and the silence surrounding addiction and dependency. That old recipe
of "more love and understanding, less guilt and judgment" came rushing
back to me. *There but for the grace of God go any of us.*

But could the federal government really dispense love and compassion? I had to think about that. Could the Golden Rule apply to our
work in the White House? Or was I just being naïve? We'd just have to
find out.

The commission held public hearings that brought together stakeholders from across the country. In my many conversations with people
much more expert in this than me, I quickly identified three areas to focus
on: Prevention and education. Treatment and recovery. Law enforcement
and interdiction.

I specifically avoided making this the Kellyanne Show. But with the
steady leadership of my chief of staff, Renee Hudson, we shepherded this
whole-of-government approach. I convened an Opioids Cabinet, which
met weekly and included people from fifteen different departments and
agencies. These experts were grateful to finally have their voice be heard
directly in the White House.

Our travels around the country brought the drug crisis into sharp
relief and took me to at least a dozen states with the president, the First
Lady, cabinet secretaries, and the nation's leading experts. We demonstrated both urgency and agency as we went from state to state, from big
cities to small towns, from factory floors to hospitals, receiving input and
delivering resources. On one trip to Cleveland with Governor Christie
and former congressman Patrick Kennedy, who spoke openly about his
own recovery, we visited veterans and were blown away by the new non-
drug treatments for non-combat-related pain. *Take a pill* wasn't the only

way anymore. The veterans I met that day were proud to demonstrate the alternative therapies that had reduced substance abuse and suicides.

In Maine, New Hampshire, Michigan, and Pennsylvania, we witnessed the conversion of fire departments into "safe havens." We talked to coroners overwhelmed by opioid deaths. We met with men and women who had worked in faith-based charities, the health system, and the public sector, helping drug addicts and their families. I also got to speak with many people in recovery. A single mom of two named Liza shared her story of survival and then hugged me. The photo of us embracing was carried by local newspapers the next day and is still etched in my mind. It was devastating to learn shortly after our visit that she'd been killed in a freak car accident. But her young children were strapped and safe in their car seats. I called Paul LePage, the governor of Maine.

"We're going to do this for Liza," I vowed. "And I want her children to know one day what motivated us. She overcame so much only to leave the world that way. They need to know their mom loved them enough to work hard at getting better."

I met Barbara Goldner, a nurse and social worker, whose husband, Brian, was the CEO of Hasbro Toys. They had lost their twenty-three-year-old son to a heroin addiction. He'd kept it hidden from his parents, as did the authorities. In the two months preceding his accidental overdose, Brandon had been revived seven times. I listened carefully, remembering my own friend's sibling, with a heart full of questions. Why is survival a crapshoot for so many? This one dies. This one lives. Addiction is a disease. We know that. Why can't we save more of these suffering people? Three of Brandon's ODs happened in a six-day period. Each time, he was discharged without substance-abuse or psychiatric screening, without any assessment of being a danger to himself or others, without referral to detox and recovery programs. Though he had provided his mother's name and phone number as an emergency contact, Barbara Goldner never received a call about any of her son's seven overdoses. The call she finally got was from a friend of Brandon's, who was at his apartment with police and the coroner. In their grief and anger at a system that failed their son, the Goldners became activists, pushing for vital changes in law and hospital protocols.

If a fifty-year-old businessman suffers a heart attack, his family gets a phone call. Why shouldn't the family of an inner-city young addict who overdoses? HIPAA privacy rules seemed to be counterproductive in cases like that. Soon the U.S. Department of Health and Human Services (HHS) issued a clarification that meant more families would be clued in before it was too late.

The opioids and poly-drug crisis was the most prominent public policy issue that Donald and Melania Trump worked on together. I'd go on to lend my staffer Catharine Cypher to help the First Lady build out her policy shop and solidify her "Be Best" initiative. In October 2017, the First Lady and I visited Lily's Place in Huntington, West Virginia, which does incredible work for neonatal abstinence syndrome (NAS), babies born chemically dependent. Melania cradled and comforted the newborns, while holding forth on the importance of keeping moms out of jail and their babies in facilities like Lily's Place. That same month, the Trump administration declared the drug crisis a public health emergency.

The evening before that announcement, the president and First Lady sat with senior staff in the Roosevelt Room as we previewed the run of show for the next day's event. "I never touched a drug in my life . . . *never!*" Trump told us. "And no alcohol, either. No cigarettes. I never touch the stuff. I know myself, and I would want more. I lost my brother Fred, more handsome, smarter, supposed to take over the family business. Lost him to alcohol at forty-two."

We'd heard this story before. But sitting in the relative quiet of this small room in the White House and knowing how we were taking on the nation's opioid crisis, I think all of us were struck by how deeply, personally moving his words were.

WE ROUTINELY REACHED out to people whose stories both informed and inspired us and invited them to the White House, often to meet with the president. Ryan Holets, a police officer from Albuquerque, New Mexico, showed what miracles can happen when people step out of their comfort zones and learn to see addicts as human beings in pain rather than nameless statistics or just a public nuisance.

Holets, we learned, had been responding to a call on September 23, 2017, about someone trying to steal beer from a gas station convenience store. That's where he spotted a couple sitting on a grassy slope out back.

He could see a syringe and a spoon, too, which the pair tried to hide as he approached. The officer's body camera captured what unfolded next:

"I'm not gonna lie to you, it looks like you guys are ready to shoot up," Holets said. Then he noticed that the woman, thirty-five-year-old Crystal Champ, was pregnant.

"How far along are you?" he asked.

"Like, seven or eight months," Crystal answered, clearly agitated.

"Oh, my gosh," Holets said, his voice shifting from that of a cop about to arrest a couple of addicts to that of an alarmed father of four.

"Why are you doing that stuff?" he admonished. "You're going to ruin your baby. You're going to kill your baby!"

Crystal buried her head in her hands and sobbed. Holets had already decided against arresting the expectant parents, but he wasn't ready to simply walk away.

"What do you think is going to happen when your child is born?" he asked.

Through her tears, Crystal said she wanted to put the baby up for adoption.

"Do you know who's going to adopt your baby?" Holets asked.

"No. No, I'm so sorry," Crystal cried.

Sitting with the president, the Albuquerque police officer picked up the story there. "Two worlds collided as I knelt down beside her, a police officer and a homeless drug addict brought together by forces outside of our control."

Certain that his wife, Rebecca, would feel the same need to make a difference, the Holetses offered to adopt the baby. After going into labor five weeks early, Crystal gave birth. Ryan Holets was present in the delivery room. Sadly, the baby girl was born addicted to heroin and meth and was forced to endure two painful weeks of withdrawal. Ryan and Rebecca took turns at the hospital to comfort the underweight infant around the clock. This was their child now. But they still hadn't decided what to call her.

"We have so much hope for you," Ryan murmured to his daughter as he gently rocked her one night.

Hope Crystal Holets was named for the family who gave her a fighting chance, the mother who ultimately chose life, and the single word that was the common goal behind every piece of legislation passed, every cent of the $6 billion in new federal funding we secured to help Americans fight opioid abuse, and every effort across party lines to turn the tide on addiction.

Unknown to almost everyone, Holets's name had been added to the secret guest list that had been assembled for the upcoming 2018 State of the Union address. He and his wife, Rebecca, along with their new baby daughter, would sit next to Melania Trump in the First Lady's box. There weren't many dry eyes when Trump asked the Holets family to stand, eliciting a rare, bipartisan standing ovation.

THIS NATIONAL CRISIS needed a national team effort.

We pulled in big names from the private sector, like Amazon, Google, Microsoft, Apple, Facebook, Leidos, Walmart, CVS, and Walgreens. Professional sports teams also joined in the effort. The Baltimore Ravens donated money toward drug packets for every tackle made and the Washington Wizards and Washington Capitals hosted an opioid awareness night. Opioids, all of them recognized, were a problem for their customers, their communities, and their employees. They all expressed a willingness to help generate creative ideas. Amazon programmed Alexa to answer questions about opioids and addiction. Emergent BioSolutions offered free NARCAN nasal spray (the drug that can reverse overdoses) to every public library and YMCA in the country. Walmart furnished a product that allows for safe drug disposal. Google invested heavily to expand the reach and success of "Take Back Day." Governors looked for ways to get their state medical schools to change the curriculum on safely prescribing drugs. Many companies turned their efforts inward, creating better systems of communication and treatment options for their own employees and their employees' families.

I liked what Belden Inc. did at its cable manufacturing plant in Richmond, Indiana, where business was booming and one-third of the workforce was expected to retire within five years. Now, when a qualified job applicant failed the pre-employment drug test, that person was sent for drug rehab on the company's dime, instead of just being shown to the sidewalk. And a job would be waiting on the other end. One forklift operator told me he owed his life to the company. Another employee confided that he was almost relieved to have failed the drug screen because he never would have entered treatment otherwise. I started telling the Belden story to employers in other communities. Great ideas are meant to be shared and duplicated.

Our cause got a major boost when the Ad Council voted unanimously to work with us, donating a massive amount of advertising time. "It's a big get," I told the president, reminding him that the Council was behind major public service campaigns like Smokey the Bear, Friends Don't Let Friends Drive Drunk, and A Mind Is a Terrible Thing to Waste. "We're going to reach so many people!"

One especially effective ad, "Treatment Box: Rebekah's Story," featured an addict going through withdrawal and recovery. It was a six-minute film that played around the clock on specially built cubed screens in New York and other major cities. No matter the time of day, people were drawn to watch, standing in one spot, taking precious moments out of their busy day. That one won an Emmy. Other ads in The Truth About Opioids series told the real stories of Americans, many who were desperately dealing with addiction and an overwhelming need to get more pills at any cost. One young man smashed his hand with a hammer. Another sped her car into a wall.

Given all the attention and goodwill we had generated, this was an issue, I was convinced, where we might find bipartisan agreement, even in thoroughly divided Washington. I got busy assembling a legislative package we called the SUPPORT for Patients and Communities Act. SUPPORT stands for Substance Use-disorder Prevention that Promotes Opioid Recovery and Treatment.

I was on Capitol Hill quite a bit in the summer and fall of 2018. Normally when Congress begins adding bills together, you lose support. But incredibly, the opposite was true this time, in part because every member had seen the need back home. One day, as I was delivering a briefing in the Capitol for eighteen senators—more Democrats than Republicans—liberal Massachusetts senator Elizabeth Warren came barreling in, ready, I was sure, to challenge whatever I had to say. But she stopped when she noticed I was surrounded by doctors in lab coats and admirals in uniform. We had a civil conversation. I happily listened to her ideas and answered her questions. Then, seeing she was invested and noncombative, I asked Senator Warren if we could count on her help.

That legislative package passed nearly unanimously. The votes were

98–1 in the Senate, including yea votes from Michael Bennet, Corey Booker, Kirsten Gillibrand, Amy Klobuchar, Kamala Harris, Bernie Sanders, and Elizabeth Warren, all Democrats already angling to run against Trump in 2020—and every single Democrat in the House. The package included a combined fifty bills and yielded $6 billion in new money for state and federal addiction prevention and treatment programs, stopping doctors from overprescribing addictive narcotics and intercepting shipments of fentanyl and other deadly drugs at U.S. borders. It also provided for intensified federal research into new pain management therapies. These changes, I was convinced, would truly save lives. And we proved something a lot of people doubted: In a bitterly partisan era, we *could* all work together for the greater good of all Americans.

"Together we are going to end the scourge of drug addiction," President Trump said in the bill-signing ceremony on October 24 at the White House. "Or at least make an extremely big dent in this terrible, terrible problem."

Over the next few years, progress on the issue continued. We tried to make *fentanyl* a part of the everyday lexicon, since it was fast becoming a lethal killer. Enough illicit drugs to kill the entire U.S. population many times over were seized through the mail, at our ports, and at our southern border. We launched an enhanced narcotics operation led by the U.S. Southern Command. Just as important, we launched FindTreatment.gov, which had sat dormant for more than a decade. This interactive website provides an easier, customizable way for people seeking addiction treatment to find providers near them. After years of work, we made it possible for those seeking treatment to customize their search as you would with most web searches, including specific treatment, inpatient/outpatient, age, private or public insurance, veteran, LGBTQ. Months later, I suggested it would be applicable for finding testing during a global pandemic.

We began to see the first decline in overdose deaths in nearly thirty years.

Part VI

House Divided

Chapter 29

Poison Keyboard

As 2018 gave way to 2019 and the second half of Donald Trump's presidency began, the nation was divided in many ways.

Nancy Pelosi was sworn in as Speaker, giving Democrats control of the House of Representatives, while Republicans maintained control of the Senate and the White House. The fruitless hunt to find conspiracy and election-shaping collusion between Russia and the 2016 Trump campaign, otherwise known as the Mueller investigation, seeped into its third calendar year. The federal government was shut down. The contentious debate over whether our southern border should be fortified was roiling Washington again and playing out in cities and towns across the nation. Brett Kavanaugh joined Neil Gorsuch as Trump-appointed associate justices of the U.S. Supreme Court, but the battle scars suffered by people on both sides of the divide during his confirmation hearings remained glaring. You could see it on people's faces and smell it in the air. A fractured White House was welcoming its third chief of staff in two years. The Democrats were also divided as fresh(man) faces like Congresswoman Alexandria Ocasio-Cortez, an overnight sensation for upsetting a Democrat stalwart in a primary, tried to move the party to the far left, while a large, disparate group of Democrats made clear they were getting serious about running to replace Trump in the White House.

My house was also divided.

George ramped up his presence on Twitter and amped up his criticism of President Trump. A thirsty press corps and a rabid anti-Trump, never-Trump, oddly-obsessed-with-Trump contingent that seems to live on social media could not get enough. Regularly furnishing fresh though often redundant content, and most days well surpassing the number of tweets and retweets sent by the tweeter in chief himself, George did not disappoint his growing fan base of Trump haters.

George, however, did disappoint me, skipping the kinds of confidential, civil conversations spouses typically have when one has a change of heart or both agree to disagree about something big. Instead of that, he chose to take his feelings public. Friends of ours watched in horror, including those who had done something George himself had not done—voted against Donald Trump. It had been a constant theme throughout my complicated life: Even if I could not understand something, I could still grow to accept it. Whatever George's rationale, it was a complete about-face from his earlier, enthusiastic support of President Trump and his partner of twenty years.

It was just so out of character for George. One of his most admirable qualities, I had always thought, was how he kept his own counsel. Weighing in smartly yet sparingly. Retaining and then repeating details from conversations that I wasn't even sure he'd been listening to. When my mouth was in mile-a-minute overdrive, George would remind me and my female-centric family in South Jersey (that is also his family) that the famous "Mars versus Venus" gender divide could be scored in daily spoken-word count. Perhaps there is no greater gender gap than this one—with our differing loves of chocolate and our heat-versus-air-conditioning debate vying for second. As his wife and closest confidante, I knew exactly what he thought about various people, places, or things, but neither he nor I would ever have divulged any of that. Clients and colleagues valued his discretion. He saved his verbosity for the sharp legal briefs and sage client advice that he was known for. Family and friends accepted and at times admired that George was quiet but present. He could surprise people with his sense of humor, impersonations, and hearty laugh, yet his natural resting place was knowledgeable but reserved. As wise in what he didn't say as in what he did say.

Going into 2019, George's daily spoken-word count at home

remained low, even as he descended deeper into the quicksand of Twitter. George was getting addicted to the sugar high of new followers, likes, tweets, retweets, trending, and the predictable *breaking news! lookie here!* reaction of the media lemmings. They had egged him on from the cheap seats as he upped his Twitter output from zero tweets during the entirety of 2016 to an average of dozens per day.

"What are you doing, George?" I asked him plainly and calmly.

I got the same answer every time we discussed his newfound love, which was not often. "You work for a madman," George would say in a loud, sinister voice, as if his finger were still on the tweet button. "He is not fit to be president, and he will destroy this country!"

I had heard all this before, of course. I have access to cable TV and social media. Trump Derangement Syndrome was real and festering and incurable. People seemed to lose their manners about the Office of the President, en route to losing their minds about President Trump.

Never Trumpers, accounting for roughly 5 percent of all actual Republicans and roughly 95 percent of the "Republican" guests on non–Fox News TV, were glorified and deified by reporters who sat on Twitter all day, lavishing praise and retweets on each other. According to the Pew Research Center, 22 percent of Americans said they were on Twitter—a number that has remained quite stable. And just 10 percent of Twitter users prior to the 2018 midterms produced 92 percent of all U.S. tweets. Of these highly prolific users, 69 percent identified as Democrats or Democratic-leaning independents. When you get right down to it, the vaunted Twittersphere is still a relative handful of people, talking mostly to each other and finding comfortable reinforcement in one another.

The Twitter bios of these "concerned citizens" often said "former" this or "former" that. These people seemed to believe that because they and President Trump both had Twitter accounts, they were just like President Trump. A hodgepodge hot mess of tweets spilled constantly forth from print "reporters," content that could never have gotten past an editor's desk and into their own publications. But there were few rules and no editors on Twitter. Just like-minded people with poisonous keyboards and a mind-boggling amount of free time.

This strange, parallel, online universe was tickled that "Kellyanne Conway's husband" was inching toward the ragtag Resistance, and then jumping in with both feet. The offline media followed, led by the *New York Times,* which happily turned over a generous parcel of its most-prime real estate to George and an odd collection of lawyers whose views might otherwise have been ignored (okay, routinely *were* ignored). Now this motley crew was high-mindedly announcing the launch of a group they called "Checks and Balances."

Never heard of it? Don't remember it? You are not alone. Three years later, they had a paltry 38,000 followers on Twitter, a website with less than a dozen statements since 2019, and hadn't really produced anything. Isn't it curious that on paper this group was more logical for a lawyer of thirty-plus years, and given the issues afoot during the Trump administration (Mueller, impeachment)? But this wouldn't be the group getting the MSNBC interviews or Twitter buzz. The group did lend a few of its wayward "advisors" and "former" something-or-others a chyron for cable TV so they could sit and spew on-screen, even as George seemed to unburden himself of the group not long after its founding. Hungry consultants, who had failed upward for years, greased each other on a new gravy train to nowhere while the political graveyard was littered with clients they had flayed for money and failed at the ballot box. None of them had ever achieved what "the wife of Kellyanne Conway's husband" had achieved, and none of them had a spouse in the West Wing of the White House. They wanted George for bigger, better things—for *them.* Bigger bank accounts and better talking-head gigs.

In all that time, the president barely mentioned George to me, except to say he'd only met the guy on a few occasions ("He was quiet in the backseat that time we went to the Mercer costume party") and had barely spoken to him. Other members of Team Trump—and a few people with Trump in their names—had decided they were no longer going to sit by as George insulted the president's work and mine. Eric Trump, accustomed to defending his father offline and online, chimed in to defend *me* against the Twitter troll who was also my husband. In December 2018, Eric tweeted: "Of all the ugliness in politics, the utter disrespect George Conway shows toward his wife, her career, place of work, and everything she has fought SO hard to achieve, might top them all. @KellyannePolls is a great person and frankly his actions are horrible."

The tweet from Eric, a loving husband and a new dad, was intended more to defend and protect me than to attack George. I appreciated his gallantry and sincerity, though I also would have preferred to just avoid the public confrontations. Eric and I spoke by phone after the tweeting episode. CNN's Dana Bash called to say she needed to do a story about the kerfuffle. *Breaking news,* no doubt! But in the same breath, she also said that if she'd known prior to our previous sit-down eight months earlier where all of this was heading, she wouldn't have tossed in that flippant question to conclude a hard news interview: "What's up with your husband's tweets?" I had not asked her anything about her ex-husbands or private life in return. I would not have done that. I could not understand why anyone would.

Cue another *New York Times* feature on this "breaking news": Two female *Times* reporters, Annie Karni and Katie Rogers, were now assigned to the "George Conway beat." Karni, who had just jumped to the paper from *Politico* after becoming a new mom, called me for a comment on her very first *Times* piece. She had been assigned to cover a brewing battle. China versus the Uyghurs? Iran versus Israel? Schumer versus McConnell? Hillary versus What Might Have Been? *Nah!* This was "the paper of record." They do serious journalism.

Eric Trump's tweets versus George Conway's tweets.

I advised Karni, who would go on to use George as a rent-a-quote in pieces about everything from COVID to constitutional law, that she might want to tell her editor it was unfair to assume she still had "baby brain" and couldn't handle the substantive assignments that went to Peter Baker or Mark Landler, her male colleagues covering the Trump White House. One of us was suddenly speechless.

I asked her, "Would you like it if Ted [Mann, her husband, also a reporter] did that to you or to your employer? Would you want your [newborn] son to read something like that about his parents one day?"

She privately tried to make amends for her published transgressions many times years later. I am many things, but I try not to be phony or a hypocrite. Many of the same reporters who sawed down the rough edges on stories about colleagues of mine or deleted this or that passage in response to a threat or a request or the promise of an inside scoop could not see the sheer creepiness, the inappropriateness of writing and discussing my marriage and my children, and the potential long-term harmful effects on those children. And now you expect me to help soothe your conscience? Pass. I didn't pile on when reporters wore corduroy overalls, flannel shirts (are you chopping down that tree on the White House North Lawn?), or wedding gowns with twisted dirty bra straps peeking out. No, I was gracious. Why would I ever mention that?

MICK MULVANEY, A former congressman from South Carolina, had spent the past two years as director of the White House Office of Management and Budget, a full cabinet position, and acting director of the Consumer Financial Protection Bureau. Mick was a major player in the administration's lower-taxes, fewer-regulations accomplishments, and he was good on TV. Less than a month into the term, he'd been the first to note that the *Morning Joe* hosts, who had hung out with Donald Trump in his hotel suite in New Hampshire after he won that state's crucial primary and had been invited just weeks earlier by Jared and Ivanka to brunch with Trump at the White House, were now outwardly questioning the president's mental fitness. Mick suggested that perhaps we should ban the show and starve them of White House guests.

Mick had had a ringside seat to the tenures of Donald Trump's first two chiefs of staff, their approaches to the job, their relationships with the president, and the mixed results each managed to achieve. He was more laid-back than General Kelly, more serious than Reince Priebus, and he wasn't trying to be POTUS's BFF, as Mark Meadows would try to be in the future. When the photographers were around, he didn't seem to care whether *he* was in the shot. Of the three, Mulvaney was most attuned to the unique dynamics of the Trump family. Where Priebus had tried to befriend Jared, and Kelly had tried to oust him, Mulvaney endeavored to build goodwill with the whole team, tolerating and trying hard to accommodate "the kids." Mulvaney also discovered—and fixed—that certain people were putting at the top of the president's pile of important documents every night a printed copy of the Drudge Report and numbering which stories they wanted the president to read; lo and behold, they happened to be the same articles they had told Drudge to run. Mulvaney endeavored to be a chief of *staff* and not just chief of president.

When President Trump and the senior staff returned to the White House from Camp David on January 7, 2019, we were ready for a busy week. The president was set to deliver his first prime-time Oval Office address to the nation, his first major speech since Democrats had assumed majority control of the House. The topic was border security and the sixteen-day-old government shutdown. For someone whose party had lost forty seats and control of Congress, the president was feeling fairly upbeat. With Trump's help, Republicans had actually gained seats in the Senate a month after Kavanaugh's confirmation and prevailed in key close races like the governorships of Florida (Ron DeSantis) and Georgia (Brian Kemp).

He knew he deserved a lot of the credit for that.

We spent the next morning working on the remarks, followed by lunch in the Roosevelt Room, where he had agreed to preview the speech in an off-the-record session with network and cable TV anchors. As the president spoke, I was reminded of the breakthrough immigration polling my firm had conducted in the summer of 2014. Two years after Romney's loss to Obama and the Republican National Committee's clueless "autopsy," we had helped reshape the Republican conversation on immigration, foreshadowed Trump's rise, and pushed the America First concept onto center stage. As most Americans saw it, the question should not be simply what is fair to the illegal immigrant but what is fair to Americans.

Before the anchors arrived, there had been some heavy, behind-the-scenes jockeying about who would represent each network and print outlet at the lunch with the president, a decision we had left to the media outlets. That had devolved into quite a competition, with network colleagues trashing and undercutting each other, not so different from what happened every year for the press lunch prior to the State of the Union address. But once the questions began, the anchors were notably more curious and less dubious or odious than in some of their TV confrontations with Trump "and his people." They ate off White House china, seemed more engaged than enraged while in Trump's presence, took notes, and asked questions that almost sounded respectful.

"What did you think, Kel?" Trump asked me back in the Oval Office after the media guests had left the complex.

"I think they recognize that Pelosi and you are in your first pitched battle of a politically divided Washington," I said, "and they want to see who will blink first. The facts about border crossings, child smuggling, the drugs, and such are on your side, and they listened."

"Yeah, they won't cover it fairly," Trump said with a shrug, "but it's good we did that and we'll talk directly to the people tonight."

"No reason to be afraid of people who seem afraid of bread, mashed potatoes, and dessert," I joked, ribbing the carb-conscious press corps who had left the best parts of the meal on their plates.

Eight of us were in the Oval with the president as he spoke that night from behind the Resolute Desk. The president referred to the economic angst of immigration.

After his address to the nation, the Democrats got screen time for a rebuttal. Pelosi and Senate Minority Leader Chuck Schumer, standing side by side, delivered an odd and fact-challenged response. "The president has them worried," I observed afterward, still in the Oval.

Pelosi had barely been elected Speaker that week, squeaking by after making concessions to brand-new members young enough to be her grandchildren, frustrated liberals, and cranky moderates. I'd watched over Trump's shoulder in amazement and amusement at how he'd handled Hillary Clinton in 2016. Now I was eager to witness his interaction with Nancy Pelosi.

I didn't need to wait long.

The very next day, the Democrat and Republican leaders of Congress filed into the White House Situation Room. Among the Democrats were Schumer and Senate Minority Whip Dick Durbin. When Speaker Pelosi walked in, our eyes met.

"I was just at Trinity for a town hall this morning," Pelosi said. She might be Speaker of the House (again) now, I thought, but she was still enough of a retail politician to remember that she and I were both graduates of Trinity College, the nation's oldest Catholic college for women. I acknowledged and congratulated her on her speakership.

The president walked in late and handed out White House candy. He immediately congratulated Speaker Pelosi on her swearing-in and remarked, somewhat over-the-top, that he was "fascinated" by her and the way she operates. Schumer also extended his congratulations. My facial expressions might have included an eye roll or two: These two tough, hardened New Yorkers, Trump and Schumer, were all mushy and gushy about the new Speaker.

Pelosi did most of the talking for the Democrats, as Schumer sat quietly and grinned from time to time. Homeland security secretary Kirstjen Nielsen, who had taken the department's top job months after its former head, General Kelly, became chief of staff, gave a detailed presentation on key facts at the border—the number of migrants, the child exploitation from traffickers, and the cartels bringing in tons of drugs.

Pelosi listened but didn't budge, maintaining that she had her own (alternative?) facts and would not give a cent for the border wall, even though that meant keeping the government shut down. The president held his ground, too. Stalemate. The president was ready to leave, but not before tasking Pence, Nielsen, Kushner, and a few others with going to Capitol Hill to negotiate.

ONE OF MY favorite responsibilities in the White House was being part of a very small group of people who help recommend the guests in the First Lady's box for the president to mention in his annual State of the Union speech.

I was thrilled that Mrs. Trump hosted Officer Holets and his wife, Rebecca (and their baby, Hope) in 2018 and, the following year, Judah Samet, a Holocaust survivor who miraculously survived nearly being shot when he was four minutes late to services at the Tree of Life synagogue in Pittsburgh where eleven people were murdered. Members of Congress sang "Happy Birthday" to Samet, who turned eighty-one the day of the State of the Union. That night the president also honored Timothy Matson, a member of the Pittsburgh SWAT team who had been shot six times when he responded to the Tree of Life massacre.

What a humbling and meaningful assignment it was, helping to research and invite these American heroes to Washington for that one night each year when the president, his cabinet, and the Congress file into the Capitol to hear the commander in chief deliver a progress report and a vision for the future, an appeal to our better angels. Perhaps my deepest and most humble gratification came from the chance to connect with the guests on a personal level. That year, marking the seventy-fifth anniversary of D-Day, we also had two American veterans who had fought on Utah Beach at Normandy, sitting alongside a Holocaust survivor whom one of the soldiers later helped liberate from Dachau. With them was ex-prisoner Alice Johnson, who had been granted clemency by President Trump. She'd been serving a mandatory life sentence for a nonviolent drug crime. I was struck by her grace and her poise.

*   *   *

MARCH WAS TOTALLY off-script. While I was busy focusing on my two jobs as mom and counselor to the president (in that order), George was still completely sucked in by Twitter and his new popularity among strangers and a whole lot of people he'd previously had little regard for.

When it came to handling George, Brad Parscale, who had been Trump's lavishly compensated 2020 reelection campaign manager for a year already, some two years before the actual reelection, was no Eric Trump. He probably should have been more focused on Georgia than on George. But Brad, like George, spent an unhealthy portion of his day online, allowing himself to be baited by my husband's latest Trump insults, including nonphysician George's armchair-and-keyboard diagnosis of his nonpatient president as mentally unfit. In a fifteen-thousand-word piece for *The Atlantic*, George cited the *Diagnostic and Statistical Manual of Mental Disorders*, or *DSM-5*, a book he had hardly relied on in thirty years of being a lawyer.

Like every American, George is entitled to his opinion and has a constitutional right to express it. But he is not entitled to his own set of facts or seemingly converting his law license into a medical license when it suits him. What exactly qualified my husband to be making mental health diagnoses? No need for a medical degree when George had one degree of separation from Kellyanne Conway. Nothing more, it seemed, than that he really, really hated Trump and was Kellyanne Conway's husband. The "facts first" media suspended standards and made space for his poison pen. George had an obligation to consider how this one-sided civil war might affect our tender-age children and what kind of example his vicious social media outbursts were setting for them.

Unfortunately, the whole thing exploded around me.

Parscale responded in kind, on Twitter: "We all know that @realDonaldTrump turned down Mr. Kellyanne Conway for a job he desperately wanted. He barely worked @TheJusticeDept and was either fired/quit, didn't want the scrutiny. Now he hurts his wife because he is jealous of her success. POTUS doesn't even know him!"

The explosions had only begun.

The president then quote-tweeted Brad and added his own "A total loser!"

The next day was even worse. Early on Wednesday morning, the president released a lengthy tweet: "George Conway, often referred to as Mr. Kellyanne Conway by those who know him, is VERY jealous of his wife's success & angry that I, with her help, didn't give him the job he so desperately wanted. I barely know him but just take a look, a stone cold LOSER & husband from hell!"

Later that day, Trump was stopped on the South Lawn by reporters as he was headed to Marine One. He said, "Kellyanne is a wonderful woman, and I call him 'Mr. Kellyanne.' The fact is that he did a tremendous disservice to his wife and family. She's a wonderful woman." That was more delicately put than the tweet but consistent with what I was hearing from him privately, where his focus was on me and my children and not on the latest Trump detractors swinging from the rafters and preening for the cameras.

It was all so foolish and, frankly, beneath both of them. But each got his wish. George finally got the president to elevate him after spending days and nights tweeting thousands of times about the president. He went viral and gained more "followers," which is often the goal of people who are superactive on social media, even those over the age of twenty. And Trump, who had held back while he had my back, got in his classic counterpunch and signaled to the world that my job was safe, but also that he worried my marriage and my family were not.

The interview offers poured in. Networks and magazines. Big names across the media. Would George and I sit for an exclusive? You can imagine the pitches.

"America is divided, and so are the two of you."

"How does your marriage really work?"

"What is the effect of all this on your children?"

"Is this all for show, or was the guy holding his wife's coat as he cheerfully joined her at Trump's inauguration festivities now a full-on member of the Resistance?"

Surely the sit-down would have been a blockbuster, couples therapy on-air. When I politely declined, it wasn't only because there was little chance George would jump from the comfort of curated tweets to the choppy waters of live TV, next to the woman he loved and who he at one point had bragged was the "best politician." If my boss and my husband were going to attack each other online, I was going to protect my children offline—otherwise known as the *real world*. I was caught in a completely impossible position. George did not want to talk about it and shut down every attempt I made to discuss it with his usual refrain: "You are working for a madman." He wanted to tweet about it and text his newfound friends on encrypted apps about it. The woman who had married him and bore his children would need to wait.

Meanwhile, he spoke to a friend at the *Washington Post*, solo, and told the reporter, "The tweeting is just the way to get it out of the way, so I can get it off my chest and move on with my life that day. That's basically it. Frankly, it's so I don't end up screaming at her about it." He wasn't jealous of my success, he insisted, because "I made it possible for her to be where she is today."

Boorish.

It was not exactly true, that notion of him harmlessly letting off steam. He still berated me about "Trump! Trump! Trump!" He didn't "go on with his day." He was tweeting around the clock, tens if not hundreds of times in a twenty-four-hour period, even as our family needed him to be more present. He loved the attention. I was sad that I—*we*—weren't enough.

At the same time, he vastly downplayed his long-standing support for the president, claiming that I was the only reason he was happy Trump was elected and that he hadn't joined the administration because it was a "shitshow." But the receipts are in public view. The anti-Trump crowd never stopped to ask George, *How did you get here? And should we trust you?* They gave automatic membership to anybody who was anti-Trump. That welcome was extended to George and many other people who had at one time happily and actively worked for the president or proudly donned MAGA hats.

Forgoing a network exclusive or a magazine spread, I did end up addressing this latest episode of what I called "Men Behaving Badly (Online)" during my next scheduled interview. I had been invited to talk policy with Maria Bartiromo on the Fox Business Network. Before the interview ended, Maria unexpectedly asked about George, and I responded, no notes and no net, sharing a statistic I still found amazing:

"In 2016, which was known as the year of the tweet, George Conway sent exactly zero tweets. So this is new. And what also is new is not supporting the agenda of the president and my work there. I was raised in a household of strong Italian Catholic women who taught me that you air your grievances like that in private, so it is very surprising to see it be so public."

I had addressed it and, to me, that should have been enough. But everywhere I went, I kept being asked about George—along with or instead of me, my job, or what the administration was doing for the people of the United States. To me that smacked of bias and sexism. He was known for *me*, the woman who had the big job with the big guy in the big White House. The media, both the "facts first" and the "Gossip Girl" wings, soon adopted George as their own. They retweeted and "liked" his posts and never showed the least bit of curiosity about how or when George got to this strange place he was in. They were all just happy that he had arrived. Moreover, they were determined to keep him there, joining in the fun of criticizing and diminishing me, never once considering what impact more media attention on George and me might have on our children, and looking past their own salacious personal lives and shortcomings.

Of which there were plenty.

I DID GET some much-needed female support inside the White House, including from a colleague who happened to be the president's daughter. Ivanka and I had a cordial relationship in the White House, though never as tight as we'd been during the 2016 campaign. Our work didn't require daily contact, but we stepped in and stepped up together in the foxhole, sometimes as the only foxes in there. On occasion I'd come to her for big decisions regarding her father, and she'd consult with me about how to handle this or that. Ivanka offered empathy and an ear.

"I am in a family of Democrats," she said, referring to at least some of the Kushners. "I get it." I got somewhat emotional, not overly personal, and was truly grateful. In that moment, Ivanka was incredibly kind and supportive, reiterating that she knew how warmly her father and their entire family felt about me.

A week after that conversation, and based on my stated openness to the idea, Ivanka came into my office (which was next to hers) and handed me a Post-it note. It had the names of two local doctors who specialized in couples therapy. I noticed she had avoided putting that in a text or an email. I appreciated the information and her thoughtfulness and wanted to pursue it. After I showed George the names, he rejected one and said a half-hearted "okay" to the other while looking at his phone.

We never went.

He spent his time exactly how he wanted to. If it was important to him, he would have made it happen.

Ivanka and I certainly had one thing in common now: Both Jared and George were often referred to as "husband of . . ."

Another Trump woman also spoke in my defense. I was in the Roosevelt Room talking with Press Secretary Sarah Huckabee Sanders and Maria Bartiromo, who was about to interview President Trump on Fox Business. I was summoned to the back dining room, where the president was seated in his usual place with his back to the windows, a jar of Starbursts and a muted TV in front of him. I'd been in there countless times and for just as many reasons. I always tried to be prepared for whatever might come up. But this was one of a handful of times that President Trump would mention George to me at all and one of just three times that he would do so in a frustrated tone of voice.

As soon as I walked in, I immediately recognized the perturbed look on the president's face—and the voice emanating from the box. It was Melania's. The First Lady was on the phone.

"Can you believe this?" Trump said, referring to George's recent eruptions. "This guy is nasty. He won't stop. And it's our Kellyanne. She's my top person. She knows a lot, too! What are we going to do?"

Melania's calm voice piped in immediately as my mouth closed and my eyes widened. "Donald," she said, "this is not her fault. And she is a big girl. Strong and confident."

Melania wasn't done.

"We don't control our husbands—and you don't control us!"

Trump couldn't argue with that. I didn't ask for any of this. I felt awkward and embarrassed that the president of the United States and the First Lady had to spend even a minute on this and yet felt relieved and protected from what was becoming an armful of harmful.

Chapter 30

Collusion Illusion Delusion

Attorney General William Barr released his summary of the long-awaited Mueller Report on March 24. Despite all the alternative non-facts being spewed by Democratic elected officials and their adjuncts in the media, insisting that Trump was a "Russian asset" or "there is ample evidence of collusion," there was simply no *there* there: no proof of any conspiracy that colored Trump's 2016 win over Hillary. Any talk of Russian interference in the election occurred when President Obama and Vice President Biden were in office. As people searched for evidence of Russian collusion, the fact that the media itself had interfered the most in the election was hiding in plain sight. Their skewed coverage and phony polls had more of an impact than Russians and $100,000 in Facebook ads. Still, like the Russians, the media couldn't impact the actual results.

That same day, I was on *Fox News Sunday* with Chris Wallace to discuss the Mueller findings and the huge letdown they represented for the Trump Derangement Syndrome crowd, who had believed their own bullshit for two and a half years.

While I was on set, a breaking news story flashed: A former Nevada state assemblywoman, a Democrat named Lucy Flores, alleged that Joe Biden had done his weirdo signature kissing, sniffing, rubbing, handsy thing to her in 2014. This especially newsy weekend also included a surge in border crossings and Trump's announcement that he was challenging Obamacare through the courts. I addressed all of that in response to Wallace's questions. I held forth with facts and figures about the southern border and the state of healthcare and insurance coverage. I also suggested that the audience type the words "Creepy Uncle Joe" into their Google search bars and see the "treasure trove" that would produce.

Wallace, a ratings-hungry anchor, had a full plate of breaking news in front of him. But he still found time to fit the other Conway into my segment. He introduced a new spin on the matter, echoing a theory from *New York Times* columnist Maureen Dowd, who had told me at the British ambassador's residence one night that she had declined an assignment from *Vanity Fair* to write a piece about George and me.

As if he were covering the fall of the Berlin Wall in 1989 or the building of the border wall in 2019, Wallace asked me a question about my husband: "Do you think he's cyberbullying here to try to get you to quit? Do you think he's jealous of your high profile?"

I had sadly and privately concluded that *yes* and *possible* were the answers to those questions, even though I was not going to be real-time and real-life bullied into discussing all this on national television. Rather, I quickly shut down the line of inquiry. My children did not need their parents attacking each other publicly. One, I thought, was more than enough. George could inhabit that unseemly space all by himself. I had recalled the old line from a Broadway musical "You should worry more about what your kids think of you when they are thirty than when they are fifteen."

"My first line of protection in this world is and will always be my four children," I told Wallace, his viewers, and the hungry Twittersphere, still in bed that Sunday morning. "So I don't really like to discuss this publicly." I was speaking as a mother, not just as a senior counselor or a spouse. But Wallace, the hard-news guy, was unmoved. He persisted and went for the clickbait. "I guess the question I have to ask, bottom line, final question: Has this hurt your marriage?"

"Oh, Chris, what are you, Oprah now?" I shot back—with all due respect to Oprah Winfrey, whom I deeply admire, and her best friend, Gayle King, who has always been one of my favorite anchors and who was one of the reporters offering George and me a more professional platform to tell our story. "I mean, what am I—on a couch and you are a psychiatrist?"

Since my modus operandi was never to draw first blood but to always get the last word, I added a capper: how surprised I'd been to see so many homewreckers and serial adulterers suddenly becoming marital experts, appearing on TV and lecturing the rest of us.

You (all) know who you are—*wink!*

Wallace texted me later and pleaded, "Are we OK?"

WITH MARCH SO full of my personal life, I was relieved when April was packed with my professional one. Now that Mick Mulvaney was chief, healthcare policy was elevated on the agenda. I'd tackled that issue for years, beginning with Hillarycare in 1993, much of which was no doubt crafted in the same West Wing office Hillary Clinton once occupied and now I did. Our administration had made some positive policy moves on healthcare, such as shoring up the Affordable Care Act (ACA) for millions of Americans. But we needed a consistent message and a concrete plan of our own beyond "repeal Obamacare!"

One of the main reasons for the blue wave in 2018 was the failure to communicate on healthcare by members of Congress who had voted to repeal the ACA multiple times without sufficiently explaining what would replace it. I said as much, armed with suggested policy prescriptions and messaging points, in a closed-door session on Capitol Hill one day when then–conference chair Liz Cheney invited me to address the Republican members of Congress. By this time we had a stronger healthcare team in place, with Joe Grogan, Larry Kudlow, Brooke Rollins, and a handful of very talented young policy staffers all reporting to Mick. Health and human services secretary Alex Azar and Medicare and Medicaid administrator Seema Verma were also involved. On April 5 we had a small staff retreat at Camp David to finalize our healthcare plan. I presented a slide deck of our plan to Mick, Grogan, and the others. Together they decided it would be best if I led the presentation of our healthcare ideas to the president. Ten days later we gathered in the Roosevelt Room with the president, vice president, cabinet members, and an expanded group of senior staffers.

Before the president joined us, a few senior advisors were taking bets on how many slides the president would get through before he got bored. The guesses were mostly in the four-to-five range. In fact, I delivered my full fifteen-slide PowerPoint deck, complete with off-script flourishes, uninterrupted for twenty-five minutes.

The president sat through it all quietly, absorbing the information. After I finished, he remarked, "Kellyanne, that is all great. There's one problem. It's hard to run against free, free, free. I know you guys think it's easy to run against this socialism and the nice-sounding 'Medicare for All.' But free sounds pretty good."

The Democrat Party was inching more and more to the left and away from the center. The uberprogressive Alexandria Ocasio-Cortez, Rashida Tlaib, and the rest of "the Squad that didn't do squat" were growing in influence. Bernie Sanders had beaten Hillary Clinton in sixteen states in 2016, and Elizabeth Warren, his socialism-loving female counterpart in the Senate, was also surging in the polls, looking toward 2020. Trump had a point. A sad-but-true good point.

Trump said the same thing the next week in an education meeting while Democratic presidential aspirants were promising to wipe out student debt. It was a fair political point and part of Trump's instinctual knack for peeking around the corner and anticipating the other side's first few punches.

Between all these policy discussions, the Mueller Report was finally released in full, minus some redactions. We all gathered in Mulvaney's office early that morning and hit print as soon as the document was released. In a divide-and-conquer strategy, each of us grabbed dozens of pages, circling and highlighting the juiciest stuff or whatever came closest. I was reading through two lenses: as a trained yet nonpracticing lawyer and as an untrained yet effective presidential communicator. I took notes of what was and what wasn't there. There was a lot more in the second category than in the first. Others were looking to see if their names were mentioned and shouting out important conclusions. I walked to the Oval Office and into the dining room, satisfied I knew what Mueller had concluded, and told the president, "Today will be an okay day for you."

"Go out and say that right now," he instructed me. "It's fine. It's midday. Why wait for the night shows?" Then he called in to Mulvaney: "Mick, get her out there now."

An extra-large press corps was waiting on Pebble Beach. They looked deflated, and not because $45 million in taxpayer money had been wasted on what the president referred to as a "witch hunt." The TV lawyers who had blustered months earlier that a "coven" of witches had already been found? They were still referring to people whom I, the campaign manager, had never even met. Carter Page. George Papadopoulos.

I described the Mueller Report as political proctology and declared that the president had emerged with a clean bill of health. As for the claim of obstruction, I said, intent matters. And the main takeaway? "The big lie that you've let fly for two years, it's over, folks."

There was no Russian collusion that swung the election. There was also no apology, of course. And I remained subpoena- and scandal-free.

"How come I never see your name in any of the scandals, subpoenas, or hauled up to Congress?" Democratic caucus chairman Hakeem Jeffries asked me at a book party for Charles Schwab that spring. And he was right. But even as the investigations and recriminations had not touched me, we had all still been slandered. The charge, no matter how discredited, implied that somehow or another the Trump 2016 campaign had won unethically if not unlawfully, and that I as campaign manager would have allowed or actually participated in such a conspiracy.

The media pressed me on when we were going to "move on," saying we seemed to be "rubbing it in."

Wasn't that rich!? They'd just spent two and a half years repeating evidence-free accusations and allegations of criminal conduct with screaming graphics and head-nodding analysts, night after night after night, until they deluded themselves into believing their own hysteria. *Moving on* might take a minute. The media were left to stew in their own toxic brew.

When confronted with malfeasance, like calling the president a Russian asset, and saying that the campaign I had managed to its successful conclusion was in the grip of Russian agents, the reporters wanted to hold on to the Pulitzer Prizes and other forms of circular self-congratulations they'd already received for those lies, but none of them volunteered to own their own mistakes.

THE PRESIDENT WANTED to advance talks with Congress about rebuilding the nation's crumbling infrastructure, and we were expecting

Nancy Pelosi to arrive at the White House. That all changed when the cameras caught up to the House Speaker as she was leaving the halls of the Capitol to come over for the discussion. She, it seemed, had caved to demands from the radical left that, despite the results of the Mueller Report, Congress should press ahead with impeaching the president. The lefties had been demanding impeachment from the moment Trump was sworn into office and even before that. Pelosi turned to the cameras and said, "We believe no one is above the law. And we believe the president of the United States is engaged in a cover-up."

If that was her idea of fair-mindedness, she might as well have toilet-papered the bushes on the South Lawn beneath the president's bedroom window. Now she was on her way to the White House.

The president saw her comments as the Cabinet Room was beginning to fill. Once the Speaker and her team arrived and everyone was seated, the president walked in. He remained standing, calmly saying he wanted to make a deal on infrastructure, but not under these circumstances.

"I don't do cover-ups," Trump said, a pointed dig at Pelosi.

He also made certain that Pelosi's Democrat colleagues all knew that she alone bore the responsibility for unexpectedly blowing up this important meeting. Trump may have briefly been fascinated by the Democratic Speaker, but she seemed flummoxed by him. Trump exited back through the door that connects the Cabinet Room and the Outer Oval as a stunned silence filled the room. We had been put upon but asked when we might move on. Yet here was the highest-ranking Democrat in the country making clear that collusion, not collaboration, was still top-of-mind. I turned to Speaker Pelosi as she got up to leave and tried to salvage, olive branch in hand, whatever discussions had preceded this awkward moment.

"Madam Speaker, is there a way we can address what the president said?"

She barked at me, "I respond to the president, not staff."

"Real pro-woman of you," I replied.

She shuffled out of the Cabinet Room muttering to herself, then ordered a twenty-one-year-old White House receptionist to retrieve her mobile phone. She had the audacity to accuse the young woman of hiding it. Always the pro-woman "Madam" Speaker! Pelosi had some explanation later, but she was not in control. Trump proceeded to the Rose Garden, with props this time, large placards that read "no collusion, no obstruction." When the press asked about all this the next day, I laughed off Pelosi's trigger temper and her poor office manners, saying that the Speaker had treated me like she does her cook, her hairdresser, her driver, her pilot, and her other personal servants—shabbily.

I'D FORGONE DOZENS of foreign trips with the president to stay with my kids. I lucked out in the one I chose to join. The state visit to the United Kingdom in early June was an out-of-this-world privilege. I'm a longtime Anglophile who once bought Queen Elizabeth tchotchkes as an undergraduate at Oxford. Now I was about to meet her in a private setting at Buckingham Palace. Her Majesty got along well with President Trump. I was humbled by the gravity of the moment when she and her grandson, Prince Harry, emerged from a movable wall to meet twenty or so of us in a reception room. Both royals were incredibly warm and engaging. These were happier times. The House of Windsor was not yet as much a House Divided as it would become when Prince Harry and his wife, Meghan, Duchess of Sussex, broke with the palace and moved to the United States with their son. Lunch with the queen followed, and a day later, wearing a gold-and-silver gown by the American designer Mac Duggal and escorted by the queen's cousin, Prince Edward, I processed into the state dinner.

Prior to our visit, the American delegation had been briefed on protocol and etiquette. One clear directive: Do not ask members of the royal family questions of a personal nature. Imagine my delight, then, when a very gracious Kate, Duchess of Cambridge, asked me if I had any children. "Four," I replied, "including a George and a Charlotte, just like you." She and her husband, William, Duke of Cambridge; Prince Edward and Sophie, Countess of Wessex; Camilla, Duchess of Cornwall; and truly everyone we encountered spent plenty of time with the Trump family and senior staff. They could not have been more lovely or more welcoming. It was a night to remember, one in which I feel blessed to have been included.

Dinner at Winfield House, the residence of the ambassador of the United States to the Court of St. James's, honoring Charles, Prince of Wales, was also extraordinary. I was seated at a table for ten with the guest of honor, the president of the United States, Sarah Huckabee Sanders, Prime Minister Theresa May, British foreign secretary Jeremy Hunt, other dignitaries, and James Goldston, a British American who, at the time, was president of ABC News. Prince Charles was wonderful company and, we were all certain, had never encountered a U.S. president quite like Trump. The prince was laughing heartily as the president told stories and showcased his own sense of humor. The conversations during cocktails and over dinner were next-level. Yet somehow George's Twitter feed, like a bad American penny, had followed me to Great Britain.

Goldston expressed regret about "your husband's tweets," saying "that mustn't be easy."

I smiled in my updo and navy gown, listening to yet another unnecessary intrusion into my privacy. "Actually," I said, "it mustn't be *news*, so one wonders why your network obsesses over it."

"Oh, well, do we? Uh, Twitter has a certain officialdom to it," he sighed, perhaps unaware of what a headache social media posts were causing traditional outlets like his.

"Not really, respectfully," I replied. "There is no fact-checking, no editors. As I noted on television way back in 2016, if what a reporter posts on Twitter could not be approved by an editor for publication or broadcast, then how do you justify that same reporter publishing it on Twitter? After all, most aren't posting in their personal capacity. They are posting at 10:22 a.m. from their desk at the *New York Times*. . . ."

Goldston nodded.

"Or at ABC." I winked, already bored with the conversation about tweets when literal royalty was there to talk with four feet away.

"Substantively, though," I added, "you are covering my personal life and should not. It's a free country. George is welcome to change his mind and disagree with the president without it being a headline."

Cue the flattery.

Goldston carried on about how I was a prominent person, a top aide to the president, trusted and listened to by the leader of the free world, so it was news.

Yeah, yeah. Of course, couples disagree all the time and about matters much more significant than politics. By definition, adultery is *also* a disagreement between spouses. No one would dare touch that. Every day, major media outlets look the other way and say, "It's none of our business." That's exactly how I felt.

ROBERT MUELLER, IT turned out, wasn't the only person kicking around Washington with *special counsel* next to his name and wasting taxpayer dollars tilting at windmills. Most Americans didn't know this, but there was also the grossly misnamed "Special Counsel" Henry Kerner, who no doubt was under enormous pressure from the political left to silence me. And so he tried.

On June 13, soon after we returned from the United Kingdom and France, I had wrapped up a healthcare meeting with the governors of Georgia, Iowa, and New Hampshire, followed by a lunch with them and the president, when I received word: This other Office of Special Counsel had published a report saying I had violated the Hatch Act as a "repeat offender" and recommended that the president fire me.

Among my alleged sins? That in television interviews, I had accused Senator Cory Booker of saying something "sexist" (he did), that I had said Joe Biden lacked "vision" (he does), that I had dissed Senator Elizabeth Warren for lying about her ethnicity (she did, for thirty-six years), and that I had criticized another failing presidential candidate and *Vanity Fair* cover model Beto O'Rourke for not thinking the women running were "good enough to be president" (a thoroughly accurate portrayal of O'Rourke).

Oh, one other thing: I had also retweeted a March 31 message referring to Joe Biden as "Creepy Uncle Joe."

There is a living, breathing, years-long catalog with accompanying video of handsy hair-sniffing to substantiate that one.

If you were already pissed off about the waste of your money and Congress's time over the fruitless Mueller investigation or wondered why the troubled and talentless grifter-drifter Hunter Biden can get away with enriching himself through his dad's connections and on taxpayer-funded planes, try this one on for size: The Hatch Act, a 1939 law that forbids executive branch employees from getting involved in overt political activities, has been invoked infrequently over the course of history and resulted in termination of a public official almost never. Obama press secretary Josh Earnest, for example, repeatedly made political comments from the White House Briefing Room disparaging Republican presidential nominee Donald Trump in the throes of a general election campaign. Yet Earnest operated free from any Hatch Act charges.

This was an inside job by a ragtag team that could have been investigated and/or terminated, if only they were worth the effort. A number of made-for-TV "experts" in the so-called nonpartisan ethics community had harassed me for years in ways that often smacked of sexism but usually were just the handiwork of middle-aged, underachieving men who spent far too much time with their hands on their . . . tweet buttons. This included a guest at our wedding who begged me to get him a meeting with Trump during the transition and later, confusing Twitter followers and MSNBC bookers with enthused voters, embarrassed himself with an overwhelming primary loss for statewide office.

Much of this was propelled by a group deceptively named CREW, Citizens for Responsibility and Ethics in Washington, whose board of advisors and employee roster reads like a who's who of Democrat politics and liberal activists. For years, CREW pretended to be nonpartisan. CREW also tweeted my name more than 375 times.

Talk about *obsessed*.

The president saw all this for what it was: attempted intimidation and harassment and the umpteenth effort to silence his favorite spokesperson, muzzle me ahead of his reelection, and erase me from the "first female" slot, which had been reserved for their girl Hillary. So much for "moving on." Trump declined to terminate me as they demanded and wanted me to defend myself in a hearing at the Capitol. I was ready right then and there. But after working with White House counsel Pat Cipollone on a rebuttal letter, I was advised to adhere to precedent and decline to testify in front of the House Oversight Committee. Ironically, this move was also designed to protect colleagues who were *not* scandal- or subpoena-free. By remaining uncharacteristically silent and not showing up to testify, I allowed the floodgates on more serious matters plaguing less serious colleagues to remain shut.

The guy who testified against me may have later regretted his fifteen minutes of fame. Henry Kerner was not a pretty sight under the klieg lights. Ranking member Jim Jordan, an Ohio Republican, made easy work of him, telling Kerner that Kellyanne Conway was good at her job "and that's why you want to get rid of her." It was a struggle to discern how, as the complaint alleged, something I said had swung electoral votes for or against presidential candidates like Seth Moulton or Cory Booker, both of whom received zero electoral votes. They had earned the embarrassment of being electoral zeroes without my help.

I watched the hearing, with my nameplate and an empty chair, as one unimpressive Democrat after the next slammed me by name. At least I had memorized the tops of their heads as they stared down at the notes prepared by their staffs (à la Mazie Hirono in Senate Judiciary Committee hearings), concocting conclusions in search of evidence on live TV.

The freshman congresswoman Alexandra Ocasio-Cortez of New York was on the Oversight Committee and was there for the taxpayer-funded Hatch Act hearing, after which she flew to New York to appear on an episode of Stephen Colbert's *Late Night* on CBS.

After she had sat in the committee room for those four hours of testimony, plied with binders of notes others had compiled, you might reasonably expect the congresswoman to possess a rudimentary, factual understanding of the Hatch Act. Instead AOC was not close to "A-OK" when she tried to explain the act to Colbert, telling the late-night host it meant that a "White House employee can't endorse a certain policy," which of course was ridiculous on its face and the opposite of what the Hatch Act was designed to protect against.

"We can fine her," the congresswoman said with feigned concern. "I believe she can go to jail," which was mean and false but achieved her only goal: having the equally clueless and partisan audience erupt in applause. No one dared check the young representative's alternative facts while appearing on a late-night comedy show. And no one asked her why she was advocating for a mother of four to "go to jail" based on my recitation of provable facts and actual statements made by U.S. senators who wanted to be president.

Was AOC MIA to her constituents during her rushed trip to NYC to appear on CBS? Did she sleep that night in her Queens district apartment or in a posh, show-provided Manhattan hotel room? There is no record, since her office does not make available her full schedule, and no one in the one-sided thirsty-for-Trump media would dare even ask, let alone call out her alternative facts.

*   *   *

AMID ALL THIS, Jared Kushner, who was lauded by the media as the "de facto campaign manager" (and de facto chief of staff), was itching to host a rally formally launching the president's 2020 reelection campaign. By then the campaign had been in operation for sixteen months, with a highly compensated campaign manager and other senior staff as well as an army of equally highly compensated fundraisers, pollsters, event teams, and other consultants.

In a meeting in the White House residence to discuss the location of the president's reelection launch, a few of us, including me, agreed with Parscale that it should be in Florida, site of Trump's so-called Southern White House and a much-needed swing state that he'd carried in 2016 and again helped carry in 2018, when he endorsed low-in-the-polls congressman Ron DeSantis in the Republican primary for governor. Jared wanted a replay of the famous Trump Tower escalator ride. But midtown Manhattan was not exactly a swing state. When I observed that such an arrangement would leave no room for supporters, he said that the rally-loving president did not need that. "This would be a worldwide media event," Jared said. "There will be enough room for press."

His rarely quite-right political instincts were overruled by the president, whose sense of people and pomp was better than all of ours.

Trump made his announcement at the packed twenty-thousand-seat Amway Center in Orlando.

Game officially on.

Chapter 31

Broken Vows, Broken Heart

T he Fourth of July fireworks arrived twenty-four hours early this year.

It was Saturday afternoon, July 3, 2019. We were down the shore in our Ventnor house and I was getting ready to make the long drive to the Hamptons for the elaborate annual party hosted by *Washington Post* heir and editor Lally Weymouth that celebrated Lally's birthday and America's birthday. Claudia had just finished helping me with hair and makeup. I was still in my room at the shore house, searching for a handbag, when I looked at George Conway and calmly told him exactly what was on my mind.

"You're the only person in this world with whom I took vows on an altar at the Basilica Cathedral of Saints Peter and Paul in Philadelphia in front of God and our loved ones and five priests."

That caught his attention. I pressed on.

"You're the only person in this world for whom I gave birth to four children."

By this point, George had a look on his face that I interpreted as expectant but dazed, like he knew the crescendo hadn't arrived yet and he wanted to take in the whole show before deciding exactly how he was going to respond.

"And so," I continued, "you're the only person who has a choice to make. You can see me mostly as your wife of eighteen years and the mother of your four children. Or you can see me mostly as senior counselor to President Donald Trump. When you wake up every morning, you have to decide how it is you see me. George, how do you see me?"

I got no thoughtful response, which isn't to say I got *no* response.

It was the same response I had been getting since my husband had begun this not-so-secret passionate fling of his with Twitter.

"You have ruined yourself," he yelled without making eye contact, "and you have embarrassed this family."

"*I've* embarrassed this family?" I shot back. "You abandoned me for Twitter, and she's not even hot. I'm not the parent who spends her day curating tweets to attack the other parent in full view of this family. I'm the one trying to raise kids to show respect and openness with a parent who spends his day tweeting juvenile 'Orangeface' or '#DerangedDonald.' It's totally beneath you!"

I tried again to explain to George why I was in the White House. That I was doing meaningful work on behalf of a country I love dearly and for a president I respected and supported, who supported and respected me.

"Over time," I continued, "I can formulate a reasonable exit strategy, if that is what we decide together is the right thing for us and our family." I continued packing my bags for my drive.

He didn't want to hear it, but he also didn't want to admit that the George I married, whom I had built a life and family with, would have had a reasonable conversation with me.

But at this point, he could not or would not. As happens in many marriages, a third person was involved. But in this case, there was no other woman.

George could barely form or finish a sentence—online or offline—that did not contain the words *Donald Trump*.

Trump never once said to me, "Choose between your job and your marriage." It was George who made me feel that way. And where were all the self-identified, "independent-thinking feminists"? Mostly they were silent when they weren't cheering George as he squeezed his wife to make a choice no woman should ever have to: her marriage or her job? They hated Donald Trump so much that they couldn't see the gaping contradiction there. Nor could George, whose unconditional love and support of my career, including on the campaign and into the White House, suddenly disappeared.

A truly independent, successful, powerful woman facing down an indifferent husband who was disrespecting her and diminishing her accomplishments. Where was *my* pink-hat parade?

I hopped in the car and drove myself to the Hamptons. I sat at the head table with Lally, a most gracious hostess, and hit the dance floor with Ron Lauder and commerce secretary Wilbur Ross. Two years earlier, at the same party, I had exchanged pleasantries with Martha Stewart and spoken to Steven Spielberg, who said, "I've wanted to meet you."

Early in the administration and continuing that summer, I was a guest at events in the homes of prominent media figures. Judy Woodruff had a party for women on both sides of the aisle, including elected officials. Shortly after that, she hosted a smaller dinner. I had admired Judy's old-school journalism and authenticity (she'd treated me nicely at CNN in 1996) and NBC's Andrea Mitchell, her best friend. Their stories of what it was like to be young female reporters in the 1970s struck a chord. They knew how to socialize with all of Washington without compromising journalistic integrity and didn't pretend that engaging with just one political party or narrowcasting one's friendships through a partisan lens was the same as objective journalism.

Sometimes I was the only "Trump White House person" at an event. Some of the other guests may not have liked my being there (or were jealous of the seating arrangements). But hosts like Ambassador Gérard Araud, Ambassador Kim Darroch, Ambassador Armando Varricchio, and David and Katherine Bradley were welcoming and engaging at elaborate dinners or book parties. Same for CBS's Norah O'Donnell, who one night years later was chatting with me at Andrea Mitchell's home for an event celebrating the launch of Susan Page's biography of the inimitable, incredible Barbara Bush. Democrat senator Amy Klobuchar, who had just announced her presidential campaign to take on Donald Trump, engaged me in polite conversation. A few new Democrat House members had no problem with me being there. Yet a few older female reporters not as accomplished as a Norah or an Andrea, and never happy-looking, apparently did. They followed George (and later Claudia) on Twitter, stood frowning in a circle that night, and grumbled the next day.

I was pleased that the doyennes of social Washington had shifted away from that boring homewrecking woman known for her husband and onto accomplished, magnetic, brilliant women like Adrienne Arsht, Hilary Geary Ross, Rima al-Sabah, Princess Lalla Joumala Alaoui, and Ambassadors Dina Kuwar, Ivonne Baki, and Dame Karen Elizabeth Pierce.

ON JULY 25, the president hosted another campaign meeting in the White House residence. It featured members of Congress, donors, officials from the Republican National Committee, campaign staff, and Jared and two of his young assistants. It did not include the 2016 campaign manager. But the president called me after 8 p.m. and said, "Kellyanne, what do you think about these candidates? Were you in the meeting?"

"You mean the political meeting in the residence?" I asked. "No, I'm already at home with the kids."

"Oh, I didn't know," he said. "They're telling me this and that about Minnesota, about Warren and Harris . . . *Ka-ma-la*."

It was just then, with Trump still on the phone, that a news alert came across my email. "Trump aides cite top threats at White House briefing: Harris, Biden, Warren," the headline said.

"Well," I said to the president, "I wasn't in the meeting. But I'm reading what happened in the meeting right now. It already leaked. It says, 'Campaign manager [and serial leaker] Brad Parscale noted that Elizabeth Warren was rising. Republican National Committee chairwoman Ronna McDaniel said Kamala Harris could pose a threat in Michigan, and Trump 2020 advisor Bill Stepien highlighted Joe Biden as a potentially formidable threat."

Trump couldn't believe it, how quickly the supposed "nonleakers" on his campaign had leaked the details of the meeting to Alex Isenstadt of *Politico*, who got so many Trump campaign scoops, he may as well have been their official scribe. That same day, I would learn a few months later, was also when the president called Volodymyr Zelenskyy, the Ukrainian president. A very busy day for leakers around the president.

The campaign people also told the Republican congressional leaders and donors in that meeting that 2020 was a *turnout* election, not a *persuasion* election, reporting that their data showed Trump would receive

72 million votes, which was all he needed. But wait. Isn't *every* election a persuasion election? And hadn't the man who wrote *The Art of the Deal* mastered the power of persuasion throughout the 2016 campaign?

As the summer wore on, I went back out on the trail. I had no official role in the reelection campaign, but the president still seemed to value my political insights and kept asking me to step in. I flew to Wyoming for a weekend fundraiser and some horse riding, white-water rafting, and rodeo watching with my kids. A week later I did a Women for Trump event in Tampa with former Florida attorney general Pam Bondi. A thousand women (and some very smart men) showed up on two days' notice. Pam and I had been friends for years. A month later after Pam was named as a lawyer to Trump's impeachment team, a Yahoo reporter emailed me, asking if I was mad that Pam was an impeachment attorney, because, the reporter claimed, I didn't like her. So I hit reply and said, "Since you are talking about Pam I thought I'd put her on the email." I continued, "We have been friends for years, in fact here is a great picture of us together last month."

I watched the 2020 Democratic field assemble. Many of them were already out on the road. There were so many of them and no one was remarkable enough to merit voter notice, let alone a Hatch Act violation for pointing out the obvious. I saw no presidential timber. I saw only wood chips.

One morning in August, the president called me asking the usual open-ended question: "How's it playing?"

"Well," I said, "Elizabeth Warren had thirteen thousand people at her rally last night in Minnesota."

That got an instant reaction. "Come down now," he said.

But I wasn't right upstairs in the West Wing. For the month, while our offices were under maintenance, I was in temporary space in the EEOB, the Eisenhower Executive Office Building, next door. I printed up an article and some photos from the Warren rally. It was scheduled to be indoors but was moved outside due to the large turnout. I knew what to expect when I got to the Oval Office and started by urging the president not to overreact. I reminded him that we had all been wrongly impressed by the twenty thousand people who'd showed up for Kamala Harris's presidential announcement rally, only to see her appeal and popularity fade almost immediately.

"So, would you rather run against Joe Biden or Elizabeth Warren?" Trump asked.

"I'd rather run against Elizabeth Warren," I said, "but I'd rather debate Joe Biden. She would be up in your grill, finger in the face, calling you every name in the book. Pig. Sexist. Xenophobe. Racist. Disgrace."

Six months later, Warren would do exactly that to hapless billionaire Michael Bloomberg, making quick work of his failed personal billion-plus-dollar investment in his own Mike-for-president campaign. His consultants may have been the biggest winners of the cycle.

Trump could not believe he'd need to face either Biden or Warren. "Is that the best they've got?" Now the president was asking the same core question many concerned Democrats were.

THAT SUMMER, GEORGE'S outrage was flipping from topic to topic, just like the Democrats in Congress. And no matter what the outrage du jour, the media genuflected to George like he was a recognized expert and quotable source on nearly anything. In early September, the gossip girls were on the hard-news beat again, devoting precious column inches not to what the actual president and his presidential advisor Kellyanne Conway were doing, but to a story about a man, Joe Walsh, who was running for the Republican presidential nomination and would never be the Republican nominee, a story that included a big photo of Walsh's presidential campaign advisor, George Conway, who had never been a presidential advisor or a campaign advisor or a presidential campaign advisor or anything close to that unless it included the phrase "husband of . . ."

This was not the legendary musician Joe Walsh, who has done meaningful things with his life and *intended* to entertain us through his work. It was a former Republican congressman from Illinois famous for saying, "I wouldn't call myself a racist, but I would say I've said racist things on Twitter."

George, the *Times* scooped, had given three hours of his time in New Jersey advising the Walsh-for-president "campaign" (yes, president of this country) and, more importantly, a check for $5,800 from *our* bank account. The Walsh "campaign" and its "advisor" got about as far as you might expect.

That September, I went at it alone to a state dinner in honor of Australia. It was truly one of the most remarkable events of my life, a somewhat intimate affair in the Rose Garden. The military bands played from the roofs of the West Wing.

I proceeded into the "book room" of the White House on my way to the state dinner the same way I had walked down the aisle on my wedding day eighteen years earlier: alone.

Photographers snapped pictures. A female reporter shouted, "Where's George?"

Where are your manners? I thought. *And why do you look like Cinderella before the ball?*

I was tempted to ask where her hairbrush was but kept smiling and held my head high.

Next in line were Deputy Chief of Staff Dan Scavino and Chief of Staff Mick Mulvaney, who walked in side by side in their tuxes, without their wives, who did not attend. No one asked them a thing.

AT THE END of September, I addressed the Ohio Republican State Convention, then rushed back to New York on the First Lady's plane to be with the president when he addressed the United Nations General Assembly. He was speaking to the world's leaders on a topic I cared a lot about, religious liberty. I had helped to arrange the speech, and I wanted to be there for the session, though I knew I'd have to break off after two days to speak on the drug crisis at the Concordia Summit, three blocks away at the Grand Hyatt.

Suddenly, stories were swirling about that call Trump made months earlier to Ukraine president Volodymyr Zelenskyy and a related whistleblower complaint. In between the religious freedom speech and multiple bilateral meetings, I tried to get up to speed. What was this about? I had access to the president's foreign calls, but I was not on that call and had never seen a transcript.

"Kellyanne," Trump said to me, "call Bill Barr. I need you to ask them about the call."

"Okay, what call?" I asked, making sure he was asking about what I was hearing.

"Ukraine."

I asked the Secret Service for a secure line and dialed the White House switchboard so I could be connected to the attorney general. As it happened, Barr was at the White House meeting with Pat Cipollone, the White House counsel. I spoke with both of them. They briefed me with some top-line details and said they needed to make a decision on whether and how we should release the transcript of the call between the U.S. and Ukrainian presidents.

Releasing the transcript could set a bad precedent. House Intelligence Committee chairman Adam Schiff, already burned by his own cable news claims of "ample evidence of Russian collusion in plain sight" (reminder: no one on TV is ever under oath) and the Democrats' failure to remove the president from office, would be slap-happy in his constant requests for transcripts for no good reason. It raised a legitimate diplomatic issue. These conversations with international leaders are private. Both nations expect confidentiality and discretion to speak freely about vexing issues. To ease some domestic uproar, did we really want to reveal the details of a private conversation with the president of Ukraine?

I reported their concerns to the president. He told me to come to Trump Tower that evening to view the transcript, as I went off to a few more bilateral meetings, including with Prime Minister Narendra Modi of India and the United Kingdom's new prime minister, Boris Johnson, who let me update a photo of the two of us that we first took in 1987.

I felt awkward when I first arrived at Trump Tower. I was the only staffer there as the family members wandered in one by one for a planned family dinner with the president and First Lady, all five kids, and their significant others. Soon the president and I went into a private corner and I finally had an opportunity to review the transcript of his call with the Ukrainian president.

"So, what do you think?" he asked. "It's perfect, right?"

"Well," I said, "it's not terrible, but maybe I don't understand it completely. Let me read it again." I skimmed the transcript for key words. "It's not perfect, but it sounds like you. It's how you talk. You never ask him to investigate [Hunter] Biden. When I speak with you privately, you're not even worried about Joe Biden [politically], which I guess you get from your campaign. Go enjoy dinner. We will talk later."

I handed him back the transcript copy and said nothing to anyone.

The next day the president delivered his address at the UN General Assembly. I broke as planned right after the speech and headed to the Concordia Summit. I had just gotten offstage at the Hyatt after my speech on the drug crisis and our public-private partnerships and planned to head back to Washington—and the president was calling. I had no private place to escape to take the call and no secure line. Reporters and random people were afoot. Security ushered out most of them. I found a corner but feared my voice was echoing through the room. The president was livid. Democrats had pounced while he was standing shoulder to shoulder with world leaders.

"They are going to impeach me over a transcript they haven't seen?" His voice thundered out of the phone. "This is ridiculous!"

His fascination with Pelosi had turned to red-hot anger.

"She has no choice," I told him. "She still owes the crazies a pound of your flesh. They missed their chance with Mueller. Maybe the transcript will clear things up."

The Trump economy was booming. Unemployment was at a fifty-year low, including among key sectors: African Americans, Asian Americans, Hispanics, women, veterans, and disabled Americans. The president had ordered the strike that killed the head of ISIS, Abu Bakr al-Baghdadi. One thing was different about this month: I had taken myself off TV for nearly all of October. To me, Ukraine wasn't Robert Mueller or porn people, where I saw or surmised the endgame. I had been campaign manager and knew to a certainty that I'd never spoken to anyone in Russia about the campaign or sanctioned anyone to do so. In this new situation, I didn't know all the facts. I knew what was in the transcript, but I didn't know what Rudy Giuliani was up to—only that he'd been to Ukraine—or who else was involved with what else or where else. Three years and three press secretaries later, it had become custom that, when trouble broke, others ran to the hills and I was forced to run to the cameras. But this time, I recognized I could not possibly have all the facts here. This time, I was watching and waiting.

Chapter 32

Office Politics

The other house divided was the White House, and Jared was ready to prove it once again in the fall of 2019.

This was early one Friday morning at a meeting in his office. He had called the meeting. The group included campaign manager Brad Parscale, RNC chairwoman Ronna McDaniel, and White House chief of staff Mick Mulvaney.

"Wow," Jared said to me soon after I walked into the room and we started talking. "I had no idea how much you hated me."

"Don't flatter yourself," I responded. "I don't hate you. I just don't understand you. Three years later, I don't understand why, when the president asks us to work together, you pretend you will with a flippant 'sure' or ignore him and roll your eyes on your way to trying to roll me."

We hadn't exactly built a trust relationship over the past three-plus years, Jared said, with no explanation and quite a bit of revisionist history, especially about the 2016 campaign. He had "trusted" and foisted some questionable characters on the rest of us, as White House personnel, and some dubious priorities and strategies that did not align with the president's. It wasn't about trust. It was about loyalty. To Jared. Where others would vomit his name to add credibility to their work, I had never cowered or capitulated to him. I was respectful, not deferential. A colleague, not a supplicant.

"Do you want Brad's job?" Jared asked me with Brad sitting right there, across from me, red-faced and rapidly sipping water.

"No," I said emphatically, "I don't want Brad's job. I want to do *my* job, and I already had Brad's job. And for God's sake, I want Brad to do his job. Look at what you've done. The only way you could exclude me was to try to convince colleagues and the president that I'm a leaker. You can't tell him I'm stupid. You can't tell him I'm disloyal and"—I pointed up to the quadrant of TVs on the wall—"and you can't tell him I suck on TV. Yet we all know how hard it is to be on TV. Right, Jared?" I glared at him. "Right, Brad?" I cocked my head around to lock eyes with Parscale. There was no reason to go down that same road with Ronna or Mick. They were very good on TV.

"Right, Jared?" I repeated. "So, instead, you tell him I'm a leaker. You can't get me on the merits. So you pull that crap. You think people don't tell me this? Cabinet officials. Congressmen. Colleagues. Tell you what, pal. If I ever became a leaker, let alone *the* leaker, you'll know right away. The content and juiciness of the leaks will improve instantly."

I looked directly at him, a man of countless life privileges and endless self-assurance. His father had donated more money to Harvard University prior to Jared's admission there than my father had made in his entire life.

At Jared's explicit direction and implicit command, I had been excluded from all sorts of things, some of which were so stupid I was grateful to be away from the mess. Other things kept blowing up in the son-in-law's face. There were quite a few situations where I could have been helpful and the president expected me to be there. So I'd get summoned toward the end, forced to play catch-up and then cleanup.

I CERTAINLY HADN'T forgotten how, months earlier, Jared thought he could spearhead his vision for full and final border security and merit-based immigration, culminating in a Rose Garden ceremony where the president announced Jared's grand initiative to an overflowing audience of press and congressional leaders. To the media, it might have looked like just another Rose Garden announcement by President Trump, but the backstory was far more complicated than that. It was a classic collision of Jared's schemes and dreams.

This time it involved more than a dozen White House staffers and the Statue of Liberty, all part of this destined-to-fail plan. The idea was to have President Trump go to Ellis Island, where he'd stand at the foot of the Statue of Liberty to lead a naturalization ceremony. It quickly became apparent that an event like that would soak up a ton of government resources and almost certainly provoke angry protests. I was excluded in the planning and policy stages for weeks, with some close White House colleagues sheepish because they liked me and liked working with me. Eventually they came to me because they wanted my messaging expertise. By then the event had been moved from the Statue of Liberty to the National Archives in Washington, about one mile from the White House. Then the Archives also was scrapped. The event ended up being where all events seemed to end up, in the White House Rose Garden. That's just one problem of focusing on style over substance.

President Trump ultimately announced a plan that was never going to pass the Congress. I found myself, about an hour before the big ceremony, speaking uninterrupted on Rush Limbaugh's inimitable radio program for two segments to detail what the president would roll out: Rush really let me go for it.

"A modern merit-based immigration system," I told Rush and his massive radio audience. "And you are right. This shifts from low-skill to high-skilled immigration. Why? Because in our country, under our current system in the U.S., approximately twelve percent of green cards are allocated on the basis of skill. Over sixty percent are allocated based on family units, and it's often extended family. In Canada, it is the exact opposite, where over sixty percent are based on skill, and a much lower percentage— one-third of that or one-fourth of that—are based on family ties."

"So, we're going to safeguard immediate families, prioritizing immediate family over distant relatives for legal immigration. It also offers a renewable nonimmigrant visa for parents. But we also have to promote national unity. This president's plan is designed to attract immigrants who love America, share our values, and want to contribute to society. We want to make sure that those industries that need workers have them, but we want to protect American workers and help raise the wage for everyone."

Rush didn't typically let people talk for long without interrupting them.

After I hung up, Rush said to his audience, "Okay. Caught your breath yet? I don't think there's anybody who says more in less time, other than me, of course, complete with facts and analysis than Kellyanne Conway. I mean, she really does define the concept of listening fast, and she's so good, you don't need to ask her any questions. I could have taken the half hour off except for the commercial break. That's why I said she can come back anytime." Rush was the gold standard, and the dozen times I was in his company over the years always felt consequential.

As soon as I was done, I went down to tell the president that I'd gone on Rush to explain this immigration shift and what the questions about it might be. I found Jared and the president alone in the dining room. All I got out of Jared was two shrugged shoulders and a mumbled "great." I guess Rush Limbaugh was more appreciative that I was willing to present our immigration plan to his large and influential audience. Certainly more than Jared sounded.

As always, I was happy to be a team player. I wasn't going to sulk or sit this out because I wasn't included from the beginning. I just had to wonder, *Why do we have to make this so complicated for ourselves?*

Two hours before the Rose Garden event, Jared instructed staff to put copies of the plan on each chair. I immediately thought, *Why do we want the press to get their hands on this for two full hours before the president takes the stage to announce it? They'll start writing about this before we have had a chance to explain it, a plan that hasn't even gotten final sign-off yet. What sense does that make?*

Now, months later in the campaign, meeting with Jared, Brad, Ronna, and Mick, I confronted Jared in his office about that document. "You instructed someone to put copies of the plan on the seats, but to this day that document has still not cleared White House counsel."

"Well," Jared said, "I'm the one who pulled it back."

Incredible! "You're the one who commanded that it be printed," I reminded him, as if we were leafletting the Rose Garden.

That's the problem with unchecked power. It is never accountable.

In that same meeting in Jared's office, I whipped out a binder that showed it was his people who had been leaking these stories, often to the detriment of the president. "Here is a selected list of times that you two"—Brad, who was already red-faced, speechless, and gulping water, and Jared—"leaked to the press. Often to these four or five same reporters."

Jared didn't exactly own it. He didn't deny it, either. His facial expression didn't change at all. Instead, falling back on one of his favorite lines for ducking the conflicts that he caused, he said, "We don't need to do this now."

"No, we actually do," I corrected him.

BACK AT MY house, George was moving on to some next alleged out-rage and basking in the media presumption that he was an expert on politics, constitutional law, psychiatry, and racism.

What could possibly be next?

Envelope, please . . .

And the winner goes to: Pelosi's long-threatened impeachment of Donald Trump.

He was an "expert" on that, too.

George moved from his usual spot behind the keyboard to join MSNBC's special impeachment coverage. It was especially amusing to hear that one of the TDSers at the cable network, Nicolle Wallace, had recommended George's appearance on the panel, given that she had called me sympathetically a few times early on to voice dismay about George's tweets. If our significant others are so relevant, why didn't the newly divorced Wallace fully identify a frequent guest on her show as her boyfriend? The chyron said "New York Times" or "Author, [book title]." Under the standard applied to "Kellyanne Conway's husband" and the sanctimonious "fight for truth and transparency" claims, shouldn't her audience be told the full story?

"I would get divorced for less than that," a married close friend of both mine and George's who voted against Trump said plainly one day. "It's abusive. Why can't George be like the rest of us who don't like Trump but who love you?"

Like everything George did during this time, I found out about it after it happened or as it was happening. It was sneaky, almost sinister. Why not own it, share it, sneer in my face with a copy of tomorrow's *Washington Post* op-ed or next week's Lincoln Project ad? Night after night, I would come home from a busy day at work and be there for the kids: dinner, homework, projects. While I was minding dishes, dogs, laundry, managing adolescent dramas and traumas, George would be just steps away from me, tucked away in his home office, plotting against my boss and me. On the television that day, he was "Constitutional law expert George Conway." The wizards at MSNBC somehow forgot that George's experience with successfully impeaching a president applied to Democrat hero Bill Clinton! In fairness, folks much less intelligent than George had been on TV bearing the same "expert" chyron. Come to think of it, some of them have daily shows bearing their name. I didn't learn anything new that day. Not about constitutional law, anyway.

The next day, November 14, I was back on TV after my own brief self-directed hiatus, speaking on set with CNN's Wolf Blitzer. The anchors, I found time and time again, liked to wait until the end of the segment to pull out the question they should have been too embarrassed to ask.

"I just have a final question, a sensitive question, and it's a political question, it's a substantive question," Wolf stammered. "I don't want to talk about your marriage. I know that there are issues there. Your husband George Conway . . ."

"I don't want to talk about your marriage," he gaslighted, while proceeding to ask about the man I had married. Then, mind-bogglingly: "I know there are issues there." It turns out Ivanka did not need to recommend marriage therapists to George and me after all. We had Wolf!

I asked him why he would say that and why he would need to play a clip of George on the screen. "Because he is a legal scholar," Wolf said.

That was a new one. But Wolf was lying about his justification. He said the magic words "your husband" and that's why he played an entire clip of George and left my face on the screen in a reaction shot, which I could see out of the corner of my eye. I asked what the relevance was. "He happens to be married to you," Wolf said minutes after saying he didn't want to talk about my marriage.

Et tu, Wolf? I did not hold back. "That is his opinion," I said of my husband. "I don't think CNN was lacking for anti-Trump voices. And we've heard things like [what George] said on CNN for three years."

I think I took a breath here. Maybe I didn't.

"And where—honestly, where is the shame? Where is the introspection of people who have said for three years, respectfully, Wolf, actually beginning in May of 2017, I'll quote 'your wife's husband' right now. I won't talk about your marriage, but I'll quote *your* wife's husband."

I wasn't close to finished.

"In 2017 you asked [Independent senator from Maine] Angus King, 'Are we getting closer to impeachment?'"

I looked straight at Wolf, who by this point seemed more like his name was Sheep.

"Does anybody ever feel badly about getting it so wrong? We sort of look the other way of how wrong everybody was here and elsewhere with the elections. I was on your network every single day as gracefully and respectfully as I could, laying out the case as to why Donald Trump would beat Hillary Clinton. I have a living, breathing video catalog, which is why I don't worry about anything when people say, 'I always knew he'd win.' I said it all the time.

"What you just quoted [by George] is said every day by other voices, but you wanted to put it in my husband's voice because you think somehow that that will help your ratings or that you're really sticking it to Kellyanne Conway. And let me be very clear. You didn't stick it to Kellyanne Conway. I think you embarrassed yourself, and I'm embarrassed for you because"— mimicking the network's famous tagline—"*this* is CNN . . . *Now?* I looked up to you when I was in college and law school. I would turn on CNN to see what Wolf Blitzer had to say about war, famine, disruption abroad. I really respected you for all those years as someone that would give you the news, and now it's what somebody's husband said on a different network."

It was truly shocking, Wolf's ill-advised question. My response was just a long time coming.

Yet the worst thing Wolf Blitzer did that day may have been when he told me, "You are welcome to come back anytime." *That* definitely would have inflamed his audience.

I had always tried to take the high road when anchors took the low road to "get Kellyanne" and, in turn, to "get Trump."

Can you imagine for one second if I had ever turned the tables?

Should I have mentioned their marriages? Their second spouse's adultery? Their drug use? I didn't and I don't because I am a gracious person, something they cannot say. They can dish it out, but they could never take it. Let's be honest, I often treated them better than they treated me, even when they didn't deserve it.

CNN's Jake Tapper had George on two months later. He mentioned that George was my husband, neglected to reveal that by then, he and George were friends, but continued and quickly said, "You have already made clear *that* is not a subject you want to talk about. So, I am not going to waste any time. I just want my viewers to be aware."

Oh, how convenient! How delightful! If the Conway who made our marriage a public issue is on set, it's a "waste of time" for CNN to discuss. And yet if I'm on, it's the entire subject. Sexism, plain and simple. I get asked and placed in a pressure cooker in every interview, but George need not be asked about *his* spouse, the one who actually worked in the White House, never pretending to be something I wasn't. It must have been nice to have (new) friends in high (horse) places.

Some in the media—male and female—refused to cover George.

In George, the cable networks had seen an opportunity to stick it to me (and Trump). But the greedy consultants had something different—and far more lucrative—in mind. In George, they saw a cash cow.

Those unsuccessful consultants, some overrated, others hardly known, saw financial opportunity in the fissures. Serial misogynists themselves, they delighted in watching George tear down his wife, who had done what they could not: help get her presidential nominee into the White House and then follow him there in a position of responsibility that these consultants all thought a bunch of tweets could quickly undo.

His platform and position could be useful to them. Wrap it up in some high-gloss, high-minded, high-anxiety packaging to "restore the soul of America" or "save the country" when what you are really doing is what you do best: pad your pockets with millions while producing precious little return on investment.

It took brass ones for Wolf Blitzer at CNN and Chris Wallace at Fox News Channel to ask me about my marriage, all the while insisting "this is not about your marriage." At least they did it to my face. Others, like late-night comedians and other unfunny people, were more cowardly.

Over at ABC's *The View*, marginally conservative yet verifiably cranky cohost Meghan McCain made George and me—two people she'd never met—a regular part of her "expert analysis." "They're both disgusting" and they have "an anti-marriage" were among the proclamations she made on a few occasions when she wasn't looking down at prewritten notes or being visibly shaken or peeved by one of her cohosts.

As is the case with most of the nasty and often sexist articles, quotes, insults in tweets or on TV, and false "statements of facts" about me written during my time in the White House, I learned about the McCain comments only after the fact. I wasn't paid to read about myself while in the White House, and I had little respect for the celebrity-journalists who spent the commercial breaks on a live TV set scrolling through their Twitter DMs and "Google Alerts—ME!" to see how what they just said was received by people they don't know. We were busy minding the country's business, including protecting the rights of the unhappy and the egotistical to enjoy free speech and lob cheap shots.

Ironically, when McCain brought up my marriage, the more liberal hosts of *The View*, like Joy Behar and Ana Navarro, would come to my defense, or at least not pile on. I'd been a guest on *The View* before McCain joined the show, on September 28 and November 2, 2016. The questions were tough but the panelists, including Whoopi Goldberg and Joy Behar, were welcoming and gracious when the cameras were off. On November 2, less than a week before Election Day, they gave me a gift from the Trump Spa and I suggested they invite me back on after Trump won the presidency.

First, Meghan McCain insulted me, and then she lied about me, telling Andy Cohen on his late-night show, "Don't call me or email me, Kellyanne, I don't care. She does that every time I say something." What?! I searched my contacts and did not see her in there. I searched my emails and did find one exchange between us, initiated by her. The email was glowing and friendly: She invited me onto the show and for George and me to have dinner with her and her husband, Ben Domenech. I sent a cordial reply and we never had dinner.

Even if it improved her mood, or improved *The View*'s ratings, to hurl invective my way with no opportunity to respond, why lie?

Maybe she was too young to remember when, a decade earlier, I was on CNN's *Larry King Live* in late February 2008, forty-one years old and nearly nine months pregnant with my third child, to defend her father after the *New York Times* ran a specious front-page piece linking Republican presidential nominee Senator John McCain and an attractive female lobbyist, Vicki Iseman.

I was outraged for the McCains. Senator McCain unwisely instructed everyone to stop talking about Rev. Jeremiah Wright, the controversial anti-Semitic 9/11 truther who just happened to be Obama's pastor of many, many years, who had married Barack and Michelle and who had baptized their daughters. Even Obama was forced to deliver the famous "race speech" in Philadelphia in March 2008 in part because of these disturbing revelations. McCain thought he took the high road, only to have the *Times* and others pull his name into the gutter with stories like this one. I went to the mat for Senator McCain that night and throughout the election cycle.

Years later, I quietly paid my respects to her late father at the U.S. Capitol in 2018 and was among the first White House officials to publicly acknowledge his death and his service to the nation. I don't recall judging or begrudging Meghan McCain when, like John's unsuccessful presidential campaign consultants, it looked like to me she cashed in on her father's two defeats for president with books like *America, You Sexy Bitch* or *Dirty Sexy Politics*. She had been born to a famous father and a rich mother, so her path to power was a hop, a skip, and a jump. Her ad nauseam, ad hominem attacks on me were uncool and unprovoked.

Like many know-it-alls, she knew nothing about me, and perhaps even less about herself. You would think someone who so easily falls apart when challenged would show a little grace to others when their own ride got a little rocky. I was reminded of this when McCain herself could not take what she dishes out, following a tough exchange with co-host Joy Behar, she recalled (in an interview): "She's [Joy] supposed to be my friend, and it's supposed to be a sisterhood." McCain added. "I'll never forget. I went back to my office and I had a panic attack. I was crying. I was hyperventilating. I threw up."

The couples dinner never happened. One half of the two couples had conversed, though. I had run into Meghan McCain's husband a few times, including on the set of *Face the Nation* and at an *Axios* party, and I had known his father, Doug Domenech, years earlier as part of the conservative movement. Ben is very smart, good on TV, and as head of *The Federalist*, lived and worked close to where he'd been raised in the Virginia suburbs of Washington, D.C. *The Federalist* was known for hiring young, beautiful, thin conservative women. One such mini-entourage surrounded him at an *Axios* event, where I had stopped on my way to a live hit with Laura Ingraham. In making polite conversation, I acknowledged his wife's fairly new gig at ABC in New York and said soothingly, "George and I did the commuting thing between Washington and New York when we were first married, just like you'll do now, with your wife up in New York on *The View*. It works out, you just—"

"Meghan McCain's husband" interrupted me with a smile. "*The View* is the worst show on television."

*   *   *

DECEMBER 17, 2019, began like most other days. I was gulping coffee
and print news, abbreviating a workout, helping the kids, dogs, and my
mom start their days, then dashing to the office. Three days before the
start of winter, it was cold enough for me to move a morning TV interview inside to the White House Press Briefing Room. Amid the morning's cheerful chaos, and with a week to go until I'd be hosting Christmas
Eve and Christmas Day at our house (Santa, this year you'd better be
real), my mind was full.

I had spoken with the president and had checked in with colleagues.
But I hadn't yet managed to absorb clearly and completely the latest
surprise from George.

For twenty years, those surprises had included romantic gifts, thoughtful gestures, and creative trips. The Concorde to Barbados. Australia for
my thirty-fifth birthday. Budding romantic but not yet boyfriend George
waiting in seat 4A on my connecting flight from Dallas to Tucson as I slid
into seat 4B and the cabin erupted in champagne-fueled applause.

Lately, the surprises had come in the form of tweets and op-eds
meant to malign my boss and, I hated to admit, to wound me. They came
without warning or advance notice or even the simplest courtesy a husband might normally give his wife of decades and the mother of his four
children. I learned about these little surprises and read them when the
whole world did, or in too many cases, well afterward. While I was doing
dishes or helping with homework, he was tucked away conspiring and
typing, choosing those who were using him over those who loved him.

That morning, the *New York Times* had an op-ed headlined "We Are
Republicans, and We Want Trump Defeated." The authors were George
Conway, Steve Schmidt, John Weaver, and Rick Wilson. It read like a
free and fawning press release, announcing a new group called the "Lincoln Project."

I knew these other men: three Republican political consultants who
were lately long on TV appearances and short on actual victories. George
knew them only by "reputation," and he'd never been a huge admirer
of the unregulated, unaccountable political consultancy. The three consultants all had something important in common: None of them had
ever successfully managed a presidential campaign, though some of them

(including Schmidt with McCain and Starbucks' Howard Schultz; and another "cofounder," Stuart Stevens, who was Romney's honcho in the embarrassing 2012 loss to Barack Obama) had tried.

As was custom after I'd finish a television interview, I took questions from the press in an unscripted gaggle that would go on for at least twenty minutes—no notes and no net. The president was increasingly dissatisfied with the press shop I had avoided running three years earlier, so there I was. In a few days, President Trump would be impeached in the House for the first time. So I was expecting *most* of the questions I got.

But twenty-nine minutes into the gaggle, a reporter in the back asked me if I had any reaction to "this super PAC funded by or started by your husband, John Weaver, and Rick Wilson."

Off the cuff, I responded, "Oh, those presidential campaign managers who failed? Who never got where I got?"

As that landed, I continued: "I don't really have a reaction except to say the *New York Times* seems overjoyed every time they can write a puff piece that includes certain people's names. They covered some group last year [Checks and Balances] that hasn't really taken off. They covered some Republican primary opponent [Joe Walsh] of the president that none of you give the time of day to anymore, I noticed.

"It's kind of disappointing to see some of the people involved, but not surprising."

Just two years earlier, George and I had sat alongside the president and First Lady for an intimate Christmas dinner with White House senior staff and spouses that he thoroughly enjoyed. Now he was in cahoots with overrated, underachieving men who had ridiculed and dismissed me for years, all for the purpose of defeating Donald Trump.

There was just one big problem in the formation of this new group: George wanted to make noise. These other guys wanted to make money. George may have been placing principle before profit, but there's no way they were, I thought.

IT WAS TRULY amazing, I came to see, how many Americans, including Hollywood figures, media stars, and loads of bored, unhappy, anonymous people, practically live on Twitter and its other social media cousins. I regretted that my own husband had become one of them. From zero tweets in 2016 to a total of 80,000 by the end of 2020, George had narrowed much of our once full and happy life into tiny Twitter tirades.

But it wasn't only social media dragging the country down this hole. The nation's major newspapers and cable and network TV were certainly doing their part, and so was late-night TV, trying to divide George from me and me from Trump, just as sure as red states were different from blue. They shape-shifted George into whatever they needed him to be to fit or generate a story. The *New York Times* mentioned George in roughly forty-eight articles over a period of three and a half years. In forty-five of those forty-eight articles, the paper referred to George as my husband. The *Washington Post* followed suit. Of the 191 times he was mentioned in that paper, he was described as my husband 165 times. Other times he simply relied on his byline as a *Washington Post* "Contributing Columnist."

When I appeared on CNN, I was often asked about my husband but not about my work. Meanwhile, George, who was unemployed through much of this, was asked about "his work" and not his wife. I asked myself again: *Where are the feminists who should be objecting to this?* Especially when I was working in the White House and George was not working anywhere.

The secrecy and duplicity stung.

If George was proud of his new role as a constitutional scholar/ campaign strategist/psychoanalyst/columnist/TV pundit, why not just own it? Why not discuss any of it with me? Instead, I kept discovering the latest op-eds and TV appearances along with the rest of the world. Now here was my own husband, taking up with the same men who had excluded me and then underperformed me. This whole Lincoln Project thing seemed an odd fit for George. This brilliant man and accomplished lawyer had gone from working with legal legends like Marty Lipton and Herb Wachtell to fronting for grifters and gadflies.

Increasingly, reporters revealing their biases and weird but also twisted people online seemed to take sick pleasure in thinking George's tweets were hurting me or bothering the president. George, in return, gave way too much to those strangers and wallowed in the attention. I read many of these for the first time long after I left the White House. A thrill for online weirdos who pretend they know George and have a relationship with him; a chill for those who actually do know him and do have a relationship with him.

The sheer amount of time George spent tweeting was alarming. Each day I got myself ready for work and my kids ready for school while George cozied up with Twitter. It became obsessive, escalating from a few legal observations or corgi memes, to defending me, Brett Kavanaugh, and Attorney General Barr, to becoming an unqualified yet unbridled psychiatrist offering diagnoses and an armchair critic hurling insults. The volume was alarming, but what concerned me most was how all-consuming it had become. Feeding the beast and one-upping one's last outlandish or outrageous post is central to gathering a following online. Like too many who slip into that vortex, George eagerly complied. George's newfound allies in the media and the odd collection of has-beens and never-will-bes in NYC and D.C. who would invite him to their homes and exclusive meetings began to take precedence over his family.

George got very personal and mean. I strived each day to keep our family together and happy, to try to keep him involved in the daily drumbeat of our lives and included in the major decisions and events. He returned the favor by attacking my boss and my colleagues. A sampling of tweets:

- Turned pollster: "And not only is he under 50 in PA, MI, WI (3 states he won by a total of 77,774 votes), he's under 50 in TX and LA (which he won by 10 and 20 percent), and in others he must win like FL, NC, GA, IN, OH, AZ. This even though the strong economy he inherited remains strong (for now)."

- Turned doctor: "We have an incoherent president who's off his rocker, and this is what we're talking about? Seriously?"

Some tweets are laugh-out-loud ironic and delicious, given now-President Biden's incoherence, obvious physical infirmities, and polls that show a majority of Americans say he is "not up to the job" and "mentally unfit."

- "Are we ready yet to have a full national conversation about the diseased mental state of the president of the United States?"

- "The media and the political establishment need to start asking the question: is @realdonaldtrump's disordered mind spiraling psychosis? Has it already?"

People who had known George for years, some even longer than I had known him, registered their concerns. Their own politics ran the spectrum from full-blown MAGA to unrelenting progressives to proudly apolitical, but all of them were worried about me and then the kids. They simply did not recognize Tweeting George, characterizing his conduct on a spectrum from inexplicable to reprehensible. I found myself reflexively defending George at first: "he also tweets about the Philadelphia Eagles and Corgis," "he's allowed to have his own opinion," and the most ironic one, "George never cared for all of Trump's tweeting, I suppose...." I was in denial. I literally did not want to see what was in front of me.

- Explaining to someone why he tweets: "My thoughts are: I suspect—just to pick two distinctions at random—that your candidate didn't (1) show signs of serious mental instability and (2) have command over the world's second-largest arsenal of nuclear weapons. Am I right?"

- Turned political analyst: "Harris would annihilate Trump."

- Discussing allegations against the president: "Everyone should listen to this. It's unpleasant. But please do. It's important. Please retweet it. And please email it to as many people as you can. Please."

- "The Liar-in-Chief and his lieutenant liars love to falsely accuse other people of lying even when overwhelmingly evidence corroborates the truthfulness of the person they are lying about."

Followers aren't friends, "likes" on Twitter aren't love in real life, yet it seemed that this was the affection and attention my husband craved. I was more numb than mad; and if I was mad, it was overtaken by sad.

- Turned personal: "No one needs him. It's just that some people haven't figured it out yet."

- "Why people persist in trashing their own personal and professional reputations for @realdonaldtrump utterly escapes me."

- Aged well: "I was never a fan of @NYGovCuomo. But he's doing a terrific job with these presentations. Imagine how much better off the country would be if @realdonaldtrump had just one-quarter of Cuomo's clear-mindedness and honesty."

Exactly no one—beginning with me—objected to George's about-face on Trump, even if I did not understand it. George was free to have opinions, even ones that were at odds with those he'd held just a short time before. The perplexing and vexing part was how public he was with those differences of opinion, how aggressive, how incessant. This was so out of character for George: the name-calling, the spitefulness, the passive-aggressive nature. Some were so shocked, they nervously asked if he and I had some plan, as if I'd be in on a ruse to let loose on the president "and the people around him." "This is all for show," people would write. All silly. If this were a show, I wanted no part in it, literally. Cancel the rest of the season—please!

- Sharing a Lincoln Project post predicting Joe Biden would get 443 electoral votes: "This would be the biggest electoral college defeat of a sitting president since 1980."

- Sharing false stories (still posted): "The Russia-bounty story is as huge a presidential scandal as there can be. It's an order of magnitude more outrageous than what he got impeached for, even though the Ukraine scandal was plainly criminal from the beginning. And it's clearly not going away."

Tagging the president in tweets suggested that George had become one of those many people who had convinced themselves that the president and he were the same: I have a Twitter feed, too! Except they weren't like him. One was the president, with the weight of the world and its chaotic, uncertain challenges on his shoulders. Trump was too busy and too uninterested to notice every comment or commentator. George is a smart man who must have recognized this. So if he wasn't trying to hurt or embarrass Donald Trump, or drive him out of the White House, then who was his intended target?

• It felt that George was moralizing while violating his marital vows to love, honor, and respect: "No one is compelled to work for, speak for, defend, explain, rationalize, or excuse this president and his incompetence, derangement, and racism. Whether to do any of that, or not, is a choice. And it's a moral choice, a crucial one, both for individuals and the nation."

As time went on, George and I barely spoke about Trump or politics.

IN THE OVEN-TO-TABLE format of Twitter-to-TV, the media kept generating content and generating eyeballs for themselves. *This will fluster her! Let's do more Conway stories!* I wasn't mad. Mad? I was sad. This was my marriage, my children, and my life. I'd kept it private for years. As had George. Now the brilliant man I respected for so many reasons, including how he kept his own counsel, was sending more than a hundred tweets a day, attacking my boss and the very things I had worked on, more clickbait grist for the media mill and connection for quite a few lonely, unhappily married, never married, or no longer married women developing unhealthy crushes on the man behind the tweet button. They could make George whatever they wanted or needed. I just wanted the old George, the loving husband and father who did not fritter away the day in an online abyss about the same stuff over and over.

Reporters who had gone out of their way to question me about George in unkind ways were now jumping to claim him as their own. In this crazy club, they all joined together in a circle of jerky mutual praise, tweeting, retweeting, insulting, and instigating.

President Trump was impeached before Christmas by a myopic, partisan Democrat House majority over his phone call with the Ukrainian president. Trump had flippantly described the phone call as "perfect," and the Democrats had foolishly treated it like the end of the world.

At least 2020 had finally arrived. Peace and prosperity abounded. My children were thriving. The elders in my life were healthy. And the president was poised for reelection.

What could possibly go wrong?

Part VII

Year from Hell

Chapter 33

Catching It

Twenty-twenty was brimming with promise.

As the New Year's ball was ready to drop in Times Square, teens Georgie and Claudia and I and two close friends who call me "Aunt Kels" watched the countdown from a hotel ballroom in Fort Lauderdale, Florida, while George had Charlotte and Vanessa skiing in Park City, Utah, where several members of the Lincoln Project happened to reside.

Absent a major unforeseen obstacle, incumbent president Trump was well poised for a second term. The overall economy continued to boom, buoyed by low unemployment, including record lows for African Americans, Hispanics, and Asian Americans. The arrows were pointing up for construction, mining, manufacturing, small business ownership, and home ownership. President Trump had reformed and modernized aspects of the North American Free Trade Agreement with Canada and Mexico, replacing it with the far more advantageous United States–Mexico–Canada Agreement. He was about to sign a major trade deal with China. The administration's policies on energy had yielded more jobs and lower prices, and meant that the United States was now a net exporter of oil and natural gas. Oh, and two Supreme Court justices, Neil Gorsuch and Brett Kavanaugh. Don't forget about those. The accomplishments of the Trump administration had truly lifted millions of Americans.

That's the kind of record that reelects incumbent presidents. Still, not everyone was on board with four more years of Donald Trump. I had talked to the president about this in the fall, as the Democratic field was ping-ponging among different front-runners. "Typically," I told him then, "incumbent presidents have a solid twenty-five to thirty percent of Americans firmly against them. For you, that number is higher. Your supporters are intractably passionate and will be there . . ."

The president nodded.

". . . but your detractors are incurably obsessed with destroying you."

He stopped nodding.

"So far, you've beaten them," I said. "Road Runner to their Wile E. Coyote. They've made it personal. They've tried to get you through Mueller, your businesses, your family, your staff, your tweets, Kavanaugh, porn people, and now through impeachment. But the ballot box is still their best bet."

Trump's critics continued to find ways to attack him incessantly and try to thwart his agenda. It seemed lost on many of them that their own bulging stock portfolios, cash positions, and freedom-through-wealth had been proximately caused by the leadership, policies, and persistence of the president they so loathed. And the media and Never Trumpers, by then living on Twitter, could not get over his tweets. But now that the new year was here, attention would increasingly focus on Election Day. The president fully understood when he called me on New Year's Day.

"Happy New Year!" bellowed the familiar voice on the phone.

"Happy, healthy New Year to you, Mr. President," I said. "Twenty-twenty—it should be phenomenal!"

Democrats had scored a Pyrrhic victory earlier that month when they impeached Trump over his call with the president of Ukraine months earlier, even as they would fall short of votes to convict him in the U.S. Senate. The presidential field for the Democrats was becoming a chaotic clown show, having featured dozens of "diverse" candidates and not a single compelling message.

"Twenty-twenty," Trump repeated. "Who do you think the Democrats will put up there?"

The lumbering Democratic presidential field resembled children chasing a slippery soccer ball all at once with no strategy to score and win. The field of candidates included several women, a black man, a black woman, a Hispanic, an American Samoan, a war veteran, the first openly gay candidate for president, and of course a few socialists ... which still must have seemed so underwhelming to billionaire Michael Bloomberg that he felt compelled to jump into the race. Once he'd spent a billion dollars to win zero states and two-thirds of the delegates of American Samoa, the only thing you could say was that his consultants fared a whole lot better than he did. Bloomberg's delegate haul was still four more than Kamala Harris's zero. Despite having twenty thousand people at her launch, her campaign went nowhere. Were the Democratic primary and caucus voters "racist" or "sexist" or both? We'll never know. Harris was out of the race before a single vote was cast.

The Democrats and their diverse field of "firsts" all trying to claim the mantle for the "future of the Democratic Party" would, of course, go on to nominate someone synonymous with the past: a seventy-seven-year-old white man who had been a career politician in Washington for four decades. Whom I would refer to as "the Loch Ness monster of the swamp"—which Don Junior would use three months later in his convention speech.

If elected, Joe Biden would make history, too, as the nation's oldest president. Biden had served for eight years side by side with President Barack Obama, who then unceremoniously passed over him to support Hillary Clinton in 2016 and, according to the *New York Times*, was skeptical and discouraging of a potential Biden White House run four years later, reportedly admonishing his former vice president, "You don't need to do this, Joe."

As I breathed in the warm ocean air, I called to wish my mom, a New Year's baby, a happy birthday. I felt there were good times ahead.

HOWEVER, WHAT SHOULD have been an exciting and triumphant year quickly turned into a punishingly horrible one for President Trump, for the nation, for the world, and for me. Within weeks, we got a terrible piece of news in our family, and within months, the world began a long struggle to confront an invisible but deadly virus sweeping the globe. But none of that was known when the year began.

As I had throughout my White House tenure, I knew I'd soon be hitting the road in my personal capacity on behalf of the president and other Republican candidates. Lincoln Day dinner speeches. Fundraisers in Florida, New Jersey, Kansas, and Iowa. Those were imminent. This trend was sure to accelerate as the election year rolled on.

On January 23, I flew with the president to the Trump National Doral Miami resort for a Republican National Committee meeting and fundraiser. The next day I was back in Washington with Trump as he became the first sitting president to address the March for Life, live and in person on the National Mall. He was fantastic, energizing the huge pro-life crowd. "They are coming after me because I am fighting for you," he roared. "And we are fighting for those who have no voice." A few days later, I flew with President Trump and three of my children, Georgie, Charlotte, and Vanessa, on Air Force One to Wildwood, New Jersey, where my family had spent my childhood summers and close by to where, thirty-two years earlier, I had caught the political bug after meeting President Ronald Reagan. Who could ever have imagined all those years ago that I'd be back home, this time traveling with my kids and the forty-fifth president? The month before, I'd personally and secretly escorted Congressman Jeff Van Drew to the president's private residence, where Van Drew would become the first sitting member of Congress to switch parties from the majority party to the minority. He said that his Democrat Party lost him over focusing on impeachment instead of on the needs of people in his district. In return, the president told him he would go do a big rally in Wildwood. At these back-to-back events, Trump called me up onstage to rally the troops, and it really got me going. I was brief but bullish: "We have two Supreme Court justices, two new trade deals, and two dead terrorists . . . that equals two terms."

It seemed clear to me: Just ten months stood between President Trump and his reelection. The campaign was so flush with cash, they had agreed to pay more than $11 million to air one Super Bowl ad and seemed utterly unfazed by whatever unknowns might be coming their way.

But *this*?

A global pandemic heading to our shores from China?

A silent, savvy killer, able to spread from person to person and then change its form to outmaneuver whatever defenses modern medicine might erect?

No, no one was prepared for that. No one had contingencies for: *Okay, this is what we do if a deadly virus upends the entire country!*

On January 27, acting chief of staff Mick Mulvaney hosted a meeting in his office with senior staff to discuss this coronavirus officially known as SARS-CoV-2 and the potentially deadly condition it is responsible for, COVID-19. Our deputies, including my own chief of staff, Renee Hudson, had been in meetings for weeks. With infectious diseases, I was worried about the unknown, but was following what our health professionals were monitoring. Two days later, President Trump announced his Coronavirus Task Force and banned travel from China. The task force would be headed by Alex Azar, secretary of the Department of Health and Human Services. Members would include Robert Redfield, director of the Centers for Disease Control and Prevention (CDC); Dr. Anthony Fauci, the top infectious-disease doctor at the National Institutes of Health; and National Security Advisor Robert O'Brien. From the beginning, it was difficult to get everyone on the same page. The doctors were either opposed to the China ban or at least skeptical about its effectiveness. A ban like that was a rare step to take against another nation, let alone a nation with whom the president had just weeks earlier finalized a major trade deal.

Joe Biden had his own opinion. He called the ban "xenophobic."

Looking back, it's scary to recall how little any of us knew yet about this deadly virus, including all the top doctors in the land.

So life went on. On February 1, I flew to Kansas with my youngest daughter, Vanessa, and retiring senator Pat Roberts to deliver the keynote address for his last state convention dinner. Later that night, Vanessa and I flew to Iowa to meet a chartered planeload of Trump surrogates who had just descended on the first-in-America caucus state. Vanessa, ten years old, and I had breakfast at the governor's residence the next morning and did a campaign event with Governor Kim Reynolds and Senator Joni Ernst.

That Sunday morning, I received devastating news.

My father had been rushed to the hospital, and we all were told, "Get to Florida to say your goodbyes."

My father had been in shaky health. But he'd just spent Christmas with us in Washington and had visited again in mid-January. Vanessa and I left Iowa immediately. A family friend jumped on a plane with Claudia from New Jersey. George and Charlotte made their way by car from a field hockey tournament in Orlando. It was a comfort to be at my father's bedside in his final days, even as it was rough on my daughters, who insisted on being there.

Claudia and I slept at the hospital, and I did play-by-play commentary of the Super Bowl for my sleeping father. As a fellow Philadelphia Eagles fan, my father had insisted he'd never live to see former Eagles head coach Andy Reid win a Super Bowl, but that night, Reid did it, guiding the Kansas City Chiefs to their first Super Bowl win in decades.

I don't remember the campaign's $11 million Super Bowl ad, but I did see a bunch of the senior campaign staff on Twitter taking selfies in suites and enjoying themselves. Good for them! I was content to sit with my father, waiting for my half brother Scott to arrive, and holding the green "#1 PopPop" shirt my children had given him weeks before. I thanked my father and thanked God again for our second chance of "meeting" each other when I was twelve.

Two days later, and after my father regained consciousness long enough to acknowledge us in the room with him, his two children and four grandchildren released him to heaven with love.

CLAUDIA AND I flew back to Washington on the night of February 4. Thanks to Delta Air Lines' live TV feed, I was able to see President Trump deliver what would be his final State of the Union address.

I had sent handwritten edits hours earlier and quadruple-checked that all the guests and their guests were accommodated. Having been a part of the small group who helped do the initial planning and vetting of the president's and First Lady's State of the Union guests (none of whom ever leaked and all of whom were inspirational), I watched the speech through my grief on the plane, gratified to see so many wonderful Americans receive recognition and praise for their contributions to this country.

The next day, February 5, the president was acquitted in the U.S. Senate. Impeaching Donald Trump in a Democrat-controlled Congress was one thing. Convicting him in a Republican-control Senate? That was something else entirely.

The morning after, I rode with the president in his armored limousine, the Beast, to the National Prayer Breakfast. On the short drive to the Washington Hilton, he asked if Ivanka was joining us. I called her and she said she would be watching on TV and would see him back at the White House. I then dialed up Tom Joannou from my office, who was briefing the president and me on the latest approval rating in Gallup, showing President Trump at a high of 49 percent that morning. Trump was reveling in his acquittal and the turning of public opinion, knowing he was just minutes away from being on the same stage with Speaker Pelosi, who thirty-six hours earlier had torn up her copy of the president's State of the Union speech in a televised hissy fit. I had something else I wanted to mention to him, and I took advantage of us being alone in the Beast to squeeze in a private thought.

"Mr. President," I said, "I'm worried about the coronavirus."

"I'm not," he answered. "The doctors told us there is a very low risk for the United States."

He was right. They had said that. Looking back, *why did the doctors say that*? Isn't the nature of infectious, respiratory-borne disease its unpredictability and contagion? Those who claim the president was not following the science should note that the president was following the scientists. Question is, what were *they* following?

When he got to the Hilton and took the stage, the president took a moment to celebrate. He held up a copy of *USA Today* with big, bold letters that said "ACQUITTED."

The Senate vote was on his mind, not a disease that was still mostly contained to China at this stage. A meeting in the Oval Office later that afternoon convinced me that I had been too excitable and emotional in raising concerns about the virus. I already regretted bringing it up. It was rushed, and he had been focused on impeachment. And what he said about the doctors downplaying it was true. So, I failed to mention it again that day or the day after that or the day after that.

After all, President Trump was just "following the science" of what was known at the time, as relayed by his doctors and experts, who went as far as to tell the president and the American public that the coronavirus posed a "low risk" and was "not a major threat."

I WASN'T THE only person in Washington who was slow to fully grasp the urgency of COVID's threat. I had tons of company on that, including some of America's greatest medical minds, parked right there beside me.

At this point, Dr. Fauci, Dr. Redfield, and other top experts, on and off the president's task force, were fairly consistent in their overall view that "we still have a low risk to the American public." Just a couple of weeks earlier, Dr. Fauci, with the very latest information available, had stated straight out that "in all the history of respiratory viruses, asymptomatic transmission has never been the driver of outbreaks. An epidemic is not driven by asymptomatic carriers."

That would certainly turn out to be wrong.

By mid-February, we had just over a dozen cases in the United States, most of them people who had traveled from Wuhan, China. But even with COVID mostly contained overseas, it was already becoming an increasing focus of mine. I spent most of February immersing myself in the topic and meeting in the Situation Room with other senior staffers, doctors, scientists, and cabinet members.

It was Melania Trump who raised some of the strongest, early concerns.

The president and First Lady were planning a trip to India. On February 14 they met with a large group from the West Wing, the East Wing, and the Coronavirus Task Force. The group gathered in the Oval Office to discuss whether the trip to India should go ahead. The president, the First Lady, Dr. Fauci, Secretary Azar, and Dr. Redfield were all around the Resolute Desk, while the rest of us were seated farther back.

Politely yet pointedly, the First Lady said to the doctors, "We have staff that will be heading to India soon and be there for at least a week before we arrive. I am worried about them with the virus. Should they go?"

It was a direct question that needed to be answered directly. And it was.

No problem. Go ahead.

The same doctors who two weeks earlier had expressed their skepticism about the president's travel ban against China were now unconcerned about the first family and the staff going to India. "India has only a couple of cases right now," one of them said, looking down at typed notes on a sheet of paper.

India has more than 1.4 billion people, I thought to myself. *How could India have "just a couple of cases" of anything?* I was no epidemiologist, but that seemed implausible. Sadly, within the year, India would be the global center of rising COVID cases and death. Nevertheless, with clearance from the doctors, the Trumps and their delegation headed to India on February 23.

With eight months left till Election Day, it would be the last foreign trip of the Trump administration.

As China continued to cover up the severity of the coronavirus, the country proceeded as normal. The media coverage was still limited. The experts were cautious but optimistic.

COVID was a story, but it wasn't *the* story. Not yet. And it was very hard to see at that point how close it was to changing the world.

THE TRUMPS WERE on Air Force One, flying back from India, as CDC official Nancy Messonnier warned the nation that the novel coronavirus could become a widespread health crisis, including in the United States. The stock market plummeted. The Dow was quickly down more than one thousand points.

Deputy National Security Advisor Matt Pottinger, an expert on China who spoke fluent Mandarin, rushed into my office. Matt and I had worked closely on President Trump's agreement with Chinese president Xi Jinping to punish manufacturers and distributors of Chinese fentanyl. Pottinger was the guy who had convened the earliest briefings about the novel coronavirus, sitting at the head of the table in the Situation Room and gathering people and assets from different cabinet agencies and the White House complex. Now Pottinger was in my office, and he had a worried look on his face.

He was deeply concerned about China's lack of transparency on the coronavirus and concerned about our nation's preparedness. He said we needed to convince the president to appoint a "coronavirus czar," someone who could lead our nation through this increasingly complicated and dangerous time.

"Some people think this could be the end of President Xi," Pottinger said to me. "But I worry it could hurt President Trump."

He recommended bringing aboard Dr. Deborah Birx, who had made a name for herself decades earlier when she'd successfully taken on another mysterious and deadly virus.

"Deborah Birx of the HIV/AIDS work?" I asked. "Is she still at State?"

"She is," Pottinger replied, "and she's terrific."

I promised to do anything I could to help.

Once the president was back, he immediately got to work on expanding and shaping the Coronavirus Task Force. I asked Secretary of State Mike Pompeo if he could spare Dr. Birx. He said sure. This was becoming an all-hands-on-deck situation. Everyone seemed to like the idea of giving her a key role in the task force, even the president's usual critics. With Drs. Birx, Fauci, and Redfield coordinating the medical side of things, the administration's coronavirus response was now being guided by a real public health A-team. President Trump considered appointing his former Food and Drug Administration commissioner, Scott Gottlieb, or former New Jersey governor Chris Christie to be the head of the task force, but he decided the effort would have a closer connection to the Oval Office with Vice President Mike Pence in charge.

When Trump and Pence were about to announce some new additions to the task force, the president looked at me in the Oval Office and asked, "Do you like Mike as the coronavirus czar?"

"I like him as the vice president," I said. "He doesn't need a Russian title." But if Pence was going to be responsible for the COVID fight, I said, it was right having the doctors and everyone else on the task force report to him, and he could then report to the president.

"It makes you both politically accountable," I said.

At that point, I don't think either of them knew—I don't think any of us did—just how much they were taking on.

THE FIRST U.S. COVID death was reported on Leap Day, February 29. Two days later we filed into the Cabinet Room and witnessed history being made. The president and the vice president had a scheduled meeting with top pharmaceutical executives from Pfizer, Moderna, Gilead Sciences, and Johnson & Johnson. They had come to Washington to discuss prescription drug pricing, an important priority for the Trump administration. But a far more pressing issue was staring us all in the face: the need to develop new therapeutics and vaccines for COVID-19. That morning the president made clear he wanted this to happen, and happen fast. Far more quickly than it normally took Big Pharma and federal regulators to get new drugs to the people who needed them. These new meds had to be safe, the president said. They had to be effective. But there was no way America could wait five or ten years.

The question, Dr. Fauci reminded everyone, wasn't how quickly a vaccine could be *made*. "The question is, 'When is it going to be *deployable?*'" Now in his fifth decade of infectious-disease work, Fauci knew just how maddeningly long the drug development cycle could take. But President Trump was unmoved. He had been dealing with bureaucratic red tape and delays for his entire career in the private sector. He knew that, when the pressure was really on, things could get done much faster without sacrificing safety. This time, dealing with even the possibility that COVID-19 could threaten Americans, the president pushed hard and consequently sparked real results much, much sooner than almost anyone else imagined was possible.

The rest of the week was our last on the road before the world practically shut down. I traveled to Tampa, Florida, with Attorney General Bill Barr to participate in an Elder Justice Summit. I went with the president a few blocks from the White House to the Latino Coalition Legislative Summit. I participated in a roundtable on child exploitation with Ivanka Trump, Attorney General Barr, and representatives from the Five Eyes intelligence alliance (Australia, Canada, New Zealand, the United Kingdom, and the United States) and the big tech companies.

Later it was confirmed that Australia's minister of home affairs tested positive for COVID-19 after being at the roundtable with us, the first time COVID hit home so directly. Thankfully, no one else tested positive. Later that day, I boarded Marine One and Air Force One with President Trump and flew to Scranton, Pennsylvania, for his first town hall of the year, an event that White House press secretary Stephanie Grisham and I helped to organize. The president received only one question from the audience about the coronavirus and two follow-ups about it from Fox News anchors Bret Baier and Martha MacCallum. There were reportedly 164 known cases of COVID-19 in the United States at the time.

Days before, as I was preparing for the March 1 Sunday shows, the doctors and other Coronavirus Task Force members debated whether the United States was still in "containment" or had entered the "mitigation" stage. "Containment" won. No one changed that assessment as we prepared the president for his March 5 town hall. That was lodged in my brain when, the next morning, a (now former) network reporter asked me if the coronavirus was "contained." I responded affirmatively, in part because of what the "experts" were saying and in part because as a layperson, I was using *containment* with a small *c*, meaning we (the White House, the nation) were aware, studying, ramping up production of personal protective equipment (PPE) and testing capacity, and taking action, like "fifteen days to slow the spread."

Somehow my repeating the doctors' assessment was a first-class felony in the eyes of the drive-by media and TwitterLosers. They weren't fact-checking; they were cherry-picking. Media work overtime twisting and spinning the doctors' actual inaccuracies and inconsistencies. But if a different messenger reflects what the doctors have said, it is a global truth pandemic.

So obsessed with messenger and not message, with political science and not actual science, the same critics seemed unbothered by the most troubling fact of all: The entity actually responsible for fighting the pandemic, the World Health Organization, was sticking by its earlier, unfathomable declaration (on Twitter, naturally): "Preliminary investigations conducted by the Chinese authorities have found no clear evidence of human-to-human transmission of the novel #coronavirus."

Nor did these critics seem to care that their favorite doctors and scientists in charge of the response to COVID-19, like Dr. Fauci, were saying at the same time that masks did not work, that the coronavirus posed a low risk to the public, and that asymptomatic spread was virtually impossible. Mixed messages from visible top experts were spreading as quickly as the invisible virus.

Chapter 34

Fighting It

The three White House chiefs of staff President Trump had chosen so far were very different men. Different backgrounds. Different kinds of experience. Different managerial styles. But all three, Reince Priebus, John Kelly, and Mick Mulvaney, had something notable in common: During the 2016 presidential campaign, they had all expressed misgivings and criticisms of candidate Donald Trump.

On March 6, 2020, you could raise that number to four.

Mick Mulvaney was out. The new chief, North Carolina congressman and House Freedom Caucus head Mark Meadows, had been no Trump fan during the primaries. But once Trump had the nomination—and especially once we were in the White House—he was all in for Trump. He helped push the America First agenda and joined with Ohio congressman Jim Jordan, at the time the ranking member of the House Oversight Committee, to poke holes in the Russian collusion delusion. Before he got the chief's job, Meadows liked to sit in Steve Bannon's office during that brief and ill-fated tenure, talking up a military transgender ban and how to screw Paul Ryan. One day over lunch in the Navy Mess, and again in his congressional office, Meadows suggested I should be chief of staff, a job he was already angling for, and I was not. He liked to pronounce earnestly that I was "being grossly underutilized" in the

White House, Meadows meant it as a compliment, even if untrue. Then, once he moved into the building where I'd worked for more than 1,100 days already, he worked doggedly to make it true.

THIS PERSONNEL CHANGE and several others that followed during COVID would negatively affect much of what would happen in the long eight months between March 6 and November 6.

Overhauling core divisions of the West Wing had serious consequences, especially in the middle of a worsening national medical crisis, and on the cusp of a reelection campaign. Trusted White House aide and deputy press secretary Judd Deere was one of the few kept on, bringing some continuity to the press shop at the start of the pandemic. Our plates were quickly becoming full with the many issues facing us, even beyond COVID. In an election year, talent usually leaves the White House to staff the campaign. But this year, many "political" people were coming *into* the White House to deal with a still-unknown virus and their own agendas.

In a *60 Minutes* interview that weekend, eight days after I repeated his and the other doctors' claims that we were still in virus "containment" and not "mitigation," Dr. Anthony Fauci made a head-scratcher of a comment. He cast doubt on the effectiveness of wearing a mask, telling Americans, "When you're in the middle of an outbreak, wearing a mask might make people feel a little bit better and it might even block a droplet. But it's not providing the perfect protection that people think that it is." The media had made Fauci a superstar, and an untouchable messenger. This was illustrative of the mixed messaging coming from a White House in flux to a nation on edge.

March 11 was the day things got real.

To many Americans, the rapid ping of news alerts that day came as a shock of reality. The NBA paused their season. The NCAA conferences canceled tournaments, and U.S. cases of the virus exceeded one thousand. Celebrity couple Tom Hanks and Rita Wilson revealed that they had COVID. The dubious, discredited World Health Organization finally called it a *pandemic*. The hits kept coming into that night. The White House was scrambling for a quick response. Throughout the day, family members and other higher-ups urged the president to deliver a prime-time Oval Office address. The president's only previous prime-time Oval Office address had occurred fourteen months earlier, with a different press and communications team. It had centered on immigration and wall funding during the government shutdown, a topic Trump had been passionate about since the primary campaign.

Now Trump would be expected to inform, assure, and guide the nation on this "invisible enemy" that our own doctors seemed to downplay in early messaging. Why that night? Was there a pressing need to speak directly to the people? Yes, there was an announcement of an additional ban on travel, this time from the Schengen Area, comprising twenty-six European countries. But that could have been issued by the State Department or through a press release, Twitter, or the regular press briefings.

This crisis was all still new, changing each day, surprising even the experts daily, so knowing what to say and when to say it was both tricky and unpredictable. The president's first concern was how best to calm a worried nation, without adding to the growing fear and uncertainty. Would the information the president provided on one day still be true on the next or the next day, once we learned more about a virus that began in China and was now ravaging Italy? I wondered, should President Trump contradict Dr. Fauci's advice on *60 Minutes* from three days earlier and encourage Americans to wear masks? Ultimately the decision was made. Trump would address the nation.

I had been intimately involved with the president's first prime-time address the year before, and was in the Oval when he delivered it live on January 8, 2019. The speechwriting and press teams supported a well-organized event that was in the president's wheelhouse.

The stakes and substance at hand on March 11, 2020, were fundamentally different. And for me, I was doing double duty. March 11 was also my daughter Charlotte's twelfth birthday. While the president delivered his remarks from the Oval Office, we celebrated Charlotte at a packed RPM Italian restaurant in Washington. It would be the last outing for a while. Later that evening, the White House canceled or postponed all events for the next two weeks.

The planned address required a few immediate and last-minute clarifications, and live cameras caught the president seeming uneasy or unenthusiastic about what had just happened. The reviews that night and into the next morning were mostly critical. The president noticed and wanted a course correction.

I VISITED THE Oval Office the next day with a suggestion.

"Mr. President," I said, "I think it would be good to engage with the four living former presidents. They each have dealt with major crises. It will show leadership, bipartisanship, and calm everyone."

"Ugh," he said. "They're all horrible to me."

"They haven't been great," I allowed, "but this is bigger than all that. Just hear me out, please. It'll take just one or two calls to get it moving, and it wouldn't be a long-term thing." I also knew it could help seal his reelection, but I didn't say that. Most people in this country are apolitical and look for consensus, collaboration, and agreement. This would be a bipartisan way of being nonpartisan.

"Jimmy Carter is in his nineties, God bless him," I continued. "He could offer his advice but may not be able to travel. In fact, with COVID, none of them may be able to travel now."

The president was listening, so I kept going.

"George W. Bush would engage, and the four of you [including First Ladies Laura Bush and Melania] genuinely got along during the time of his father's funeral," I said. "He'll help. Barack Obama would not decline. He dealt with Ebola and swine flu, and this is serious, too. More serious, it seems. Bush and Obama would help and then go back to their lives. The only one who may be tough to get rid of is Bill Clinton. He'll enjoy the spotlight again, loves this stuff, and"—I smiled—"may want to be your best buddy."

Looking at Trump across the Resolute Desk, I could picture all five presidents standing there, lending their support to him as he tackled this "once in a century" pandemic.

Trump declined.

I didn't take it personally, and I didn't take it as a final no. These things take time. I was suggesting the president reach out to men who had been openly critical of him, and none of whom had voted for him or been much help in the three years he'd been there. I knew the idea might take some convincing.

I returned to my desk upstairs and dialed Mark Meadows. The new chief of staff had yet to even appear on campus. He was quarantining from exposure to someone at CPAC who'd been infected. I told him what had just happened. Meadows said he "liked" the idea, asked how Trump reacted, and said maybe we could revisit it with "POTUS." I told him I was not sharing it beyond our conversation and that I was continuing my practice of keeping the chief of staff apprised of need-to-know conversations with the president.

Following Trump's uneven Oval Office address, a Rose Garden event was being planned for Friday the thirteenth. Some of the country's biggest retailers and tech companies would be there, pledging cooperation and support in our fight against the virus. It was impressive, but again, the rush to fight a virus we couldn't see or understand led to the president's remarks including incomplete claims, this time a pledge from Google that was not yet fully developed.

The country hunkered down at home, and we hunkered down at the White House.

Trump called as I was driving in that Saturday for a task force meeting. He said he was joining, too. Shortly after we hung up, he showed up in the Situation Room in a baseball cap and no tie. After the task force meeting, the president mentioned he would sit on the side in the staff section during the scheduled briefing. After talking it through, he decided it was best for him to kick off the briefing, then turn it over to the vice president, and leave the Q-and-A to the doctors. That was a strategy that was maintained daily for a little while and the country was clearly appreciative of hearing directly from the president and vice president, surrounded by the experts. Trump was leading and meeting the challenge, even declaring himself a "wartime president" later that week.

A few days later, a new initiative was introduced: 15 Days to Slow the Spread. The idea was that if Americans just hunkered down at home for fifteen days, we could beat this virus in one collective action, just stomp it down all together and be done with it.

I was in the Roosevelt Room with the doctors and others trying to tighten and clarify the mixed public messaging. The president was in the Situation Room on a videoconference with other leaders of the G7 nations. At this point our experts were still saying "the American public is at low risk." Dr. Fauci was pleading with Americans not to panic or buy masks.

With Vice President Pence leading the discussion, the health professionals had the floor. I learned a great deal, and when we met afterward, I raised a few concerns about the messaging on masks, the confidence in 15 Days to Slow the Spread, and setting expectations among the public about testing.

When I was brought in for messaging, I always applied "RPI." *Real people impact.* I tried to picture how the people I grew up with might react if they were told to spend "fifteen days out of work and out of school to slow the spread" and then were asked to tack on fifteen or thirty days more. Or if we said "COVID testing is available" at Walmart and Walgreens, failing to make clear that such testing was for healthcare workers and other first responders, not for the general public (yet), what type of confusion or chaos might ensue. I also questioned why, if, as the doctors were saying, the risks of hospitalization and death increased with age and with co-morbidities like diabetes, hypertension, or obesity, we weren't saying so. Someone mumbled that this was no time to shame Americans, but it wasn't as if we were naming or blaming them, so why not be transparent and truthful?

For the next thirty days, with a day off for Easter, we spent seven days a week in the Situation Room and overflow rooms with the Coronavirus Task Force. Vice President Pence spent much of March leading briefings.

Despite some people playing politics, a majority of the country was willing to go along with the fight as we asked for fifteen days to slow the spread. Entire cities were closed down, something we'd never seen before. But Americans sacrificed when they were asked. I was on our weekly calls with the governors. The president's most hardened critics were among the most appreciative, since many of their states were being hit the hardest.

During one task force phone call that March, Governor Kate Brown of Maine, Mayor Muriel Bowser of Washington, D.C., Governor Laura Kelly of Kansas, and Governor Michelle Lujan Grisham of New Mexico, and the Governor of Guam, all Democrats, expressed their gratitude directly to the president for surging supplies like PPE and testing capacity, for making available federally provided meals for stuck-at-home schoolchildren who relied upon them, for coordinating with FEMA regional administrators (Governor Gretchen Whitmer of Michigan did not seem to know how they operated, in an earlier call). The process seemed free from "political science."

The president also had support from the public, who, given that the nation was under assault, was rallying around the flag. The morning of March 25, Gallup reported that President Trump had a 49 percent job approval rating, a record high for him, and 60 percent approved of his handling of the coronavirus. I brought that poll down to the Oval Office to show the president. I wanted him to know the country was with him. He had a live town hall planned in the Rose Garden with Fox News later that day. The president seemed pleased with the poll but then said something that made me nervous. He said he was going to declare the country would "open up by Easter."

I pleaded with him that we shouldn't declare any end dates right now. The country was listening and making the sacrifices. I made the point that "you have never had sixty percent on anything, including your handling of the economy, which you surely deserve."

"I haven't?"

"No, you have not had anywhere close to that number on *any* issue. The country is divided, and Americans expect that businessman Donald Trump would create a good economy. They did not expect you to be dealt a once-in-a-century pandemic. Right now, you have a grace period. They want this country to beat the virus. If you put an artificial date on it, they will try to make you own every death after that."

I walked out of the Oval still worried.

I road-tested my thoughts individually with two of my second-floor West Wing colleagues, Larry Kudlow and Ivanka Trump. I first went to Larry to make the same appeal. I knew the economic folks were looking to open up the country, and we all wanted that to happen as quickly and safely as possible. But I worried about declaring premature victory over an enemy we could not see.

Next I went to Ivanka's office. She listened intently, as I sought an ally to talk with the president about providing a struggling and fearful America with immediate economic relief and a promise/plan to reopen safely but without arbitrary deadlines like Easter Sunday.

The president said it anyway. Soon after, though, he clarified things, describing Easter more as a goal than a deadline. Moreover, he said, it was the governors who would decide on behalf of their own states when to reopen.

The next day, I joined the president, Secretary of Defense Mark Esper, National Security Advisor Robert O'Brien, and Meadows in Norfolk, Virginia, to set sail the USNS *Comfort*. The Navy's traveling hospital would head to New York. Critics said it would take weeks for the needed help to arrive, but the ship was on Trump speed and got to New York in a few days. The USNS *Mercy* had already docked in California to help that hard-hit state minister to the overflow of COVID patients. Unfortunately, the governor of New York, Andrew Cuomo, never made much use of the *Comfort*. President Trump smartly called New Jersey governor Phil Murphy and offered it to his residents.

Murphy was thrilled.

THE CASES CONTINUED to rise. Most people in the West Wing were focused on ways to slow the pandemic.

Our lives and work turned upside down much like the rest of America. Schooltime had become screentime, dream vacations were canceled, and long-planned celebrations, including weddings, shelved. One such couple, Sarah Trevor from my office and Will Russell, one of the president's traveling aides, had their wedding canceled. This was sad, yet there was perhaps one place better than the Trump International Hotel to celebrate your planned nuptials: the Trump White House. Trump found time to bring them into the Oval Office for a celebration. Trump was always pleased to see that if not for his presidency, two people might not have found each other.

Hope Hicks had returned to the White House a few weeks earlier, after a two-year hiatus, to be the liaison between the campaign, the Republican National Committee, and the White House, an important duty in any campaign year. But Hope's role quickly transitioned into helping with the COVID crisis, from communications strategy to the president's daily schedule. I had taken calls with heavyweights Bob Iger of Disney and Bill Gates of Microsoft, asking how they could be helpful. Jared Kushner got the Federal Emergency Management Agency (FEMA) to take the lead on emergency management pieces and brought in some of his friends from the private sector to apply best practices in securing PPE and ramping up testing capacity and ventilator production. Almost everyone was doing his or her part.

After a week or two of the country unifying, the media and other leading Democrats had reverted to form and grew more critical. Every ten or twenty years, an event seems to unite this country. The pandemic didn't. We had a nationwide response, working hand in glove with every governor, some of whom sounded frighteningly ignorant about emergency management response protocol in their own states, and some of whom could not resist the excitement of being on the Sunday shows criticizing the president.

The pandemic, one would think, should have been a unifier. Maybe it was the president's high approval ratings over his handling of it, or maybe it was just people reflexively going back to their partisan comfort zones. Some on the left clearly saw the pandemic as an opportunity to undermine Donald Trump's reelection prospects, echoing President Obama's chief of staff Rahm Emanuel, who famously said in 2008, "You never want a serious crisis to go to waste. I mean, it's an opportunity to do things that you think you could not do before." But the goodwill we had fostered helping states and their people get the help they needed was gone and the obvious reason was that 2020 was an election year. The Democrats quickly pivoted to blaming Trump for acting too late. Yet the Democrats hadn't been fast to react, either. In late 2019 and early 2020, they'd been hyperfocused on impeaching President Trump and then finding a Democrat who could beat him. When Democratic officeholders did speak up, it wasn't just to urge caution. It was people like Nancy Pelosi telling Americans to go visit Chinatown in San Francisco as a rebuke to Trump's China travel ban, and Mayor Bill de Blasio riding the New York City subway and suggesting Broadway plays to see to prove that the fears over COVID early on were overblown.

Hindsight as twenty-twenty does not apply to the willfully blind.

I WENT ON television and called out the Democrats for their partisanship during this time. There was plenty of it, including from the presumptive Democrat nominee and the Democrat governors who came to the task force saying they were deeply grateful for how much we were doing. They promptly turned around and went on MSNBC and CNN and trashed the administration. From Joe Biden to Andrew Cuomo to Gavin Newsom, their eyes were far more focused on the poll numbers than infection counts. Once the pandemic was politicized, there was no turning back.

I had wished Trump had engaged the four living ex-presidents, but the man who next wanted to have that title, Joe Biden, did come calling. Lately, Biden and many other Democrats had been criticizing the administration for not helping, and then taking credit for help that the administration was providing. Biden seemed unengaged and unpresidential, popping up intermittently like a groundhog on February 2 to give a rambling or cringeworthy interview and scurry back into the basement.

This is what's wrong with politics. Biden, with forty-seven years in elective office in Washington, and angling for Trump's job, couldn't be bothered to participate or offer any real insights into how he would handle the pandemic response? On Wednesday, April 1, I called out Biden on TV. "I think it's really disappointing to have President Obama's number two, who apparently doesn't talk much to him, out there criticizing instead of saying, hey, here's what we did that we thought was effective," I said. "Why doesn't Vice President Biden call the White House today and offer some support? He's in his bunker in Wilmington . . . we're not talking about politics here at the White House at all. We're talking about ventilators and vaccines, not Biden and Bernie."

Someone in Biden-land heard me and later that night Kate Bedingfield, Biden's deputy campaign manager, released a statement: "Our teams will be in touch and we will arrange a call."

Not so fast. Five days passed—radio silence. On April 6, 2020, President Trump tweaked Biden, tweeting, "What ever happened to that phone call he told the Fake News he wanted to make to me?" Within an hour, longtime Obama and Biden advisor Anita Dunn reached out to me and we set about arranging the call.

The Trump-Biden call lasted no more than ten or fifteen minutes, and Biden did most of the talking. He had prepared, maybe practiced his pitch, as if a Disney World animatronic had been flicked to "on." Biden suggested four measures to combat COVID: fully implement the Defense Production Act, appoint a supply commander to oversee it, ramp up testing, and open a new enrollment period for the Affordable Care Act. Thanks, Joe, but every single one of these "fresh ideas" was already weeks in development, except the Obamacare enrollment period. We had decided weeks earlier to instead cover all costs for the uninsured with respect to COVID testing and treatment up to ninety days rather than reopen enrollment, a fact I wished President Trump had flagged and bragged about more.

It was a cordial conversation, which I witnessed, and Biden was especially engaged. So much so that, after the call, President Trump looked at me and to my surprise declared: "Everyone is wrong. He hasn't lost it." Biden was clear and to the point. The stumbling and bumbling we saw on television were not nearly as evident on the phone—but they would return soon enough. Imagine if Trump had fallen up the stairs of Air Force One several times in a matter of seconds, as Biden did! But that day, Biden got to do what he had not done much of lately: offer his advice rather than attack the president.

In fact, there was no getting away from COVID. On April 16, I walked back upstairs and into my office to find Dr. Birx writing a note to me on my desk. She thought I had left for the night, although I could hardly remember the last time I had managed to escape for home at a decent hour. She reiterated her thanks for how I'd backed her. I certainly supported her work, as I did the others' on the task force. I also knew that during this crisis, she was separated from her parents and her children and grandchildren. A month in, I saw in her what I saw in my own life for decades. She was the workhorse. She was the one at the White House in early morning and late at night. In task force meetings, she reviewed data and delivered status reports and projections. Dr. Fauci would chime in here and there, but it was Dr. Birx who had the most "words" and "paper" in the Situation Room. Fauci saved most of his observations and advice for his regular public-facing appearances on TV.

I had known of Dr. Fauci for decades and had met him a few times. It was always cordial and respectful. I was fascinated by his work in infectious diseases, most specifically his early and sustained work on AIDS and HIV. I was in high school and college when AIDS killed tens of thousands of Americans, including friends and family members.

One Saturday afternoon about a year before COVID hit, Dr. Fauci had approached me at a supermarket on Wisconsin Avenue, on the edge of Georgetown. For years that store had been known as Washington's "Social Safeway," where the young and single could encounter each other. Now it was a place for me to meet the voracious demands of my high-consumption household.

"Hi, Kellyanne. I can't believe you do your own grocery shopping," he said. I was ninety minutes into that day's excursion and had two carts going, feeling briefly nostalgic for those Saturdays of running six miles and reading a book for pleasure.

I looked at him and matched his smile. "Dr. Fauci, how else would my family eat?" We chuckled, and he invited me to call him "Tony."

"I doubt I can do that, sir, but thanks for all you've done over so many years." Dr. Fauci had been a key player in America's fight against AIDS and several other public health emergencies. I hoped that had prepared him and his team for this latest public health challenge.

Chapter 35

Vaxxing It

Some stains just can't be bleached out.

On April 23, Bill Bryan, the acting undersecretary at the Department of Homeland Security for science and technology, had already spent two days sitting in the Situation Room with the Coronavirus Task Force as a guest of acting homeland security secretary Chad Wolf. It was somehow decided—how or by whom, I am not altogether certain—that Bryan should join the president at the podium for a press briefing that was set to start within the hour. Bryan would present his findings on how LED lights, sunlight, higher temperatures, and disinfectants applied to surfaces could shorten the half-life of the virus.

It struck me as nice-to-know, but also as nonessential, if not potentially confusing.

As we exited the Situation Room, Bryan, Dr. Fauci, and I and a few others tucked into a side office around the corner, on the ground floor of the West Wing, past the security guard, Navy Mess, and near the staircase that leads to the Press Briefing Room straight ahead, or the Cabinet Room and Oval Office at the end of a hairpin turn. We would review Bryan's materials before he presented them to a president he had never met and faced a public thirsty for information about a fast-moving, invisible virus that had kept them locked at home for more than a month.

Dr. Fauci made key edits to the medical and scientific claims, while I gave a couple of communications recommendations to mitigate confusion and offer clarity.

"Are the industrial-strength disinfectants you recommend for surface cleaning accessible and affordable to regular Americans?" I asked.

"Yes."

"Can people buy them at the store? Are you talking familiar over-the-counter brands like Lysol and Clorox?"

"Yes."

"Okay, good," I replied. "Just don't promote actual brands in the Briefing Room. I did that once, and it didn't go so well. People lost their minds."

It was unclear to me if Trump had ever met Bill Bryan or if anyone had told the president about this late addition to the press conference lineup. Such a sudden atypical addition would be all too typical.

I excused myself to head back to the Oval Office and speak directly with the president about the timing and blending of this guest presentation. The door to the Oval was closed. I quickly mumbled something to the Outer Oval officials about needing to see the president, looked through the peephole as I knocked, and opened it.

A "private" meeting was under way. Brian Jack, the young political director, was ticking through races and endorsements. He is a smart guy who had much more experience than many of the other eight people in the room. He wasn't the issue. The issue was timing.

No wonder they mark these clusters private, I thought to myself, as I approached Mark Meadows and said, "I need you to see this and hear this to make sure you're comfortable before the briefing."

Meadows obliged and directed me hurriedly down the hall toward his office.

"I just want you to be aware we are going to have someone the president hasn't met before, who will present his findings at the press briefing," I said to a nodding Meadows as we arrived at the corridor that intersects the offices of the chief of staff and the vice president. "I think it's a little rushed, since the president wasn't briefed on it. The guy is nice, and his message is fine. Fauci approved it. It's just a matter of timing and cohesion."

Bill Bryan caught up to us and with a few others walked into the chief's office. Bryan did a dry run of the presentation and ably handled a few mock questions he could expect from the press or the president.

Meadows and Bryan then went to the Oval to meet briefly with the president just before they'd head to the Briefing Room to take the stage. I went back upstairs to the Cool Kids Wing to take an unrelated meeting. I did not watch or hear the briefing live.

But boy, did I hear about it afterward!

As soon as Bryan had finished, the president started riffing.

"So," he said, "supposedly we hit the body with a tremendous, whether it's ultraviolet or just very powerful light, and I think you said that hasn't been checked, but you're going to test it. And then I said supposing you brought the light inside the body, which you can do either through the skin or in some other way. And I think you said you're going to test that, too. Sounds interesting, right? And then I see the [surface] disinfectant, where it knocks it out in a minute, one minute."

That's where he began conflating the two.

"And is there a way we can do something like that, by injection inside or almost a cleaning, because you see it gets in the lungs and it does a tremendous number on the lungs, so it'd be interesting to check that, so that you're going to have to use medical doctors with, but it sounds interesting to me."

Then he seamlessly returned to: "So, we'll see, but the whole concept of the light, the way it kills it in one minute. That's pretty powerful."

Had Donald Trump just suggested that Americans put bleach in their bodies?

Not exactly. But that's sure how some people heard it, and not for no reason, and that was the strong impression a lot of the breathless media coverage dished up, conflating, as the president unwittingly did, the injection of light and the surface use of disinfectants.

This was not good.

I ran down to the Oval Office, where Bill Bryan was taking pictures with the president and no one was raising alarm. I described what was already splashed all over TV and burning up the internet.

"This needs to be cleaned up immediately," I told the president. "I think you were talking about bleach when you meant to talk about light."

It was an unfortunate briefing and an unforced error. Legitimate concerns emerged that some Trump followers might try what they thought he was suggesting, at genuine risk to their lives. This was just a month after the president had recorded his highest overall approval rating. All communications from the podium and elsewhere should have centered on everything he had done that "only a president could do."

Now, instead of an incumbent president appearing in command and control of the COVID challenge, the nation was drowning in bleach stories about an unfortunate and unconscionable comment from the president of the United States. Bad for Trump. Great for a media obsessed with eradicating Trump and eradicating COVID, preferably in that order.

The president clearly misspoke by confusing the light therapy and the disinfectants. As I had warned less than two hours earlier, there was no reason to rush this particular message or this particular messenger to the podium. Furthermore, the medical team and the press team should have sprung into action without a moment's delay and made clear that no one should inhale or inject bleach or other disinfectants into the body. Major companies like Lysol and Clorox had to step into the breach.

THE REELECTION CAMPAIGN chose a line of attack that was fair game but overdone and unimaginative. By constantly mocking "Beijing Biden in the Basement" and his lack of mental acuity, the campaign risked alienating millions of seniors, who were doing their utmost to stay safe through the pandemic and were also unlikely to appreciate the attacks on the brainpower of a seventy-seven-year-old they were seeing briefly each week. All those millions of dollars for polling and micro-targeting and data mining, and this was the best message? It didn't help that the sprawling staff at campaign headquarters in Virginia was now working from home like most of America. That wasn't much of a change for Brad Parscale, the newly rich campaign manager who spent most of his (pre-COVID) time in Florida, a state whose residents don't pay state income taxes. He was scarce in the campaign HQ—a complete 180 from the way I operated in 2016. Some campaign staffers joked that they saw Brad on Tuesdays, and whenever a reporter wanted to profile him. He had a standing "book" appointment with the *Wall Street Journal*'s

Michael Bender, who drove his Vespa right into the campaign office and who penned a scathing, bestselling book about Trump, apparently with Parscale's help.

Facing a deadline at the U.S. Supreme Court the first week of May, President Trump had to decide if he would continue trying to toss out all of Barack Obama's Affordable Care Act. The pressing question: Should COVID put the brakes on that? I thought maybe so, and so did Attorney General Bill Barr. So did Jared Kushner and deputy chief of staff Chris Liddell. It didn't seem to me like the right time to be seen as taking health benefits away from frightened Americans. It had long been a political winner but now seemed like a political loser. Now it was time for a final decision.

Twenty people were seated around the table in the Cabinet Room on May 4: the president, the vice president, senior staff, and several cabinet officials, though only seven or eight of us spoke. It quickly became apparent that Barr and I were on the losing end of this debate. "We run Obamacare really, really great," the president said. "But running it great, it's still lousy healthcare."

He said he felt like his people expected him to carry on the fight. Then he turned and looked at me. "Do you mind being in the minority?" he asked in front of everyone.

"I never mind being in the minority, Mr. President, so long as I'm in the vocal minority."

"Wow, you're flying a little too high, Kellyannepolls," Trump teased me, using my Twitter handle. "You forgot those people."

"Yes, you've got me," I said. "I feel so high on my government salary away from my kids, trying to sort out a once-in-a-lifetime pandemic, Mr. President." I smiled. I think he knew I was being a little sarcastic. "Do you know what the most important issue to your base is, sir?"

"Abortion?" he asked.

"No."

"Guns?"

"No."

"National security?"

"No."

"The economy."

"No, sir. The most important issue to your base is that one year from now, two years from now, three, four, five years from now, that you are still sitting in that chair, that you are still president." And he had so much to run on. "*You* took the heart out of the Affordable Care Act by eliminating the individual mandate. You are running Obamacare better than Obama did. You don't need to take this to the Supreme Court right before the election and have healthcare benefits taken away in the middle of a pandemic. But if you choose to do so, I will make you the 'healthcare president.' You have lowered the cost of prescription drugs, expanded Health Savings Accounts and short-term limited-duration plans, and on and on. We'll just have to make that case."

And so we did.

On May 26, Centers for Medicare & Medicaid Services (CMS) administrator Seema Verma and I had arranged for an announcement in the Rose Garden that had been two years in the making: lowering the cost of insulin for seniors. The heads of the three main insulin manufacturers and representatives from senior advocacy groups joined the president and vice president to announce a maximum cost to recipients of Medicare Part D of thirty-five dollars per month for insulin. And this was just a start. Our goal was to extend this policy to other Americans, too.

As we were preparing to head into the sweltering sunshine for the speech, Democratic nominee Joe Biden was participating in his first live event in a long time. The president and I were watching it on the TV in the Outer Oval. Biden was talking to a dozen people sitting inside circles in a gymnasium or a barn and was using a teleprompter.

"What do you think?" the president asked me, both of us watching Biden.

"I think if we lose to this guy, we are pathetic."

THROUGHOUT THE WEST Wing and across the administration, there were many people on staff who were focusing more and more on the pandemic while trying to tend to their vast policy portfolios. Ivanka Trump leveraged her contacts and success with economic development to address COVID in the workforce and the economy. Setting a precedent that would be duplicated in states, cities, and small towns, she teamed up with the U.S. Department of Agriculture to provide fresh food to underserved communities. The vice president asked me to reengage with the Ad Council, which had helped us bring awareness and engagement to the opioid crisis. They jumped right in, placing public service announcement (PSA) and direct-to-camera videos from Dr. Fauci, Dr. Birx, and Surgeon General Jerome Adams on all forms of media. The campaign produced $112 million in donated media, viewed more than 3.3 billion times, with 6.8 million direct hits to coronavirus.gov. We also turned our attention to what was becoming a "pandemic within a pandemic," the drug addiction, alcohol abuse, depression, domestic violence, suicide, and other mental challenges that people face when spending so much time at home.

Pre-COVID, we were already making progress on different aspects of expanding access and coverage. My pitch to the president: As he and the doctors and FEMA addressed COVID, don't forget all those other parts of healthcare. In too many cases, the pandemic was a rapidly spreading national mental health crisis.

One day in the middle of all this, I was exiting the EEOB after getting my daily COVID test when I turned the corner and ran into Governor Andrew Cuomo, who was getting tested ahead of his meeting with President Trump. The governor was all smiles, hugs, and compliments—about me, his brother "Christopher" at CNN, and about himself.

"We miss you on those governors' calls," I ribbed him, given that he was the only governor in the country who was regularly absent from the weekly sessions with Vice President Pence and, on occasion, President Trump.

"You know, we're pretty busy tackling this virus," Cuomo replied. I guess he was referring to his daily press conferences, which had made him a national sensation, provoked lots of "eligible bachelor" speculation, and introduced his three grown daughters to the nation. We now know he was busy with a lucrative book, too.

"My numbers nationwide are the highest of any Democrat, including Biden," Cuomo crowed.

Congratulations?

"Good to see you," I said. "Take care of yourself. The girls—the young women—are beautiful. God bless them."

* * *

LIKE MILLIONS OF other Americans, I truly could not believe my eyes.

I had heard about what happened in Minneapolis to a man named George Floyd. I had read the news reports. But none of that prepared me for actually watching the video. The man was on the ground. Four city police officers were there. One had his knee on George Floyd's neck. For eight minutes and forty-six seconds.

"I can't breathe," Floyd is heard saying repeatedly on the video. Then, he said nothing at all.

People were outraged, and rightly so. Large protests in Minnesota began to form. Some were peaceful and principled. Some descended into violence and vandalism.

Reasonable people would acknowledge that there had been an increase in incidents—or at least an increase in the awareness and footage of incidents—where men, and some women, of color were dying in police custody. Likewise, there had also been a rise in incidents where police officers were threatened and killed. "Pigs in a blanket—fry 'em like bacon," to quote a popular Black Lives Matter chant from years earlier.

I sat in my backyard and called two trusted, wired, smart acquaintances: Donna Brazile and Van Jones. One of them crystallized it perfectly: "Kellyanne, this *is* different. Everyone saw this with their own eyes. Young black men and women will see themselves in this video and feel disconsolate."

I was the first senior staffer in the White House to say George Floyd was "murdered." Responding to reporters' questions on Pebble Beach, I was unequivocal: "We watched a man be murdered before our eyes on a videotape. As painful as it is to watch, I think most people should bring themselves to watch all eight minutes and forty-six seconds or so of George Floyd's *murder*. I don't have another word for it."

I talked to President Trump about the video. He too was incredulous, sympathetic, and shaken, as I knew he would be. While in the Oval with a few other staffers on the afternoon of May 29, I asked him how his call with Floyd's family had gone. There hadn't yet been one, he said.

"Come on," I implored, "that needs to get done. Definitely call his brother." Moments later, the president and George Floyd's deeply grieving brother, Philonise, were on the phone. I witnessed it from the president's side. My heart broke for the Floyd family.

"The death of George Floyd on the streets of Minneapolis was a grave tragedy," Trump said the next day in Cape Canaveral, Florida, where he had gone to witness the launch of SpaceX Dragon, the first civilian-built manned flight to space. "It should never have happened. It has filled Americans all over the country with horror, anger, and grief. Yesterday, I spoke to George's family and expressed the sorrow of our entire nation for their loss. Healing, not hatred, justice, not chaos, is the mission at hand. The police officers involved in this incident have been fired from their jobs. One officer has already been arrested and charged with murder. In addition, my administration has opened a civil rights investigation and I have asked the attorney general and the Justice Department to expedite it."

Of course, his full speech received little fair coverage and the protests began to spread nationwide, including in front of the White House. The authorities seemed outnumbered, and some were assaulted as they tried to hold the line. The White House complex closed early, and staff had to be escorted off the property. The unofficial start to summer 2020 was marked by social unrest.

After criticism of the president's perceived inaction to stop the spreading violence and a leak that the president had been rushed to the "bunker," White House staff decided it was time to issue a stronger response. The weekend leading up to June 1 was marked by more protests and violence, some that struck close to home. Someone set a fire at the historic St. John's Episcopal Church, near the White House. Why turn a 204-year-old church into a target? The president told me on Sunday night how outraged he was to see that church, where he and dozens of presidents had worshipped, fall victim to the chaos and destruction.

By Monday morning, some of my colleagues had cooked up a plan.

As the president delivered one of his regular COVID updates in the Rose Garden, law enforcement began preparing in Lafayette Park, which is situated between the White House and the now boarded-up St. John's. When the president finished his speech, he walked directly out the front door of the White House and headed to the church, followed by nearly half his cabinet, most of his senior staff, including his daughter and son-in-law, along with General Mark Milley, Attorney General Bill Barr, Secretary of Defense Mark Esper, Hope Hicks, Pat Cipollone,

Alyssa Farah, Hogan Gidley, Kayleigh McEnany, and security. Twenty-nine people in all.

Mike Pence was not there. Melania Trump was not there. I was not there.

An attempt at police reform with Senator Tim Scott of South Carolina and others, announced in the Rose Garden, went nowhere with Democrats. After all, they were too busy staring at that election calendar. My chief of staff said something that gave me an idea to pitch to the president. "Camp David is the traditional site for peace talks," I said to Trump. "Why not host 'Domestic Peace Talks' there and see if there is a way to unify and heal?"

"Hmm, Camp David," he said. "Maybe. Let's talk about it."

"I think some of the activists and family members might come along with pastors, community leaders, and the like. I'll talk to Jared about it."

Those peace talks never happened. The peace never came.

NOW, A MEETING and a briefing were set for June 26 at Health and Human Services headquarters. According to two of the doctors, the White House press team didn't want the briefing in "their" Briefing Room. Alyssa Farah, the communications director and a Mark Meadows protégée, had taken her well-known eye-rolling about the doctors and the science and made them go somewhere else. As the task force discussed policy and new findings and then transitioned to prep for the press briefing, CMS administrator Verma surveyed the others: "So, are we going to walk to the podium with our masks on or not?"

Fair question, since Fauci and the doctors did not wear masks during the actual meeting (Secretary Alex Azar often did).

No masks was standard fare in the White House Situation Room, where Dr. Fauci was more likely to wear "Dr. Fauci" socks than a mask. Then, like magic, when D. Myles Cullen, the vice president's photographer, came into the room, masks would suddenly appear. The truth is that everyone in that room was being tested and cleared for COVID every day and there was some false sense of security in knowing that. It was decided: For the indoor press conference, masks on. Indoor mask-wearing was important visual affirmation.

*   *   *

I HAD NEVER met a mom who thought her child needed more "screen time," and now, everywhere across the country, we were referring to screen time as school time. This had mixed results for my own kids, and they didn't live in a broadband desert or have outdated textbooks or a lack of parental supervision. With safety and physical health as the primary concern, millions of parents like me wondered if and when the "old normal" might return and our kids could get back to school, lest their emotional well-being and mental health be at risk, too.

No one seemed to know.

In July we hosted a roundtable in the East Room led by the first and second couples, Donald and Melania Trump and Mike and Karen Pence. We heard from moms, dads, students, and educators on how to get our kids safely back to school in the fall. Then, in August, I questioned President Trump, Vice President Pence, and Secretary of Education Betsy DeVos at a town hall in the State Dining Room with parents, educators, and kids. With expert direction we weren't just talking and listening. Now we were providing reopening guidance. How to accommodate teachers and other staff who were at increased risk being on campus, how to stagger curricula, athletics, and enrichment programs, and addressing head-on how COVID had increased demand for alternatives to shuttered schools through school choice, charters, and opportunity scholarships. COVID's severity was undeniable, and, despite the knowledge available at the time that it was primarily our senior citizens at risk, the health and welfare of the children was weighing heavily on the president and his staff.

The pandemic wasn't easing its grip on the country. The usual suspects smelled blood and sought to politicize the deadly virus. Unity and nonpartisanship were a quaint memory. Even without the traditional campaign trips, party conventions were happening soon, and then voting would begin. Inside the White House, the president was hearing from Dr. Scott Atlas, who was floating around the first floor of the West Wing in Jared's office and elsewhere for a while before the media had a clue. Atlas made some fine if not obvious points about the low risk of COVID infection to schoolchildren and the negative impacts of sustained lockdowns. But he also made obvious points we discussed months earlier, as when he announced one day that this virus affects the overweight and the immunocompromised and those with hypertension. Also, he wanted to relitigate mask-wearing, and often contradicted policies that had been discussed and decided by the medical experts, the vice president, and president months earlier. Atlas loved seeing himself on TV, and the young staffers loved seeing his Bentley with the California plates parked on the White House complex.

Inviting Scott Atlas in invited POTUS to pick the science he wanted. The president could have ignored those who were telling him that "wearing a mask is like Dukakis with the helmet in the tank." He could have followed his mask-wearing wife and the orders in one of his own popular tweets to "wear a mask" (featuring him wearing a mask). In fairness, the doctors downplayed the virus at first and, for a while, did not consistently wear masks themselves and were skeptical that therapeutics, let alone a vaccine, could be developed in Trump Time.

Both were.

All of the doctors, including Atlas, were attending task force meetings and appearing regularly on TV. Dr. Fauci was asked in most interviews when he had last spoken with the president. The media would never let a global pandemic get in the way of palace intrigue. One day I dialed in to the task force meeting from my desk's secure line. About halfway through, I heard Dr. Atlas objecting to every point made by Drs. Fauci and Birx. They were pushing back as well. The conversation started to resemble, a little too closely, teenage skirmishes, with which I was familiar, and I went down to the Oval Office. I asked the president if he would host the task force following its meeting. He agreed.

I went down to the Situation Room, where Vice President Pence was leading the meeting, and told his chief of staff, Marc Short, that the president was expecting the group as soon as they finished. Soon everyone came upstairs to the Oval Office and quickly found a seat, everyone except for me. I stood and started the conversation, firmly yet respectfully saying that I was just a staffer but we were all a team, fighting the virus and not each other. Withholding information from other task force members only to share it on live TV, and then contradict each other, was helping no one. Then I added, "If you want to say something to the president, here's your chance. And if he wants to say something to you, we know he surely will."

The ensuing discussion was substantive and spirited. And needed. Maybe it was time for the doctors to get off the TV, where they were causing confusion, and back into the lab to cure disease. The task force continued to meet for many months after that under the leadership of the vice president.

ON FRIDAY, AUGUST 21, 2020, I parked at the West Wing entrance and headed directly to the East Wing to join President Trump. For the second consecutive presidential cycle, he had agreed to do an interview with AARP, the nation's largest seniors' group, which publishes the nation's most widely distributed magazine. He and I had discussed the interview over the phone as I drove to work. I had assured him that all the materials he needed were already in his briefing book and I reminded him that we'd done a similar exercise in 2016, when AARP's Myrna Blyth brought to my attention, days into my becoming manager, that the campaign had been unresponsive.

As I walked across the colonnade, I studied my notes and spoke with Seema Verma on the phone. A member of my staff intercepted me to say that Mark Meadows needed to cancel the interview. He was in a meeting, but his office would call mine once that was finished. I pivoted toward my office, immediately thought better of it, and bounded down the stairs.

I'm a pecking-order-and-protocol kind of gal, which is why I had gone through all the proper channels to get the AARP interview with President Trump scheduled in the first place. At moments like this, I would not stand on ceremony. I knocked and walked right into the chief's office. He was flanked by Kayleigh McEnany, Alyssa Farah, Hope Hicks, and Jared Kushner.

"Excuse me, Mark, but what is going on? The president is ready for this interview with AARP. Biden has already provided an interview. It will be featured in a widely distributed magazine. I just can't imagine why we'd give up an opportunity to talk to seniors, let alone in the middle of a pandemic and an election."

"When I was on Capitol Hill, AARP was so terrible to us and . . ."

"You're not on Capitol Hill anymore, Mark, and the president's standing with seniors is down."

He kept talking. ". . . some of us were talking and just think it's a bad idea."

He was looking in the direction of Alyssa Farah, who in four years had worked for him on the Freedom Caucus, for Vice President Pence, for the Pentagon, and now as Meadows's handpicked White House communications director. She is the daughter of Joseph Farah, the editor in chief of the online media organization WorldNetDaily (WND).

"Oh, this was your idea, but you couldn't bring it to me?" I asked Farah, a skilled and ambitious young woman who was cozy with the press corps and not so cozy with the doctors, only sporadically attending COVID meetings and routinely trashing them to POTUS when she'd tag along into the Oval with people who were invited to the meetings.

Before she could answer, her work dad sprang to his feet and got red-faced. Pointing at me from across the coffee table, Meadows raised his voice: "It wasn't her idea. It was my idea, and you can take your anger and your bitterness and go somewhere else."

"*My* anger and bitterness?" I shot back with a wide smile. "You're the one screaming at me because you didn't bother to read the president's schedule and briefing book until two seconds ago."

I wasn't done. And I wasn't done smiling. "I'm the jackass who follows protocol and rules around here."

A soft voice intervened.

"No, Kellyanne, it's fine," said Jared Kushner, who by then was standing over my right shoulder. "And we appreciate that you go through the channels and the rules."

Meadows suddenly backed down, changed his tone, and changed his tune. "The interview is fine," he relented. "I just wanted to make sure he's prepared, and everybody's eyes are wide open."

My eyes were already wide open. The president was being underserved, poorly advised, and, ironically, ignored by "senior staff." Like in June of that year, when the First Lady was finalizing a plan to light up the White House in the pride colors and send out a tweet that the president planned to retweet. All of a sudden when the day came, nothing happened—the whole plan had been blocked. It would have been great to do it for many reasons, including that Donald Trump never got or took the credit for the amazing fact that he was the first president to come to office already in support of gay marriage.

Some of the staff egos were bigger than the enormous tasks confronting us. Others acted like adolescents in cliques or hungry sharks with agendas separate from that of the nation. People could not even agree on a mask policy. Most of them were insisting he would win reelection in a landslide before "Sleepy Joe" ever awoke.

Meadows, the self-described "chief's chief," was the fourth person to serve in that role, and the only one during the most fraught time for the president and for the nation. The man did not match the moment. I could have been angry, but mostly I felt worried. Trump can be as good a listener as he is a talker, so quality of counsel and pureness of advice are imperative. Personnel could be a blind spot for him. Facing the twin challenges of COVID and a reelection campaign, he deserved the best and the brightest.

I was worried.

Chapter 36

More Mama

I was also leaving.

Just a few hours after Mark Meadows's red-faced freak-out on me, I was sipping cappuccino and nibbling on cookies in the East Wing of the White House with Melania Trump. In a few minutes, we'd be heading into the Map Room to work on her prime-time, Tuesday night address to the Republican National Convention. Only a handful of us had read the speech and heard her practice it. Others in the White House feared Melania almost as much as her husband did and didn't dare ask for an advance copy of her remarks. They would need to wait, like the rest of the world.

Melania knew that this small group of confidantes—Stephanie Grisham, Emma Doyle, Marcia Lee Kelly, and me—would neither breach her trust nor leak the contents of her remarks.

"It's a powerful speech," I told her. "A compelling review of the people you've met, the causes you've championed, the societal problems you've helped to surface and solve. And the people you single out for praise or recognition. It's like the State of the Union on steroids!"

The First Lady and I had lived in the trenches together, and I was thrilled that she would spend forty-five minutes speaking directly from the heart to the country, making the case for four more years and outfoxing the critics yet again who insisted she would speak for a few minutes.

Placing her cup on the saucer, the First Lady asked how my children were, each by name. Tears welled in my eyes. I had already made the decision to let her in on something I had struggled with on my own. I reached into my bag, pulled out a folded piece of paper, and handed it to her. It was a draft of my resignation announcement.

"Actually," I said, swallowing hard, "I'm leaving. I'm leaving to be with the children."

Her eyes widened. She leaned forward just an inch or two. "I'm sorry, Kellyanne," she said, calmly and sympathetically. "Are you sure? That's too bad. Does the president know?"

"No, I wanted to wait until after the funeral today."

Trump's younger brother, Robert, had a died week earlier, eleven days before his seventy-second birthday. They had held a funeral service that morning in the East Room of the White House, the first time a president's relative had gotten that kind of send-off in nearly one hundred years. "I'll tell him this weekend."

"We will miss you and will always be here for you and your family," Melania said with a reassurance that always seemed to come naturally to her. She was gently nodding and looking me squarely in the eyes. "You will be back. You can come back in the future."

WHAT AN UNSETTLING year 2020 had been, and we weren't even through eight months of it. A strange mood hovered over the White House and over America that entire summer like a vast storm system with no reliable forecast. There was uncertainty and fear over the mounting number of COVID cases. There were all the mixed messages from some members of the task force about mitigation, containment, and masks.

Most Americans had been holed up at home, including millions of kids for whom screen time had become school time. The country complied with online learning when the virus was new, understanding that from March to June it was reasonable to keep the kids safe at home. Now, after a summer of relaxed requirements and record number of vacations by car, school districts were murmuring about starting the school year off-line and off campus. And there was anger in the streets—literally. It was palpable, and it compounded by the effects of the virus. Thousands of people, including my oldest daughter, were still marching in the streets for Black Lives Matter. Most of the protestors were peaceful; some were not. Nobody knew for certain what was going to happen next.

Donald Trump loved administering the element of surprise, but these surprising elements were being administered unto him.

I had been going about my daily life and my work as normally as I was able to, trusting my instincts and relying on experience to guide me through whatever unforeseeable challenges lay ahead. COVID consumed most of my attention at the office, and at home, as we all tried to adjust to the ever-changing protocols of the three different schools my children attended in different jurisdictions. There was no working from home for me. My responsibilities at the White House meant *more* time at the office, not less time. Nesting with my children meant coming home from work and starting the second part of my day. Why were so many people complaining about extra time with their families when previously they had complained about never having enough time with their families? I tried to learn from the doctors and scientists, to support the Coronavirus Task Force, to coordinate with the other health professionals, the emergency management officials, the president and the vice president, the cabinet, and the First Lady, whose focus included mental health and mask-wearing, and help all of them educate and engage the public. This was especially vital given that many "leaders" at the White House had become COVID truthers and many members of the press had found new reasons to criticize the White House.

WITH FOUR TEENS and tweens, you can count on a party platter of emotions nearly every day, let alone a long pandemic. I was like any other parent navigating emotions and uncertainties while trying to provide stability and sanctuary.

I tried to get everyone started online in the morning. Then I was off to the office, where I took many calls and FaceTimes from each of them throughout the day, ran home and back when I needed to (the roads were deserted, totally clear), and supervised homework while trying to actually enjoy our evenings together. My oldest daughter, Claudia, was already going through a difficult year not of her making. But things escalated in the summer of 2020.

We all think we know what being a teenager means, because, after all, we were all teenagers once. But we don't have a clue what it's like now. I feel for this generation of young people. It looks to adults—and to the teens themselves—like they have more freedom, more access, more knowledge, more opportunity—and all that's true. But there is also more confusion, more exposure, more pressure, more unreasonable expectations, and, sometimes, more pure poison. Social media didn't just change the landscape. It changed the planet.

Claudia had become active about social justice on social media after George Floyd's murder. She and her friends joined the Black Lives Matter protests. When I drove them near Black Lives Matter Plaza in Washington, I bypassed the blocked-off streets and afterward pulled into my White House parking spot. As the kids headed off into the chanting crowd wearing their COVID masks and waving their homemade posters, I implored nearby officers—"Can you please keep an eye on those girls?"

Claudia had been away briefly at boarding school and had of late become a self-proclaimed progressive, which neither surprised me nor bothered me. We locked horns on things that mothers and teenage daughters typically do. The First Amendment wasn't one of them. When I tell my children to form their opinions, seek their own adventures, and be their own individual self, I mean it. My belief in the sanctity of life, limited government, more individual freedom, and the hypocrisy I see in the political left's wanting to defund the police but still wanting them to protect them, in forcing kids to wear masks and then going maskless at elite parties, in foisting the Green New Deal on the rest of us as they fly around on private planes, buttressed my own political underpinnings. I was proud of Claudia for expressing herself, and she was not alone. A steady cluster of my friends, children's friends, and my friends' children have always come to me for support and advice. Those nonpolitical adult conversations about real-life struggles and torturous decisions I'd witnessed around our dinner table (or eavesdropping under it) in Atco came in handy when the twenty-first-century versions of those issues presented themselves. I shared the outrage over Floyd's death, in fact I was the first person in the White House to refer to it as murder. I feared for safety, too, with huge, heavy statues being pulled to the ground and stores being burned and ransacked in cities across the nation.

I have raised my kids to be strong, independent thinkers. They've grown up in a two-lawyer household and know how to do their own research, form their own opinions, then express themselves freely but respectfully—or not at all, if they choose. I am deeply proud of each of them and their journeys, and I learn from them daily.

For today's adolescents, including my own children, opinions can be formed free from maternal influence, but not free from social media influence and expectation, which is almost always hyped up and opinion masquerading as fact. Peer pressure and mob persuasion are real. They are never more than a couple of clicks away, now that phones are an extension of kids' arms and iPads and video games are never out of reach. That was compounded in those six months in 2020 when kids were on computers for school. I had never met a mother anywhere who said "You know what my kid needs more of, his phone or her computer." Yet there we were having it masquerade as school.

It was obvious at the time that youth would bear the brunt of the emotional toll of COVID. They lost learning time, friendship develop-ment, and the connection and growth that come with regular physical interaction. Polls prove this. Gen Z (ages thirteen to twenty-four) above all says the pandemic has increased their stress and has had a negative impact on relationships, education, and mental health.

For my kids it was all compounded. Their mother was regularly sav-aged on left-wing social media (I did not read it, but my kids did) and their father was one of its newest superstars, some days tweeting and retweeting hundreds of times. George went from zero to sixty (thousand tweets) in no time, crowding out what used to be phones down, family time.

It wasn't just Twitter, which statistics prove is populated mostly by a group of people talking to each other. By 2020, the much more main-stream and successful app TikTok had been downloaded to phones and iPads more than 2.6 billion times, making it the most popular social media app on the planet. It is an open forum where individuals of any age can post short videos of themselves doing anything. Claudia was one of them.

TikTok was a platform where she could showcase her musical tal-ents, goof around with her friends, strike poses, and project a level of maturity beyond her years. She also used it, as millions of teens do, to trash-talk her parents and public figures and to spout opinions about trending topics. Her posts, like all those on TikTok, were available for anyone to see. None of this is unusual. This is what it means to be young today.

By any objective measure, and not just according to her biased, love-her-unconditionally mom, Claudia is a beautiful, brilliant, articulate, talented adolescent. People noticed her once camera shy and now twice bitten by Twitter father, in one of her TikToks and realized who she was. Among them was a thirty-five-year-old internet culture and technology "reporter" from the *New York Times* named Miss Taylor Lorenz, who has blue blood and thin skin. Raised among the privileged in Greenwich, Connecticut, the unmarried and childless Lorenz spent most days trolling other people's kids on social media, occasionally slandering them, and often adding nothing to a conversation that rose to the level of the *Times*'s motto, "All the news that's fit to print." Whenever Lorenz's tactics or veracity are challenged or the slightest bit of her own foul medicine is placed on her lips, she screams sexism, sends up a distress call to the *Times* mother ship, and retreats. Lorenz prefers Twitter, as she explains in one of her own videos posted from her bed, because "with Twitter, I can just literally lie here and post shit." In today's media industry, this is considered a job, even at America's most august newspaper. And that was *before* the pandemic, which excused so many other "reporters" from shoe-leather reporting out on the beat and replaced it with "posting shit" in bed.

GEORGE AND I had just switched places at the Jersey Shore house so a parent would always be around to chaperone as Claudia consecutively hosted two different groups of visiting friends. Georgie, Charlotte, and Vanessa had all opted for a mini-vacay with close friends in a different state. I'd been at the shore all weekend with Claudia and four of her friends from Washington and was back in D.C. with Bonnie and Skipper when a reporter from Yahoo News texted me late:

"Are you following the reporter coverage of Claudia's TikToks?"

I wasn't, but the text made me look.

I was surprised to see Claudia trending on Twitter.

Lorenz had assembled a thread of all of Claudia's TikToks and posted the whole thing for her 200,000 followers, any one of whom could now paw through the daily details of my teenage daughter's life and whatever thoughts and emotions might have passed through her active mind.

Apparently, quite a few of them did.

Claudia's likes, comments, and number of followers exploded—she became an overnight sensation, as they say. This is of course the dream of every teenage girl who is on social media, but a parent's nightmare. Neither Lorenz—nor anyone else at the *New York Times* tried to contact either of Claudia's easy-to-find parents. Lorenz did contact our minor daughter, though, egging her on to talk more about her family and whatnot. A thirty-five-year-old lying in her bed was conversing with, confusing, and cajoling our *child*. Would you be more comfortable if Lorenz were a thirty-five-year-old male doing this? Of course you wouldn't. That makes you decent, but also by "woke" standards, a sexist. Her gender should not have mattered. Her lack of ethics does.

My first reaction to all this was utter terror. Terror for Claudia's safety. Instant fame brings instant chaos, as I well know. I routinely ignored the trolls and haters who came for me online and let the Secret Service agents do their job when the threats warranted attention. But now the mainstream media in pure lemming-like mob fashion had all but sent an engraved invitation to all those nutjobs to come for my child. This started as a calculated move by an unethical, childless journalist who would go on to sloppily defend her misdeeds by creepily claiming that she, thirty-five years old, and Claudia, fifteen years old, were "mutuals" and "peers" and that she had "spoken with Claudia," apparently with the approval of her editors, but not with the approval of either George or me. With the esteemed *New York Times* placing its imprimatur on the story, other outlets felt justified to contact my fifteen-year-old directly. Rather than stop, think, and take a stand to turn off the spigot, these cowardly lions of American journalism ripped it off its moorings and added to the flood. Adults were using a child for their perverse pursuits. Taylor Lorenz—and dozens of other "reporters" like her—sent *direct messages* to our fifteen-year-old daughter beginning on June 30, 2020. Our fifteen-year-old!

I've heard various opinions about the legality of that. But I know it is a class of "journalism" the *New York Times* should not feel proud of. As a mom and an adult who strives to be a decent human being, I know it is wrong. And so should you.

I called George. He was indifferent.

"What do you want me to do?" he asked before hanging up the phone.

Then, when I tried repeatedly to reach him about what I saw as an urgent issue of safety, he would not answer another call or any of my desperate texts.

I called Claudia, who was on the boardwalk with three of her friends from New Jersey.

"I finally got my fame!" she announced. "I'm trending! I'm not taking it down!"

Those words were the holy grail for a teenage girl who, like others, had succumbed to the seductive, addictive nature of social media and had now conquered it by becoming "TikTok Famous."

I tried not to scold her. Instead I told her I was worried for her safety because, now that she had been surfaced, anyone could find her.

I SLEPT FOR all of ninety minutes that first night. The president called in the morning at my desk and asked if my daughter was okay. The phone message I had left for Lorenz's editor, Choire Sicha, went ignored. So I sent him an email from my White House account, with George copied, registering my objections and asking to speak with him about their coverage of Claudia and their unsupervised contact with her. No response. When I nudged him hours later, he responded in a cynical and aloof way, doubling down on his reporter's outrageous conduct.

"Taylor would love to know more about your family," was his snark-filled response. Then he topped himself. "Taylor of course spoke to Claudia to make sure that she felt okay with being discussed, and also told Claudia that if she had any concerns, she should pass on Taylor's phone number to you as well."

Read that again. Lorenz, a stranger dangling fame to a fifteen-year-old, felt she was justified in asking *our* underage daughter if she was "comfortable" and suggested that our daughter share the adult reporter's number with us, her parents, if the fifteen-year-old minor wanted to? That is the *New York Times*'s idea of responsible journalism and human decency?

She should have been out of a job, even a job as phony as hers.

Enabling this evil reporter, the heartless Styles section editor essentially declared that Claudia's brand-new popularity on TikTok, a popularity the *New York Times* had created, made her a public figure and fair game. That editor, possibly also emailing us from his bed like his hapless supplicant, was not long for his job. When he departed the *Times* in 2021, the bizarre and aloof behavior I had witnessed continued in an interview in which he suggested that he sometimes thought of death as preferable to running the popular section devoted to fashion, culture, and romance.

George stepped up, and he and I were of a single mind on this in the moment. He emailed the chain and made clear that we were not consenting to any communication between the *Times* and any of our minor children. Sicha again defended the shady actions of his teen-trolling reporter as appropriate journalism. I wasn't finished. I moved up the food chain, firing off additional emails to higher-ranking *Times* editors Sam Sifton and Phil Corbett, emphasizing what a problem they had on their hands. Only then did the editors say their reporters would no longer reach out to Claudia without our consent and that suddenly, "We aren't going to write a story about this."

They weren't gracious. They were scared.

"It's quaint," I wrote to the *Times* editors, "that you've now instructed Taylor not to contact Claudia directly, but the damage is done. Her public statements make clear Taylor was proud of surfacing Claudia, and felt it completely appropriate to 'speak to' a 15-year-old girl, after midnight and without notice to, or consent from, her easy-to-find parents. She bragged that she and a 15-year-old girl are 'mutuals' on social media. As many have noted, that is creepy, completely inappropriate, and possibly actionable."

I wasn't finished.

"Most reputable 'reporters' and other reliably anti-Trump outlets refused to touch the issue since it required touching our daughter in the process, especially before Taylor's tweet storm and subsequent conversation with our minor daughter. Fred Ryan, publisher at the *Washington Post*, was especially helpful when one of his overnight reporters lied, saying his editors insisted he write an article about Claudia. *Times's* claim that this was acceptable because 1) Claudia is a 'popular TikToker' ironically fails to note that the fame came AFTER Taylor's lonely, late-night tweet binge and that 2) a FIFTEEN YEAR OLD said she was 'OK' talking to an adult stranger. As George notes, Claudia's parents, not Claudia, should consent to such communication—and BEFOREHAND."

I went on to say that I wasn't surprised that the *Times* would change its tune, but that the initial blow-off revealed how the "journalists" really felt. I reiterated that their initial actions and reactions showed "no 'care' for Claudia or her three minor siblings so much as an intention to continue this coverage, and an implication that we should next submit our 10- and 12-year-old daughters to the *Times*'s exploitation of minor children."

This was different from all the snotty coverage I had gotten used to, including from the *Times*, who cling to their ill-gotten Pulitzers from reporting on Russian collusion they could not seem to find. "It is well-known that including 'Kellyanne Conway' in a headline is great for kicks and clicks. You're welcome. I'm an expert in ignoring the misguided, the vitriolic, the inaccuracies (have all the editors quit?), and even the presumption that our personal lives are any of your business. But the *Times* crossed a line by entangling itself so directly and recklessly with a 15-year-old minor whose own health was compromised by the heady events of yesterday."

And I was right. The damage *had* been done.

By now, Claudia was trying to manage all the incoming. *"Exclusive network interview! . . . We'll send a car! . . . Do you need something to wear? . . . Do you have an agent? . . . Is this your right address (reading the address of our shore house)? . . . Why weren't you wearing a mask in those TikToks? . . . We want to give you a comfortable platform to discuss your feelings toward the president, how your mom's job affects you and other family issues."*

The *Times*'s big "scoop" about a teenager using social media had unleashed a mob of other reporters salivating over the viral story of "Kellyanne Conway's daughter" following in the footsteps of "Kellyanne Conway's husband" to publicly denounce President Trump. Yes, George had also taken a path that would lead to fame and likes, a path that had caused its own havoc in our family. But he was fifty-six years old, a Yale-educated attorney with a long legal career. Claudia wasn't even old enough to vote or to drink or even to drive. But her age was never the media's concern. Her lineage was.

The *Times* was the first and the worst, but they were not alone.

Once the *Times* opened the door, other media outlets blew right through their own internal protocols—assuming they had any—to get to Claudia, DMing our fifteen-year-old child and flooding her with interview requests and promises of other goodies. Claudia shared many of these with me, and they are embarrassing. Another *USA Today* reporter direct-messaged Claudia on Instagram and said, "Hey I am contacting you on behalf of IG-less colleague of mine, Jeanine Santucci, who would like to interview you." Going to extremes to interview our fifteen-year-old daughter, when all they could have and in fact should have done was contact her parents. I have many examples like this, as does Claudia. They are reprehensible. Some reporters failed to adhere to formal standards. Other reporters failed to exercise sound judgment. All who were parents failed to put themselves in the shoes of George and me, choosing to dishonor that unspoken but well-understood rule that all decent parents look out for each other's children. Or the popular rule usually uniformly accepted from reporters of not talking about politicians' children like Malia and Sasha Obama, Chelsea Clinton, and Jenna and Barbara Bush.

Through their correspondence with George and me, the *New York Times* editors proved that hating Trump could justify anything, including the exploitation of a child by a reporter—who would later have the audacity to complain about being harassed on social media and singled out by Tucker Carlson.

Top TV reporters and anchors also began following Claudia on social media and still do (weirdos), apparently hoping . . . *what exactly?* That she might reach into my purse and produce the "smoking gun" that proved Russian collusion that changed the election results or evidence that COVID-19 was leaked from a lab at Trump Tower? Nope. They just wanted her to keep on insulting Trump and Mom.

The Conways are real people. A real family. This was beyond.

They made false, confusing, manipulative, and seductive statements to Claudia and then offered, in exchange, some odd mix of fame, refuge, and platform, never once considering how damaging all this might be to a teenage girl at a fraught time for all teens.

She is A CHILD, dumbasses.

She is MY CHILD.

I made a pledge to protect and love her unconditionally, the moment she came out of my body and into this world. That pledge has no limits and no end date. It prevents me from setting some things straight publicly. But it empowers me to make sure she gets justice and feels whole.

I'm the one charged with cleaning up the collateral damage here. I'm the one who must continue to guard against the emotional shrapnel this malfeasance wrought. Those who are guilty will not be forgiven. Or forgotten. Ever.

The attempts of some of them to apologize to me later, the sheepish requests that we "move on"—all of that is hereby rejected and denied. I've got your number, folks (and your direct messages). We're not done here.

SURE, AT SOME point earlier Claudia could have stopped the madness, even as the insane adults were running the asylum. She has expressed regret for some of the things she said and did online, which makes her bigger, bolder, and more mature than many adults. I thank God that she and I are close and can talk lovingly and candidly. I'm proud of how she has survived and thrived since then, privately, where I see it, and publicly, such as when she shared her talents with the world as a contestant on *American Idol*. Claudia was a kid feeding the beast. And as beasts often do, this one began feasting on her.

She was suddenly handed what all teenagers on social media crave.

Attention. Celebrity. Fame. A future bigger than the norm. She's begun to learn over time that the beast is never satisfied. It cares more about drama than people. And when you get too big, as Claudia quickly did, the beast tends to bite back.

Consider this: In 2020, Claudia Marie Conway, fifteen, got more media coverage than Hunter Biden, fifty-one. My underage daughter became news, but not Joe Biden's dirtbag adult son, who had flown to Ukraine, China, and God knows where else, reportedly more than eighty times on the taxpayer dime, to coerce tens of millions in contracts and capital. Hunter, who had an affair with his deceased brother's wife, fathered a child with a different woman, and had a laptop with pornographic content that was more verifiable than the Steele Dossier ever was. Hunter's father, a former vice president, made sure his son was off-limits to the media that showered him with a ton of "he's just misunderstood" sympathy due to the son's drug addiction and, yes, lineage. If we are going to revisit if it is appropriate to scrutinize kids, should we not focus mostly on adult children of people in power who are making money off their parents' position, like Hunter, Paul Pelosi Jr., or Maxine Waters's daughter?

Hunter Biden was fifty-one. Claudia was fifteen. Those of you who censored the facts about a fifty-one-year-old son of a man running to be president and exploited a teenage girl whose mother was a staffer are reprehensible. And to coin your own phrases, the stink will never get off of you, and history will judge.

It was one of the biggest stories of the summer. Yet when the *New York Post* put Hunter and his laptop on page one, the mainstream media blacked out the story and the *Post* lost its Twitter privileges for two weeks. No one would pick up the story, even though the media covered Claudia like she was the love child of Deep Throat and Greta Thunberg.

Here's the deal: Why would Big Tech allow a fifteen-year-old child of a staffer to trend on Twitter but censor stories about a fifty-one-year-old adult son of a man who wished to be president? Jack Dorsey of Twitter later admitted that his platform's censoring of the *Post* story was wrong. Too little and too late. Some say that, if reporters had done their job, and Trump's Justice Department had done its job, the outcome of the election might have been different.

Some judgey parents and some relatives wanted me to be more upset with Claudia. But I saw the heavy cost of all of this on her. My support of my children is unbowed. My love for her is infinite and unconditional. I was left to deal with a vulnerable teenager who had enormous pressure fall on her overnight, and three other kids exposed to all the twisted interpretations, public dissections, and outright lies about our family.

Like my own mom, who was very loving and devoted, I can sometimes lose my temper and sometimes curse like a truck driver. Love comes naturally to a parent. Patience is acquired, yet essential.

I worried about my children's physical safety and emotional health. The fools calling Child Protective Services and the police on us further harmed, not helped, Claudia, and no doubt diverted precious resources away from at-risk children in actual need of such protection and intervention.

I found strength and comfort in some family members and a sisterhood of some friends who stepped up and stepped in. Acquaintances who do not care for Trump came to our defense, too, wanting to help. Trump himself offered "whatever you need," and the First Lady reached out daily as well.

Sadly, I learned that others I had trusted weren't so loyal or sincere. Some "friends" who had leaned on me for heavy-duty headaches and heartbreaks, legal jeopardy, and medical scares went dark in our hour of need. This was especially true of those with teenage daughters of their own who craved the kind of fame, celebrity, and attention that Claudia had just received. Some of them couldn't look past that. It seemed like adults were jealous of my daughter. Ditto for those who had happily benefited from my White House position, enjoying unique events and making memories of a lifetime, and likely benefited financially from administration policies as many Americans did.

It would have been a good time for George to step away from social media and the Lincoln Project, even though they needed his name and marriage to help raise the millions they pocketed from Trump Derangement Syndrome–addled donors. George's one useful tweet, nicking the media who had elevated him to his own celebrity perch, was an improvement, at least, over authorizing interview requests with Claudia in the first flush of viral fame without even discussing it with me. Claudia, typical of teenage girls, including me many decades before, yearned for her dad's attention and approval. One of her most popular tweets, before she migrated to TikTok, was "I can see why my father @GTConway3d trolls @realdonaldtrump. This shit is so much fun!"

IRONICALLY, WHILE THIS was transpiring and with no direct connection to any of it, President Trump issued an executive order attempting to ban TikTok for its unregulated mining of user data.

"This data collection threatens to allow the Chinese Communist Party access to Americans' personal and proprietary information, potentially allowing China to track the locations of Federal employees, contractors, build dossiers of personal information for blackmail and conduct corporate espionage," Trump stated.

Claudia certainly had an opinion about that. "Tell Donald Trump not to ban TikTok," she implored me. "Please, Mom, just call him."

My early advice to the president was to have American companies acquire TikTok.

Sure, in an ideal world, no TikTok or Twitter would mean no daughter, husband, or boss causing havoc on social media. But in the real world, I believe in free speech. I'd say all the members of my family have learned that "free speech" is not always as free as it seems.

"Just take away her phone!" adults beholden to their phones, with kids beholden to their phones, often demanded.

"Delete Donald Trump's Twitter!" some people urged. "Put a fake bluebird on there," others cried, only to suggest self-beneficial tweets they wished he would send.

My own wish is for everyone online to spend more time offline. It's where life happens, human connections are made, eye contact occurs, and genuine emotions (not just outrage) are expressed. Living offline looks, smells, sounds, tastes, feels, and *is* better. It forces us to be held to account for our online behavior, since there are no editors or arbiters in that free-for-all space where social media muscle and self-loathing propel people to say and do things they wouldn't dare say or do face-to-face. Why be constantly enraged when you can be happily engaged?

I HAD ALREADY told one Trump. Now I needed to tell the other. There was no good time to do it and no easy way to say it, but it had to be done.

The reason I was leaving the White House was the same reason I had hesitated to work there in the first place: my four children.

Others had tried to force me out of my position. Early on it had been duplicitous, insecure, or jealous colleagues. Then it was George, whose tweets increasingly targeted me without naming me. The Democrats and their allies thought they had found a way when they dusted off the ancient Hatch Act, insisting that what I had blurted out in a TV interview required my firing and the silence of the president's most effective spokesperson. When they weren't wasting taxpayer dollars with that charade, some "reporters" ravenously dove into my marriage and targeted my children and pretended that was news, despite their own thin skin and glass houses. They had spent the nearly four years since Trump's historic victory trying to embarrass me or harass me out the door.

Yet I refused to let them purge me from power, steal my sunshine, or make me as aimless and miserable as they were. After all that, I was going to leave under my own terms.

In Washington, when public officials say they are leaving "to spend more time with the family," the cynical question always is, "Whose family?"

Often that explanation is thin cover for a simmering sex scandal, lost power, or some other untenable situation that is forcing a prominent person out of a job. But in this case, it really was about my family.

It wasn't that the jackals and jackasses had gotten the better of my kids. It was that all those predators weren't *worthy* of my kids. As I had written in the statement I had tucked in my bag that morning before seeing Melania, my children needed "less drama, more mama."

And so did I.

After enjoying some pool time and a barbecue with Charlotte and Vanessa on Sunday afternoon, I waited until evening fell and then drove my minivan the two and a half miles from home to the White House, through the eerily empty pandemic streets of the nation's capital.

"A product of my choices, not a victim of my circumstances."

I repeated that phrase to myself and sang along with the radio as I drove the familiar route to 1600 Pennsylvania Avenue. *A product of my choices, not a victim of my circumstances.* That was the advice I'd given to countless other women and girls. It was the gut check I always tried to do when making decisions or reevaluating them, the legacy I wanted to pass on to my own daughters and their daughters, too.

I passed through the Secret Service checkpoints that I had sailed through every day, waving and chatting with the same agents at their usual posts. On Sunday evening, I knew from the president's private schedule that he would soon be back in the Oval Office, which was enough of a guarantee that I could grab a window of time to talk to him alone.

There were separate hives of activity in the Cabinet Room, the Outer Oval, and the Oval. The Republican National Convention, which had shifted from Charlotte, North Carolina, to Washington, D.C., because of COVID, would begin the next day. On Thursday, the president would formally accept the 2020 Republican Party nomination for president. Once in the Oval, I asked two of my favorite White House colleagues, Hope Hicks and Dan Scavino, who were seated in the yellow chairs in front of the fireplace, if they could give POTUS and me a private moment. I followed them past the grandfather clock and to the door, closed it behind them, then turned and walked to the other side of the Oval, offering a faint smile and small wave to the president's valet as I closed the door leading to the president's private bathroom and dining room.

The president was watching me ping-pong past the Resolute Desk and across the rug that both he and President Reagan had in the Oval Office during their presidencies.

"What's going on?"

He leaned in slightly, a look of concern on his face that I'd seen many times before.

"Mr. President, I am leaving," I said. Just like that. No preamble. No equivocation. No delay. "My kids need me."

"What? No. No, you can't leave now. What do you mean?"

I always appreciated the way Donald Trump looked people straight in the eye, but now it was adding to my guilt and my grief. I could already feel it.

"It's time," I said. "With virtual school again, they need a parent with them at all times, and that's me. They need their mom."

"Honey, don't worry about it," he said, literally waving away my need to leave. "You don't have to go. Just take all the time you need and come back. I know what you mean. We have Barron on computer school, too."

It was a warm and human reaction. He meant it. He had stood by me when colleagues tried to turn him against me, when my own husband was diminishing and deriding me for online kicks and clicks. But I held firm, even as my voice got a little wobbly. "I have to," I said. "I have a statement written already. It'll be announced tonight. It'll pop as a big story tonight and tomorrow morning and then, hopefully, it will fade away because our convention begins and that will consume the news cycle. I am speaking on Wednesday and will still be a part of the whole week."

"Oh, okay, good," he said. "You should speak. Great. But are you sure?"

I nodded. I started to read my statement, and he interrupted me.

"Are your kids okay? What do you need?"

I did have one ask. I had held it together the whole time since I'd walked in to speak with him. But now I got emotional, bringing up the three staffers who were my West Wing Squad. "They are incredible," I said. "Please be good to them."

He immediately opened a drawer of the Resolute Desk and took out his Sharpie and a piece of "President of the United States" stationery to write a note to himself with their names. "Honey," he said. "They are great. Don't worry. They will be taken care of."

And that was it.

After informing the president, I told the world.

My public statement was a tribute to the beauty of America and her people, a message of gratitude to those who had made it possible to work in the White House and had touched me along the way. And I made clear that the move was my choice. I felt resolved, and then I felt relieved. My Twitter post boiled it all down into something appropriately Twitter-brief. "I'm Leaving the White House. Gratefully & Humbly." "In time, I will announce future plans. For now, and for my beloved children, it will be 'less drama, more mama.'"

The potency and immediacy of social media meant that messages of support poured in immediately from CEOs, conservative and liberal activists, young and old, media figures, strangers, colleagues, members of Congress from both parties, and the cabinet. I especially appreciated the messages from other moms. I'm sure plenty of bark and snark poured in as well, but I ignored it the same way I had since I'd turned off my notifications on Twitter years earlier. Even now, I chuckle thinking of all the wasted energy and venom hurled into a vacuum from anonymous haters and well-known figures that I've not read and don't intend to read. Let the haters stew in the cesspool while I dance and sing through life.

The next day, someone was selling "Less Drama, More Mama" T-shirts on Etsy.

NATIONAL POLITICAL CONVENTIONS are carefully orchestrated affairs.

When the list of featured speakers was released, showing I had five prime-time minutes at the podium on Wednesday night, George was furious. He confronted me with a sinister ultimatum, demanding that I cancel my speech, or else he would embarrass the president and me.

Embarrass me? More than what he'd tried to do on a daily basis? It didn't seem fair that George could spend a big part of his day, every day, performing for the insatiable audience, sending tweets that got over 100,000 likes and were either flatly false (Russian bounties on American soldiers; troops are "suckers and losers") or downright mean and seen as anti-wife. He wielded his Twitter posts like a sword, ostensibly slashing at Trump but aiming at everything I worked for and believed in, knowing those cuts could deeply wound me and our children. Was he threatening even more and caustic ridiculing of his wife—mother of Claudia, Georgie, Charlotte, and Vanessa? He had ignored me for months, and now he'd lifted his head up long enough to bully his own wife to keep her from attaining the very thing he coveted most, a platform bigger than his Twitter account.

I ignored his insults, turned away his threats, and denied his demand, viewing this as my swan song and a unique opportunity to pay homage to the amazing women who had raised me and the incredible men and women who had touched me during my four years on the campaign and at the White House. I would speak my truth, as the kids are taught to do, in my own words, on my own terms, to stand the test of time. My entire career, I had resisted men bullying me into doing something or not doing something, and I wasn't about to let that happen now, let alone on the hundredth anniversary of women securing the right to vote. The campaign offered to write my speech, but I wrote every word myself. My intention was to be uplifting and unifying.

"A hundred years ago," I began, "courageous warriors helped women secure the right to vote. This has been a century worth celebrating, but also a reminder that our democracy is young and fragile. A woman in a leadership role can still seem novel. Not so for President Trump. For decades, he has elevated women to senior positions in business and in government. He confides in and consults us, respects our opinions, and insists that we are on equal footing with the men."

This would pass any fact-check. It seemed obvious to me, but I still believed that a lot of people needed to hear it and that, sadly, many women in their own workplaces would never experience it.

"President Trump helped me shatter a barrier in the world of politics by empowering me to manage his campaign to its successful conclusion. With the help of millions of Americans, our team defied the critics, the naysayers, the conventional wisdom, and we won. For many of us, women's empowerment is not a slogan. It comes not from strangers on social media or sanitized language in a corporate handbook. It comes from the everyday heroes who nurture us, who shape us, and who believe in us."

I certainly knew about that firsthand.

"I was raised in a household of all women," I said. "They were self-reliant and resilient. Their lives were not easy, but they never complained. Money was tight, but we had an abundance of what mattered most: family, faith, and freedom. *In America*, I learned, *limited means does not make for limited dreams*. The promise of America belongs to us all. This is a land of inventors and innovators, of entrepreneurs and educators, of pioneers and parents, each contributing to the success and the future of a great nation and her people. These everyday heroes have a champion in President Trump. The teacher who took extra time to help students adjust to months of virtual learning. The nurse who finished a twelve-hour COVID shift and then took a brief break only to change her mask, gown, and gloves to do it all over again. The small business owner striving to reopen after the lockdown was lifted and then again after her store was vandalized and looted. The single mom with two kids, two jobs, two commutes, who ten years after that empty promise, finally has health insurance."

Those people and millions of others were the reason I came to work every day. They are how I retained my optimism about the sheer beauty, sturdiness, and resilience of Americans.

"President Trump and Vice President Pence have lifted Americans, provided them with dignity, opportunity, and results," I said. "I have seen firsthand many times the president comforting and encouraging a child who has lost a parent, a parent who has lost a child, a worker who lost his job, an adolescent who lost her way to drugs. 'Don't lose hope,' he has told them, assuring them that they are not alone and that they matter. *There always will be people who have far more than we do. Our responsibility is to focus on those who have far less than we have.* President Trump has done precisely that in taking unprecedented action to combat this nation's drug crisis. He told me, 'This is so important, Kellyanne.' So many lives have been ruined by addiction and we'll never even know it because people are ashamed to reach out for help, and they're not even sure who to turn to in their toughest hour."

I wanted to end on a high note and hoped that someone listening would find some genuine encouragement in what they heard.

"Rather than look the other way," I said, "President Trump stared directly at this drug crisis next door, and through landmark bipartisan legislation, has helped secure historic investments in surveillance, inter-diction, education, prevention, treatment, and recovery. We have a long way to go, but the political inertia that costs lives, and the silence and the stigma that prevents people in need from coming forward is melting away. This is the man I know, and the president we need for four more years. He picks the toughest fights and tackles the most complex problems. He has stood by me, and he will stand up for you. In honor of the women who empowered me and for the future of the children we all cherish, thank you, and God bless you always."

When I finished my speech, I hopped onto Marine One with the Trumps and flew to Fort McHenry in Baltimore, where Vice President Pence was delivering his convention address. On the way there, the president, First Lady, and I were reminiscing and Scavino, a one-man digital avatar for the president, took my phone and snapped a photo to commemorate my final journey on Marine One.

I spent another week getting my things in order, handwriting more than one hundred thank-you notes, including to the permanent staff, and loading my minivan with mementos of a blessed and busy period in my life. President Trump and I spent an hour alone together in the dining room off the Oval Office, talking candidly, laughing heartily, and him signing photos and mementos.

I collected my belongings and my emotions, gathered up my children, corgis, and mother, and headed to the stone rancher that had been my life's refuge, my childhood home in Atco. Determined to trade in stilettos for sneakers, that weekend I dove into the thirteenth annual scrum of back-to-school paperwork and preparation. The kids would begin a new academic year differently. So would I.

At fifty-three, I became a stay-at-home mom.

Chapter 37

A Tale of Two Outcomes

The storm had finally broken, and I had gotten through it.

I had outlasted many of my colleagues, defying the odds by keeping my job and keeping my wits intact for more than four uninterrupted years, from campaign through the White House.

Trump Speed is not found in nature. He works with a volume and velocity that is not for everyone. I thrived on it and loved most minutes of trying to help the amazing people of this incredible country. But as heady and humbling as all that was, it was nothing compared to being a mom. These four kids are the aortas and ventricles in my heart. My babies are the best. Knowing I'd be with them more as a new, (ab)normal, COVID-addled school year began softened the sadness of leaving the White House and invigorated me.

One-on-one homework assistance. Dinners together around the kitchen table. Closer parental supervision. Face time, not FaceTime.

When I announced the big move toward "less drama, more mama," George said he too would be stepping back from his (unpaid) Trump-bashing duties on Twitter and at the Lincoln Project, which had raised $100 million in the 2020 cycle from the likes of Chuck Schumer's PAC, Hollywood and tech titans, billionaires, and smaller donors. No doubt the other male founders could not believe their fortune—literally—

when the brilliant guy who helped form and get next-level press infatu-ation and adoration—Kellyanne Conway's Husband—did not share in the tens of millions of dollars that one of its cofounders bragged could generate "generational wealth."

A hypocrisy of misogyny had taken root. Unlike in the Trump White House, the women of the Lincoln Project were not treated the same as the men. They did not share equally in the power or in the profits and, it was revealed later, were not clued in to basic information about the operation, strategy, direction, and finances of the group. Some of the little-known consultants raked in millions even as their small firms had never shown anything close to that level of annual income previously. The misogyny included publication of the private, internal communica-tions of their sole female founder, a move that George noted on Twitter might be a crime, and the absence of any females representing the group when its principals—four middle-aged, stout, balding white guys—sat for a *60 Minutes* puff piece in October 2020. One of the men chosen over the women (including two women of color who had been my friends for years) for the interview was married-with-children John Weaver, even though the principals knew he had been accused of sexually harassing men and promised other young men professional opportunities (through the Lincoln Project) in exchange for sex, through publicly released DMs.

When George had retired suddenly from the law firm, I had hoped that he'd make good on his goals: get healthy and spend more time with me and the kids. Hadn't I paid it forward during all those years of George's job coming first? In this new period, he did do more, but never more than I did. Ladies, does this sound familiar? All those days patiently accepting when he couldn't be expected to do much for the kids or the house (or for me) because he was so busy in Manhattan in his high-powered job? I still vividly remembered those crazy months in early 2010, with a newborn and three toddlers while George was off in (my) Washington preparing for a Supreme Court oral argument that would take place three months later. I was deeply proud of George but would tease him: "I'm the worker, and you're the breadwinner." I also felt a tinge of jealousy that he had a free pass to reduce or relinquish the bulk of other responsibilities anytime his work demanded it. Working moms typically get no such forbearance.

But now that George had more time for daily, active fatherhood, the major competitor for his time and attention was not another woman. It was Donald Trump. Yes, I am the Conway who worked with Donald Trump, until I resigned, but George was the one who could not quit him.

BRAD PARSCALE'S TWO-AND-A-HALF-YEAR (!) reign as campaign manager of the president's reelection exceeded the tenure of many cabinet members, who weren't making the millions Brad was and were performing more ably. The Trump-Pence 2020 campaign's $1.4 billion budget did rival some of those agencies' budgets! The axe fell on Brad on July 15, and Jared Kushner was swinging the handle. A month or so after Brad overpromised and underdelivered at a rally in Tulsa, Oklahoma, just as Trump was itching to return to his usual style of campaigning with COVID still in the air, Trump and Jared ushered him out the door. But the shakiness of Brad's position could have been divined far earlier than that. Right from the day he had gotten this important job, way back in February 2018, the press release contained effusive praise from Jared Kushner and Eric Trump but nothing at all from the president.

Brad would weirdly brag he was part of the family. He'd been around for years, developing websites for the Trump Organization and helping with other tech matters. But he was not born a Trump, nor had he married one. Neither had I, of course, which is why despite all of the intimate moments I shared and all the private information I'd been trusted with, I would never refer to myself as "family."

Still, Brad was close enough to some members of the Trump family to keep his job for far longer than he should have. Well into summer 2020, members of the Trump campaign were wasting precious airtime on TV talking about Parscale instead of the people: "Brad's job is safe! Brad's part of the family." As late as July 12, 2020, a top Republican leader insisted Parscale was "absolutely the right man for the job," asserting that the campaign manager's "work ethic and command of what it takes to run a successful campaign in 2020 is second to none."

Three days later, Parscale was fired. But it hadn't been the job security of Brad Parscale that was concerning me. It was the president's.

I had tried to be helpful. The first piece of advice I gave Brad when he asked me to dinner one night in 2019, following a Rose Garden ceremony honoring Tiger Woods and my address to Leader Kevin

McCarthy's donors, was, "You need to build your own relationship with the president. Your relationship with him can't be through Jared."

There's an old joke that says the fastest way to make a small fortune is to have a very large one and waste most of it. Hillary 2016. Trump 2020. Real-life examples of the punch line.

The reelection campaign blew through $830 million before Labor Day, with two months still to go, and most of that happened under Brad's direction.

Brad was showy in a nouveau-riche sort of way with his fancy cars and multiple houses, private security, and mini motorcade "protecting" his six-foot-ten-inch frame. It is easy to conclude of Brad, *height is not depth*. But there was something earnest and sweet about him. The one place Brad was less showy was at the actual campaign headquarters in Arlington, Virginia, unless he was sitting for a media profile. "Don't do the Sunday shows," Jared had cautioned Brad, with no such ban on magazine cover stories for either of them. Many staffers felt frustrated at their leader's chronic absences and lack of engagement. He wanted to be a Florida resident, ostensibly for tax purposes. "We never saw Brad on Mondays," a campaign staffer announced. Worse, he was too much of a control freak to delegate responsibility to people who were actually there. Unlike this sibling wannabe, the Trump kids never took advantage of their dad, never directed millions from his campaign to their own companies, never let their father down. Brad was a self-described part of "the family" until the patriarch and the princely son-in-law decided on July 15 that he was expendable.

The 2016 election victory was dramatic, a media-shocking come-back in the final one hundred days. As digital director, Brad Parscale was a notable part of it. A successful reelection would need to reignite the "down in the polls but never out of the game" spirit of 2016, the indefati-gability and inimitable connection between the people and the candidate. After we won, I was hopeful we would use the next four years to ready ourselves for 2020. Once Brad was gone, Trump announced on Facebook that he was turning to another New Jerseyean late in the game, former White House political director Bill Stepien. "Step" was a former senior aide to Governor Chris Christie and already deputy campaign manager. Stepien is a master tactician who was part of the 2016 dream team. By the time he was promoted to the top spot in 2020, the resilience, swagger, and hunger of the 2016 effort had been replaced by self-assurance and a sense that COVID would go away, and a roaring economy would again be the top issue to crow about to voters.

The $1.4 billion reelect, with its often-absent campaign "manager" was more solipsistic than scrappy. The legend that Jared was the actual campaign manager and the myth that Brad was a competent campaign manager deprived some of the most talented and hardest-working people there (Chris Carr, Emily Moreno, Zach Parkinson, Nick Trainer, John Pence, James O'Connell, Matt Wolking, and Hogan Gidley) from Trump's notice and briefing schedule. Trump would have benefited from—and enjoyed—the data modeling and other cutting-edge marketing techniques. Good leaders elevate colleagues and engage in conversation with as many smart, vested players as makes sense.

As I told him, "You were the underdog both times even though you were the president of the United States the second time. But what you didn't have this time was the hunger and the swagger. And you weren't underresourced and understaffed. If anything, Arlington became Brooklyn. Trump 2020 resembled Hillary 2016. There was too much money, too much time, too much ego."

"Beijing Biden" was a foolish attack line. It lacked the Trumpy one-two punch and resonance of "Crooked Hillary," which was easy to discern, and people felt actually affected them. It also suggested a dearth of seriousness during a national crisis where folks were more concerned about another city in China: Wuhan, and the deadly virus that originated from there. The wartime president, in control, commanding private companies, government agencies, and pharmaceutical innovators, surging supplies, providing resources and information daily to a worried nation: Now, that would have made an easy-to-understand and compelling ad! I tried to make the point discreetly by telling the Washington Post exactly that. But as an anonymous Trump campaign official (Brad) put it to the same Post reporter: "Positive ads do nothing for Trump." That was ridiculous on its face, as it would be for any sitting president running for reelection. There are endless reels of footage of being the commander in chief, helping Americans, standing shoulder to shoulder or going toe-to-toe with foreign leaders, making things happen that soften even your most hardened critics who selfishly vote for you in the privacy of the booth.

I was also vocally concerned about seniors. Yes, the administration had increased the number of telemedicine visits by Medicare recipients from 14,000 to 1.7 million a week. We sent the National Guard to sanitize and provide PPE to the nation's nursing homes and reduced the price of insulin for them. Yet I was worried about the effectiveness of relentlessly mocking the seventy-seven-year-old Biden's mental acuity. Seniors were scared of COVID. Statistically speaking, they were more likely to be hospitalized. In states like New York and New Jersey, many were dying in nursing homes and veterans homes. They may well have been sympathetic with Biden's age and gaffes. Was Biden not up to the job? Or was too much being made of his minor gaffes? It was hard for voters to tell when he only emerged from his basement about an hour a week.

Politics 101: You don't tell the American people what's important to them. They tell you. On some days, it seemed the campaign viewed the COVID pandemic the same way they viewed Hillary, Comey, or Big Tech—just another political enemy standing between Trump and reelection.

Even though Trump wasn't president in 2016, we showed voters that he was up to the task, up to the fight, up to the job. The day after I assumed campaign manager duties Trump called me on his way to New York's LaGuardia Airport. I had planned to be on calls all day, talking to our state directors and pollsters, but I hung up immediately once I saw who was calling. I ran through what was happening back at the campaign and detailed the upcoming schedule and events.

"Governor Pence will be in Baton Rouge, Louisiana, tomorrow to survey the devastating floods and offer assistance," I said. Trump sounded intrigued. "That's good, that's good. Should I go, too?"

"Well," I said, "we have you in Minnesota, and I don't want two of our best assets in the same state. But President Obama is refusing to cut his vacation short in Martha's Vineyard, and Hillary's Hamptons aren't a swing state either."

"Tell Mike I'll go with him," Trump responded. The next morning, as the media focused on Paul Manafort's firing, Trump and Pence were in Baton Rouge comforting and assisting flood victims. Louisiana wasn't a swing state. That wasn't the point. It was the right thing to do and showed compassionate leadership. The TV coverage was decent and far-reaching.

When you feel like you have nothing to lose, you can actually win.

And we started to feel that by the end of August 2016. While Trump was looking presidential, Hillary was looking petty, delivering a speech in Reno, Nevada, focused solely on the "alt-right." She called out Steve Bannon and Breitbart, a conservative news site that he oversaw. Hillary was in Nevada snarling about a website while Trump stood side by side with a foreign leader who must have known a President Trump would challenge him on border security, illegal immigration, and trade. She was the one who'd been a U.S. senator and secretary of state, but it was the businessman with no political or diplomatic experience who projected confidence and competence on a world stage that day.

On September 18, 2020, Claudia and her friend yelled to me in the adjacent kitchen in Alpine the sad news that U.S. Supreme Court justice Ruth Bader Ginsburg had died. I was sad and yet smiled, remembering the privilege to speak with Justice Ginsburg at the White House on two separate occasions, and also years earlier over dinner with her and her adoring husband, Martin Ginsburg. On the night of Justice Kavanaugh's swearing in, the petite justice was a booming presence, entering the White House residence, her lace-gloved hand reaching for a glass of champagne. As happened with the sudden death of Justice Antonin Scalia in February 2016, Trump's focus was adjusted to the newly open Supreme Court seat.

In 2016, Senate Majority Leader Mitch McConnell held off for months as the pressure mounted to fill Justice Scalia's seat, citing a 1992 speech from Senate Judiciary Committee chairman Joe Biden that nominations should not happen in a lame-duck, presidential election year. In 2016, rank-and-file conservatives worried that Trump, if elected, might revert to governing as the bawdy pro-choice Democrat he'd long been. They were no less comforted following the *Access Hollywood* incident. But we doubled our list of potential Supreme Court nominees from ten to twenty-one. These were actual men and women whom Americans could research if they chose to. Hillary had refused to release a similar list, allowing us to fill in the blanks of what kind of radical person she might put on the federal bench. The list eased the minds of conservatives across the country who were still undecided, and it proved to be a deciding factor for many when they pulled the lever for Donald J. Trump.

In 2020, Americans already knew Trump's record of nominating conservative judges, but Ginsburg's death served as a reminder of what was at stake. Immediately, the name Amy Coney Barrett was floated. She was a young working mom of seven, already a judge on the U.S. Court of Appeals for the Seventh Circuit. The decision for President Trump was the quickest and easiest of the three Supreme Court nominees he selected during his term. Barrett's name, in fact, had surfaced during the previous two confirmation battles, which resulted in Justices Gorsuch and Kavanaugh.

Weeks after I had officially resigned, I was invited back to the White House to meet with Pat Cipollone, the White House counsel, and discuss Barrett's path to confirmation. When I arrived in his office, which was adjacent to mine, Chief of Staff Mark Meadows was seated there as well. He went on about how great it would be if I were involved in this process: "You're a lawyer and have been helping with judges throughout."

I nodded until Meadows started gesticulating about the significance of me being "in the shot" (meaning the photo that would be released to the world) when Barrett arrived to the Capitol and walked the halls of Congress to meet with senators. *Why is that relevant?* I thought, recalling the perfectly majestic and staff-free photos of Justices Gorsuch and Kavanaugh alighting from a vehicle with Vice President Pence, who had escorted them and who happened also to be the president of the Senate. Surely, the third time could also be the charm, with Amy Coney Barrett alongside Pence on the steps of the Capitol, greeted by Leader McConnell and other Republican senators who would shepherd her through the meetings and prepare for the confirmation hearings.

The other favor Meadows asked of me, I was happy to deliver: Would my former team be willing to move so Amy Coney Barrett could work out of my old office in the West Wing during her confirmation hearing? That was a no-brainer. Renee Hudson, Tom Joannou, and Sarah Trevor were dedicated workhorses, well respected in the White House and, along with Pranay Udutha, key to my success there. By then they were part of the Domestic Policy Council, headed in the final months by Brooke Rollins, a dynamo mother of four with a heart and brain as big as her native Texas. I did appreciate that Rollins and Meadows and the others recognized how valuable they were. Renee, Tom, and Sarah didn't care where they worked as long as the work involved serving the country and serving this president. I'd later go and visit Judge Barrett in my former office, offering help. She was on the verge of becoming a U.S. Supreme Court justice for life. Yet there we were in Hillary Clinton's former West Wing office, chatting like any other two moms.

Barrett needed no one's help, including mine. Her execution in the confirmation hearings was a master class in confidence and competence. She was patient and compliant, even in the face of the more predictable and insufferable questions being posed by some U.S. senators who had no intention of listening carefully to her responses or treating her nomination fairly. I smiled watching her "no notes (on her notepad), no net" performance. She was my kind of girl: a mom of multiples, non–Ivy League educated, Catholic, self-made, close to her family. Her primetime swearing in on the veranda above the White House lawn was an incredible moment. Her husband held the Bible and was beaming. As I watched them, I recalled the new justice's description of her husband in the Rose Garden a month earlier. "He asks me every day how he can make my life easier, what he can do for me. . . ."

Trump's judicial record bore potentially powerful political currency. In 2016, 21 percent of voters who supported Trump said in one postelection poll that "judges" was a top issue. Four years later, Trump wasn't just promising on the judiciary. He was delivering. In his four years as president, Trump would preside over the confirmation of 230 federal judges, including 3 to the U.S. Supreme Court and 54 to the U.S. circuit courts. He often marveled in private about the number of vacancies he inherited from Obama: 128.

Amy Coney Barrett was the latest example, and a high-profile one at that, of Trump's fulfilled promise to place men and women on the federal judiciary who would treat the Constitution not as a paper towel but as the law of the land, one of the most important ways a president can safeguard our God-given rights and man-made freedoms. The campaign cited the success but never truly capitalized on it.

Following that ceremony and the announcement by the president and First Lady that they had tested positive for COVID, I went on Friday to get tested. I had tested negative every morning before debate prep and the Barrett ceremony. As I was sitting in the doctor's office, I also got an email from another medical firm, saying that my son and I had tested negative from a test we'd taken days earlier to attend an NFL game. Within the hour, I got a call from the doctor's office I had just left, telling me I had tested positive. I got into my van alone and drove fourteen miles, more than ninety minutes in traffic from New Jersey to NYU Langone Health on the East Side of Manhattan to get a more accurate test. That test confirmed I was positive. Claudia tested positive two days later, and we quarantined for twelve days together, which I affectionately referred to as *bonding*. We stayed together in a guest bedroom on the lower level of our house, with friends leaving food at the side door for us. George, Georgie, and the corgis had fled to D.C. When my son realized he couldn't taste his spicy chicken wings, we knew instantly that he, too, had been infected. Thankfully, Charlotte and Vanessa did not get the virus and stayed with godparents in Philadelphia until it was safe to reunite. As a mother, I was more concerned for my children than for myself and grateful that we all recovered in two weeks' time.

I rejected the therapeutics offered to Claudia and me, given how rare they were then and how healthy she and I were pre-COVID, and kept close tabs on two other COVID-inflicted men about whom I cared deeply. I watched as the president was sent to Walter Reed National Military Medical Center. I was pleased to see him walk to Marine One on his own, but I was also worried for him. I checked in daily with Chris Christie, who was hospitalized in New Jersey, and forced him to FaceTime me so I could see for myself how he was. I was grateful to see he was recovering steadily. I checked in with the president, who said he felt fine and was getting out of there soon. He asked how I was recovering and joked to me, "Well, you know, they say if you have zero percent body fat, you'll be fine." It was great to hear the president sound like himself but very strange to see Meadows spending the night at Walter Reed. I long ago realized he wanted to be the president's BFF or the second most important person in the White House, which meant more important than the duly-elected vice president, but now it seemed like he wanted to be the First Lady. He's most famous for that weekend in leaking, off the record but on camera, the president's actual health condition and later writing about it in a book, which the president told me personally he was disappointed in.

I HAD LEFT the White House but like that famous line from *The Godfather*, just when I thought I was out, they kept pulling me back in . . . first for Amy Coney Barrett and then for debate prep. There was also the superstitious president. He had confided in me that he felt he had the "yips." As a nongolfer, I learned that meant "nervousness that causes a golfer to miss an easy putt." He felt one way to cure the yips was to bring back the team that had helped him cross the finish line the last time. By reclaiming my chair in debate prep in 2020, I could at least satisfy that superstition.

I had run debate prep in 2016 along with Reince Priebus and Chris Christie. With the first debate set for September 29, I returned to the White House several times in the week leading up to it. Governor Christie, a smart and skilled debater, had been doing informal prep sessions with the president for a few weeks. Now he would play the role of Joe Biden, just as he had played Hillary in 2016. With me as the "moderator" and Stepien next to us, there was plenty of Jersey in the room.

I knew Trump's strengths on the stage, and the tripwires and quagmires the moderators might set up for him. I was fluent in Trump. Trump was fluid in his answers. Many things were similar to 2016, but many more were different and distinctive. On the positive, Trump was the president, not an aspirant. As a candidate seeking the public's votes, he was no longer promising what he would do. He had actually done much of it.

On the other side, people had learned how to get under his skin, though the ones who claimed to were not actually the ones who succeeded.

It was essential that he speak to the accomplishments of the past four years, not just try to slam Biden. He should make clear that he shared a nation's grief rather than express his own about the unexpected year. I had supplied my favorite line of the fall: "Trump has done more in forty-seven months than Joe Biden has done in forty-seven years," a remark I made first on live TV (*Hannity*, August 19), and that the president himself would repeat many times to show the contrast between the consummate Washington insider Joe Biden and the president—yet still political outsider—Donald J. Trump. It truly encapsulated the two candidates. Democrats claimed they wanted a person of color or a woman and ended up with . . . Joe Biden. The progressive, pro-youth, pro-energy, pro-future, pro-inclusion party nominated exactly the opposite, the brightest illustration the Democrats had of someone who had been in office too long, had accomplished too little, and wasn't given to either eloquence or enthusiasm.

Soon after I arrived, I sat down with Christie, Hope Hicks, Bill Stepien, Jason Miller, Stephen Miller, and the president for our first formal debate session. Our strategy focused on letting Biden talk—which often left him with participles dangling and coherent sentences hanging. And numbers would numb him completely.

The next day, I was back at the White House for another debate prep session with the president just before he would go outside to the White House Rose Garden, where he announced the nomination of Amy Coney Barrett to U.S. Supreme Court Associate Justice. I tried to focus the session on two things—one defensive and one offensive. The president had done so much for this country on COVID. But for a man who usually loved to brag and take credit, for some reason he ceded the mantle to the governors. When he was being attacked on the issue, he invariably fell back on the China travel ban, a decision his administration's health experts had resisted and Biden had denounced. It was the right call. But people already knew that. Now he needed to go further. Another principle of Politics 101 is to not tell people what they already know and can see, tell them what they don't know and can't see. They love being in the loop and appreciate the transparency and accountability that accompanies that.

I recommended that, once he mentioned the China travel ban, he follow up with six key points with which the public was not as familiar: He had led HHS, FEMA, and the private sector to come up with 100 million N95 masks, 250 million face coverings, 345 million surgical gowns, and nearly 100 million gloves. He procured more than 100,000 ventilators and distributed them to states so no one who needed a ventilator would be without one. He had vaccines and therapeutics being produced at a rapid pace. He used the Defense Production Act more than thirty times to provide $3.2 billion in critical support for essential medical resources. He sent the Army Corps of Engineers to build field hospitals, deployed thousands of National Guardsmen, sent CDC staff into every state, and deployed the USNS *Comfort* and *Mercy*. He made available federally provided meals for stuck-at-home schoolchildren who relied upon them. He took more than seven hundred actions to suspend regulations that would have slowed our response. He signed three bills from Congress totaling $3 trillion in relief for Americans. I had assembled and memorized these facts and knew he could place them in his own words, with cadence and potency.

Bang, bang, bang, bang, bang, bang. Just like that.

I also urged the president to use the Supreme Court opening to our advantage. Many in the media and on Team Biden thought we would be defensive over the pro-life Amy Coney Barrett. My advice in 2020 was to have President Trump flip that Supreme Court discussion on its head to expose Joe Biden, the Senate Judiciary Committee chairman of three decades earlier. For decades, Supreme Court nominees were noncontroversial. Antonin Scalia was confirmed 98–0, and Ruth Bader Ginsburg confirmed 96–3. But that changed when Biden was the Judiciary chairman thirty years earlier and led what Clarence Thomas called a "high-tech lynching." In fact, Biden had consistently used his perch as chairman to politicize Supreme Court nominations. By revisiting Biden's past on the Thomas hearing, the president could also highlight Biden's sketchy history on race issues, which also included supporting crime and sentencing laws that disproportionately affected people of color, palling around with southern Democrat segregationist senators, and sharing his creepy "Corn Pop" story with a group of African American children. (Corn Pop, Biden said, was the name of a "gangster" he and his "hairy blond legs" fought during his youthful lifeguarding days.) After all, this was the same dude who described Senator Barack Obama thusly: "You got the first mainstream African American who is articulate and bright and clean and a nice-looking guy. I mean, that's a storybook, man."

"Geez, she's brutal," the president responded as I was peppering him with examples of this all-but-guaranteed question about race.

I told the president I'd rather he hear it from me in the privacy of the Map Room than on the debate stage for the first time.

"You are going to get a race question or three," I assured him. "However they ask you, you have to be ready to give the same answer."

"Mr. President," I said, playing the debate moderator, "the Bidens have a guest here tonight. Her daughter, Heather Heyer, was killed by one of your supporters who purposefully drove his car into a crowd at Charlottesville. Would you please tell Heather's mother how you justify her daughter being killed by someone who supported you?"

"Whoa! Are they going to ask that?" the president snapped back.

"They won't ask the question that rudely, maybe. So let's get it out here in the family. They may ask about Charlottesville or 'shithole countries' or how COVID disproportionately affected African Americans or the Proud Boys. You can be asked seventeen different ways. But whenever it comes, you need to identify it immediately. I know you will talk about the lowest unemployment among African Americans. You can also mention your record on HBCU [historically black colleges and universities] funding, school choice, opportunity zones, breaking the back of the opioid crisis, criminal justice reform, and an economy that lifts everyone.

But you should also hit Biden on his troubling record and tumultuous comments about race."

Debate prep was meant to be tight. Tom Joannou had prepared red and blue cards and posterboard with quick hitters for the president that I detailed in debate prep. But crowd control in the debate prep room was no competition for all the straphangers who wanted to cram in, sit down uninvited, and leak to the press "I was there" or pipe up unhelpfully with lines that sounded like a cable news food fight and not a presidential debate.

IN THE FIRST debate of 2016, I was the last person to speak to Donald Trump before he took to the stage in front of a worldwide audience of millions, as I'd been at the Commander-in-Chief Forum weeks earlier. I was the busiest guest in the spin room after each event. But now I was like millions of others: watching from my home. There was a sort of peace about it. Two things caught me by surprise. The first was how aggressive Biden and then Trump were almost from the get-go, talking over and about each other with ferocity. Fierce is fine. Passionate is preferred. But the interruptions, accusations, and yelling by both of them did not match the moment. Of course, it allowed the spinmeisters to pin it on Trump even as Biden did his fair share of interrupting. Trump had gone a bit rogue and did not adhere as closely to the debate strategy that we had all agreed upon previously. He had been advised to just let Biden do all the talking, let the man ramble, stumble, and mumble without interruption. Could Biden outlast the ninety-minute clock? Would he win the war of attrition or seem evenly matched in energy with Trump, whose indefatigability was the stuff of legend?

The second surprise was that I didn't expect Joe Biden to mention me by name.

In one of his shots at the president, Biden said, "And by the way, you know, his own former spokesperson said, 'You know, riots and chaos and violence help his cause.' That's what this is all about." When Trump asked who said that, Biden, in front of millions of people, said, "Kellyanne Conway."

"I don't think she said that," Trump answered, defending me immediately.

Trump was right. I didn't. In response to a claim by Pete Buttigieg that the riots were happening "on Donald Trump's watch," I noted that the riots were happening in Democrat-run cities that rejected Trump's help to send in the National Guard. I quoted an anti-Trump restaurateur who was yelling at the looters that they were trying to get Trump reelected. Then I noted that Trump was the one calling for law and order in these cities, not the Democrat mayors and governors, the same point that was being made by the anti-Trump restaurateur whose neighborhood was burned and looted.

The second debate was canceled because Trump was recovering from COVID. But that wasn't the only reason. Months earlier, the president's campaign team had demanded more and earlier debates. But now, when it really mattered, the campaign shied away from the second debate because they didn't like the moderators' anti-Trump tweets and didn't want to do the debate virtually. In 2016, Trump had benefited from all three debates to make his case to undecided voters, especially the second one, two days after *Access Hollywood*. Trump's strong, unflappable performance helped settle the ground.

In 2020, he needed those debates for similar—and different—reasons. He could have used the second one to highlight his own remarkable recovery from COVID. It presented an excellent opportunity to remind the public of his administration's work in securing vaccines and therapeutics and show that even people of his age could come back strong from the virus. Sadly, none of that happened. Instead the campaign reverted to the old Bill Clinton playbook: "It's the economy, stupid!" That is nearly always true. But in the face of a once-in-a-century pandemic, people really were worried about COVID, both as an excuse for lockdowns, closures, mandates but also as a legitimate health concern. Compounding this was the belief by many voters that Biden was a moderate who would use his experience in Washington to unify the Beltway and the country and negotiate good deals for America. There was no punch left in attacking Biden as a progressive. That strategy would have worked against Bernie Sanders or even Elizabeth Warren, but it did not play well against affable, enigmatic Joe Biden, who used COVID as an excuse to bury himself in his basement.

In 2016, Donald Trump's campaign message was known by all. He repeated it countless times at rallies, during interviews, and in tweets. Trade and manufacturing. Stop illegal immigration. Fairness. America First. Forgotten men and women. Jobs. Lower taxes. Repeal Common

Core. Build the wall. Stop drugs and crime. Take on China. Rebuild the military. Take care of our vets and military spouses. At the same time, Hillary was seen as the establishment favorite. In her case, the candidacy represented change, but the candidate did not. An ABC poll showed that 62 percent of Americans said she was not trustworthy. What could possibly follow the "... but I'll vote for her anyway" that would make any sense?

In 2020, winning became hard, but the message was uncomplicated: Revive the prosperity, opportunity, and security that President Trump had delivered before COVID hit, and emphasize how he met the challenges posed by a once-in-a-century pandemic that no one saw coming, and that was still, as he put it, "the invisible enemy."

For a man who loves to brag, Trump sure had a lot to say: Border security. Economic prosperity for all Americans. Tax cuts and deregulation. New fair and reciprocal trade deals with Korea, Japan, Mexico, Canada, and China. A strong national defense. Peace abroad. No new wars. Energy independence. Less income inequality. Fewer Americans on welfare or food stamps. More healthcare choices at lower prices. Two hundred and eighty new conservative judges. A rebuilt military. Major investments in our veterans. A strong response to the opioid crisis. Criminal justice reform. Support for school choice and educational freedom. Therapeutics to mitigate and, soon, vaccines to eradicate this pandemic. Soleimani and al-Baghdadi dead. Hostages and detainees returned home to the United States. Record-low unemployment rates for blacks and Hispanics, and a fifty-year low for women. Record-high median household income, including the largest gains for minority groups. Poverty at a record low, including an all-time record low for every race and ethnic group.

It was a long, hot list and a highly impressive one.

THE SECOND DEBATE, which was really the scheduled third debate, took place on October 22 at Belmont University in Nashville. It went much better than the first one, hewing closer to the original plan. It also helped that in the vice presidential debate, Mike Pence had delivered a master class in how to message the accomplishments of the Trump administration and defend against an ill-prepared, unimpressive Kamala Harris (a harbinger of her awful early tenure as vice president). Pence knew how to brag about Trump and challenge the shopworn sound bites that Harris delivered.

Minutes after the final debate, my phone rang. First Lady Melania Trump was calling, but it was her husband who grabbed the phone as they loaded into the Beast.

"Did you see that, Kel? How did we do?"

"Congratulations, sir," I said. "You just got many steps closer to reelection."

Still, for all his love of hitting the stump, Trump never lost his affection for hitting the Send button. In the spring of 2020, when I entered the Oval Office one day, the president was seated at the Resolute Desk with phone in hand, and he remarked, "I think without this, I wouldn't have got elected." True enough, but as I reminded him, with respect to social media, "Make sure it doesn't get you unelected."

In the closing months of 2020, Trump needed all the help he could get. The campaign was pulling back ads, not just in the states we were trying to flip but also in traditional red states, like Georgia, that we were unexpectedly defending. Despite having a substantially larger budget in 2020, much of the money had evaporated before the crucial final days leading up to November 3. This affected the morale of the campaign. Playing offense is always more invigorating than playing defense.

My practice in 2016 was to be sure that statements were backed by strategy. When I said we would perform well with women, I reminded the audience that *all* issues were women's issues and that it was insulting to think women cared only about issues from the waist down. Women were the small business owners, I pointed out. They did the household budgets. From womb to tomb, they directed the family's healthcare dollars and decisions. They cared about public safety and national security. They had watched loved ones lose jobs or get buried under mountains of student loan and credit card debt. They had wondered when Americans stopped apologizing to each other and started apologizing for America.

As I tried to get my head around that, I looked back to April, when Fox News anchor Martha MacCallum challenged Brad Parscale with public polls showing Trump getting crushed by Biden among women. Brad's answer needs to be reread to understand the campaign's limited imagination:

When women see that Biden stands for free healthcare for illegal immigrants, not closing China's border. [They will vote for Trump]

No wonder Jared Kushner, the putative campaign manager, told Brad, the actual campaign manager, to stay off TV.

With two years to prepare and nearly $2 billion to spend, was this wonky mishmash the best the campaign could come up with to reassure the millions of women locked down at home, unable to return to work because all of a sudden they became the tutors, teachers, and taskmasters for kids who were learning from home because of a global pandemic? The messaging never improved. Apparently the campaign needed time "to overcome the media's biased message." Time was the least of their limitations. In the fall of 2020, Trump was regularly addressing "suburban housewives," a turn of phrase that would have made even June Cleaver, and certainly the ladies on Wisteria Lane, cringe. And the team was citing a phrase I coined in 2016: "the hidden undercover Trump voter." But in 2020, if you were a Trump voter, you weren't undercover; you were loud and proud because you had won against all odds. Trump voters were donning their red hats now, going to rallies, and having boat parades. Yet the reelection campaign was underestimating the depth and width of a not-so-hidden anti-Trump voter. For four years, these people had been waiting to make Trump pay for his 2016 victory. Many of them lined up early to vote in person in states like North Carolina as early as September 2020. They wanted to erase Donald Trump from the presidency, even though they oddly couldn't quit him. After that big surprise in 2016 and the ubiquitous presence of a president you could not ignore, even if you wanted to, they weren't about to stay home this year.

Chapter 38

Uncheerful Chaos

I woke up in New Jersey early on Election Day 2020, got the kids settled (three for online school, one in person), and cast my vote the old-fashioned way.

In person. At my local polling place in Borough Hall.

Later that day, I drove four hours solo to attend the Election Night party at the White House, reflecting in the car on what was to come. Although less certain this time around, I still had hope. The president had made up considerable ground. The energy was back on his side. The rally crowds were huge and happy. But I couldn't help feeling the same way I'd been feeling for months—was all of it too late?

Nearly 100 million votes had been cast before Election Day. Would the day-of voters be enough to make up the ground the president had likely lost from the mail-ins?

There was no precedent for this. What was going on across the country? What did we not know? What could we not see? Ronna McDaniel and the Republican National Committee, along with mobilizing record campaign outreach, volunteers, door knocking and data, had litigated fifty-two lawsuits prior to Election Day, including before the U.S. Supreme Court, over ballot access and election integrity and unknown factors like universal mail-in ballots, drop boxes, and extended time periods for voting. A once-in-a-century pandemic meant that creative measures and unknown factors dominated. More people had more time to vote in more ways than ever before. This would make it easier to vote. One fear is that it also could make it easier to cheat.

Donald Trump had had that fear ever since COVID arrived and states across America started to change their election rules. As far back as April, he was firing off tweets that warned especially about the dangers of mail-in ballots. In June, *Politico* interviewed the president and headlined the piece: "'My biggest risk': Trump says mail-in voting could cost him reelection."

People on the campaign had nodded when he said that, but had they been listening? Maybe not.

I arrived in the Washington area shortly after 7 p.m. and headed right to the campaign headquarters in Rosslyn, Virginia. There I did a few interviews, telling reporters from ABC and NBC News that a tight race with uncounted mail-in ballots suggested that we might not have a final result right away.

"I can wait," I told ABC News's George Stephanopoulos on live TV. "I'm a patient person. Our democracy deserves nothing less." To NBC's Savannah Guthrie and Lester Holt, I said that President Trump could afford to lose a few states he carried in 2016 and still win reelection. This was realistic, not fatalistic. For weeks, some in the president's campaign and White House had been insisting, "Landslide!" and then jumping on Air Force One daily to preen and revel rather than redouble efforts to make it true.

As the polls began to close across the country, I was at the White House in and out of the Map Room, where the war room was set up. We felt pretty comfortable as the night wore on. The president was running up impressive numbers in some swing states that were projected to be close. Florida. Iowa. Texas. Ohio. A total of ninety-one electoral votes. The vote tallies of already-reporting states put us way ahead, but I still couldn't shake the feeling that I had had for months that we might be behind. In 2016, I was highly confident, projecting daily we would win. I had never felt that way this time around.

The numbers evened out over time, but the constant flow of votes in all forms did not relent. This was shaping up to be a monster turn-out election. Parscale was never right that this was a "base" election and not a "persuasion" election. But was he correct that if Trump received 72 million votes, he would be the winner?

Ohio was called for Trump at 11 p.m., when he was up by half a million votes. Florida was called for him at 11:10, with Trump up by 400,000. Both of those seemed solid, and both states had deftly calculated and reported all votes that nights. But when Fox News called Arizona for Biden at 11:20, they called it way too soon. The Map Room exploded. Jason Miller said it was dead wrong. Relying on our data, we demanded a retraction. Jared promised to call Rupert Murdoch. I texted Bret Baier and Martha MacCallum, asking how they could be so sure. Arizona governor Doug Ducey called to say his top guys thought it was a premature call because of the high number of outstanding, uncounted ballots.

In 2016, Pennsylvania had been called for President Trump at 1:35 a.m. Within an hour of that, Huma Abedin rang my cell phone and handed hers to Hillary to concede. Shortly before 3 a.m., President-elect Donald Trump had been making his victory speech. In 2020, at 1:35 a.m. we were still discussing President Trump's path forward, particularly in Pennsylvania. We had seen votes trickle in for Biden late across many states, none more important than the Keystone State. Suddenly the president was demanding, "Stop the count."

"Mr. President," I said, "you won Pennsylvania by 44,000 votes last time. You are up by over 700,000 votes with more than seventy percent of the vote in. Let's let them finish the count." He and the First Lady went upstairs. The rest of us called it a night, and I left the White House at 5 a.m. Which ended up being a miscalculation on our part. Twenty-twenty had more people voting in more ways over more time than ever before. The results were still coming in through the morning. In 2016, Hillary was worried Trump would not accept the election results. It turned out that she was the one who, after conceding her loss, repeatedly called the 2016 results into question. In 2020, the daily traveling clique on Air Force One was certain of his big win. They never thought he might lose. So they did not expect him to reject the results.

But he did.

*   *   *

ON WEDNESDAY, PRESIDENT Trump was asking how in the world he could have lost to Sleepy Joe. He wasn't angling for a sophisticated analysis of turnout and the Electoral College. He meant he literally could not believe it.

The same people who assured him he *would win* were assuring him he *had won*. This was becoming less sustainable as more votes were counted.

On Thursday, November 5, I walked into campaign headquarters in Virginia just after dawn. I was scheduled to go on *Fox & Friends* for the first time in months. I'd been in the headquarters building just a handful of times and never took a single penny from the $1.4 billion reelection fund. That morning, I wanted to get a candid, in-person briefing on the nature of the votes yet to be counted. They appeared to be from Democratic strongholds, and viable legal challenges were being prepared. The race had not yet been called for Trump or Biden. There was time. Shortly before the cameras started rolling, someone handed me a sheet of paper: "Here's your backgrounder."

At the very top, the paper made a claim that the campaign had put on the record as well: "President Trump Won Pennsylvania. Period."

It wasn't dated 2016. Votes were still being counted. I ignored it.

Through the glass, a familiar scene was unfolding. Kushner & Clique, the long-running and revolving group of men Jared had collected around him to reinforce his instincts and praise his understated brilliance, were in a deep hush. They looked worried. Mark Meadows made an entrance— in a mask, oddly enough. It turned out Meadows had COVID. They were scurrying about, closing doors behind them to have some secret meeting so inane and inconsequential that it might have been best for them all if it stayed secret. I'd seen this movie too many times. Long on drama, low on impact. Was there a plan? That was also a secret. With the clock ticking, and the lead eroding, lots of head-nodding and no plan wouldn't just be annoying, it would be fatal.

As I prepared to leave campaign headquarters, Jared Kushner, who forty-five minutes earlier had shooed me away from Bill Stepien's office when I tried to tell them the president was on my phone asking a question the lawyers might want to answer, approached me, emotionless except for a tinge of worry, and asked a strange question: "What do you think your highest and best use is?"

I held my tongue and leveled my gaze at him. "Normally," I said, "I'm asked that before Election Day and not after it. I'm going to the Oval to offer help."

I left the campaign headquarters with Hope Hicks and never returned.

Hope and I headed to the White House. I walked into the Oval to see Ivanka with her father. They were working on the president's statement. Ivanka was focusing on how her father had grown the party, winning in Democrat counties and expanding numbers in the House. I had already suggested to him that he include a line that said, "Every legal vote should be counted, and no illegal votes should be counted." He added the sentence: "If you do that, I win."

Jared walked in and said, "Oh, you guys take care of the messaging. I have to deal with the mayor. They are cooking something up."

"Oh, what does she want?" I asked, thinking he was referring to Mayor Muriel Bowser of D.C.

"No," Jared responded. "Rudy Giuliani."

"WHERE'S KELLYANNE?" THE president had been asking a shocked and befuddled throng of advisors, days after the election they had guaranteed he would win.

It was a reasonable question. The ubiquitous-on-TV campaign manager from 2016 was absent from the Oval Office and the airwaves. Soon the president and I were on the phone and he had a question for me. "Oh, so you don't like the fraud and theft thing, then?" he asked.

"Mr. President," I replied calmly, "fraud and theft are crimes that require a high standard of proof and evidence. People know that elections are subject to irregularities, improprieties, honest mistakes, and, yes, deliberate malfeasance. But proving conspiracy and fraud is tough."

"We're hearing all kinds of crazy stories," he countered. "Our people not being able to watch them count the votes. Boxes and boxes of ballots coming through the back door in the middle of the night.

Democrats going to people's houses to get their ballots and changing the rules."

"Get those people to sign sworn affidavits," I advised him. "This needs whistle-blowers, video footage, something that slows down the acceptance of a Biden win. You have every right to file credible legal challenges, but the judges will rule quickly. Are we ready?"

The precious hours and days following Election Day provided a reasonable time frame to prove that widespread, systemic fraud had robbed Donald Trump of reelection. No, this wasn't "something only Trump would do," as Never Trump pundits complained. Al Gore challenged the results in 2000. Hillary Clinton did in 2016 and, a few paragraphs in her book notwithstanding, continues to cast doubt on her loss to this day.

Indeed, there were some credible accounts that seemed worth investigating, even litigating. In Wisconsin and Pennsylvania, local election officials changed the rules on who could vote and how they could vote, late in the game. The U.S. Supreme Court should have taken the Pennsylvania case. Georgia was headed to an automatic audit. Sworn affidavits from eyewitnesses were coming out of Nevada, Arizona, and Michigan. North Carolina was called late and for Trump, but that was the only late call that went his way.

"Look, this is very different from *Bush v. Gore*," I told the president, recalling the landmark 2000 election that was finally decided on a 5–4 vote in the U.S. Supreme Court. "That involved one issue, in one state, and really just a few counties. The irony here is that the more widespread the problems, the harder it is to hold the public's attention. People need one or two big things to focus on, like a court invalidating ballots or ordering a revote."

I told him the story of what had happened in 2018 after a special congressional election in North Carolina. The winner was Republican Mark Harris. There were credible allegations of ballot harvesting in Pender County. So in that county only, the original results were tossed out, and a new vote was scheduled. "It was just one county, Mr. President, and the revote did not affect the original outcome of the election. But election officials did not need to prove fraud or theft. They just needed to assure the voters their votes counted and that the process was fair."

In the 2018 midterms, votes did come in late, and some races were decided after the fact. In 2020, however, 100 million ballots were cast early, a majority of them by mail. Improprieties were inevitable. "One or two favorable court rulings in a few of these places," I continued, "and people might listen."

Those favorable court cases never came.

In the weeks that followed, I participated in zero interviews, tweets, or retweets about "stopping the steal." I hoped and prayed that evidence would surface, judges would reconsider, votes would be recounted. Stuck in a parallel universe, many Trump supporters deluded themselves into thinking that somehow the president would remain in office or be reinstated once gone. Trump was more shocked to lose in 2020, I think, than he was to win in 2016.

I MAY HAVE been the first person Donald Trump trusted in his inner circle who told him that he had come up short this time. It wasn't the result I wanted. It wasn't the result some 74 million Americans—by far the largest number of people ever to vote for an incumbent president—wanted. Equally sad and troubling was the missed opportunity he may have had to win a second term outright and, overwhelmingly, to avoid lawsuits, recounts, audits, legal challenges, assorted machinations over a stretch of months, and January 6, and to spend the enormous campaign fund's $1.4 billion more wisely, including on a postelection legal strategy and team worthy of an incumbent president facing enormous resistance and once-in-a-century, global-pandemic-compelled changes to who can vote, how, and for how long.

I told the president he had every right to contest the results. Again, Al Gore and Hillary Clinton had. He had a right to try to prove his case. But to have a chance of prevailing, the actions needed to conclude by December 14, the date when the electors would certify the results. If solid evidence wasn't pulled quickly, I worried, the campaign might run out of time. Yet they had six weeks.

Stop the Steal was the rallying cry for those challenging the election results. Yet long before Election Day, the *steal* that needed to be stopped was the one that put an obscene amount of money in the pockets of campaign consultants who failed to focus on Trump's winning outright and overwhelmingly.

Losing campaigns are often studied but rarely scrutinized. This one should be. A campaign that had more than three years to prepare for Joe Biden, that raised more than a billion dollars, but that reportedly ran out of ad money two months before Election Day: we deserve answers, and might demand an audit.

President Trump deserved a better campaign than what Brad and Jared ran for two and a half years.

Also, here was something truly maddening: After those in charge of the 2020 campaign failed so convincingly, they tried to change history and take credit for 2016, the tougher campaign and the only clear win. Fired campaign manager Brad Parscale took to Fox News to announce that he was the "semi-quasi campaign manager" of 2016 and Jared was the "real campaign manager" in 2016.

It was so sad, I felt bad chuckling.

President Trump called me the next morning. He said, "Can you believe this guy? He is so weak. I had to get rid of him. Weak. A dumbass.

"Did you see him in that video with the police? With the beer shirt on the lawn?" Trump was referring to the body-cam footage from the Fort Lauderdale Police Department of a domestic dispute at Parscale's home earlier that fall, where Parscale was tackled by the police.

He continued: "And the whole wife thing? That was horrible!"

"Yes, I did, sir. Yet it was he who was so obsessed with *my* marriage. And just to be clear, it was an open beer with no shirt. Anywazy . . ."

"Honey, don't worry about a thing. He's so weak. With you, I am 1 and 0. . . ."

"And Brad is 0 for 1," I finished.

"Well, let's see what happens. We may still win this thing."

"That would make Stepien 1 and 0. Jared and you fired Brad months ago. He's 0 for 1, come what may."

Even Jared reached out. He texted while he was in the Middle East and called me the next morning after returning. "Brad shouldn't have done the interview," he said. "I don't know why he did."

"Sure you do," I said. "Brad said to the country what you and Brad tried to tell the press and tell the president for four years."

"Well, Kellyanne," Jared said, "it was great to work with you those last few months, and I wish we had done more together."

"You pegged me as a leaker for four years," I reminded him. "You never gave me a break."

"Looking back," he chuckled, "it was Brad who got that in my head."

THE TWO MONTHS between November 6, 2020, and January 6, 2021, marked the least active period for me politically and professionally in decades. I took myself off TV and somewhat off the grid. I was helping a few clients and delivering a few paid speeches, but mostly I was keeping the central commitment I'd made months earlier.

More mama.

Long before my December 4 appearance, I had agreed to join the "19th News," an independent newsroom "reporting on gender, politics, and policy." Our topic was "the year of the Republican woman" and the role of women in our politics, culture, and such. I spoke for the Republicans. Valerie Jarrett spoke for the Democrats. While there, I stated the obvious, which somehow was news.

"The president wants to exhaust all of his legal avenues, as he has made clear many times," I said. "His team is doing that, and that is his right. . . . If you look at the vote totals in the Electoral College tally, it looks like Joe Biden and Kamala Harris will prevail. I assume the electors will certify that and it will be official. We, as a nation, will move forward, because we always do. . . . You always need a peaceful transfer of democracy, no matter whose administration goes into whose administration."

I understood the concerns that President Trump and millions of other Americans had about the election results. It's okay—even American—to question whether your sacred vote has been counted properly. And just because you question election results or distrust partisan activists fueled by "Zuck Bucks" does not mean you are the "QAnon Shaman." In fact, casting doubt on the election results would put you in the company of plenty of Democrats, *who have not accepted a Republican presidential victory this century!* There were Democrat members in the House who voted against certifying Electoral College wins on January 6 in 2000, 2004, and 2016, sowing distrust in the election results each time.

In 2016, the left and the media went even further, concocting a four-year "Russia" conspiracy to diminish a fair election in 2016. In 2017,

Nancy Pelosi went as far as to say, "Our election was hijacked" and "There is no question. Congress has a duty to #ProtectOurDemocracy & #FollowTheFacts." Talk about reckless! Furthermore, in 2019, Kamala Harris said we needed to secure our elections and go back to paper ballots because machines could be hacked. Rich!

Ensuring that votes are cast freely and counted fairly is a long-standing, bipartisan, nonpartisan practice. Not until 2020 was expressing a smidge of doubt about election results practically banned from public discussion, and widely banned from social media platforms.

What happened in 2020 can never be fully understood. There has been no silver bullet that proves Donald Trump was the rightful winner, as many have claimed. Some people want to "move on" rather than look under the hood to examine why, in election after election, voters lack faith in the results. Those who do look back have never proven that or how a presidential election was rigged. If you ask ten Republicans, "How do you think the 2020 election was rigged?" you may get ten different answers. In 2016, Democrat voters could vomit *Russia, Russia, Russia.* In 2000, they pointed to Florida. Twenty-twenty was a year of many unknowns, and the confusion of the election was just another one.

Certainly, there were legitimate gripes with the way this election was conducted. There were transparency issues. How do you get people to not trust the results of an election? By changing the rules at the last minute, by accepting ballots long past the legal deadline, by sending people mail-in ballots they did not request for elections they do not seem interested in until you show up at their door offering to help them complete and deliver it, by states giving you two months before Election Day to vote and then taking until two weeks after Election Day to count the ballots. With every minute that goes by without tallied and reported results, the way states like Ohio, Florida, and Vermont did on Election Night, the doubts will grow stronger. When a batch of votes comes in overwhelmingly for one candidate in the middle of the night, that creates doubt. When poll workers put up cardboard to block poll watchers from watching, that creates doubt. None of that is evidence of fraud or proof that the results are wrong. But all of it undermines public faith in our elections. We must make it easier to vote and harder to cheat. Stop pretending that presenting valid identification before you vote is burdensome or racist. It is a common practice that allows you to engage in much more mundane daily activities (like entering office buildings). One must present proof of being fully vaccinated before entering a restaurant in Manhattan, but one must not present proof that he is who he says he is before voting?

The disinformation was to be expected. In the closing months of the 2020 election, media outlets were jammed with flimsy, leaked stories about the president, such as the debunked story of Trump calling troops "suckers and losers." (Even John Bolton denied Trump said this.) Or that Russia had put a bounty on U.S. troops and Trump didn't do anything about it. (The Biden administration has even said they assessed that intelligence with "low to moderate confidence.") The difference in 2020 was Big Tech and media censorship. There was a blanket censorship of negative, truthful stories about Hunter Biden and the Biden family's sketchy ties to China. When has the country ever banned any story? Why now? Do we not think Americans are smart enough to suss out the facts and make their own judgments? A year later, it is now accepted that Hunter Biden is not the most credible or ethical person and likely was making money off his father's name from foreign nations. Many mainstream outlets now freely probe Hunter Biden's sketchy ties, including his own father's knowledge and involvement. Was this covered up to ensure a Joe Biden victory? Was it an overcorrection for the media's willingness to cover Hillary Clinton's email controversy in the closing months of the 2016 election? I believe so. Furthermore, a *Washington Post* poll showed Joe Biden with a 17-point lead in Wisconsin days before the election. That was never true (Wisconsin is a swing state for a reason). Trump lost Wisconsin by less than 1 percent, 20,000 votes. Does that have an impact on trust?

In 2016, Mark Zuckerberg stayed neutral, allowing us to run 5.9 million Facebook ads, offering embeds to our campaign (and Hillary's). We used it to our advantage to compete with Hillary's massive TV ad campaign. The 2020 elections witnessed an entirely different type and level of engagement. Through the Center for Technology and Civic Life and the Center for Election Innovation & Research, Mark Zuckerberg donated more than $400 million to election offices. Studies have shown of the twenty-five "Zuck Bucks" gifts of $1 million or more to cities and counties in Arizona, Georgia, Michigan, North Carolina, Pennsylvania, Texas, and Virginia, twenty-three went to places Joe Biden

won. Now many state attorneys general are banning these private dona-
tions due to the partisan implications.

Finally, there's just something wrong about changing the way we
conduct an election mere months out from Election Day. Trump's many
warnings about mail-in ballots were warranted, and should have been
heeded by his own flush campaign. We have never elected a president
with mass-mailed ballots to voters who never asked for a ballot. This
time also brought a massive uptick in drop-box locations and changed
signature-matching and ballot-harvesting rules.

All those changes took place within months of electing a new president. None of them seem to rise to the level of curiosity you might expect
from a media obsessed with my husband and daughter.

As reporter Mollie Hemingway has noted in her excellent book
Rigged, "Some of these changes were enacted by state legislatures,
some by courts, and others by state and county election officials. Many
changes, allegedly justified by the global pandemic, were broad reforms
that Democrats had long desired. The crisis was their chance to sneak in
contentious policies through the back door."

While I had certainly hoped the lawyers and election watchers could
find enough irregularities and fraud to force a revote or a recount, it had
been over a month of dead ends with no real lead, confirming the reality
of Biden's presidency.

On December 22, 2020, at his invitation, I had lunch at the White
House with President Trump. I accepted the invitation weeks after publicly acknowledging Biden as the winner. The president had just recorded
a video expressing support for stimulus checks of $2,000, not the much
lower amount of $600 that Republicans in Congress were advocating.
We spoke about that at length, with him insisting, correctly, that "small
businesses can't make it on that," saying "we should be doing better for
these people."

This was the populist president I knew.

He asked about my children, and I asked about his. We spent a quick
minute on the 2020 election challenges, more time on the stimulus, and
the balance on his policy accomplishments, prospects for the final month,
and the future.

January 6 was never mentioned during our lunch on December 22.

To my relief, January 5 was. The president confirmed that he would visit Georgia again to fire up his voters the night before the runoff elections that would decide the winners of the two U.S. Senate seats in Georgia and, by extension, control of the U.S. Senate.

"Excellent," I declared. "I'm going the day before that. Kelly [Loeffler] and David [Perdue] must win. We need them there. So much of your legacy has run through the Senate. Protecting them is protecting you as well."

The president and I discussed pardons and clemency. I repeated what I had told him previously: "You shine when you bring liberty and freedom to men and women who have long been forgotten, those who languish in prison long after they've paid their debt to society."

I understood why presidents pardon high-profile household names or allies. But I made the case for those who have no voice and less hope.

"Do you want one?" President Trump asked me as I dug into my roast chicken and mashed potatoes in the presidential dining room.

"One what?" I asked, wondering if he meant a Diet Coke or a dinner roll.

"A pardon. Do you want a pardon?"

"Do you know something I don't?" I asked him, a little surprised. "Why would I need a pardon?"

"Because they go after everyone, honey. It doesn't matter."

I politely declined.

As we walked out of the dining room together and headed to the Oval Office, he motioned me into the room where presidential memorabilia were kept. He made me the same offer he'd made to a ten-year-old Claudia at his Virginia golf course in May 2015: "Take whatever you want. Go ahead. Get it all."

I walked away with a silver-plated tray and a trip down memory lane with the boss who had changed my life.

ON JANUARY 3, 2021, I headed to Georgia, joining Senators Tim Scott, Mike Lee, and Ted Cruz, Matt and Mercedes Schlapp, and a few other notable surrogates for a bus tour with the Club for Growth. I was introduced to loud applause from a large crowd at the Bowl at Sugar Hill. I focused my remarks on why we needed to get out the vote for Georgia senators Perdue and Loeffler, who were in runoff elections that would determine which party controlled the U.S. Senate.

The next day, I campaigned for the two Senate candidates. As I was sitting in the Savannah airport, I got a call from the president, who was on his way to Georgia.

"Kel, are you coming with us tonight?"

"No, Mr. President. I've been in Georgia for two days, and I am heading home now."

"Come on," he said. "We can give you a ride home."

"I am boarding soon," I told him. "It's great that you are coming. Make clear to your voters that they need to get out there. They must protect your legacy and our futures." We then discussed a few pardons.

The president campaigned, but Senators Perdue and Loeffler did not prevail. The Republican consultants who made high six- and seven-figure fees off the runoffs race immediately shifted blame to the president. In the Republican Party, candidates often lose but consultants always win. This particular losing streak was as maddening as they come. They lost five races in two months in one state? What kind of genius is that?

JANUARY 6, 2021, was supposed to be much like January 6, 2017, a procedural event, the day Congress convenes and counts the votes already certified by the states on December 14. The role of the sitting vice president in this process is similarly ceremonial. Joe Biden certified Mike Pence's results on January 6, 2017, and Mike Pence was set to certify Joe Biden's results four years later. The 2021 version took on outsized importance after a ragtag assemblage of lawyers, outside agitators, and senior administration officials convinced the president that Pence could block certification of results from an election that had occurred two months earlier.

For the week before that day, the media had been working overtime to suggest that Vice President Pence would ruin his reputation and destroy his own political future by acceding to his boss and refusing to certify the election results showing Biden-Harris as the winners.

Pence was not going to do that. The media were mistaken again.

I was in Dallas enjoying the Cotton and Rose Bowl games with my son just before New Year's 2021 when I asked Marc Short, Pence's chief of staff, how I might help with the latest round of "What will Mike Pence do?" stories circulating ahead of the January 6 certification.

"Just tell them the truth," Marc said. "The VP has no authority to do what the White House is asking him to do."

Short did not say "president."

But clearly, others were still feeding the frenzy and demanding that the vice president of the United States do what lawyers for two months had failed to do.

"We've got a shot, Kel," the president said to me when we spoke by phone. "One state here, another there, then they keep going."

For a president who many thought surrounded himself with yes-men, that was never the case until 2020. And it proved costly from November to January. In Obama's final months, he was instituting policies to handcuff his successors and cement his own legacy. He had the entire national security apparatus in the Oval Office, laying the traps of the Big Lie of Russian collusion. In Trump's final days, a few in the senior staff were doing nothing to cement or communicate his impressive policy legacy and were ushering in conspiracy theorist after kook after conniver.

Over the protracted course of these hopeless challenges, with a paint-by-numbers, revolving-door collection of lawyers pleading the cases, some ninety judges, including some the president had nominated to the bench, rejected all the arguments. But the fatal legal blow had landed before Election Day. On October 28, the U.S. Supreme Court refused a plea from Pennsylvania Republicans who wanted the court to decide before Election Day whether the state could continue counting absentee ballots for three days afterward.

To Trump, that had stung.

For him, "judges" had been a shorthand reference for why on-the-fence conservatives and libertarians should vote for candidate Trump. It was something we used in the 2016 campaign. By 2020, that same term, "judges," was in the top three of President Trump's most durable accomplishments. In this dismal period, judges, including many he had appointed, were sealing Trump's electoral fate.

*   *   *

WHEN I WOKE up on the morning of January 6, it was all over the media: Vice President Pence had informed President Trump that he had no legal basis—and therefore, no intention—to block the certification of the election.

Then I went into my Alpine cave. Getting the kids going on their schoolwork. Strategizing in the kitchen. Retreating to my home office, where I purposely had no TVs. But I did have my phone. Don Jr.'s tweet popped as an alert at 2:17 p.m. It seemed cryptic and urgent, both at once.

"This is wrong and not who we are," the president's oldest son wrote. "Be peaceful and use your 1st Amendment rights, but don't start acting like the other side. We have a country to save and this doesn't help anyone."

I hadn't watched a single moment of the earlier rally or the subsequent events. The first inkling I had about what was happening at the Capitol that afternoon was Don Jr.'s tweet. It was my fourth month as a stay-at-home mom, mostly disconnected from the daily political conversation that had been my soundtrack for decades, surprisingly at peace without it. I rapid-scrolled through Twitter to learn more and ran down the stairs to flip on a TV.

I was late to witness the mystifying events. But like many others, I immediately understood the gravity. As I scanned my phone for further updates, a familiar number popped up. An ally of D.C. mayor Muriel Bowser, her words frantically spilling forth.

"We've requested the National Guard and were denied," she said. "Can you help?"

"What? What happened?"

"SecDef declined the request," she said, meaning Acting Secretary of Defense Christopher Miller, "and we don't know if he was acting alone or at the direction of the president."

"Let me make sure the president even knows this," I said. "Sometimes people act on their own, and sometimes people do things based on what they think he wants them to do, without bothering to ask."

I hung up and dialed the cell phone of an aide I knew would be next to the president. Typically, I would call the switchboard to get a secure line. But time was of the essence.

"Do you want to talk to him?" the president's loyal aide asked me, right after *hello*.

"*NO!*" I answered. "We're in crisis. People need him. He can call me later if he wants. Please, tell him three things from me."

I had never before called his aide's cell phone as a way to reach the president. But the urgency demanded speed and clarity.

"First," I said, speaking quickly, "add me to the chorus of people calling to urge the president to tell the people at the Capitol to stop. Just stop. Get out of there. Maybe there are loudspeakers. Someone could livestream him. They need to hear *his voice*. People in riot gear rifling through desks and turning over trash cans are not stopping to check Twitter.

"Second, there are requests to deploy the National Guard," I said. "Some confusion, but just be sure the president knows this and based on what I see, that's a solid call and a reasonable request by the officials in D.C., Maryland, and Virginia.

"And finally," I said, "can he please clarify his Twitter feed."

If the people inside the Capitol had actually read the president's tweets, they would have been totally confused and not deterred. Some of them read like an annual fundraising appeal: "Please support our Capitol Police and Law Enforcement. They are truly on the side of our Country. Stay peaceful!" Others had the opposite message: "Mike Pence didn't have the courage to do what should have been done to protect our Country and our Constitution, giving States a chance to certify a corrected set of facts, not the fraudulent or inaccurate ones which they were asked to previously certify. USA demands the truth!"

To hear Pence explain it, the issue was not of courage but of the Constitution.

To hear Trump explain it, all his vice president had to do was send the matters back to a few state legislatures.

I spent the rest of the afternoon watching events unfold and adding my own voice to the calls for calm and retreat.

"STOP," I tweeted. "Just STOP. Peace. Law and Order. Safety for All." To those who broke into Speaker Pelosi's office, I wrote: "This is not appropriate, not legal and not funny. Get out."

ABC News had asked me to call in for a live reaction, as a bystander no longer involved in the White House. Since I couldn't run down to the Oval Office anymore to help, I made my plea on TV. "I want to tell everyone, particularly people who support President Trump, if you condemned looting and rioting this summer, you need to do it now."

What was happening at the Capitol, I knew, wasn't what so many Americans had fought for. This wasn't what had made them stick by Donald Trump as he had defied all odds, beaten Hillary Clinton, and soldiered on through attack after attack. They had stuck their necks out for him, despite losing friends and family members. This wasn't the payback they deserved.

In that same ABC interview, I said, "I think they give a bad look to the president's legacy and also the seventy-four million people who voted for him."

It left me wondering what the point was of the January 6 rally that day. The viral video of Trump family members (and others who fancy themselves Trump family members) backstage before the president addressed the crowd lacked the most notable and most popular one: Melania Trump. As was her practice, the First Lady shared her opinions and advice with the president privately—and freely. She had tweeted on November 9: "The American people deserve fair elections. Every legal—not illegal—vote should be counted. We must protect our democracy with complete transparency."

Big changes were already taking place a thousand miles from the Capitol, in the Trumps' new home state of Florida. Jared and Ivanka had just paid $30 million for a lot in an exclusive community in Miami. Their kids were enrolled in a nearby school. With the moving vans and future plans all pointing south, I wondered: What exactly was everyone trying to "stop" in D.C. on January 6?

DESPITE THE MOUNTAINS of money Trump had raised, his team simply failed to get the job done. A job that was doable and had a clear path, if followed. Rather than accepting responsibility for the loss, they played along and lent full-throated encouragement (privately, not on TV) when Trump kept insisting he had won.

The team failed on November 3, and they failed again afterward. By not confronting their candidate with the grim reality of his situation, that the proof had not surfaced to support the claims, they denied him the evidence he sought and the respect he was due. Instead, supplicant after sycophant after showman genuflected in front of the Resolute Desk and promised the president goods they could not deliver.

Fixated on the heartbreaking events of January 6, many people missed January 19. The president started a two-day tranche of pardons, some of which seemed justified, some of which seemed pushed by the usual suspects, and some of which were mind-boggling. Well-connected people were reportedly getting paid in the high six figures to lobby for others' liberty.

President Trump called and asked me to call Steve Bannon. The president said I was the only one holding up the pardons. That was news to me. I knew that others in the White House, like Jared, Ivanka, and Eric Herschmann, were active in the pardon discussions, but I was not.

I told the president that I would not call Bannon and that I didn't know I had that much power. By then the president and I had both gone years without talking to or talking about Steve Bannon. Probably since Bannon last walked out the White House door.

Hours later, I got a call from an unknown number. It was Bannon, who pretended to want to talk. He was the same unpaternal, paternalistic bore of a boor. "I called you because I thought you wanted to be on my podcast," he said.

"I didn't know you had a podcast," I snarked.

"Very funny, girl."

"Well," I said, "the president keeps calling me to call you about a pardon. I didn't know I wield that much power and, frankly, I haven't thought about you since you left."

"I didn't ask for one, a pardon," Bannon said.

"Well, I tell you what I told the president: He doesn't owe you a thing, including a pardon. You were a leaker. You were terrible to him in the press. You were terrible to his son. You were the only source for at least two books riddled with lies." There was the time Bannon called Donald Trump Jr. "treasonous" and the time Bannon said he was "sick of being a wet nurse to a seventy-one-year-old man."

"When did Bannon say that?" the president had asked me.

"When you were seventy-one," I retorted sharply.

Admitting defeat would have required these advisors to forgo future paydays. The Trump campaign raised $200 million *after* November 3 to prove the election had been stolen. A smooth transition and a focus on the president's legacy would have served him and the country better.

The final days of the Trump presidency were a study in contrast. On January 8, Twitter banned @realDonaldTrump. Steve Bannon and others of questionable character got their pardons. Congress, meanwhile, was busily impeaching the president once again—the self-anointed "history will judge" mob was trying to erase him altogether. Despite all these distractions, the president seemed lighter, more at peace with the coming reality, and strangely relieved that he didn't need to constantly keep up with Twitter.

The day before the president left office, the White House released a list of one thousand accomplishments, a list that should have been released in stages throughout the entire transition. I knew what I would have done. These accomplishments could have been rolling on Jumbo-trons across the nation during a Thank You, I'll Be Back Tour, a much better idea than whatever January 6 was designed to be. And whatever January 6 was designed to be, it wasn't that at all. What it became was destruction of the Capitol and a second impeachment.

On my fiftieth birthday, I watched Donald Trump take the oath of office. On my fifty-fourth, I watched Joe Biden do the same.

It didn't have to be this way.

Chapter 39

Beautiful Night

Donald and Melania Trump and I had dinner together on an especially gorgeous night in Palm Beach in the spring of 2021. The change of scenery and escape from the daily grind clearly agreed with them.

The main patio at Mar-a-Lago was bustling. They both looked fantastic. As was our custom, the conversation ranged from the personal to the political to the professional. Laughter and candor were on the menu.

"Bring her the shrimp," the president said to a waiter. "We have the best shrimp."

And why stop with shrimp?

"Do you like steak?"

"Yes, sir, medium rare."

Back to the waiter. "That, too."

Back to me. "Is this the best food? Best place?" He looked up and around and then at Melania and me.

"Spectacular, sir. The smartest eight million dollars anyone ever spent on anything."

I was referencing his original, 1985 purchase of the extraordinary property that fronts the Atlantic Ocean and the Intracoastal Waterway and was known as the "Winter White House" long before Donald Trump became president.

"But it's not the Oval Office," I said ruefully. "As nice as this is, I wish you were still there."

"We'll be back, honey. We'll all be back."

One of the great things about these conversations with the Trumps is that almost nothing is off-limits. After all we've been through together, we are comfortable sharing just about anything and speaking our minds. We keep it real. I keep it respectful, never presuming I am their friend, and never mistaking their trust in me and concern for me as me being a member of their family.

Later in the evening, President Trump suddenly switched topics. "You weren't much of a Jared person, were you? Because he says nothing but great things about you!"

I chuckled at the irony, realizing that passive-aggressive Jared was clever enough never to trash me outright to the president, and I was classy enough to have never bothered the leader of the free world with years' worth of petty asides and exclusions.

"Mr. President," I said, "we don't need to talk about that. I just don't understand why you gave him so much power and why he meddled in every single thing."

"I didn't *give* him all that power. He just happens to have a very good relationship with my daughter."

"She's brilliant, and kind," I said, "but . . ."

"The Abraham Accords are fantastic, don't you think?" he asked me.

"Yes, I do, sir, and I am grateful to the many people involved with those agreements, including the actual secretary of state, Mike Pompeo. But why does Jared get to pick and choose what his legacy is when you can't?"

Repeatedly referred to as the "de facto chief of staff," the "shadow secretary of state," and the "real 2020 campaign manager," Jared had hightailed it to the Mideast just as soon as the campaign Brad and he ran lost the Midwest and the election victory he had so confidently predicted had not materialized.

"Maybe you have it backward, Donald," offered Melania, the original counselor to the president. "Maybe Jared was not much of a Kellyanne person."

We moved on to key lime pie.

At some point, President Trump mentioned the implosion of the anti-Trump Lincoln Project, which took me by surprise, since this was probably the third time we had ever discussed them. Liberal groups were questioning their effectiveness. Assorted malfeasance and missing funds. Alleged predatory sexual behavior by one of the founders. A cover-up by the other principals.

"You've helped make many people rich, Mr. President, both for and against you."

"That's true."

"They never elevated women into positions of authority and responsibility," I said. "You did. Always have. They treated the women terribly. None of the women had major equity or went on *60 Minutes*. They sent a bunch of middle-aged white guys instead."

Trump smiled.

"George resigned and publicly said the group should disband," I continued, "George never took a dime from the Lincoln Project," I said. "He—"

"Well, that wasn't smart!" the main target of the group's activities replied. "That was dumb. All that money and he let the other people have it?"

Melania laughed at that.

"George could have been your neighbor in Palm Beach, and I'd like to be!" I told them. "Those grifters and drifters got all the money. They are the original 'money for nothing' crew. They never achieved what you and I did together."

Trump nodded and leaned in: "Write a great book, honey. You made history. You were the first woman. You did a fantastic job. You should talk about it."

Afterword

T hat's my story. It's not a tell-all-and-bore-most riddled with lies, deceptions, and exaggerations to redeem or enrich myself, as others have done—conveniently, after they were forced out or slinked away in shame or irrelevance. I am not speaking up now because I didn't speak up then. God knows, *I spoke up then.* This book shows I have been vulnerable, but I am not a victim. I've made mistakes, both professionally and personally, for which I've sought forgiveness and mercy. I've loved and I've lost. I've also gained appreciation and perspective from those with whom I agree or disagree. I have found out who my real friends are, who, along with my cousins and family, will continue to hold my hand through the journey of life. I've enjoyed one-of-a-kind experiences and met, hugged, helped, engaged, encouraged—and snapped photos with!—thousands and thousands of Americans who represent the best of our beautiful nation.

Strangers stop me often to ask how I am, how my family is, and to thank me for my service. I thank them back, saying how grateful I am to have worked for the country I love so truly, madly, deeply. I was one of very few who worked in the White House in 2017–21 and departed on their own terms, on their own timeline, scandal-free and subpoena-free. I am proud to be the first female to successfully manage a U.S. presidential campaign and to have served as senior counselor to the president.

That gave me the opportunity in some modest way to give back to the country that has given so much to me. Even after nearly five hundred pages later, it seems both incredible and indescribable to have had a ringside seat to history. Sure, some moments were fraught. Some days were tumultuous. Some decisions were maddening. Some words and actions were a cause of head shaking. People should have kept their paws off my marriage and my children. Yet there were many more highs than lows, more successes than setbacks, and results that improved many individuals' lives. Throughout it all, I felt honored and humbled to be there.

Many ask me what Donald Trump is really like. Those who are devastated that he is no longer president want to hear more about the man behind the mission, the inside scoop about his humor, his toughness, his relentlessness in getting things done. Those who are thrilled he is no longer president wonder why I stayed so long, why I fought so strong. Their viewpoint is typically dressed up in compliments for me and criticism for him.

Donald Trump is a complicated person with simple ideas. Many people, including in politics, are the reverse.

He is an excellent storyteller and can be a patient listener. He rarely forgets people, places, or things, even the ones you wish he would. He gave me my shot, and I wasn't going to throw it away. He treated me with respect, empowered and emboldened me. He defended me from enemies both "foreign and domestic." I disagreed and dissented plenty. If I was disappointed or disgusted, I did not need to conceal it. Neither did he. Some of his tweets and off-the-cuff remarks created chaos. He could be open to persuasion yet obstinate. He could be focused yet obstreperous. He could be repetitive yet choosing the right word to explain to everyone what it means and how it affects them. Some of the personal insults were unfunny and unnecessary, even as he was responding to someone else who had drawn first blood. He is a person who doesn't use any conversation fillers, and if you keep talking without the "uh" and "you know" like other politicians, you can get yourself in trouble. But on balance, people had more access to their government and more transparency from the man in the Oval Office. The number of policy achievements is breathtaking. No one ever had to wonder where Donald Trump stood or who was actually the president.

He always put America first.

He also put his people first. When he asked how my mother or my kids were, he waited for an answer and seemed genuinely interested in it. I heard him say numerous times to people of differing needs, "Look at me. Anything we can do, you tell me. Call me directly." He was generous and solicitous when the cameras were off, when the only payback he'd get would be the great feeling of knowing he had eased another's burden.

President Trump could have asked me to leave. Who could have faulted him if one of those times he summoned me to the Oval Office it was to say "Look, honey, you're great. We love you. You'll always be part of our group, but I can't worry about George Conway when I've got to worry about Kim Jong Un and ISIS and now COVID. You understand, don't you?" He didn't say that. Others pressured him to. I can understand why, given how constant and gratuitously nasty George was to the president and those close to him. Trump would often call me a *warrior*. "She's fierce—did you see what she did to that guy on CNN?" He wasn't worried about George. He was worried about me. Worried this George-on-Twitter thing was a mountain too steep for even me to scale.

The Donald Trump I knew treated me and other working moms with respect. I've been alone with him countless times, even though in my life I've been grabbed, groped, cornered, propositioned, punished for being noncompliant, and worse. I've been denied a seat at the big-boys' table, dismissed when pregnant, and derided when I dared to succeed a little. But never by Donald J. Trump. I'm not mad at ALL men for that licentious behavior; I'm mad at THOSE men. I'm also forever grateful that Donald Trump never treated me that way or made me feel that way. It confirmed that I was promoted and empowered on merit. He gives people "second, third, and hundredth chances," to quote one of Taylor Swift's most memorable lines. (Another Swift line I love is, "If you say it on the street, it's a knockout. If you put it in a tweet, it's a cop-out.") A funny thing happened on the way to the petty partisans, jealous jerks, and unimpressive underachievers who were trying to diminish, if not to destroy, me. God had bigger plans for me. What God had made, no man can cancel. People who call you names don't want to know your name. They don't want you to have a name, to be real and relatable, human and humble; they want to indulge in their convenient assumptions, presumptive negativity, wishful thinking, and worst possible fictitious concoctions about who you are, what you believe, how you feel, why you exist, when you should and should not speak to whom and about what.

Every day, I faced an approachable boss, slow to anger, asking how we might help this one or that one, a boss who had joy on the job and love in his heart for this incredible country and her amazing people. A man much bigger and smarter than his tweets might allow. He was good to me, and great for America.

SINCE I LEFT the White House, I have had time to reflect. I watched from a distance, at home in New Jersey, the closing months of the 2020 election, the transition from Trump-Pence to Biden-Harris, and January 6. The awful events were unnerving and unnecessary. I am still in shock, and not in awe.

So where does that leave the Trump movement? The 74 million Trump voters? The forgotten men and women? This divided country? My own house divided?

In 2016, 79,646 votes in three states pushed Donald Trump over Hillary Clinton to become the forty-fifth president of the United States. In 2020, about 45,000 votes in three states ultimately shifted the presidency from Trump to Joe Biden. The Democrats also gained control of the Senate, albeit 50–50, and the House had its slimmest majority in nearly a century. Our divisions at the ballot box are laid bare every few years, but our divisions at home, work, school, and play are uglier by the day. This seems unwise and unsustainable.

Yet all the signs say that the people who could help unify us are dividing us instead. Redistricting means fewer and fewer "swing" districts, places where politicians need to speak to both sides and forge compromise. In too many parts of America, there is no political risk to divisive rhetoric and no political incentive to seek common ground. That is already true online, but my fear is it is happening offline, too. Half the Congress hardly speaks to the other half of Congress. They should be calling each other by name, not calling each other names. How are they truly "representing" the country when out in the real world, few people want to live in their "red" or "blue" uniforms 24/7/365 and never be able to change those clothes or change the channel or change the conversation to something nonpolitical? A growing number of voters (and nonvoters) identify with no party, trust no one, and have grown deeply suspicious of the very notion that political leaders of any stripe will ever solve the issues that divide our nation or find ways to improve people's lives. It brings me back to a quote from former president Bill Clinton, sixteen years after he left the White House, this time on the campaign trail in 2016 to help his wife in her second run. When asked about the even rougher and tougher twenty-first-century campaign, he wondered aloud whether he had the temperament for the current political climate: "I don't fit anymore. First of all, I'm a happy grandfather. I'm not mad at anybody." He had a point.

Thomas Jefferson was right. "Opinion is power." Showing up, standing up, and speaking up are vital to the health of our democracy. I believe that certain ideas should prevail and others should fail. So do you. But that does not preclude trying to build on what binds us and not what breaks us. The elusive word *unity* may be unattainable in this political climate, so let's attempt it in nonpolitical settings: in our places of work and worship; in our kids' schools and playgrounds; in our communities.

"Unity" was Joe Biden's 2020 promise to America. Barely a year into his term, the nation's divisions are raw, and the most unifying thing seems to be how unpopular he and his vice president are. At one point, his approval rating was 33 percent and hers was 28 percent. The dismal news comes from polls conducted not by "right-wing revolutionaries" but by mainstream media outlets that pushed (a little too hard) for Biden-Harris's victory. Biden-Harris swiftly lost the political center, America has lost confidence in their competence, and their personal attributes (for example, cares about people like me, has a plan, is compassionate) have declined. The most bipartisan action of the Democrats during Biden's first year, that time when Democrats seemed genuinely interested in attracting Republican support, was . . . the impeachment of President Trump.

Look at the political parties, the social media slop, the cable news chatter, our own families. Maybe unity seems elusive because it must be preceded by civility. Common decency and respect. Listening. Asking why, not assuming why not. Most Americans seek out "news" that they believe reinforces their own beliefs. The don't simply disagree with people who are different; they seek to diminish them and destroy them. This has hit too close to home for me. It is only recently that I have read a sampling of George's ninety thousand tweets. For once, Kellyanne Conway is speechless. It's tough to stomach or reconcile some of the gratuitous meanness of some of the tweets with the man I married and for whom our family came first for so long.

The rest of us would do well to listen respectfully. And once in a while shutting up already. It can be lost on politicos like me, but here's a fact: Most Americans are sick and tired of politics. For years, my job was to make the political personal. Now, too much of what should be personal has become political. Most people don't want to think about politics 24/7, watch political shows, or debate politics day and night. When did politics seep into every conversation or consideration, every friendship and relationship? Most people certainly don't want to be pressured into taking sides on every new issue that comes along. *Enough*, they're saying. *Enough! I'll vote on Election Day.* Yet even Election "Day" now begins two months before—and goes three weeks after—Election Day. There seems no escape.

I was fortunate to contribute to some policies that were (and should be) decidedly nonpartisan and unifying or widely beneficial to so many. Military spouses and veterans. Child exploitation and drug dependency. Deregulation and tax cuts. And hundreds of judges. Therapeutics and vaccines. The media paid little mind. They preferred heat to light.

It's easy to be a naysayer and a critic. It's effortless to fire off a rude or insulting social media post aimed at making someone else feel "less than." That's trash, not talent. Grandmom was right: "Kill them with kindness." Similarly, you can take one look at some people and verify the saying "Hate corrodes the container in which it lives."

DONALD TRUMP WAS a unique candidate who did not run a conventional campaign. He built a movement. Trump channeled a message that spoke to voters who had been dismissed for decades. They, too, were outsiders to a corrupt and sclerotic system that varies between being broke, woke, and a joke. Trump gave them a voice and a different choice. The result was an historic 74 million voters in 2020, the highest number for a sitting president in U.S. history.

The lessons from the MAGA movement are important. Some candidates around the country are trying to emulate Trump but in the wrong way, mimicking his personality or social media posts instead of his policies. Trump won in part because he was a political outsider, a first-time candidate, and a successful businessman. He made regular, strategic, and brilliant use of an unsuspecting and willing media. He led a democratization of information, where all Americans received frequent presidential communications instantly at no charge, absent a middleman manipulating or denigrating the message. Mostly he won because he did what every leader must do: He connected with people, demonstrated market distinction, offered a better and different way, ignored the vicious critics, exposed his opponents' hypocrisy and vulnerability, embraced the forgotten man, woman, and child, and made promises he intended to keep. And let's face it, folks, he did the work. The implications are playing out in 2022 and will play out in 2024. As I've told President Trump, elections are about the future, not the past, and many of the same people who benefited from his having been in the White House are now suffering because he is not.

Some of the same advice I offered in 2016 I would offer now. It is timeless, and now we should listen to it again. The job description of the next contender is not who but what. That person has got to articulate, advance, and explain to the people the America First agenda, whether it is Donald Trump or if he chooses not to run, another candidate. People want a fighter, and not to simply fight with others or for a narrow cause, or when the cameras are on, but a fighter who fights for them. Americans often speak as a group, but we vote as individuals. We ruminate about what offends us. We act according to what affects us.

Biden won because he wasn't Trump. That left him with a pyrrhic victory, no mandate, and no core constituency. Biden began his first year in office inheriting three vaccines developed during the Trump administration, and he ended his first year with three COVID variants overwhelming the nation. In four years, Trump started no new war. In just one year, Biden's feckless and reckless foreign policy emboldened no less than Russia, China, Iran, and the Taliban. The deadly and chaotic withdrawal in Afghanistan against the advice of his generals and ceding the country to Taliban control. Leaving behind $85 billion worth of equipment and intelligence within the reach of China. Six months later and a full year after Biden began his march toward energy re-dependence, Ukraine became the first sovereign nation in Europe to be invaded in eighty years.

There's more—the dissipation of energy independence and the jobs and sovereignty that go along with it, too. There are unanswered questions about the 2020 elections that affect future elections, yet half the country seems incurious and the other inconsolable about it. The prices of gas and goods are up while morale and life expectancy are down. Fentanyl is the number one killer of 18- to 44-year-olds across the country. Our high school and college students, facing a never ending-episode of *Life, Interrupted* have been negatively impacted with respect to their mental and emotional health and their ability to focus on their careers. This is America; we are hearty and resilient. We must do better, because we are better.

President Joe Biden is in daily conflict with Senator Joe Biden of the previous five decades, who presented as more moderate and more open to working with the other side. His forty-seven-year career in Washington seems more a liability than an asset.

As polls show, the voters already feel buyer's remorse and do not think Biden is up to the fight. This is not a Joe Biden problem, it's a Democrat Party problem. In less time than it takes to have a baby, Biden, Harris, Pelosi, Schumer, and their crew ended policies that were working. They attempted policies that will never work and left America, Americans, American industry, interests, individuals, and ingenuity vulnerable and threatened.

Republicans would be shortsighted to simply ride this wave of disapproval. True, polling shows a lack of confidence in Biden's competence, a loss of trust among Independents, and a sharp decline in positive personal attributes. In polls, voters think Biden is not "mentally sharp." But if we solely blame his unfitness on his mental acuities, we are excusing his policy decisions. Joe Biden is the president. He should eat and own every decision.

I have launched a new firm, KAConsulting. It feels good going back to my roots and listening to Americans all across this country. In my surveys and focus groups, I learn valuable information and hear simple wisdom from people across the country. True to my own advice, I prefer to approach people first through a nonpolitical lens, and let them tell me who they are, what burdens they bear, and what advice they wish to share. These conversations can be had free from presumption or politics. It builds familiarity.

In focus groups I have conducted across the country, many of the most toxic issues are pillars of the Democrat Party: defund the police, exclude parents from their children's education, open borders, tax hikes, overregulation, and mindless spending of money we don't have on things we don't need. These voters think Democrats want to control you, your actions, your children, your money, your life . . . but take no responsibility of their own.

The strength of the Republican Party lies in its policies and its people. Voters applaud the GOP's commitment to fiscal issues, national security, and social issues. A "SAFE" agenda means Security, Affordability, Foreign policy, and Education. The Republican Party has credibly become the party of the worker, putting forth policies that help job creators, job seekers, and job holders. America is not just another country. It is an extraordinary, blessed nation destined to lead. Republicans believe parents should have a say as to where their children go to school and what is taught there. Sixty or so years after some Democrats stood in the schoolhouse door, refusing to allow children of color inside, they are standing in the schoolhouse door refusing to allow children of all backgrounds out of failing institutions to find an alternative worthy of them. Democrats say no arrests, no prosecutions, no bail demands; law-and-order Republicans wish to more deeply respect and more generously resource those who literally take bullets for us on our streets and on our battlefields. A commonsense plan that encourages and rewards work and promotes policies that help the American family, the middle-class taxpayer, and the small business owner/employee is a freedom agenda and a winning platform.

The Democrats pretend to be the party of youth, energy, diversity, and fresh faces, yet they are led by—seventy-nine-year-old white male career politician Joe Biden. He is the head and the face of the Democrat Party. Who is the heart? Republicans have an increasingly impressive list of leaders whose choices and circumstances, faces and places look more like America. Let's elevate them, and if they have the courage to run, let's elect them. We need to learn to finish our sentences and broaden our stable of messengers. Voters ask, "Do I like you?" which is the classic "Do I want to see you in my living room?" Yet the more important voter calculus is, "Are you like me?" That connective tissue with people is the key to winning and governing, and possibly to unifying.

When I speak with or visit former president Trump, it is obvious that he feels there is unfinished business in this country and this world that he would be tackling and that his successors are hardly touching or, in many ways, making worse. Typically, voter disappointment in a presidency becomes "I hope it gets better." But in this case, many Americans are saying, "It *was* better." Millions are longing for what they had not so long ago.

DEMOCRACY WILL SURVIVE. America will survive. George and I may not survive. MiMi once told me that we hurt as deeply as we love, that our joy and grief are in proportion. I learned that when she and my father, my childhood friend Christine, and other people I adored passed away, and I've learned it again recently. I will always love George. Even if I don't fully understand what happened or why it was worth the high cost to him. I thought we were stronger than that. Perhaps "for better or for worse" does not anticipate every possibility. And what about the vows to honor and to respect? For me, our main difference is not about Trump. It's about time. And how each of us chooses to spend it, with whom and doing what. Apparently I can't compete with the tweet. Or ninety thousand of them. And why would I even try? She has no personality and she's not even hot. I can't imagine relying upon the odd opaque online world for comfort, friendship, or validation.

I will be ever grateful to have built a life and a family together. Nothing can change or touch that. George has been kind and generous to my family, who is his family, too. Come what may, the ugliness of differing politics is no match for the beauty of shared parenthood. Take it from me. If you are on the outs with a loved one because of politics, reassess. And if you must, express regret and remorse. At least reflect: Is politics *that* important? Will your gain outweigh your loss? Do you wish to be right or to be loved?

As far as the Conway Six are concerned, we will always have each other, the most extraordinary gift imaginable. We have used this time to step away from the limelight and unwanted attention. Hopefully, those who suspended common decency and violated that unspoken, understood rule that kids are off-limits have allowed themselves reflection and regret. They've not been fully held to account. They've not offered an apology. You know who you are. And so do we. No sense debasing my memoir by naming, blaming, or shaming you. There is always tomorrow.

My favorite and most important role—mom—is the greatest. Always an adventure. Cheerful chaos and simple pleasures. I highly recommend it. There are fewer women having fewer children than at practically any point in our nation's history. But I will forever be overwhelmed with gratitude to have the gift of motherhood. My four children are my four favorite people in the entire world. I wistfully miss those early years with the kids, when life seemed less complicated. Play dates and playmates, backyard BBQs, pool days, Jersey Shore summers, weekends of kids' games, kids' parties, kids' costume parades. Now these skinned knees turn into broken hearts. And those toy cars become all too real. Now my children are at the ages where I encourage independence and self-designation while making sure they know I am there to listen, to make it all better, to catch them when they fall and cheer them when they soar. The four of them will always be my first priority. I laugh out loud when I think of the reverse pyramid of my life, coming from a household of four adult women and one child to a household of one adult woman and four children. Those Golden Girls of South Jersey furnished more instruction and inspiration than I could ever repay.

George is an only child, and so am I. Yet we have four incredible children together. No one can touch or change that. Georgie, Claudia, Charlotte, and Vanessa will always have each other. As will their children and children's children. It is the greatest, purest gift imaginable. My children are my heart. New parents learn a love they didn't know existed and are forever transformed. There is a daily amazement and an indescribable joy I feel in just being their mom, life's hassles, hiccups, twists, and turns notwithstanding. I love all of my children equally and unconditionally. Yet I respond to each of them individually for the unique people they are and are becoming.

Here's the deal: It's been quite a story, quite a ride, quite a journey, quite a life. God has been so good to me. He tested me yet trusted me. He has asked me to bear burdens that did not break me. He has bestowed blessings on me beyond what I imagined—or deserved. Amen.

Acknowledgments

A memoir at my age feels unusual in that, God willing, I have decades of life ahead of me. Still, it was not difficult to fill five hundred pages, twice the length of similar books, and with plenty of additional content to spare. It was time I spoke for myself, rather than have others speak for me or about me.

An undertaking like this required many months of relentless research, writing, editing, rewriting, cutting, condensing, and curating. I am grateful to those who believed in the project from the beginning and helped it come to fruition, including Keith Urbahn at Javelin; executives Jon Karp, Jen Bergstrom, Jennifer Long, and Jennifer Robinson, and editor Natasha Simons at Simon & Schuster. They kept saying yes, offering enthusiasm and expertise to push me to work harder and smarter.

Book doctor Ellis Henican listened patiently, read diligently, critiqued, polished, and lent his professional expertise without changing me or my voice.

The deepest thanks for the day-to-day marshalling and muscle memory of this book goes to Tom Joannou. For years he has been by my side, riding shotgun, helping to navigate the open and unpaved roads, and sometimes taking the wheel. He is wise beyond his years, as fun as he is smart, perceptive and intuitive, dogged and decent. I admire his humility and appreciate his honesty. Tom believed in this book and kept faith and focus to see it through to its conclusion.

I am grateful to everyone who has touched me and has been part of my life's journey. Many of you are named in the book rather than in these acknowledgments, while others fell unintentionally to an editor's pen. Every single one of you is in my heart and part of my life story. Those etchings are permanent, beyond the reach of time, and continue to impact me.

So many people placed their faith in me, took a chance on me, mentored me, or provided me with professional opportunities that allowed me to get established and evolve, including: Donald and Melania Trump, Mike and Karen Pence, Dan and Marilyn Quayle, Newt Gingrich, Arthur Mason, Len Sanderson, Susan Goodenow, Heidi Diamond, Myrna Blyth, Raul Fernandez, Tom Borelli, J. Patrick Rooney, Grover Norquist, Karen Kerrigan, Pat Pizzella, Marjorie Dannenfelser, Diana Holman, Matt Lashey, Chris Christie, Rebekah Mercer, Larry Kudlow, Sean Hannity, Dave Bossie, and Ronna McDaniel. Those who work in TV and radio put me on the map, elevated my voice, provided a platform that has allowed me to connect with millions of people to deliver information they otherwise may not have.

Thank you to my colleagues at The Wirthlin Group; Luntz Research; *the polling company, inc./* WomanTrend, KAConsulting LLC, the Trump-Pence 2016 campaign, and the White House.

I have an unusually large extended family for an only child, and it is the gift that keeps on giving. My ancestors chose the greatest country in the world when they sought a better life and a brighter future. Every day of my journey is a continuation of theirs.

My family loved and cared for me, shaped me, and believed in me longer and stronger than anyone else. I can never repay them, and I will never stop loving them. They are named and featured throughout the book. Thank you to my mother, Diane; father, John; grandmothers, Antoinette and Claire; aunts Marie, Rita, and Angela; uncles Eddie and Joe; cousins Renee, Ron, Jay, Angel, Alexa, Michael, Astin, Bryn, Giovanna, John, and Jimmy; Scott and Kim, and my extended family, whom I'm so deeply blessed to have.

I feel affection and appreciation for the dozens of friends from childhood, high school, college, law school, adulthood, and parenthood who are my chosen family. Several of my friends actively encouraged me to tell my story or tried to make other parts of my life easier so that I could focus on this book, including Michaela, Donna, Marina, Marleen, Andrea, Allison, and Maryana. The sudden loss of my lifelong friend Christine opened my eyes and my heart that much more.

Someone once told me that it's easier to deliver a book than to deliver a baby. It struck me as odd at the time, but having done both, I now understand the comparison. The baby arrives on or near its due date, but the book blows past the nine-month mark, especially when the author loves to think, type, and talk. Almost as if to prove the point, the next generation and littlest members of my immediate family were born while I was working on this book: Weston, Fabrizio, Hudson, and Jack.

Thank you, George T. Conway III, for the many happy years and extraordinary memories. Your love brought me to marriage and motherhood. Your support of my career allowed me to work and strive and to take my shot in 2016 and to make the move together to Washington, DC.

Georgie, Claudia, Charlotte, and Vanessa, you are the four chambers of my heart. You made me a mom, and you make every moment more meaningful, every decision more consequential, and every aspect of my life more colorful and more beautiful. You may be the only four individuals who have ever left me truly speechless. You have endured much and made sacrifices. You are strong, brave, resilient, brilliant, generous, and kind, each charting your own path through adolescence and destined to make this world better and brighter. You are gifts from God who will always have my unconditional support and unshakable love.

Index